FILL THE EARTH

FILL THE EARTH

*The Creation Mandate
and the Church's Call
to Missions*

Matthew Newkirk

◥PICKWICK *Publications* · Eugene, Oregon

FILL THE EARTH
The Creation Mandate and the Church's Call to Missions

Copyright © 2020 Matthew Newkirk. All rights reserved. Except for brief quotations in critical publications or reviews, no part of this book may be reproduced in any manner without prior written permission from the publisher. Write: Permissions, Wipf and Stock Publishers, 199 W. 8th Ave., Suite 3, Eugene, OR 97401.

Pickwick Publications
An Imprint of Wipf and Stock Publishers
199 W. 8th Ave., Suite 3
Eugene, OR 97401

www.wipfandstock.com

PAPERBACK ISBN: 978-1-5326-9340-3
HARDCOVER ISBN: 978-1-5326-9341-0
EBOOK ISBN: 978-1-5326-9342-7

Cataloguing-in-Publication data:

Names: Newkirk, Matthew, author.

Title: Fill the earth : the creation mandate and the church's call to missions / Matthew Newkirk

Description: Eugene, OR: Pickwick Publications, 2020 | Includes bibliographical references and index.

Identifiers: ISBN 978-1-5326-9340-3 (paperback) | ISBN 978-1-5326-9341-0 (hardcover) | ISBN 978-1-5326-9342-7 (ebook)

Subjects: LCSH: Mission of the church | Mission of the church—Biblical teaching | Missions—Biblical teaching

Classification: BV2073 N495 2020 (paperback) | BV2073 (ebook)

Manufactured in the U.S.A. 04/07/20

To my parents

CONTENTS

List of Tables | ix
Permissions | xi
Preface | xiii
Acknowledgments | xv
Abbreviations | xvii

1 MISSION MANDATED | 1
   Creation

2 MISSION FRUSTRATED | 22
   The Primeval History

3 MISSION RESUMED | 46
   The Call of Abram

4 MISSION ORGANIZED | 66
   The Call of Israel

5 MISSION FAILED | 101
   The Fall of Israel

6 MISSION INTEGRATED | 130
   Tying the Old Testament Threads Together

7 MISSION REDEEMED | 167
   Jesus and the Missional Roles of the Old Testament

8 MISSION REINSTATED | 188
   The Call and Equipping of the Church

9 MISSION EXECUTED | 219
The Expansion of the Church

10 MISSION FULFILLED | 249
The New Creation

11 MISSION TODAY | 265
The Church's Call to Missions

Bibliography | 287
Scripture Index | 303

TABLES

Table 1. The Old Testament Background to New Testament Missions | 10
Table 2. Enoch and Lamech in the Lines of Cain and Seth | 43
Table 3. Creation Mandate, Land, and Blessing in the Patriarchal Narratives | 63
Table 4. Conditional vs. Definitional If/Then Statements | 73
Table 5. The Foreign Sailors' Escalating Fear in Jonah | 136
Table 6. Jesus' First Temptation (Matt 4:3–4) | 174
Table 7. Jesus' Second Temptation (Matt 4:5–7) | 174
Table 8. Jesus' Third Temptation (Matt 4:8–10) | 175
Table 9. The Creation Mandate and the Spread of the Word of God in Acts | 225

PERMISSIONS

Unless otherwise noted, all Scripture quotations are taken from The Holy Bible, English Standard Version® (ESV®), Copyright © 2001 by Crossway, a publishing ministry of Good News Publishers. Used by permission. All rights reserved.

Scripture quotations marked "ASV" are taken from the American Standard Version (1901).

Scripture quotations marked "CSB" are taken from the Christian Standard Bible, Copyright © 2017 by Holman Bible Publishers. Used by permission. Christian Standard Bible and CSB are federally registered trademarks of Holman Bible Publishers.

Scripture quotations marked "HCSB" are taken from the Holman Christian Standard Bible®, Copyright © 1999, 2000, 2002, 2003, 2010 by Holman Bible Publishers. All rights reserved.

Scripture quotations marked "KJV" are taken from The King James Version.

Scripture quotations marked "NASB" are taken from the New American Standard Bible®, copyright © 1960, 1962, 1963, 1968, 1971, 1972, 1973, 1975, 1977, 1995 by The Lockman Foundation. Used by permission.

Scripture quotations marked "NIV" are taken from the HOLY BIBLE, NEW INTERNATIONAL VERSION®. NIV®. Copyright © 1973, 1978, 1984, 2011 by International Bible Society. Used by permission of Zondervan. All rights reserved worldwide.

Scripture quotations marked "NLT" are taken from the Holy Bible, New Living Translation. Copyright © 1996, 2004, 2007, 2013, 2015 by Tyndale House Foundation. Used by permission of Tyndale House Publishers Inc., Carol Stream, Illinois 60188. All rights reserved.

PERMISSIONS

Scripture quotations marked "NKJV" are taken from the New King James Version. Copyright © 1982 by Thomas Nelson, Inc. Used by permission. All rights reserved.

Scripture quotations marked "NRSV" are taken from the New Revised Standard Version Bible, copyright © 1989, Division of Christian Education of the National Council of the Churches of Christ in the United States of America. Used by permission. All rights reserved.

PREFACE

In the fall of 2005, I entered Reformed Theological Seminary in Orlando, Florida, fully expecting to earn a master's degree, go on to complete a PhD, and then pursue a career in academia. What I did not expect was to have my understanding of the Bible, the church, and the world so dramatically transformed that I would leave seminary with a passion to see Jesus' name proclaimed among the nations. But that's exactly what happened. In God's providence my first year in seminary was Richard Pratt's last year on resident faculty, and it is no understatement to say that the two courses I took from him during that year have forever changed the course of my life.

Richard is an Old Testament scholar by training, yet the way he explained the metanarrative of the entire Bible as an account of the kingdom of God coming to earth was both deeply fascinating and utterly convincing to me. It was he who first exposed me to the idea that biblical mission begins in Genesis 1, that it pertains fundamentally to the establishment of God's kingdom on earth, and that the work of missions is a central mechanism by which this mission is executed throughout history.

For many years these ideas simmered on the back burner of my mind as seminary work gave way to PhD studies, dissertation writing, pastoring, and teaching. Yet throughout those years my interest in reading the Bible as a missional metanarrative grounded in creation never faded. When the time came for my family and I to begin our journey to the mission field, I wanted to explore in more detail the breadth and depth of this missional thinking that had shaped my life in such a significant way. This book is the result of that exploration.

Unintentionally the compositional process of this book reflects the centrality of the Christ event for the mission of the church. Just as the Old Testament anticipates Jesus' coming and the New Testament reflects back upon it, so it happened that I wrote chapters 1–6 on the Old Testament while preparing to move to Japan and chapters 7–11 on the New Testament while serving here on the mission field. Inasmuch as the Scriptures find their central pivot on the redeeming work of Jesus, so was the writing of this book punctuated by my moving to a foreign land for the sake of his name.

My hope is that the theology of mission outlined in this book will encourage you to see how the church of Jesus Christ is caught up in the sweep of the biblical story, and that this story is simultaneously God-centered, global, and glorious in nature. My prayer is that whether your calling is to "go" or to "send," you will see that the work of missions is the contemporary expression of a much larger mission that is as ancient as creation itself, and that by seeing this you will reflect in fresh ways on how you might participate in the spread of the gospel to all nations. May Jesus receive all praise, honor, and glory as his people seek to represent his kingship to the ends of the earth.

ACKNOWLEDGMENTS

Any book project benefits from the ideas, efforts, and sacrifices of many people besides the author, and this book is no different. Above all I am grateful to God for extending his mercy to me, including me in his mission in this world, and enabling me to complete this study. I am thankful for my teachers who have sparked my interest in this subject and have continued to fan its flame through their preaching, teaching, and writing. In particular I am indebted to Richard Pratt, Greg Beale, and Daniel Block for the indelible imprint that their collective influence has had on my thinking. These men have spent their lives investing in future leaders of the church, among whom I count myself blessed to be a beneficiary.

I also wish to express gratitude to the congregations of St. Paul's Presbyterian Church in Orlando, FL and Redeemer Presbyterian Church in Raleigh, NC, as well as my students at Christ Bible Seminary in Nagoya, Japan. I have had the privilege of teaching much of this material in these different contexts and have had my thinking sharpened and refined in the process by students and congregants alike. There is no better place than the body of Christ to help one understand the word of God more clearly, and I have benefitted greatly from the wide variety of perspectives on these matters that I have encountered over the years. In particular I am thankful to my colleagues Eric Ortlund and Damon Cha for reading portions of this manuscript and offering helpful feedback for improvement. Any remaining deficiencies are my responsibility alone.

My wife, Caroline, has always been a believer in this project. She has had a missionary heart since her youth and never required the depth of argument that I did in order to leave family and familiarity for the sake of the gospel. Although she understands well the analysis in these pages, she has always been more eager than I to serve Jesus to the ends of the earth simply because he commanded his followers to "go." Our children—Lydia, Silas, Ethan, and Chloe—are missionaries by birth, yet their love for our host country and its people is contagious and continues to encourage me as the years go on. I am so very thankful to be a missionary with this precious crew that God has given me.

Lastly, I dedicate this book to my parents, Mike and Marcia Newkirk. Since I was a boy they have modeled what Christ-like love and leadership looks like, they were the first to teach me the essential truths of the Scriptures, and they have never wavered in their support as I grew up and decided to take their grandchildren across the world. Their commitment to seeing Jesus' kingdom spread supersedes their affections for the good things of this world, which is not simply a lesson they have taught me through their words but that which I have observed in them over the four decades of my life. They have been the primary instrument that God has used to shape me and have invested in me more than I will ever have the capacity to repay. This volume is but a modest contribution that I offer in gratitude to them, and I pray it brings glory to the God they esteem above all else.

ABBREVIATIONS

AB	Anchor Bible
AOTC	Apollos Old Testament Commentary
ASMS	American Society of Missiology Series
BBR	*Bulletin for Biblical Research*
BCOTWP	Baker Commentary on the Old Testament Wisdom and Psalms
BECNT	Baker Exegetical Commentary on the New Testament
Bib	*Biblica*
BIS	Biblical Interpretation Series
BJS	Biblical and Judaic Studies
BSac	*Bibliotheca sacra*
BST	Bible Speaks Today
BZAW	Beihefte zur Zeitschrift für die alttestamentliche Wissenschaft
BZNW	Beihefte zur Zeitschrift für die neutestamentliche Wissenschaft
CBQ	*Catholic Biblical Quarterly*
CTJ	*Calvin Theological Journal*
CTR	*Criswell Theological Review*
CurTM	*Currents in Theology and Mission*
ECC	Eerdmans Critical Commentary
ETL	*Ephemerides theologicae lovanienses*
FRLANT	Forschungen zur Religion und Literatur des Alten und Neuen Testaments
HBM	Hebrew Bible Monographs
HBT	*Horizons in Biblical Theology*
HS	Hebrew Studies

IBC	Interpretation: A Bible Commentary for Teaching and Preaching
IBMR	*International Bulletin of Missionary Research*
IBS	*Irish Biblical Studies*
IJFM	*International Journal of Frontier Missions*
ITC	International Theological Commentary
ITSS	Invitation to Theological Studies Series
JBL	*Journal of Biblical Literature*
JCTR	*Journal for Christian Theological Research*
JETS	*Journal of the Evangelical Theological Society*
JPT	*Journal of Pentecostal Theology*
JSNT	*Journal for the Study of the New Testament*
JSNTSup	Journal for the Study of the New Testament: Supplement Series
JSOT	*Journal for the Study of the Old Testament*
JSOTSup	Journal for the Study of the Old Testament: Supplement Series
JTAK	*Journal of Theta Alpha Kappa*
JTI	*Journal of Theological Interpretation*
JTSA	*Journal of Theology for Southern Africa*
KEL	Kregel Exegetical Library
LBS	Library of Biblical Studies
LHBOTS	Library of Hebrew Bible / Old Testament Studies
LNTS	Library of New Testament Studies
LXX	Septuagint
Missiology	*Missiology: An International Review*
MNTSS	McMaster New Testament Studies Series
MSJ	*The Master's Seminary Journal*
MT	Masoretic Text
NAC	New American Commentary
NICNT	New International Commentary on the New Testament
NICOT	New International Commentary on the Old Testament
NIDOTTE	*New International Dictionary of Old Testament Theology and Exegesis.* 5 Vols. Edited by Willem A. VanGemeren. Grand Rapids: Zondervan, 1997.
NIGTC	New International Greek Testament Commentary
NIVAC	New International Version Application Commentary

NovT	*Novum Testamentum*
NSBT	New Studies in Biblical Theology
NTL	New Testament Library
NTS	*New Testament Studies*
OTE	Old Testament Essays
OTL	Old Testament Library
PBM	Paternoster Biblical Monographs
PNTC	The Pillar New Testament Commentary
PRSt	*Perspectives in Religious Studies*
ResQ	*Restoration Quarterly*
RevExp	*Review and Expositor*
RTR	*Reformed Theological Review*
SHBC	Smyth & Helwys Bible Commentary
SJT	*Southwestern Journal of Theology*
SMT	*Swedish Missiological Themes*
THOTC	The Two Horizons Old Testament Commentary
TLOT	*Theological Lexicon of the Old Testament.* 3 vols. Edited by Ernst Jenni and Claus Westermann. Translated by Mark Biddle. Peabody, MA: Hendrickson, 1997.
TNTC	Tyndale New Testament Commentary
TOTC	Tyndale Old Testament Commentary
TTC	Teach the Text Commentary Series
TynBul	*Tyndale Bulletin*
VT	*Vetus Testamentum*
WBC	Word Biblical Commentary
WCF	Westminster Confession of Faith
WLC	Westminster Larger Catechism
WSC	Westminster Shorter Catechism
WTJ	*Westminster Theological Journal*
WUNT	Wissenschaftliche Untersuchungen zum Neuen Testament
ZAW	Zeitschrift für die alttestamentliche Wissenschaft

1 MISSION MANDATED
Creation

I can still hear the pounding thump of the kick drum. Steady quarter notes came bellowing through the sound system as the worship leader led the crowd, hands lifted high, clapping our hands to the same beat. I was an undergraduate student attending the winter conference of a prominent evangelical campus ministry. This particular evening we had just heard a rousing talk exhorting us to commit ourselves to God's purposes for the world as outlined in the Great Commission. The speaker's challenge that night was bold and specific: would we devote at least one year of our life to the work of missions? To the side of the stage was a giant white poster with "The Great Commission" written at the top and the text of Matt 28:18-20 written in smaller font beneath. As the kick drum thumped and the crowd clapped, the speaker returned to the stage and invited everyone who would heed Jesus' departing command to come down and write their names on the poster. Hundreds of students eagerly descended to the side of the stage and signed their names, thereby committing themselves to a season of missionary service. It was an exciting night. The energy in the room was palpable. Hugs were exchanged. High fives were given. This was a conference that people would remember.

But I did not sign my name.

Looking back, several factors explain my lack of participation that evening. By disposition I am not one to make impulsive decisions, and to sign my name on such a poster felt quite impulsive to me. I am also a bit of a contrarian, so the fact that such a large group responded in such an overwhelmingly positive way made me hesitant to participate at the time. However, the primary reason I did not sign my name that evening was my perception that the speaker was making too much of missions. "This is just one passage," I thought. "What about the rest of the Bible? If missions is so significant, why doesn't the Bible talk more about it?"

Years later I continue to find validity in those questions. That is, the rest of the Bible is important, and if missions is so significant we should expect the Bible to devote more space to it than a few scattered verses here and there. However, in the years since that college conference I have also come to realize that the Bible *does* talk more about missions than a few scattered verses. In fact, I am now persuaded that *the entire Bible* provides compelling rationale for the work of missions, though such a whole-Bible basis for the missionary task is rarely explicated in the church today. Such is the burden of this book: to show how the church's call to missions is based not simply on Jesus' most famous post-resurrection command, or even on a few "missions verses," but on a biblical theology that begins with God's first mandate to humanity at creation. My goal is to highlight this missional thread that begins in the creation account and show how it weaves its way throughout the Scriptures, reaching its apex in Jesus' Great Commission and finding its fulfillment in the new creation. In so doing we will see that, far from being a tangential responsibility of the church, missions is an endeavor that is grounded in the entire breadth of Scripture and therefore is of central importance for the people of God today.

DEFINITIONS

Before we embark on this study, however, we must first define our terms. Throughout the following discussion I will use two similar terms that missiologists have long distinguished—*mission* and *missions*.[1] Etymologically the word "mission" derives from the Latin word *missio*, which means "sending." Therefore when we talk about "the *mission* of the church" we are discussing what the church has been sent into this world to do. Why does the church exist, and what should we be hoping to accomplish? Or to use Christopher Wright's language, what is the church's "long-term purpose or goal that is to be achieved through proximate objectives and planned actions"?[2] The church's mission is therefore the big-picture concept; it is the overall task that the church as a whole is called to carry out in this world.

In order to fulfill this mission, as Wright notes, several "proximate objectives and planned actions" must be executed. Activities such as evangelism, discipleship, and worship are no doubt to be included on this list, as is

---

1. See, e.g., Bosch, *Transforming Mission*, 10; Moreau et al., *Introducing World Missions*, 72–73; Goheen, *Introducing Christian Mission Today*, 85–86.
2. Wright, *Mission of God*, 23.

the work of *missions*. On a popular level, "missions" used to be understood as ministering the gospel in a foreign country, and therefore "missionaries" were those who went to foreign lands and ministered.[3] In recent years, however, the label "missions" has come to be applied to a whole spectrum of ministries, both foreign and domestic. These days it is common for everyone from church planters to campus ministers to prison chaplains to be referred to as "missionaries." Some churches even have signs at the exits of their parking lots that read, "Now entering the mission field," implying that *every believer* is a missionary.

In contrast to this, an important stream of missiology has defined "missions" more narrowly and distinguished it from other types of ministry. William Carey, "the father of modern missions" (1761–1834), argued that for missiological purposes we should distinguish between (1) those who do not believe the gospel but have access to it, and (2) those who have no access to the gospel. In his groundbreaking pamphlet, *An Enquiry into the Obligations of Christians to Use Means for the Conversion of the Heathens*, Carey wrote:

> Our own countrymen have the means of grace, and may attend on the word preached if they choose it. They have the means of knowing and truth, and faithful ministers are placed in almost every part of the land, whose spheres of action might be much extended if their congregations were but more hearty and active in the cause; but with them the case is widely different, who have no Bible, no written language (which many of them have not), no ministers.[4]

It is this latter group in Carey's description—those who have *no access* to the gospel—that missions is directed toward. Every people group in the world has unbelievers within it and therefore gospel witness is needed everywhere. However, people groups without a sufficient indigenous gospel witness have no immediate access to the good news of Jesus. The work of missions seeks to establish a gospel witness in such places. Accordingly, a "missionary" is one who follows the example of Paul, who said, "I make it my ambition to preach the gospel, *not where Christ has already been named*, lest I build on someone else's foundation" (Rom 15:20). On this definition, missions should not be viewed simply as ministering the gospel in a foreign land or starting new ministries in places where the indigenous church already has a sufficient presence. Rather, as Michael Goheen writes, the goal of missions

---

3. See the description in Stott, *Christian Mission in the Modern World*, 15–16.

4. Carey, *Enquiry*, 13. See also the very helpful discussion of Carey's view by Tennent, "William Carey as a Missiologist," 23–26.

is "to establish a witness to the gospel in places or among peoples where there is none or where it is very weak."[5] This is the definition I will use throughout this study. The reason for doing so is not to downplay other avenues of ministry or to elevate the work of missions above them, but to distinguish the geographical and ethnolinguistic spread of the gospel from other forms of ministry in order to analyze how it is presented throughout the canon.

METHOD

In order to establish this whole-Bible rationale for missions, I will proceed in this study by a three-step process. First I will summarize the mission of God in this world. What is God's long-term purpose or goal for this world? What does God want to accomplish? As we will see, the creation account reveals God's original mission for this world, and this *missio Dei*[6]—or mission of God—provides the necessary context for us to proceed to the second step of our process: assessing the mission of God's people. Why did God create a people for himself on the earth? What are we supposed to be doing in this world? As will become clear, God has seen fit to execute his mission through his people, and therefore the mission of God's people may be viewed as the mechanism by which the mission of God is accomplished. Since God's people began neither with the New Testament church nor with Old Testament Israel—but with humanity at creation—it follows that to understand the mission of God's people today we must go back to the creation account and examine humanity's mission in the garden. As I will seek to show, the mission of humanity at creation is the theological precursor both to the mission of Israel and the mission of the church, and it is only by examining this mission of God's people across the canon that we will properly understand the mission of God's people today.

This will then enable us to move to the third and final step of our process: seeing how the mission of the church ought to direct the work of missions today. As mentioned above, missions is only one component among many within the church's broader mission. However, as I hope to

---

5. Goheen, *Introducing Christian Mission Today*, 402.

6. The Latin phrase *missio Dei* is popular in missiological literature, and those who employ it hold to a wide spectrum of views concerning the nature and scope of Christian mission. Peter Pikkert has rightly raised concerns over the emphases of some whose missiology may be classified by this phrase (see *Essence and Implications of Missio Dei*). Although I use this phrase here at the outset due to a conviction that Christian mission must flow from divine mission, I share many of Pikkert's concerns over certain aspects of this diverse theology of missions that has been characterized by this phrase.

show throughout this study, missions is a component of critical and strategic necessity without which the church's mission will not be fulfilled. Consequently, if we do not allow our overall *mission* as God's people to direct the way we execute the work of *missions*, we will serve God neither wisely nor strategically. The logic of this study may therefore be depicted as follows:

Figure 1. The Mission of God and the Mission of God's People

Mission of God
↓
Mission of God's People
Mission of humanity at creation
Mission of Israel
Mission of the church

Evangelism – Discipleship – Worship – **Missions** – et al

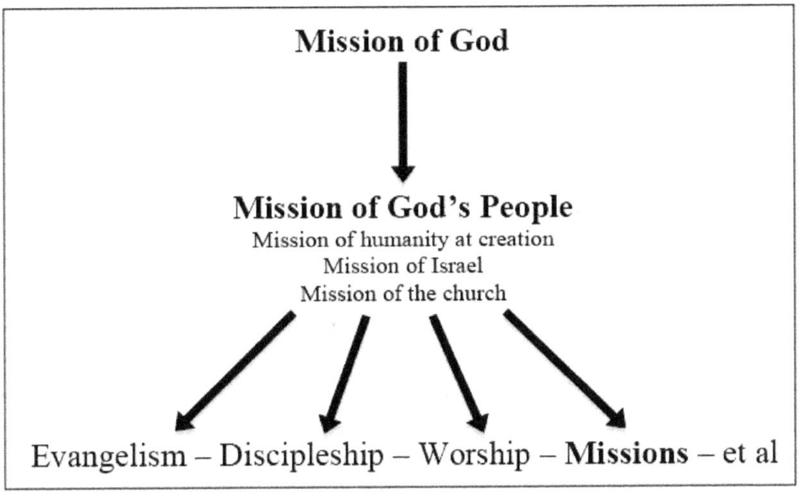

Based on this logic, in order to gain a firm, whole-Bible grounding for the work of missions, we must begin by summarizing the mission of God in this world and see how God has chosen to execute this mission through his people.

THE MISSION OF GOD AND THE MISSION OF GOD'S PEOPLE

Any attempt to summarize a theme as massive as "the mission of God" is surely prone to reductionism at some level. Nevertheless, it is still instructive to articulate this concept as best as we can in order to discuss profitably what God wants to accomplish in this world. With that caveat, what I will attempt to substantiate throughout this book is that *God's mission in the world is for his kingship to be represented to the ends of the earth.* This statement has three primary components that must be demonstrated throughout the course of our study.

First, we must see that God fundamentally reveals himself in Scripture as *King.* Modern Western Christians find it easy to think of God as "Father" or even as "friend,"[7] labels that the Bible certainly uses to describe God at various points (e.g., Matt 7:11; Luke 11:13; Jas 2:23). However, first and foremost the Scriptures portray God as the sovereign King of creation who demands exclusive allegiance from his creatures. Recognizing this royal portrayal is critical for understanding what God expects the church to be doing in the world.

Second, we need to see that, as King, God desires to be *represented* in this world. Kings rule over realms, and these realms must be defined by some recognizable means. In some cases natural geographical boundaries have defined realms (e.g., oceans, mountain ranges, etc.), while in others artificially constructed borders have marked the extent of kingdoms. As we will see, God has seen fit to establish his realm not through natural boundaries or man-made borders but through the presence of *representatives*. These representatives are God's faithful and allegiant people, and God's kingship is represented rightly only where these authorized representatives treat him as King.

Third, we must see that God desires this royal representation to be extended *to the ends of the earth*. All earthly rulers have geographically limited realms, but God has decreed that his kingdom should be limitless, encompassing the entire earth. Since this is God's mission in the world, by extension the mission of God's people is *to fill the earth as God's representatives and thereby demonstrate that his kingship extends over the entire earth*.[8] As we progress in our analysis we will survey how the biblical text introduces and unfolds this theology of mission, which will then provide a biblical orientation for grounding the work of missions today.

A THEOCENTRIC MOTIVE FOR MISSIONS

If the above theology of mission can be substantiated, what results is a thoroughly theocentric motive for missions. I have attended many missions conferences and read many books on missions where the appeal for the listener/reader to get involved in missionary activity goes something like this: "There are billions of people in the world who have never heard the gospel, and unless we go and preach to them, they are doomed to a Christless

---

7. See the discussion of Luhrmann, *When God Talks Back*, 3–5.

8. Throughout this book, whenever I speak of humanity filling the earth, I am assuming that human representation of God's kingship is only required in places that God has made habitable for human life. So, for example, God does not expect his people to live in Antarctica or in the middle of the Pacific Ocean where there is no sufficiently large land mass suitable for human dwelling.

eternity."⁹ While this is true, throughout this book I hope to show that such an argument should not be our primary rationale for the work of missions. It is not that compassion for the lost and a desire to see them saved is wrong. On the contrary, it is right and necessary for believers to care about the welfare of unbelievers—such concern reflects God's own posture toward those who are lost (see, e.g., Jonah 4:11; 1 Tim 2:3–4). However, such a concern, as good as it is, can at best be considered a penultimate motive for missions because it is fundamentally anthropocentric.¹⁰

To develop a theocentric motive for missions, we need to situate the work of missions within the larger framework of the mission of God. If God's mission in the world is for his kingship to be represented to the ends of the earth, then the ultimate motive for missions must be to advance this divine agenda. That is, we preach the gospel to peoples with little or no access to it (*missions*) so they will come to represent God's kingship through faithful allegiance to him (*mission*). Although concern for the lost is right and good, our ultimate preoccupation as we consider the missionary task should be nothing less than the spread of God's kingly glory over the entire creation. This distinction is important, since our ultimate motive will be the prime driver of our strategies as we seek to fulfill the mission God has given us. Before contemplating how this mission is fulfilled, however, we must first substantiate our choice to begin this study of missions with the creation account.

THE SCRIPTURAL BASIS FOR A THEOLOGY OF MISSIONS

When I was a freshman in high school I wanted to try out for the school's golf team. It seemed like a great way to spend time outside and develop skills at a sport I could play throughout my life. There was just one problem: I wasn't very good at it. No matter how much I practiced, I was simply not skilled at hitting the ball straight. I tended to hit the ball at an angle, and

---

9. One example of this may be found in Platt, *Radical*. Although Platt rightly acknowledges that humanity's chief calling from creation is to spread God's glory throughout the earth (64–65), most of the argumentation for missions throughout the book appeals to the fate of the billions of unbelievers throughout the world (e.g., 14, 19, 76, 105, 154, 155, 157, 186, 200).

10. Contra Pikkert, for example, who says, "The eternal wellbeing of the human soul really, really matters—ultimately more than anything else" (*Essence and Implications of Missio Dei*, 52). On the contrary, although we must affirm the great importance of the eternal wellbeing of the human soul, more important than this is the glory of God manifested and recognized throughout his creation.

therefore it didn't matter how hard I hit it or how far it went; because the ball's flight did not start off properly, it never had an accurate trajectory and thus was more likely to land in the woods than on the green. These lousy golf skills of mine provide a helpful analogy as we embark on our study of missions. Unless our biblical analysis starts off properly, we will not have an accurate trajectory and thus will not reach our desired destination. Rather than landing on the green of proper understanding, we will end up in the woods of missional misperception. Consequently, choosing where in the Bible to begin our study of missions is crucial for our efforts to be successful.

The most common passage used to support the work of missions is doubtless Jesus' Great Commission to his disciples, recorded in its most famous form in Matt 28:18–20. This was the passage employed by that dynamic speaker I heard in my college days. It was also this passage that William Carey used to ground the argument of his missiological pamphlet quoted above. More recently, Kevin DeYoung and Greg Gilbert have surveyed three other passages that have been suggested as offering firmer starting points for understanding the church's mission: Gen 12:1–3, Exod 19:5–6, and Luke 4:16–21.[11] DeYoung and Gilbert examine these texts, find them insufficient as starting points for a missional theology, and then proceed to make their case for using the Great Commission texts of the New Testament to articulate the mission of the church.[12] In arguing for their New Testament-centered approach, they suggest that "the Old Testament is concerned mainly with the nation of Israel" and therefore is inadequate to ground a missional theology.[13] They further argue that

> God's old covenant people are never exhorted to engage in intentional cross-cultural mission. Their mission light shines by attraction, not active invitation. For all these reasons the New Testament is a better place to look for a strong missionary impulse.[14]

In response, although it is true that the majority of the *content* of the Old Testament focuses on Israel, it is hardly the case that the primary *concern* of the Old Testament is Israel in a parochial manner.[15] Moreover, although we may agree that Israel's cross-cultural mission was to be centripetal rather

---

11. DeYoung and Gilbert, *What Is the Mission of the Church?*, 29–40.

12. DeYoung and Gilbert, *What Is the Mission of the Church?*, 40–45. By "Great Commission texts" they include not only Matt 28:18–20 but also Mark 13:10; 14:9; Luke 24:44–49; Acts 1:8; and John 20:21.

13. DeYoung and Gilbert, *What Is the Mission of the Church?*, 42.

14. DeYoung and Gilbert, *What Is the Mission of the Church?*, 42–43.

15. See the helpful discussion of Bavinck, *Science of Missions*, 11–17.

than centrifugal—that is, they were to attract the nations rather than go out to them—we must challenge DeYoung and Gilbert's conclusion that the Old Testament therefore does not provide "a strong missionary impulse" for the church.

Do the Scriptures of the apostolic church really have nothing meaningful to teach us about the church's call to missions? When Paul says that "All Scripture (which at that point meant the Old Testament!) is breathed out by God and profitable . . . that the man of God may be complete, equipped for *every* good work" (2 Tim 3:16–17), does this not include the good work of missions? Indeed, Paul himself, the "apostle to the Gentiles" (Rom 11:13), grounded his own missionary calling in Isa 49:6 (Acts 13:47). In line with this, James later ratified the Gentile mission at the Jerusalem Council by quoting Amos 9:11–12 (Acts 15:13–18). These passages show that the earliest Christians most certainly viewed the Old Testament as informative for a theology of missions. But perhaps the most important question we should ask is if Jesus saw the Old Testament as providing a strong missionary impulse for the church. How did Jesus view the Old Testament as it relates to the theme of missions?

It is common these days for people to engage in a "Christocentric" interpretation of the Old Testament, by which Christ is viewed as the "center" of the Bible's message.[16] It is also becoming prevalent among interpreters to approach the Old Testament in a "Christotelic" fashion, whereby Christ is viewed as the *telos* or culmination of Scripture.[17] However, in seeking a starting point for our theology of missions, we will employ a "Christoscopic" approach; that is, how did Jesus *view* the Old Testament as it relates to the theme of missions? The clearest answer to this question is found in Luke 24. After his resurrection, Jesus appears to his disciples and says to them,

> "These are my words that I spoke to you while I was still with you, that everything written about me in the Law of Moses and the Prophets and the Psalms must be fulfilled." Then he opened their minds to understand the Scriptures, and said to them, "Thus it is written, that the Christ should suffer and on the third day rise from the dead, *and that repentance and forgiveness of sins should be proclaimed in his name to all nations*, beginning from Jerusalem." (vv. 44–47)[18]

16. E.g., Greidanus, *Preaching Christ from the Old Testament*, 227–78.

17. E.g., Enns, *Inspiration and Incarnation*, 177–78; Green, "LORD Is Christ's Shepherd," 33–46.

18. Others who note the significance of this passage for understanding the Old Testament's missional character include Wright, *Mission of God*, 29–30; McKenzie, "Hebrew Bible and the Nations," 146.

In this passage, Luke first notes that Jesus "opened their minds to *understand* the Scriptures" (v. 45), which at that point referred to the Old Testament. This implies that without recognizing what Jesus says next, one does not understand the Old Testament properly. Jesus goes on to say that what is written in the Old Testament climaxes with repentance and forgiveness being proclaimed "to all nations" (v. 47). According to Jesus, therefore, understanding the Old Testament properly means recognizing that it has an *international missionary message.*

The apostle Paul also affirms this missional understanding of the Old Testament. When defending himself to Herod Agrippa and Festus the Roman governor, Paul argues that he is "saying nothing but what the prophets and Moses said would come to pass: that the Christ must suffer and that, by being the first to rise from the dead, *he would proclaim light both to our people and to the Gentiles*" (Acts 26:22–23). In this passage, the word translated "Gentiles" is the same as "nations" in Luke 24:47 (*ethnos*), which is also the term Jesus uses in the Great Commission when commanding his followers to "make disciples of all *nations*" (Matt 28:19). What all this means is that, according to both Jesus and Paul, what Jesus commands his disciples in the Great Commission has already been attested to in the Old Testament Scriptures.

Table 1. The Old Testament Background to New Testament Missions

	Luke 24	Acts 26	Matt 28
Source	"Thus it is written [in the Scriptures]" (v. 46)	"the prophets and Moses said [this] would come to pass" (v. 22)	"Jesus came and said to them" (v. 18)
Content	That "repentance and forgiveness" would be proclaimed "to all nations (*ethnos*)" (v. 47)	That "light" would be proclaimed "to the Gentiles (*ethnos*)" (v. 23)	"Go . . . and make disciples of all nations (*ethnos*)" (v. 19).

As this table shows, in all three passages the *content* relayed concerns international missions. In the first two passages, however, the *source* of this content is the Old Testament. It follows that to understand fully both the concept of God's mission and our role in missions, we need to pursue a *whole-Bible, biblical theology of mission.* In light of these statements by Jesus and Paul we must incorporate both the Law of Moses and the Prophets, which in the first century was likely shorthand for the entire Hebrew canon.[19] This means that

---

19. Witherington, *Indelible Image*, 137. The Hebrew canon is divided into three

if we want to reach our desired destination of a well-grounded theology of missions, rather than starting with the first book of the New Testament, we need to begin with the first book of the Old Testament.

MISSION MANDATED: GENESIS 1:1—2:3

With this background in place we may now begin our study by looking at the opening scene of the first book of the Bible: the creation account of Genesis 1:1—2:3. We begin with creation because God has had a mission in this world and a representative people on the earth ever since the beginning. God's mission did not begin after humanity sinned or even when he called Abram and entered into a covenant with him—important as these events are.[20] Rather, God created the world with a mission that he wanted to see accomplished from the very beginning. This mission is reflected in what God commands humanity to do at creation, and therefore it is incumbent upon us to begin our analysis of mission in this opening account of Genesis.[21] In exploring this passage I will briefly examine how the creation account portrays both God and humanity, after which I will summarize the original mission that God gives humanity at creation.

God as King of Creation and Humanity as His Representative Images

When examining the opening account of Genesis, we may easily highlight numerous aspects of God's portrayal at creation. God is depicted as

---

major sections: (1) *The Law* (Genesis to Deuteronomy); (2) *The Prophets* (which is further subdivided into the Former Prophets [Joshua to 2 Kings minus Ruth] and the Latter Prophets [Isaiah to Malachi]); and (3) *The Writings* (everything else). For a comprehensive study of the Old Testament canon, see Beckwith, *Old Testament Canon of the New Testament Church*.

20. Contra, e.g., Kaiser, who states, "[Genesis 12:3] is where mission really begins in a formal way. Here is the first Great Commission mandate of the Bible" (*Mission in the Old Testament*, xix), and Wright, who isolates Gen 12:3 as "the foundation of biblical mission, inasmuch as it presents the mission of God" (*Mission of God*, 328).

21. To my knowledge, the only other biblical-theological survey of mission that begins with Genesis 1 and traces the ongoing significance of the creation mandate throughout Scripture is Beale, *Temple and the Church's Mission*. This scholarly treatment has been simplified and streamlined in Beale and Kim, *God Dwells Among Us*. Whereas these two works use Gen 1:28 to focus primarily on the missional significance of the temple from creation to new creation, the present study complements this emphasis by focusing on how the creation mandate provides the theological foundation for the subsequent missional calls of Abram, Israel, and the church.

sovereign, personal, intentional, and wholly distinct from the created order. However, one aspect of God's portrayal is especially relevant for our purposes: *in creation God is depicted as King*. This is evident first of all by God's creating everything simply by issuing commands. Genesis 1:3 says, "And God said, 'Let there be light,' and there was light." Throughout the rest of the chapter we repeatedly read, "And God said,"[22] followed by "And it was so."[23] God speaks and creation obeys. This is the way a king rules.

Moreover, by naming and evaluating everything in creation, God reveals his authority as King.[24] God names the "day" and "night" (v. 5), the "Heaven" (v. 8), the "Earth" (v. 10a), and the "Seas" (v. 10b), and he repeatedly evaluates creation, conveyed by the six-fold refrain, "And God saw that it was good" (vv. 4, 10, 12, 18, 21, 25), followed by the climactic evaluation, "And God saw everything that he had made, and behold, it was very good" (v. 31). Only one who has authority over something may name and evaluate it in a meaningful way, and thus by naming and evaluating the fundamental elements of creation, God reveals his supreme authority over the created order. This is the authority that a king wields.

In addition to commanding, naming, and evaluating, God reveals his kingship in creation by resting on the seventh day (Gen 2:2–3). This seventh-day rest serves as the culmination to which the entire creation account builds and depicts God not as exhausted by creation but as exalted over it in his kingly splendor. Prior to describing God as "resting" from his creative work (v. 2b), the text notes that "on the seventh day God *finished* his work that he had done" (v. 2a). This sequence indicates that God's seventh-day rest is not a matter of his taking a break from creation but rather his enjoying its finality. In conjunction with the other imagery in this opening account, the picture that emerges here is of God powerfully and authoritatively bringing creation into being and then resting on his throne as King over the cosmos. As God will say later, "Heaven is my throne, and the earth is my footstool; what is the house that you would build for me, *and what is the place of my rest?*" (Isa 66:1; cf. Acts 7:49).[25] For God to "rest," therefore, portrays him sitting upon his heavenly throne with ultimate sovereignty over the created order.

---

22. Verses 5, 9a, 11a, 14, 20, 24a, 26
23. Verses 7, 9b, 11b, 15, 24b, 30
24. Turner, *Genesis*, 20.
25. The term in Isa 66:1 translated "rest" (*minûḥâ*) is different than that used in Gen 2:2–3 (*šāḇaṯ*), though the semantic ranges of these two terms overlap, as is evidenced by the fourth command of the Decalogue, which recalls God's creative "rest" in Gen 2:2–3 by using *nûaḥ*, the verbal form of *minûḥâ*.

Although Genesis 1 only implies God's kingship by these various creative actions, other biblical texts explicitly connect God's work of creation with his status as King. For example, Psalm 74 begins by asking why God has allowed Israel to experience the pain of exile without exacting judgment on their enemies (vv. 1–11), following this with a declaration of God's kingship as Creator:

> Yet God *my King* is from of old,
>   working salvation in the midst of the earth.
> You divided the sea by your might;
>   you broke the heads of the sea monsters on the waters.
> You crushed the heads of Leviathan;
>   you gave him as food for the creatures of the wilderness.
> You split open springs and brooks;
>   you dried up ever-flowing streams.
> Yours is the day, yours also the night;
>   you have established the heavenly lights and the sun.
> You have fixed all the boundaries of the earth;
>   you have made summer and winter. (vv. 12–17)

This passage associates God's kingship (v. 12) with his powerful division of the sea at creation (v. 13a; cf. Gen 1:9–10)—here characterized by reference to the mythic sea beast Leviathan (vv. 13b–14)—as well as his authority over the "day" and "night" (v. 16a; cf. Gen 1:5) and "the heavenly lights and the sun" (v. 16b; cf. Gen 1:14–19).

Similarly, Psalm 89 calls the heavens to praise God for his incomparability among the celestial beings (vv. 5–8), after which it describes God's kingly reign in the context of creation:

> You *rule* the raging of the sea;
>   when its waves rise, you still them.
> You crushed Rahab like a carcass;
>   you scattered your enemies with your mighty arm.
> The heavens are yours; the earth also is yours;
>   the world and all that is in it, you have *founded* them.
> The north and the south, you have *created* them;
>   Tabor and Hermon joyously praise your name.
> You have a mighty arm;
>   strong is your hand, high your right hand.
> Righteousness and justice are the foundation of *your throne*;
>   steadfast love and faithfulness go before you. (vv. 9–14)

This text describes God as "ruling" (*māšal*) over the seas (v. 9) and destroying the primordial sea monster "Rahab" (v. 10) in another allusion to Canaanite cosmogony. By means of two merisms that each denote the entirety of creation ("heavens" and "earth"; "north" and "south"), the psalmist depicts God as the sovereign owner of all things because he "founded"/"created" them (vv. 11–12), following this with descriptions of God's power ("mighty arm," "strong is your hand"; v. 13) and his kingship ("your throne"; v. 14). These texts make explicit the implicit portrayal of God as King in the creation account of Genesis. By creating, naming, evaluating, and resting above all things, God reveals his kingly authority over the entire created order.

In addition to this, and most significant for our purposes, in the Genesis account God reveals himself as King by setting up images of himself. On the sixth day of creation, God creates humanity by saying,

> Let us make man in our image, after our likeness. And let them have dominion over the fish of the sea and over the birds of the heavens and over the livestock and over all the earth and over every creeping thing that creeps on the earth. (Gen 1:26)

Throughout history most interpreters have explained the significance of the image of God as pertaining either to humanity's rational ability or our ethical responsibility before God.[26] These conclusions are not derived exegetically from the text of Genesis but are based upon the broader insights of systematic theology and/or perceived similarities between God and humanity as compared to the animal kingdom. However, it is widely recognized today that the use of the term "image" (ṣelem) in Genesis 1 has clear parallels in other ancient Near Eastern cultures. Israel's neighbors employed the word "image" in two relevant contexts: (1) deities had "images" on earth in the form of idols and/or the nation's king, which respectively embodied the deity's presence and mediated their reign, and (2) kings would erect and distribute "images" (i.e., statues) of themselves throughout their territories to mark the extent of their realms.[27] In both cases the presence of the image represented the reign of the deity or king. Although the significance of humanity as God's image undoubtedly includes additional elements,[28] it certainly contains no less than what this ancient Near Eastern context suggests.

---

26. For a concise survey of the history of interpretation, see Middleton, *Liberating Image*, 17–24.

27. See the discussion of Niehaus, *Ancient Near Eastern Themes*, 99–110. See also Middleton, *Liberating Image*, 26–27; Schmutzer, *Be Fruitful and Multiply*, 176–77.

28. For example, Col 3:10 describes "the new self" as being "renewed in knowledge after the image of its creator," and Eph 4:24 associates "the new self, created after the likeness of God," with "true righteousness and holiness." Therefore the Westminster Larger and Shorter Catechisms are justified in associating humanity's creation as God's image with "knowledge, righteousness, and holiness" (WLC 17; WSC 10). However, while this broader canonical perspective is true, the focus in Genesis and its ancient

The implications of this cultural background for our understanding of humanity as God's image are profound. In other ancient cultures, among humanity only the king was viewed as the image of God, the one who was responsible to represent the deity on earth. The book of Genesis, however, applies this royal title to all humanity and thus ascribes great dignity and responsibility to all people.[29] Moreover, this cultural background shows that for humanity to be created as God's image means that we are designed to serve as God's royal representatives on the earth. God is portrayed as the divine King, and humans are portrayed as his vice-regents, created to represent and mediate his reign upon the earth.[30]

God's Mission for Humanity

After creating humanity as his image, God gives them a mission, telling the first humans exactly how far and wide he wants them to spread and represent his kingship:

> And God blessed them. And God said to them, "Be fruitful and multiply and *fill the earth* and subdue it, and have dominion over the fish of the sea and over the birds of the heavens and over every living thing that moves on the earth." (v. 28)

Throughout this book I will refer to this verse as *the creation mandate*, and it will serve as our foundational text for understanding the mission of God's

---

Near Eastern context is not on cognitive and ethical capacities but rather on holistic, royal representation.

29. For a full-length study of this topic, see Pratt, *Designed for Dignity*.

30. I am not persuaded by Briggs's argument that this interpretation of the "image of God" in Genesis suffers because its "driving force ... lies outside the canon of scripture in toto" ("Humans in the Image of God," 116). On the contrary, we regularly rely on extrabiblical evidence for understanding biblical references to topography, foreign kings, or even for comprehending the semantics of certain Hebrew words based on their cognate use in other ancient languages. The Old Testament writers often did not explain their terminology or imagery precisely because they were operating within what John Walton calls the "cognitive environment" of the ancient Near East (*Ancient Near Eastern Thought*, 19–23). That is, they shared certain language, ideas, and assumptions with their audience that, while readily apparent to them, are not apparent to us given our temporal, cultural, and linguistic distance from them. For this reason it is incumbent upon us to enter their cognitive environment as best we can in order to understand the language and imagery they used to communicate to their audience. Therefore, gaining insight into the Old Testament's cognitive environment by means of literature from Israel's neighbors is a viable and indeed necessary means to understanding the language of the Old Testament.

people. In order to understand this text fully we will briefly explore each of its parts.

"And God blessed them"

In addition to the "creation mandate"[31] and the "cultural mandate,"[32] this verse has been called the "primaeval blessing"[33] and the "progeny blessing."[34] These latter two labels reflect the narrator's description of God's speech here as a *blessing*. In the Old Testament, a "blessing" such as this was often viewed as actualizing or enabling its content.[35] For example, when Rebekah convinces Jacob to disguise himself so he might receive Isaac's blessing instead of Esau (Gen 27:6–10), the content of Isaac's blessing describes Jacob becoming lord over his brothers: "Let peoples serve you, and nations bow down to you. Be lord over your brothers, and may your mother's sons bow down to you" (v. 29). When Esau later arrives and the ruse is uncovered, he demands that Isaac bless him too, but Isaac replies: "Behold, *I have made him lord over you*, and all his brothers *I have given to him* for servants, and with grain and wine *I have sustained him*. What then can I do for you, my son?" (v. 37). Since the blessing was viewed as actualizing its content, Isaac could say that by this blessing he had already made Jacob lord and therefore there was nothing he could do for Esau.

Similarly, in the creation account God blesses humanity, the content of which is introduced by, "And God said to them." In so doing God begins a process of actualizing the content of this blessing in the lives of its recipients. As the following clauses demonstrate, the content of this blessing pertains to human proliferation and governance over the earth, and therefore by *blessing* humanity this way God is enabling them to experience fertility and dominion. As Andrew Schmutzer says, in this verse humanity receives "a bestowal of life-force whereby the power-for-life possessed by God is generously transferred."[36]

---

31. E.g., Ott et al., *Encountering Theology of Mission*, 150; Schmutzer, *Be Fruitful and Multiply*, 20.
32. E.g., Hoekema, *Created in God's Image*, 79; Plantinga, *Engaging God's World*, 32.
33. E.g., Kaminski, *From Noah to Israel*.
34. E.g., Viands, *I Will Surely Multiply Your Offspring*.
35. Brown, "ברך," 758.
36. Schmutzer, *Be Fruitful and Multiply*, 66.

"Be fruitful and multiply"

Just as Isaac's blessing of Jacob consists of imperatives (Gen 27:29), so does God's blessing of humanity. The initial sequence of imperatives—"be fruitful (*pārâ*) and multiply (*rabbâ*)"—is best understood as a hendiadys, which is a syntactic arrangement in which multiple verbs combine to refer to a single, compound action. The collective sense of these first two imperatives is therefore "be abundantly fruitful."[37] God commands humanity to procreate abundantly and thereby multiply the number of his representative images on the earth.

Some have argued that, as blessings, these imperatives should not be viewed as commands to be obeyed but rather as privileges to be enjoyed. Theoretically this would seem to make these imperatives optional. For example, John Walton argues that

> granting a blessing (as in 1:28–30) must be recognized as delineating a privilege, not an obligation. In the ancient world, the ability to reproduce was seen as a gift from God. No one in that world would have considered foregoing the opportunity.[38]

Similarly, Jamie Viands says, "To command a blessing is inappropriate since all blessings are inherently desirable."[39] However, it does not follow that a privilege or desirable action may not be commanded. Carol Kaminski points to Moses' "blessing" on the Israelites in Deuteronomy 33 in which he commands Naphtali to "possess the lake and the south" (v. 23).[40] We may also point to Paul's command that fathers "bring them [i.e., their children] up in the discipline and instruction of the Lord" (Eph 6:4). Both of these examples—possessing land and raising godly children—may easily be described as desirable privileges, and yet both are commanded in their respective contexts. Consequently, that being abundantly fruitful was a desirable privilege in antiquity does not preclude this verse from being understood as a command. Although it seems possible *grammatically* that the imperatives in Gen 1:28 may be understood simply as granting permission, as I hope to show throughout this study, from a biblical-theological perspective it seems

---

37. Cohen, *Be Fertile and Increase*, 14; Schmutzer, *Be Fruitful and Multiply*, 76; Viands, *I Will Surely Multiply Your Offspring*, 15.

38. Walton, *Genesis*, 134.

39. Viands, *I Will Surely Multiply Your Offspring*, 27. Schmutzer also views the "blessing" of Gen 1:28 as precluding it from being a command (*Be Fruitful and Multiply*, 156n337), but later he refers to humanity's call to "subdue" and "rule" in this same verse as "obligations" (192, 203).

40. Kaminski, *From Noah to Israel*, 27.

that humanity is indeed obligated to be fruitful and multiply in order to spread God's representative kingship *and* that such an obligation is a blessing and a privilege.[41]

"Fill the earth"

After commissioning humanity to multiply, God commands them to "fill the earth," that is, expand geographically across the entirety of creation. This act of filling the earth is the logical result of God's prior command to multiply abundantly, and as the title of this book suggests, the missiological significance of this concept can scarcely be overstated. Since humans represent God's kingship, and since God's creation mandate is for humanity to be abundantly fruitful and *fill the earth*, it follows that God's mission in creation is for his kingship to be represented to the ends of the earth. Humanity's mission, therefore, is to *fill the earth as God's representatives and thereby demonstrate that his kingship extends over the entire earth*. This representation of God's kingship is also reflected in humanity's call to govern creation on his behalf, which the remainder of the mandate addresses.

"Subdue it"

The first element in humanity's call to govern is to "subdue" the earth. The verb "subdue" (*kabāš*) has the general sense of "make subservient,"[42] and therefore to subdue *the earth* indicates that humanity is to make the earth subservient to their needs (i.e., habitable). In the worldview of Genesis this subduing is not to be destructive or exploitative but rather an exercise of responsible dominion and control. Indeed, a healthy and well cared-for earth provides the most habitable environment for humanity to dwell in; therefore, rather than legitimating any abuse of the earth, this mandate commends creation care. In line with this, Schmutzer summarizes the concept of subduing the earth as "harnessing" and "developing" creation.[43] Humanity is to bring creation under their responsible control as they multiply and fill it.

---

41. Others who view Gen 1:28 as a command include Wenham, *Genesis 1–15*, 33; Hamilton, *Genesis: Chapters 1–17*, 139; Turner, *Announcements of Plot*, 22–23n1; Kaminski, *From Noah to Israel*, 11–12.

42. See Nel, "כבש," 596.

43. Schmutzer, *Be Fruitful and Multiply*, 229.

"Have dominion"

Lastly, part of humanity's subduing the earth involves having dominion "over the fish of the sea and over the birds of the heavens and over every living thing that moves on the earth." As many observe, the verb "have dominion" (*rādâ*) denotes an authoritative rule such as kings exercise over subjects or masters over servants.[44] The three-sphere description of the objects of humanity's dominion—the aquatic, aerial, and earth-bound creatures—recalls God's creation of the entire animal kingdom on the fifth and sixth days (Gen 1:20–21, 24–25). This reveals that, as God's vice-regents over creation, humanity is not only to harness creation's resources in such a way that human life flourishes but also rule over all the other creatures. God's kingship *over* the earth is thereby to be reflected by humanity's kingship *on* the earth.

By multiplying numerically and filling the earth this way, humanity is to represent the fact that God is King over all the earth. This is the picture of humanity's mission at creation, and as we move forward in this study we will see that this mission of God's people has never changed. Although the governance aspects of this mandate are important elements in humanity's creational rule that we will touch on when especially relevant, as we progress in this study we will focus primarily on how the proliferative aspects of this text are alluded to and elaborated upon throughout the biblical canon.[45]

HUMANITY AS THE IMAGE OF GOD

As we proceed in this study grounded on the creation mandate, it is important to make clear at the outset that the image of God is not something that is *in* humanity; rather, we *are* God's image. In some Christian traditions the image of God has been viewed merely as one part of what constitutes a human being. For example, the medieval theologian Thomas Aquinas argued that God's image refers primarily to human intellectual capacity.[46] This view has persisted in certain quarters up to the present, leading one recent study to describe the image of God as "not speaking of mankind's

---

44. Dempster, *Dominion and Dynasty*, 59; Cohen, *Be Fertile and Increase*, 16; Turner, *Announcements of Plot*, 42.

45. The Masoretic accents divide Gen 1:28 after "subdue," which precludes a neat separation between the proliferation and governance aspects of the mandate. Nevertheless, that a conceptual distinction exists between the two is supported by the repetition of "Be fruitful and multiply and fill the earth" in God's postdiluvian commission to Noah and his sons, without a corresponding command to subdue (Gen 9:1) (so also Turner, *Announcements of Plot*, 33).

46. Aquinas, *Summa Theologica*, Ia.93.6.

outward appearance or body structure" but only of "our metaphysical and moral attributes."[47] Yet this approach to understanding the image stems largely from a misunderstanding of the language of Gen 1:26. In that verse, God says, "Let us make man *in our image* (b^eṣalmēnû)." English translations typically use the phrase "in our image" because the Hebrew preposition in this sentence (*beth*) most often means "in." However, this does not mean that the image of God is "in" us. Note that God does not say, "Let us put our image *in* man." Rather, he says, "Let us make man *in* (*beth*) our image."

Hebrew prepositions function in a variety of ways, and in this instance the *beth* is best classified as a "*beth* of identity."[48] In this function, the object of the *beth* is identified with what precedes it. A clear example of this usage is found in Exod 6:3, where God says to Moses, "I appeared to Abraham, to Isaac, and to Jacob, *as* (*beth*) God Almighty." In this context, the object of *beth* ("God Almighty") is identified with the subject that precedes it ("I"). Similarly, in Gen 1:26, the object of *beth* ("our image") is identified with what precedes it ("man"). In line with this translation of Exod 6:3, therefore, Gen 1:26 could be rendered, "Let us make man *as our image*."[49] That is, "Let us make humanity as our officially sanctioned royal representatives." Understood this way, we see that the image of God is not something that is "in" us; rather, we *are* God's image.

Further reinforcing this conclusion is the meaning of the noun "image" (ṣelem). It is widely recognized today that this term refers primarily to physical, three-dimensional objects, not immaterial attributes.[50] For example, in 1 Samuel, when the Philistines capture the ark of the covenant, God afflicts them with tumors wherever they transport it (1 Sam 5:6, 9, 12). To find relief, the Philistines decide to return the ark to Israel along with an offering. Concerning this offering, the Philistine diviners say, "you must make *images* (ṣelāmîm) of your tumors and *images* (ṣelāmîm) of your mice that ravage the land, and give glory to the God of Israel" (1 Sam 6:5). The context specifies that these "images" were golden replications of these objects (vv. 4, 8). Collectively this indicates that, contrary to the quotation above, being created as God's image *does* include our physical appearance and body structure. We are God's image in the entirety of our person, both body and spirit. This is not to say that we *resemble* God physically; rather,

---

47. Ashbaucher, *Made in the Image of God*, 132.

48. So also conclude Arnold and Choi, *Biblical Hebrew Syntax*, 106; Middleton, *Liberating Image*, 88–89n116; Viands, *I Will Surely Multiply Your Offspring*, 30–31n36. This is also known as the "*beth* of essence" or "*beth essentiae*."

49. I live and serve in Japan, and this is precisely how the 2017 Shinkaiyaku Japanese translation renders this phrase (人をわれわれのかたちとして... 造ろう).

50. Middleton, *Liberating Image*, 45–46.

we *represent* him as whole persons. Another way of saying this is that our creation as God's image refers to our *function* more than our *form*, though our form is necessary to carry out our function.[51] Therefore it is not an overstatement to say that our whole identity as human beings, both physically and spiritually, is bound up with our function as God's royal representatives on the earth. To be human is to be designed for mission.

SUMMARY

In this chapter I have argued that a biblical understanding of missions must be situated within the broader framework of the mission of God and the mission of God's people. I suggested that God's mission in the world is for his kingship to be represented to the ends of the earth, and that the mission of God's people is to fill the earth as God's representatives and thereby demonstrate that his kingship extends over the entire earth. The mission of God's people is therefore the vehicle through which the mission of God is fulfilled in this world. After exploring how the New Testament points us back to the Old Testament to ground the work of missions, we examined the opening account of Genesis and saw how the creation story introduces both the mission of God and the mission of God's people. God creates humanity as his representative images and commissions them to "be fruitful and multiply and *fill the earth*" (Gen 1:28) and thereby demonstrate that the entire earth is the realm of his kingship. As I will seek to show throughout the remainder of this study, this creation mandate is the theological engine that drives the mission of God's people throughout the canon and therefore is fundamental for our understanding of the church's call to missions today.

---

51. See further the discussion of Schmutzer, *Be Fruitful and Multiply*, 175–79.

2 MISSION FRUSTRATED
The Primeval History

Having defined mission and explored God's creation mandate to humanity, in this chapter we will turn our attention to the remainder of the Primeval History. In these chapters humanity rebels against God and brings sin into the world, thereby frustrating our ability to fulfill our mission. As a gracious King, God responds by promising to redeem humanity from the effects of our sin, and as these narratives illustrate, the only proper response to this promise is faith demonstrated by obedience. In looking at this section we will first explore the fall of humanity and see how it fundamentally involves a rejection of God's kingship. Then we will survey how humanity further declines in sin throughout Genesis 4–11, observing how a rejection of God's kingship leads naturally to a rejection of his mission. Finally, we will see that in the midst of the fall God promises to redeem sinful humanity. This promise of redemption provides a note of hope that reverberates throughout these chapters, revealing that humanity's sin and missional failure are not the final word.

THE FALL OF HUMANITY: REJECTION OF GOD'S KINGSHIP

Discussions of the fall of humanity traditionally summarize it as resulting in a guilty status and a corrupted nature for all people.[1] While this is true, the book of Genesis also depicts humanity's fall as directly affecting our ability to fulfill our mission. Before looking at the fall itself, however, we must first examine God's pre-fall interactions with humanity to understand fully the implications of our rebellion.

---

1. E.g., Frame, *Salvation Belongs to the Lord*, 102–14; WCF 6:2–3.

Pre-Fall: God's Gifts of Grace and Responsibility

In Genesis 1–2, after God creates humanity and issues the creation mandate, he extends to humanity both *grace* and *responsibility*. Immediately after giving the creation mandate God says to humanity, "Behold, I have given you every plant yielding seed that is on the face of all the earth, and every tree with seed in its fruit. You shall have them for food" (Gen 1:29). Rather than requiring humanity to earn their sustenance, God begins his relationship with them by graciously providing for their physical needs.

In Genesis 2 we see creation re-depicted with a sharper focus on humanity. This chapter describes how God forms the man from the dust of the earth, breathes life into him, and then places him in the newly-planted garden of Eden (vv. 7–8). Further reflecting God's grace, this garden is portrayed as a place of tranquility and vitality, a ready-made paradise in which humanity may thrive and find enjoyment. We are then reminded that "out of the ground the LORD God made to spring up every tree that is pleasant to the sight and good for food" (v. 9a), reiterating God's gracious provision for humanity's physical needs. Finally, in the midst of this garden are the tree of life and the tree of the knowledge of good and evil (v. 9b), representing respectively God's grace and responsibility. Humanity is given free access to the tree of life, which would enable them to live forever in this garden paradise (see Gen 3:22), but they are also responsible to obey God's word and refrain from partaking of the tree of the knowledge of good and evil.

God's next interaction with humanity comes in Gen 2:15: "The LORD God took the man and put him in the garden of Eden to work it and keep it." It is widely recognized that these two verbs—"work" (*'ābad*) and "keep" (*šāmar*)—are used together elsewhere in the Pentateuch only to describe the priests and Levites "working" and "keeping" the tabernacle (Num 3:7–8; 8:26; 18:5–7).[2] By using this terminology to describe Adam's responsibilities, the author is depicting him as having the high calling of a priest, one who ministers in the special presence of God on earth, with Eden depicted as the first earthly temple.[3] This is a privileged responsibility, and together with humanity's creation as God's image portrays Adam as the first royal priest, a role that will recur in the calling of both Israel and the church.[4] Moreover, the verb (*šāmar*) may also be translated as "guard" and implies that, as God's priest, Adam is not only called to tend and cultivate the garden agriculturally but also maintain its holiness by prohibiting anything

---

2. See, e.g., Dumbrell, *Faith of Israel*, 21–22; Beale, *Temple and the Church's Mission*, 67.

3. For a different perspective on these data, see Block, "Eden: A Temple?," 3–32.

4. See the discussions in chapters 4 and 9, respectively.

unclean from entering it (see, e.g., Lev 10:10; 13:40–46). All this indicates that humanity's responsibility in creation is both royal and priestly—both representative of God's kingship and reverential of his presence.[5]

This calling of humanity to work and keep the garden may also be viewed as a further outworking of the creation mandate. As we saw in chapter 1, part of the creation mandate involves humanity subduing the earth by harnessing and developing it and having dominion over all the creatures. In the present section we see that humanity is to begin carrying out this governing responsibility in the garden. Consequently, should any unauthorized creature be found within the confines of the garden (such as a serpent!), as royal subduer Adam is to rule over it, and as priestly guard he is to protect the garden from it.

As the account moves forward we encounter the first occurrence of the verb "command" (*ṣiwwâ*) in Scripture: "And the LORD God commanded the man, saying, 'You may surely eat of every tree of the garden, but of the tree of the knowledge of good and evil you shall not eat, for in the day that you eat of it you shall surely die'" (Gen 2:16–17). Continuing the pattern we have observed so far, this command contains elements of both grace and responsibility. On the one hand, God extends grace by commanding humanity to eat freely of every tree in the garden. Although an exception immediately follows, it is significant that this initial portion of the command is gracious, which continues to highlight God's unmerited benevolence shown to humanity at creation.[6] On the other hand, God extends responsibility to humanity by prohibiting them from eating of only one tree (v. 17). Correspondent with humanity's reception of God's gracious provision is their call to obey him as their King. Just as creation obeyed God's voice and thus reflected his kingship, so must humanity. This is the way God's images rightly represent him as King.

Finally, in the garden God graciously determines to give the man "a helper fit for him" (Gen 2:18), which results in the creation of woman (vv. 21–23). The creation account then ends by describing the idyllic environment of relational unity that existed between the man and the woman (v. 25), allowing the note of God's grace and provision to reverberate in our ears as we turn the page to chapter 3. God has extended grace upon grace

---

5. Therefore I disagree with Wright, who in his study of the church's mission concludes from this verse that "humans are put into God's created environment to serve it and to look after it" and therefore "the main point of our ruling the earth is for *its* benefit" (*Mission of God's People*, 51 [emphasis original]). On the contrary, based on the priestly overtones of this language, our serving and ruling the earth is most centrally for *God's* benefit.

6. Kissling, *Genesis*, 166, 188; Waltke, *Old Testament Theology*, 262.

to humanity as the pinnacle of his creation, and as long as they respond obediently to God's word, they will remain blessed in their relationship with him and one another. As we quickly see, however, things do not remain in this idyllic state for long.

The Fall: Humanity's Rejection of God's Grace and Responsibility

Despite God's grace, in the account of the fall humanity rejects God's authoritative word and instead follows the word of the serpent, functionally treating him as king. Although Adam should have exercised dominion over the serpent and guarded the garden from him, instead he becomes a silent participant in humanity's fall. As we examine this account it is important to observe the ways in which both the serpent and the woman twist God's words. As we just observed, the first occurrence of the verb "command" in Scripture pertains to God's generous instruction to humanity to eat freely from every tree in the garden minus one. However, as chapter 3 begins, the serpent's first speech to the woman misrepresents God's word. Below I translate woodenly God's command to humanity and the serpent's recollection of it in order to highlight the serpent's subtle distortion:

God (2:16)	Serpent (3:1)
	"Did God actually say,
"You shall *surely eat* (*'ākōl tō'kel*) of every tree in the garden."	'You shall *not eat* (*lō' tō'kᵉlû*) of every tree in the garden?'"

The serpent quotes God nearly verbatim, the major exception being the insertion of the negative particle "not" (*lō'*) in his deceptive question. Although God has been abundantly generous to humanity, by this question the serpent implies that God has been comprehensively restrictive. Following suit, in responding to the serpent the woman also makes God more restrictive than he has been:

God (2:17)	Woman (3:2b–3)
	"We may eat of the fruit of the trees in the garden, but God said,
"but of the tree of the knowledge of good and evil you shall not eat,	'You shall not eat of the fruit of the tree that is in the midst of the garden,
	neither shall you touch it,
for in the day that you eat of it you shall surely die."	lest you die.'"

In contrast to the woman's recollection, God never prohibited humanity from touching the fruit, only from eating it. This reveals that (1) the woman does not know God's word accurately, and (2) she is (whether inadvertently or not) following the serpent's lead in making God more restrictive than he is.

In response, the serpent once again directly contradicts God's word, which I translate woodenly once more to highlight the contrast between the two speeches:

God (2:17b)	Serpent (3:4)
"in the day that you eat of it you shall *surely* die (*môt tāmût*)."	"But the serpent said to the woman, 'You shall *not* surely die (*lōʾ-môt tᵉmutûn*).'"

As was the case in 3:1, here the serpent uses God's exact words except for inserting the negative particle "not" (*lōʾ*) in order to contravene God's warning. By presenting the direct speech this way, the text has set the serpent's speech directly at odds with God's speech. This emphasizes that for humanity to follow the serpent's word will entail a full-scale rejection of God's word. As the narrative continues, humanity chooses to believe the serpent's word rather than God's word and in so doing functionally treats the serpent as king instead of God (vv. 6–7).[7] As royal subduer and priestly guard, Adam should have ruled over the serpent and cast him out of the garden. However, instead of responding in faithful obedience to God, humanity rejects God's kingship, gives their allegiance to the serpent, and therefore receives judgment rather than blessing (vv. 8–19). By thus rejecting God's kingship, humanity does not rightly represent him as King over the earth.

---

7. This explains how Satan can offer Jesus "all the kingdoms of the world" during his temptation (Matt 4:8). In a certain sense, after the fall, Satan became the ruler of the sinful world due to humanity's allegiance to him. In several places the New Testament describes Satan this way (John 12:31; 14:30; 16:11; 2 Cor 4:4; Eph 2:1–2; 1 John 5:19; see also France, *Matthew*, 135). This also explains the exclamation at the seventh trumpet blast in Rev 11:15, which marks the finale of God's redemptive work, where a loud heavenly chorus declares, "The kingdom of the world has become the kingdom of our Lord and of his Christ, and he shall reign forever and ever." Whereas Satan has ruled over the kingdom of the world from the time of the fall, God is increasingly reclaiming this kingdom for himself and will consummate this reclamation at the end of history.

Post-Fall: Humanity's Pain in the Mission

After humanity sins, God curses the serpent (vv. 14–15) and pronounces judgments on the man and the woman that directly affect their ability to carry out the creation mandate (vv. 16–19). First God addresses the woman:

> To the woman he said, "*I will surely multiply (harbâ ʾarbê)* your pain in childbearing; in pain you shall bring forth children. Your desire shall be for your husband, and he shall rule over you." (Gen 3:16)

In the creation mandate God had commissioned humanity to "be fruitful and *multiply (rabbâ)*." This judgment on the woman contains the next occurrence of the verb "multiply" (*rabbâ*) in the text, though here God declares that he will "multiply" the woman's pain in being fruitful. With the entrance of sin in the world, the replication of God's image will now be a painful process, which is a direct frustration of humanity's mission.[8] After addressing the woman, God turns to confront the man:

> And to Adam he said, "Because you have listened to the voice of your wife and have eaten of the tree of which I commanded you, 'You shall not eat of it,' cursed is the ground because of you; in pain you shall eat of it all the days of your life; thorns and thistles it shall bring forth for you; and you shall eat the plants of the field." (Gen 3:17–18)

The pre-fall narrative emphasized God's gracious provision of sustenance for humanity, but now the man will struggle to find food as the cursed ground produces thorns and thistles. Just as the woman will now experience pain in being fruitful and multiplying—humanity's means of filling the earth—so the man will experience pain in subduing the earth into a habitable and life-sustaining environment. Both the proliferative and governing aspects of the mandate are therefore directly affected by sin.

From this brief survey it is clear how God's judgment on humanity after the fall frustrates our ability to fulfill the creation mandate. This reveals that our fallen state is not simply a matter of having a guilty status and corrupted nature—true though this may be—but also being debilitated in our ability to carry out our mission. This is a significant point, as it sets the stage for us to view redemption not simply as reconciliation with God but also as restoration for mission.

---

8. So also Turner, *Announcements of Plot*, 23–24.

THE DECLINE OF HUMANITY: REJECTION OF GOD'S MISSION

The remainder of the Primeval History portrays humanity as further declining in sin by increasingly acting in ways contrary to the creation mandate. Specifically, Genesis 4–11 depicts humanity as inclined toward two major activities—murder and centralization—which together represent a wholesale rejection of God's command to be fruitful and multiply and fill the earth.

Murder in the Post-Fall World

A dominant theme throughout Genesis 4–9 is the prevalence of murder in the post-fall world, which represents the opposite of the command to "be fruitful and multiply." At creation God had commissioned humanity to multiply the number of his images on earth, but murder reduces the number of God's images. The first post-fall story, in fact, narrates the first murder in history between the first procreated images in history. Due to his jealousy of Abel, Cain kills him (Gen 4:8) and then expresses fear that someone else will kill him as revenge (v. 14). In response, God puts a mark on Cain to protect him from being killed (v. 15), though murder continues as a major theme throughout the narrative. A brief genealogy takes us from Cain to Lamech (vv. 17–18), who kills someone and boasts to his wives about it:

> Lamech said to his wives: "Adah and Zillah, hear my voice; you wives of Lamech, listen to what I say: I have killed a *man* (*'îš*) for wounding me, a *young man* (*yeled*) for striking me. If Cain's revenge is sevenfold, then Lamech's is seventy-sevenfold." (Gen 4:23–24)

A striking element in Lamech's speech here is the language he uses to describe his victim. The first word he uses (*'îš*) is the regular Hebrew noun that denotes a man as opposed to a woman (e.g., Gen 2:23). The parallel term— *yeled*—can refer to people across a range of ages, including a "child" (e.g., 2 Sam 12:15). This is significant because the verbal form of this same root—*yālad*—means "to give birth." This root first appears in 3:16 during the judgment on the woman, where God says, "in pain you shall *bring forth children* (*yālad*)," and every other occurrence of this root up to this point refers to the act of procreation (Gen 4:1, 2, 17, 18, 20, 22). All this suggests at least two things: (1) Lamech has likely killed a boy,[9] which portrays

---

9. Cf. NASB, which translates *yeled* as "boy" here.

his murder as an escalation of Cain's sin,[10] and (2) his murder alludes to the judgment on the woman and is therefore depicted as a reversal of the procreative activity commanded in the creation mandate. The first observation is supported by Lamech's closing comment, in which he describes his vengeance as an escalation of Cain's murder (v. 24), as well as the fact that, though Cain tried to conceal his murder (Gen 4:9), Lamech openly boasts about his. The second observation is reinforced by the next major narrative block—the flood account—which similarly depicts humanity's sin as a reversal of the creation mandate.

The account of the flood begins by describing humanity's multiplication: "When man began to *multiply* (*rābab*) on the face of the land and daughters were born to them . . ." (Gen 6:1). What follows is the cryptic account of the "sons of God" marrying the "daughters of man" (vv. 2–4), which has proven to be one of the most difficult passages for Old Testament interpreters to explain.[11] Although an analysis of the particulars of this passage is beyond the scope of this study, the text is clear that God disapproves of the actions described here and determines to destroy humanity in one hundred twenty years (v. 3). The narrator then pans out and summarizes the ethical situation of humanity as a whole: "The LORD saw that the wickedness of man was *great* (lit. 'multiplied' [*rabbâ*]) in the earth, and that every intention of the thoughts of his heart was only evil continually" (v. 5). Rather than multiplying and filling the earth as obedient, God-representing images, humanity is multiplying *wickedness*. The term "wickedness" (*rāʿâ*) is from the same root as the word "evil" (*rāʿ*) that occurs at the end of verse 5. Concerning this root, David Baker observes, "The foundational meaning . . . concerns an action or state that is detrimental to life or its fullness."[12] Hans Stoebe similarly concludes, "The concept of an inflicted injury or the resulting harmful situation underlies *rāʿ*."[13] Consequently, the multiplication of wickedness in this passage continues the same pattern we have observed throughout the narratives of Cain and Lamech: people are being violent and harmful toward one another, which is the opposite of the creation mandate.

---

10. While the noun *yeled* can refer to a "young man," such as the young men with whom Rehoboam grew up and whom he consulted as he acceded to the throne (1 Kgs 12:8, 10, 14), as Hamilton notes, nowhere else does the Old Testament place *yeled* in synonymous parallelism with *ʾîš*. If a grown man were intended as the referent, one would expect either *ʾĕnôš* or *ben ʾāḏām* in the second colon (*Genesis: Chapters 1–17*, 240–41).

11. For a survey of the interpretive issues, see Walton, *Genesis*, 291–97.

12. Baker, "רעע," 1154.

13. Stoebe, "רעע," 1251.

This pattern persists until humanity's proclivity toward violence becomes a worldwide epidemic. Genesis 6:11 and 6:13 climactically describe humanity's rebellion against God's creation mandate, demonstrated clearly when placed side-by-side with Gen 1:28:

Gen 1:28	**Gen 6:11, 13**
	"Now the earth was corrupt in God's sight, and *the earth was filled with violence*" (v. 11)
"Be fruitful and multiply and *fill the earth.*"	
	"And God said to Noah, 'I have determined to make an end of all flesh, for *the earth is filled with violence* through them'" (v. 13)

After 1:28, these verses contain the next two references to the "earth" being "filled," only now it is "filled *with violence.*" Collectively, these opening verses of the flood account depict humanity in full-fledged rebellion against God's mission for them. Rather than being fruitful and multiplying God's image in order to fill the earth with obedient representatives, humanity is multiplying wickedness and filling the earth with violence. The reason God brings the great flood, therefore, is not simply the prevalence of sin in general, but specifically the sin of *violence*, which is the reduction of God's image rather than its multiplication.

It is clear that the reduction of God's image is at the heart of humanity's sin here because of what God says to Noah and his sons after the flood. After promising never again to strike down every creature as he has done in the flood (Gen 8:20–22), God reissues the creation mandate: "And God blessed Noah and his sons and said to them, 'Be fruitful and multiply and fill the earth'" (9:1). This reveals that God's mission for humanity has not changed despite humanity's sinful rebellion against him. Following this, God stipulates consequences for the sin of murder that has escalated throughout the pre-flood narrative:

> Whoever sheds the blood of man, by man shall his blood be shed, *for as the image of God did he make man*. But you, be fruitful and multiply, increase greatly on the earth and multiply on it. (Gen 9:6–7, author's translation)

According to this passage, God prescribes capital punishment for murder *because* humanity is his image. This supports the conclusion above that the central sin throughout the pre-flood narrative is murder as the reduction of God's image. To murder another human is both a horizontal and vertical offense; it wrongs the human victim who loses life and wrongs God by diminishing his representation on earth.

Furthermore, as was the case with God's judgment at the fall, both the judgment of the flood and the sanction of capital punishment frustrate humanity's mission. Both reduce the number of God's images, though in both cases the images judged are those who have been disobedient to God by engaging in murder and violence. In contrast to this,[14] Noah and his sons again receive the same mission that humanity received at creation. However, in this third iteration of the creation mandate, the verbs themselves are multiplied: "be fruitful and multiply, increase greatly on the earth and multiply on it." Repetition is a common literary technique in the Old Testament to call attention or express emphasis,[15] and thus this passage emphatically highlights the call for humanity as God's image to multiply on the earth.

Centralization in the Post-Fall World

While Genesis 4–11 begins by emphasizing the prevalence of murder, which is the opposite of the command to "be fruitful and multiply," it ends by noting humanity's desire to centralize, which is the opposite of the command to "fill the earth." This intent to centralize is depicted in the account of the tower of Babel, which begins by saying, "Now the whole earth had one language and the same words. And as people migrated from the east, they found a plain in the land of Shinar and settled there" (Gen 11:1–2). By settling in this single location, "the whole earth" (i.e., everyone on the earth) is ironically portrayed as refusing to fill the earth according to God's

---

14. I have translated the beginning of verse 7 disjunctively ("But you") instead of rendering it conjunctively ("And you"). The Hebrew here ($w^{e}attem$) contains the conjunction *waw* immediately followed by the second-person plural pronoun *'attem*. This construction—*waw* plus non-verbal constituent—typically has a disjunctive force, and thus in such situations the conjunction is often referred to simply as "disjunctive *waw*" (e.g., Waltke and O'Connor, *Biblical Hebrew Syntax*, 650–52). For this reason, concerning verse 7 Hamilton rightly states, "This verse contrasts vividly with v. 6. Noah and his sons are to be life producers, not life takers" (*Genesis: Chapters 1–17*, 316). Another example of this construction translated disjunctively is found in Deut 4:22. After Moses reminds Israel that God is prohibiting him from entering the promised land, he says, "For I must die in this land; I must not go over the Jordan. *But you* ($w^{e}attem$) shall go over and take possession of that good land." See also Gen 15:15; 32:12; Exod 9:30; Deut 1:40; 4:4; 5:30–31; Josh 1:14, et al.

15. See the discussions of Alter, *Art of Biblical Narrative*, 111–41; Fokkelman, *Reading Biblical Narrative*, 112–22.

command in 1:28, 9:1, and implicitly in 9:7.[16] This refusal to obey the creation mandate becomes explicit by what the people say in verse 4: "Then they said, 'Come, let us build ourselves a city and a tower with its top in the heavens, and let us make a name for ourselves, *lest we be dispersed over the face of the whole earth.*'" Rather than filling the earth and representing God's worldwide kingship as his image-representatives, these people desire to centralize and make a name for themselves. The way they attempt to do this is through their tower.

In the literature of ancient Mesopotamia, the phrase "a tower with its top in the heavens" was a standard way of describing a ziggurat, which was a tall, pyramid-shaped structure with a staircase stretching from top to bottom. At the top of the ziggurat was typically a room for the deity to find rest and refreshment as he traveled from heaven to the temple, which was at the foot of the ziggurat. The function of a ziggurat was therefore *not* for humanity to ascend to heaven but for deity to descend to earth.[17] Supporting this is the fact that in Akkadian, the language of ancient Babylon, "Babel" meant "gate of God." This suggests that the edifice of Genesis 11 is most likely designed to be the place where God would descend from heaven to earth. Consequently, despite popular interpretation, it seems improbable that the people in this account are trying to "get to heaven by their own efforts."[18] Rather, it appears that these people are trying to centralize themselves and localize God to the place they have chosen.[19] Instead of filling the earth in order to represent the glory of God's name, they desire to "make a name for themselves" by building the "gate of God" and thereby restricting God's earthly representation.[20] However, whether one understands the tower as an attempt to enter heaven or as an effort to localize God, it is clear that these people are centralizing in rejection of the creation mandate, evidenced by

---

16. As Waltke says, "This [i.e., 'settling there'] represents the theological opposite of God's command to fill the earth (9:1) and the lexical opposite of 'scattered from' (11:8)" (*Genesis*, 178); see also Turner, *Announcements of Plot*, 31.

17. Walton, *Ancient Near Eastern Thought*, 120–21.

18. Contra, e.g., Wenham, *Genesis 1–15*, 245; Wright, *Mission of God's People*, 65.

19. So also Harland, "Vertical or Horizontal: The Sin of Babel," 527.

20. This is what distinguishes this effort at Babel from the subsequent building of God's temple in Israel. Whereas the people of Babel are seeking to localize God for their name's sake, in his temple prayer Solomon recognizes that the temple does not contain God (1 Kgs 8:27), foresees foreigners coming to the temple "from a far country for *your name's sake*" (v. 41), and petitions God to hear their prayers "in order that all the peoples of the earth may know *your name* and fear you" (v. 43). Israel's temple is therefore theocentric with a worldwide scope while the tower of Babel is anthropocentric with a local scope.

their stated reason for building in verse 4: "lest we be dispersed over the face of the whole earth."[21]

In response, God comes down and does exactly what these people do not want him to do. God says,

> "Come, let us go down and there confuse their language, so that they may not understand one another's speech." So the LORD dispersed them from there over the face of all the earth, and they left off building the city. (vv. 7–8)

In these verses God does two things: (1) he confuses the people's language, thereby creating the nations, and (2) he disperses the nations over the face of the earth. This confusion and dispersal of the nations is then reemphasized through repetition in the closing verse (v. 9), which reinterprets the significance of the name "Babel" by a play-on-words. As mentioned above, in Akkadian "Babel" means "gate of God" and implies that this is the location where God descends from heaven to earth. Although the people of Babel undoubtedly called their city "Babel" because they attempted to localize God to this single place, the text of Genesis provides a different explanation: "Therefore its name was called Babel (*bābel*), because there the LORD *confused* (*bālal*) the language of all the earth. And from there the LORD dispersed them over the face of all the earth" (v. 9). In addition to repeating the keyword "dispersed," which has now occurred three times in this narrative (vv. 4, 8, 9), this verse presents a significant irony. The words *bābel* and *bālal* sound similar, and through this homophony the writer highlights the main point. Rather than being the "gate of God," a single place on earth where God would descend and make a name for the people of Babel, "Babel" is the

---

21. Carol Kaminski has argued at length that the people of Babel are not resisting the creation mandate to fill the earth. She suggests that because the command to fill the earth is presented as a blessing in 1:28 and 9:1, it is unlikely that the people of Babel "would have seen it in a negative light or rejected it" (*From Noah to Israel*, 27–28). However, her analysis does not seem to take sufficient account of the pervasive role that sin has on the human heart and the proclivity to reject God's commands that it engenders (cf. John 8:34; Rom 7:14; 8:7). She also does not see God's dispersal of the people of Babel as advancing the creation mandate, arguing that while "filling the earth" is presented as a blessing, being "dispersed" is commonly associated with divine punishment in the Old Testament (*From Noah to Israel*, 28). Yet she does not seem to consider that the same action (humans spreading to the ends of the earth) could be described both positively ("filling the earth") from the perspective of the narrator and negatively ("scattering/dispersing") from the perspective of the people of Babel. It is plausible to conclude that God desires humanity to fill the earth (which is a blessing [Gen 1:28; 9:1]), but when humanity rebels against God and views his blessing as judgment (i.e., as scattering/dispersing [Gen 11:4]), he judges them for their rebellion by dispersing them (Gen 11:7–8).

location where God "confused" the nations and dispersed them throughout the earth in order to make a name for himself.[22]

With the nations thus confused and dispersed, the means by which God will accomplish his mission now is by setting apart a people for himself and through them revealing himself to the nations. We noted earlier that to represent God properly his images must treat him as King, which involves giving him exclusive allegiance and obeying his word. In the wake of Babel all humanity has now been dispersed throughout the earth, but there remains in humanity a deep-seated disposition to rebel against God and resist his kingship, which has been aptly demonstrated throughout the Primeval History. Therefore, in order to represent God properly and fulfill their mission, what humanity needs is for God to (1) free them from the dominion of the serpent, to whom they have given their allegiance, (2) forgive them of their sin against him, and (3) show them how he expects them to live. These redemptive needs are addressed in part when God calls Abram and promises to bless the nations through him, but they are also addressed within the Primeval History itself.

THE SEED OF SALVATION: REDEMPTION IN THE PRIMEVAL HISTORY

In discussions of mission and redemption, the Primeval History is often viewed primarily as background to the call of Abram, where redemption is viewed as truly beginning. For example, Gerald Janzen states, "Genesis 12–50 is indeed the beginning of salvation history."[23] Similarly, after briefly

---

22. Kaminski argues that God's dispersal of the people of Babel does not fulfill the creation mandate, but rather observes that the use of the verb "scatter/disperse" (*pûṣ*) elsewhere "seems to result in populations being depleted" (e.g., Deut 4:27; 28:62, 64; Isa 24:1, 6; Ezek 29:12) (*From Noah to Israel*, 40). Therefore, according to Kaminski, "one could argue . . . that YHWH's scattering Noah's descendants does have an *adverse* effect on the realization of the primaeval blessing" (*From Noah to Israel*, 40 [emphasis original]). We may agree that the dispersal at Babel does not *fulfill* the creation mandate, since the nations are still in rebellion against God, but it does seem to *advance* its fulfillment by dispersing them across the earth. Concerning scattering/dispersing resulting in population decimation, in most of the examples Kaminski provides it is not clear that the scattering itself is the mechanism that reduces the population. For example, in the Deuteronomy texts, both scattering away from the land *and* decimation are curses that follow from covenant disobedience (Deut 4:27; 28:62, 64). In Ezekiel 29:12, God says that *the land of Egypt* will be desolate *and* that the people will be scattered; logically the former results from the latter. In none of these cases does the scattering itself *involve* decimation and therefore without further data we may not conclude that the scattering at Babel involves decimation either.

23. Janzen, *Abraham and All the Families of the Earth*, 11.

mentioning certain redemptive events in the Primeval History in only a few sentences, Christopher Wright says, "The call of Abram is the beginning of God's answer to the evil of human hearts . . . It is the beginning of the mission of God and the mission of God's people."[24]

However, as we have seen, the mission of God does not begin in Genesis 12 but in Genesis 1. Moreover, although Genesis 3–11 portrays humanity as falling into sin and declining in that sin through escalating violence and centralization, these chapters also introduce the redemptive movement of God amidst and through his people. This movement goes through a substantial surge in the call of Abram, to be sure, but it is important to acknowledge that God's redemptive activity began right when sin entered the world and has been active ever since. In exploring redemption in the Primeval History, we will first examine God's foundational promise of redemption in the midst of his curse on the serpent. We will then explore how this promise is carried throughout the Primeval History from Adam to the call of Abram. Finally, we will briefly survey how the Primeval History portrays the appropriate response to this promise.

The Offspring of the Woman: Redemption Promised

After humanity rebels against God and aligns themselves with the serpent, God curses the serpent, in the midst of which he says,

> I will put enmity between you and the woman,
> and between your offspring (*zeraʿ*) and her offspring (*zeraʿ*);
> he shall bruise your head,
> and you shall bruise his heel. (Gen 3:15)

This verse is known as the *protoevangelium*, or the first announcement of the gospel. Here God declares that (1) he will put enmity between the serpent and the woman and between their offspring, (2) the woman's offspring[25] and the serpent will each "bruise" the other, and (3) while the woman's offspring will bruise the serpent's "head," the latter will only bruise the former's "heel."

---

24. Wright, *Mission of God's People*, 66. Later Wright specifies that Genesis 12 is where "we have the launch of God's *redemptive* mission" (*Mission of God's People*, 212 [emphasis original]).

25. The Hebrew word translated "offspring" (*zeraʿ*), like its English counterpart, can refer either to an individual or multiple descendants. However, Collins has shown that the pronouns associated with *zeraʿ* in 3:15 indicate a singular referent ("Syntactical Note," 139–48; *Genesis 1–4*, 156). Since singular pronouns are used to refer to the offspring of the woman, the text presents an *individual* as defeating the serpent. For further support, see Alexander, "Further Observations," 363–67.

This verse prepares us to look for these two lines of offspring in the ensuing narrative, and the third point reveals that the severity of the woman's offspring's bruising of the serpent will be significantly greater than the other way around. In other words, this verse records God's promise that the woman's offspring will ultimately defeat the serpent, though not without experiencing a measure of pain in the process. From this promise humanity could look forward to a human offspring who would defeat the serpent this way—a victory through suffering—and thereby do to the serpent what Adam should have done as royal subduer and priestly guard. Significantly, this redemption will come through the same means that humanity is to carry out the creation mandate: the multiplication of human offspring.

As the narrative continues, Eve gives birth to two sons: Cain and Abel. Based on their birth accounts we are initially inclined to view Cain as the promised offspring: "Now Adam knew Eve his wife, and she conceived and bore Cain, saying, 'I have gotten a man with the help of the LORD.' And again, she bore his brother Abel" (Gen 4:1–2a). Eve bursts out in joyful exclamation at Cain's birth, though she does not even comment when Abel is born—we are left for the narrator to inform us of his birth. This initial focus on Cain is then reinforced by the meanings of the two brothers' names. Cain means "spear," a weapon of power and might, while Abel means "vapor" or "breath"—something insubstantial. From a human perspective, therefore, Cain is greatly favored over Abel at birth; he seems like the type of powerful offspring who could crush the head of the serpent. By his words and actions, however, Cain proves himself to be an offspring of the serpent rather than his subduer.

In the account of the fall, the serpent both lied and murdered; he lied by contradicting God's word (Gen 3:4) and murdered by deceiving humanity unto their death (3:6; cf. 2:17). Following the serpent's lead, Cain also lies and murders: he murders Abel (4:8) and lies to God about it (4:9), thereby revealing that his allegiance is still with the serpent. Significantly, Jesus will later identify the offspring of the devil in precisely these terms:

> You are of your father the devil, and your will is to do your father's desires. He was a *murderer* from the beginning, and does not stand in the truth, because there is no truth in him. When he *lies*, he speaks out of his own character, for *he is a liar and the father of lies.* (John 8:44)

As does the father, so does the offspring, thus revealing whose offspring Cain is. For this reason, the apostle John warns his readers, "We should not be like Cain, *who was of the evil one* and murdered his brother" (1 John 3:12). In contrast to this, despite presenting Abel as an afterthought at birth, upon his death the text portrays him as the initial offspring of the woman. When Eve bears her third son, Seth, she says, "God has appointed for me another *offspring (zeraʿ)* instead of Abel, for Cain killed him" (4:25). After 3:15 this is the next occurrence of *zeraʿ* in the narrative, revealing that Abel was first in the line of the woman's offspring, and now that he is dead this promised line will extend through Seth. This sets the stage for us to read the genealogies of Genesis as the pathway for God's promised offspring to arrive.

The Gospel in Genealogies: Promise Transmitted

Biblical genealogies are among passages that even the most dutiful readers of Scripture are tempted to skim over. However, the prominence of the Sethite line as the pathway of the woman's offspring is reflected in the literary presentation of the Genesis genealogies. The book of Genesis as a whole exhibits a pattern in which the less prominent offspring are introduced first, followed by the more significant offspring. This is evident especially in the structure of the patriarchal narratives. It is well known that the book of Genesis contains ten *tôlĕdōt*, or introductions of "generations," that provide an infrastructure for the book as a whole.[26] In the patriarchal narratives, the *tôlĕdōt* of Abraham's less prominent offspring (Ishmael [25:12–18] and Esau [36:1–43]) each precedes the *tôlĕdōt* of his primary, covenantal offspring in their respective generations (Isaac [25:19—35:29] and Jacob [37:2—50:26]). Carol Kaminski has shown how this pattern of presenting the less prominent offspring first and the primary offspring last is also present in the genealogies of the Primeval History.[27]

As mentioned above, Gen 4:25 reveals that Seth, rather than Cain, will carry on the line of the woman's offspring. Supporting this, following the pattern reflected in the patriarchal *tôlĕdōt*, Cain's genealogy is given first (4:17-22), followed by Seth's (5:1-32), demonstrating that Seth's is the primary line. This Sethite genealogy extends all the way to Noah and his sons (v. 32) and is resumed after the flood in the Table of Nations, which begins by saying, "These are the generations of the sons of Noah, Shem, Ham, and Japheth. Sons were born to them after the flood" (Gen 10:1).

---

26. These introductory *tôlĕdōt* occur at Gen 2:4; 5:1; 6:9; 10:1; 11:10, 27; 25:12, 19; 36:1; 37:2. The noun *tôlĕdōt* also occurs at 10:32 and 36:9, but these do not serve the introductory function that the other ten do. See Bandstra, *Reading the Old Testament*, 108–10.

27. In the discussion that follows I am greatly indebted to the insightful analysis found in Kaminski, *From Noah to Israel*, 60–66.

Prior to the genealogical data in the Table that follows, whenever Noah's sons are mentioned together, Shem is always listed first: "Shem, Ham, and Japheth."[28] However, the order of *genealogical presentation* of Noah's sons in the Table reverses this sequence: Japheth (10:2–5), Ham (10:6–20), and Shem (10:21–31). Since Ham is the youngest (cf. 9:24), neither of these orders is based on primogeniture. This suggests that Shem's line has been intentionally placed at the end of the genealogies in order to focus on it as the primary line.[29] This accords with Noah's post-flood declaration in which he foretells the primacy of Shem over his brothers (9:25–27). Since this genealogy is explicitly connected to Seth's genealogy (5:32; 10:1), it follows that Shem's line is portrayed as the continuation of the line of the woman that is initially transmitted through Seth.

To support the primacy of Shem's line further, Kaminski observes that within the Table of Nations, the genealogies of Japheth and Ham consistently maintain the order of primogeniture.[30] Japheth has seven sons ("Gomer, Magog, Madai, Javan, Tubal, Meshech, and Tiras" [10:2]), and genealogies are given of the *first* (Gomer [v. 3]) and the *fourth* (Javan [v. 4]), following their birth order. Similarly, Ham has four sons ("Cush, Egypt, Put, and Canaan" [v. 6]), and genealogies are given of the *first* (Cush [vv. 7–12]), *second* (Egypt [vv. 13–14]), and *fourth* (Canaan [vv. 15–19]), again following the order of primogeniture. Once we arrive at Shem's genealogy (vv. 21–31), however, this presentation according to primogeniture is disrupted. Shem has five sons ("Elam, Asshur, Arpachshad, Lud, and Aram" [v. 22]), but what follow are genealogies of the *fifth* (Aram [v. 23]) and the *third* (Arpachshad [v. 24]). This reversal indicates that Aram is the less prominent offspring and that Arpachshad is the primary one, which further suggests that the line of the woman's offspring, going thus far from Seth to Shem, also extends through Arpachshad. Continuing this pattern, another reversal occurs among Arpachshad's offspring. His descendant Eber has two sons—Peleg and Joktan (vv. 24–25)—and even though Peleg is mentioned first, Joktan's genealogy is listed first (vv. 26–29); Peleg's does not appear until 11:18. This suggests that the primary line—that of the woman's offspring—goes from Seth through Shem, Arpachshad, and now through Peleg. This pathway of the woman's offspring within the Table of Nations may therefore be displayed pictorially as follows:

---

28. Gen 5:32; 6:10; 7:13; 9:18; 10:1.
29. Waltke, *Genesis*, 164; Kaminski, *From Noah to Israel*, 60.
30. Kaminski, *From Noah to Israel*, 63.

Figure 2. The Woman's Offspring in the Table of Nations

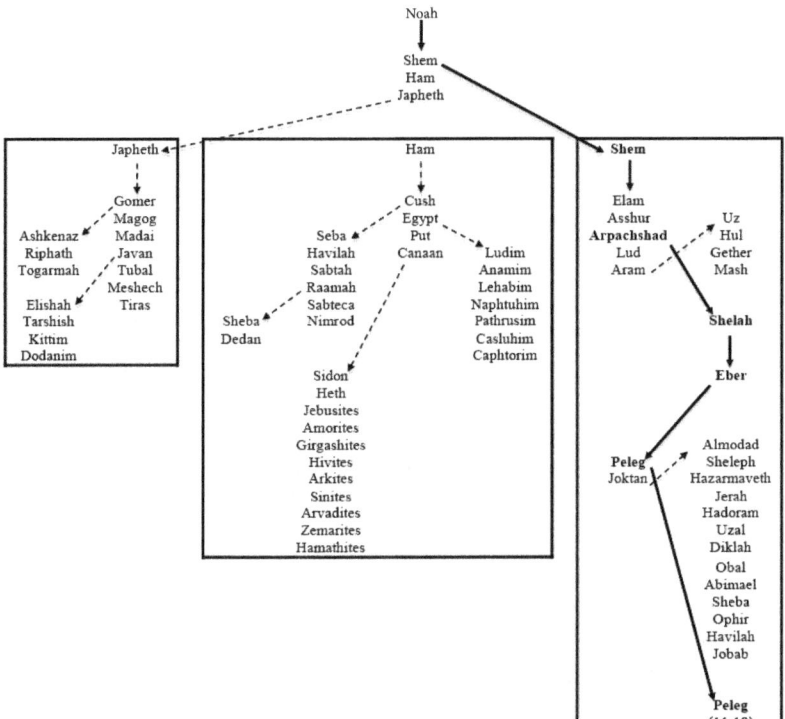

By this means the Table portrays the line of the woman's offspring progressing by a genealogical equivalent of the maxim later articulated by Jesus, "If anyone would be first, he must be last" (Mark 9:35). Confirming this pathway of the promised offspring is the linear genealogy of Shem that appears after the account of the tower of Babel (11:10–26).

This final genealogy of the Primeval History presents a direct line from Shem to Terah's family, within which are included the generations emphasized by reversal of primogeniture in the Table of Nations:

Figure 3. The Linear Genealogy of Shem

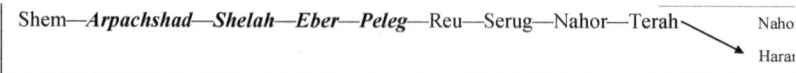

Shem—*Arpachshad*—*Shelah*—*Eber*—*Peleg*—Reu—Serug—Nahor—Terah → Nahor

→ Haran

All of this demonstrates that rather than being a dry presentation of Adam's descendants, the genealogies of Genesis are a sophisticated literary device through which the *protoevangelium* is channeled. Within the narrative of Genesis, we now expect God's gospel promise of redemption to be carried out where Shem's genealogy ends: among Terah's sons—Abram, Nahor, and Haran (11:26). Furthermore, by bracketing the tower of Babel account (11:1–9) with Shem's genealogies (10:21–31; 11:10–26), the text has enveloped the climactic rebellion at Babel with the redemptive line of the woman's offspring, thereby providing a note of hope as the Primeval History comes to an end.[31]

This analysis shows that God's redemptive activity does not begin in Genesis 12, but extends as far *back* as the curse is found.[32] As soon as humanity merits God's judgment, God immediately promises their salvation and consistently maintains this promise through their progeny and by his providence. This then raises a question: how should humanity respond to God's promise? What does he expect of them?

Faith in God: Promise Received

Throughout the Primeval History, the text portrays faith as the appropriate response to God's promise. After humanity falls, God promises redemption through the woman (3:15) and pronounces the penalties of pain and death for both the woman and Adam (3:16–19). Surprisingly, Adam then names his wife Eve, "because she was the mother of all living" (3:20). The name "Eve" ($\d{h}aww\^{a}$) sounds like the adjective "living" ($\d{h}\=ay$), and is best understood as a proper noun with a causative nuance: "Life giver."[33] Therefore, upon receiving this divine death sentence, Adam responds by naming

---

31. This contrasts with the well-known approach of Gerhard von Rad, who argued that while God's prior judgments in the Primeval History are all followed by grace, "the Tower of Babel ends without grace" (*Old Testament Theology*, 163). Kaminski also sees the Shemite genealogical brackets as God's grace to humanity amidst the rebellion at Babel (*From Noah to Israel*, 80–91).

32. To modify the famous words of Isaac Watts from "Joy to the World."

33. Layton, "Remarks on the Canaanite Origin of Eve," 31. See also ESV text note.

his wife—whom he has just blamed for this occasion a few verses earlier (3:12)—"Life giver." In so doing he expresses the belief that life, rather than death, comes through her. What best explains this change in Adam's perspective is that he is now trusting God's promise of 3:15, that an offspring of the woman will defeat the serpent.[34]

The next person in the narrative to demonstrate faith in God is Abel. In describing Cain's worship, the text nondescriptly presents him as bringing an offering "of the fruit of the ground" (Gen 4:3). In contrast, Abel brings an offering to God "of the firstborn of his flock and of their fat portions" (v. 4). This best-of-the-best offering by Abel reflects his faith in God, as the writer of Hebrews says: "By faith Abel offered to God a more acceptable sacrifice than Cain, through which he was commended as righteous, God commending him by accepting his gifts" (Heb 11:4).[35] Significantly, this faithful disposition toward God only reappears among the descendants of Seth, who, as argued above, represent the line of the woman's offspring.

Immediately after recording Seth's birth, the narrator says, "To Seth also a son was born, and he called his name Enosh. At that time people began to call upon the name of the LORD" (Gen 4:26). Elsewhere in the Old Testament, the phrase "call upon the name of the LORD" is associated with sacrifice,[36] salvation,[37] thanksgiving,[38] and covenant relationship.[39] All of these are aspects of faithful relationship with God, which suggests that by "calling upon the name of the LORD" people in Enosh's generation are being depicted in faithful relationship with God.[40]

This faithful relationship is then powerfully portrayed in the Sethite genealogy. In the garden, God warned humanity that if they ate from the forbidden tree, they would surely "die" (2:17). After Eve and the serpent misquote (3:3) and contradict (3:4) God concerning this, the verb "die" next appears in the Sethite genealogy, where it functions as an eight-fold refrain to describe humanity's mortality from generation to generation: "and he died" (5:5, 8, 11, 14, 17, 20, 27, 31). The standard formula throughout this chapter to describe each generation is as follows:

---

34. See also, e.g., Mathews, *Genesis 1:1–11:26*, 254; Waltke, *Genesis*, 95.

35. For a stimulating discussion of worship in this passage see Block, *For the Glory of God*, 60–62.

36. Gen 12:8; 13:4; 26:25; 1 Kgs 18:24; Ps 116:17.

37. Isa 12:2–4; Joel 2:32; Pss 99:6–8; 116:4.

38. Ps 105:1; 1 Chr 16:8.

39. Zech 13:9.

40. So similarly Walton, *Genesis*, 279.

(1) When A had lived B years, he fathered C.

(2) A lived after he fathered C D years and had other sons and daughters.

(3) Thus all the days of A were B + D years,

(4) and he died.

However, two men in Seth's genealogy break from this formula and recall men with identical names in the line of Cain: Enoch and Lamech. In chapter 4, Cain builds a city and names it after his son, Enoch (v. 17), seemingly rejecting God's decree that he must live as a wanderer (v. 12).[41] This rebellion that results in the city of Enoch contrasts sharply with the Enoch of Seth's line:

(1) When Enoch had lived 65 years, he fathered Methuselah.

(2) Enoch *walked with God* after he fathered Methuselah 300 years and had other sons and daughters.

(3) Thus all the days of Enoch were 365 years.

(4) *Enoch walked with God, and he was not, for God took him* (Gen 5:21–24).

In the text above I have italicized the elements that differ from the standard formula. Sections (1) and (3) follow the regular format, while (2) and (4) vary, highlighting that (a) Enoch "walked with God," which is mentioned twice for emphasis, and (b) Enoch did not die, because God took him. In contrast to Cain, who built the city of Enoch "away from the presence of the LORD" (4:16), Enoch of Seth's line "walked with God" and was taken to his presence. As was the case with Abel, the writer of Hebrews summarizes Enoch's actions here as reflecting his faith: "By faith Enoch was taken up so that he should not see death, and he was not found, because God had taken him" (Heb 11:5).

The second deviation from the standard formula in Genesis 5 is found in the account of Lamech. In contrast to the murderous boasting of Cainite Lamech, Sethite Lamech longs for a removal of the effects of the fall:

(1) When Lamech had lived 182 years, he fathered *a son and called his name Noah, saying, "Out of the ground that the LORD has cursed, this*

---

41. Hamilton, *Genesis: Chapters 1–17*, 238. It is also significant that Cain and the people of Babel are the only figures in the Primeval History who are said to "settle" (*yāšab*) in a location associated with the "east" (Gen 4:16; 11:2). This further supports the view that, by building this city, Cain is rebelling against God, much like the people of Babel will later do.

> *one shall bring us relief from our work and from the painful toil of our hands."*
>
> (2) Lamech lived after he fathered Noah 595 years and had other sons and daughters.
>
> (3) Thus all the days of Lamech were 777 years,
>
> (4) and he died (Gen 5:28–31).

In this account, sections (2), (3), and (4) all follow the standard formula, while section (1) contains the only direct speech in all of Genesis 5. In this speech, Lamech recalls the curse on the ground that God pronounced at the fall, which ended with humanity returning to the ground in death. God had said to Adam,

> Because you have listened to the voice of your wife and have eaten of the tree of which I commanded you, "You shall not eat of it," *cursed is the ground because of you*; in pain you shall eat of it all the days of your life; thorns and thistles it shall bring forth for you; and you shall eat the plants of the field. By the sweat of your face you shall eat bread, till you return to the ground, for out of it you were taken; for you are dust, and to dust you shall return. (3:17–19)

In contrast to Cainite Lamech, who boasted about causing death (4:23–24), Sethite Lamech expresses hope that Noah will bring relief from the curse that leads to death. In this way, both Enoch and Lamech in Seth's line contrast directly with their namesakes in chapter 4.

Table 2. Enoch and Lamech in the Lines of Cain and Seth

Line of Cain	Line of Seth
Enoch: a city "away from the presence of the LORD" (4:16)	**Enoch**: "walked with God," who then "took him" to his presence (5:22, 24)
Lamech: boasts in causing death (4:23–24)	**Lamech**: longs for removal of the curse that leads to death (5:29)

Based on these contrasts we may conclude that like his ancestor Enoch, Sethite Lamech is portrayed as living in faithful relationship with God.

This portrayal is further supported by the depiction of Lamech's son, Noah. When humanity multiplies their wickedness to the point that God regrets making them and resolves to destroy them (Gen 6:5–7), a significant contrast follows: "But Noah found favor in the eyes of the LORD" (v. 8). Although some believe that Noah receives divine favor here because of his righteousness, which the text highlights later (6:9; 7:1),[42] it is important to note that the narrative introduces God's favor to Noah *before* mentioning his righteousness. Moreover, Gen 6:8 closes the *tôledōt* of Adam, which provides a structural separation that further distances Noah's righteousness as the grounds for God's favor. Instead, this structural break between verses 8 and 9 emphasizes that, although the *tôledōt* of Adam begins by focusing on death for Adam's posterity (5:1–32), it ends by highlighting God's "favor" or "grace" (*ḥēn*) to Noah. In an exhaustive study of Noah's "goodness," Carol Kaminski similarly concludes that just as God shows grace after the flood by not destroying humanity even though "the intention of man's heart is evil from his youth" (8:21), so 6:8 reveals that God shows grace to Noah before the flood.[43] This divine grace, then, is best viewed as the *source* of Noah's righteousness rather than as a response to it.

The text's subsequent description of Noah as "a righteous man, blameless in his generation" (6:9a) does not indicate that Noah was without fault of any kind. To be "righteous" (*ṣaddîq*) refers to acting *rightly* in a relational context,[44] and "blameless" (*tāmîm*) describes something that is acceptable to God (e.g., Lev 1:3; Deut 18:13). The implication of Gen 6:9a is that, in contrast to those "in his generation" who are violent and unacceptable to God, Noah treats others rightly and is accepted because of his faith. Supporting this, the narrator describes Noah's relationship with God in the same terms used to describe Enoch: "Noah walked with God" (6:9b). Reading with the flow of the narrative, therefore, we see that after God shows grace to Noah, the latter faithfully walks with God and acts rightly and acceptably before him. As was the case with Abel and Enoch, the writer of Hebrews holds up Noah's righteous acts as evidence of his faith:

> By faith Noah, being warned by God concerning events as yet unseen, in reverent fear constructed an ark for the saving of his household. By this he condemned the world and became an heir of the righteousness that comes by faith. (Heb 11:7)

Therefore it is not overstating the case to say that when the floodwaters come, Noah is saved by grace through faith, which is manifested by his actions (cf. Eph 2:8–10). This is the proper response to God's gracious promise of redemption.

---

42. See, e.g., Sarna, *Genesis*, 47; Kessler and Deurloo, *Genesis*, 80; Kaiser, *Mission in the Old Testament*, 6.

43. Kaminski, *Was Noah Good?*, 200.

44. Wright, *Old Testament Ethics*, 255–56.

SUMMARY

In this chapter we have seen that despite God's benevolence to humanity at creation, the first couple rejects God's kingship and instead shows allegiance to the serpent. In response, God pronounces judgments against humanity that frustrate our ability to fulfill our mission. The narratives that follow characterize humanity as disposed toward two sinful activities in particular—murder and centralization—which together represent the opposite of the creation mandate. This rebellion climaxes with humanity centralizing at the tower of Babel and God responding by confusing humanity's language—thereby creating the nations—and then dispersing them throughout the earth. Alongside this sinful decline, we also observed that God promises redemption for humanity through the offspring of the woman (Gen 3:15), and that the only appropriate response to this promise is faith that is manifested in action. The line of the woman's offspring was seen to extend from Seth's genealogy (Gen 5:1–32) through Shem's genealogy (Gen 11:10–26), which ends by introducing Terah's sons: Abram, Nahor, and Haran (v. 26). This sets the stage for us to explore the life and calling of Abram, where the two threads we have examined so far—God's mission through humanity and God's redemption of humanity—coalesce into a unified movement: through Abram God will now accomplish his mission *through* the redemption of humanity.

3 MISSION RESUMED
The Call of Abram

After the climactic rebellion at Babel, God resumes his mission by calling Abram. Although many view the call of Abram as the beginning of God's mission in the world, as we have seen, the Primeval History provides indispensable revelation regarding God's original mission for humanity, humanity's rejection of that mission, and God's gracious promise in light of that rejection. In this chapter we will examine the structure and significance of Abram's call, paying special attention to how this pivotal passage serves as God's response to the sin at Babel. Then we will observe how subsequent reiterations of Abram's call emphasize the catalytic role that Abram's obedience plays in the extension of God's blessing to the nations. Finally, we will see how the text of Genesis portrays the call of Abram as a redemptive reassertion of the creation mandate; through Abram, God resumes his mission for humanity to represent his kingship to the ends of the earth.

THE STRUCTURE OF ABRAM'S CALL

In looking at the Table of Nations, we observed that the line of the woman's offspring progressed by a reversal of the order of primogeniture in the genealogical presentations. When we arrive at the *tôlĕdōt* of Terah (Gen 11:27), therefore, we are poised to see which of his three sons—Abram, Nahor, or Haran—will carry on God's promise of redemption. Immediately we are told that "Haran fathered Lot" (v. 27), which serves as a brief, two-generation genealogy. This placement of the genealogy of the last son first continues the pattern observed in the Primeval History and leads us to anticipate either Abram or Nahor as the primary line. Verse 29 then reports that both Abram and Nahor married and introduces their wives by name: "The name of Abram's wife was Sarai, and the name of Nahor's wife, Milcah, the daughter of Haran the father of Milcah and Iscah." This increases the reader's suspense as we wait to see which of these married sons will carry on the line of the woman's offspring. Verse 30 then seems to shut the door on Abram: "Now Sarai was barren; she had no child." This lack of offspring and thus lack of genealogy on Abram's part leads us to expect that Nahor's will be the primary line through which God's promise of redemption will pass.[1] As the narrative continues, however, we read nothing of Nahor until chapter 22, and even then he is only mentioned in passing, never appearing as an active character in the plot. Instead, the story narrows and focuses on God's relationship with Abram and his family. This emphasis on Abram indicates that, Sarai's infertility notwithstanding, God intends to continue the line of the woman's offspring through him.

This focus on Abram begins in Gen 12:1–3, where God calls him to leave his homeland and promises to bless the nations through him. Although all agree that this passage is a highly significant juncture in redemptive history, interpreters disagree over its structure and relation to the mission of God's people. Much of this disagreement relates to how one understands the imperatives in these verses. Grammatically, this passage is structured around two imperatives: "Go" and "be a blessing." Wright translates both imperatives as direct commands, resulting in the following structure:

> And YHWH said to Abram,
> Get yourself up and go
> from your land, and from your kindred, and from your father's house,
> to the land that I will show you.
> And I will make you into a great nation;
> and I will bless you;
> and I will make your name great.
> And be a blessing.
> And I will bless those who bless you;
> whereas the one who belittles you, I will curse;
> and in you will be blessed all kinship groups on the earth.[2]

On this reading, Abram is commanded both to "go" and to "be a blessing."[3] Based on this interpretation Wright concludes, "The Abrahamic covenant is

---

1. Turner argues that Sarai's barrenness would not have affected Abram's ability to have progeny, since other avenues existed for Abram if he wanted offspring (*Announcements of Plot*, 61–62). However, the redundancy in 11:30, which mentions both that "Sarai was barren" *and* that "she had no child," suggests that, from a narrative standpoint, Sarai's barrenness is being introduced as significant to the plot.

2. Wright, *Mission of God*, 200. For a similar structure see also Peskett and Ramachandra, *Message of Mission*, 90.

3. Others who interpret the second imperative as a command include Turner,

a moral agenda for God's people as well as a mission statement by God,"[4] and therefore, for those who trust in Christ and are Abraham's offspring, "the Abrahamic commission becomes ours also—'be a blessing.'"[5] In contrast to this approach, Kevin DeYoung and Greg Gilbert argue that "the 'missional' reading of the text says too much."[6] They quote Wright's observation that

> it is a feature of Hebrew (as indeed it is in English) that when two imperatives occur together the second imperative may sometimes express either the expected result or the intended purpose of carrying out the first imperative.[7]

Based on this insight, DeYoung and Gilbert argue that the second imperative should be understood as a result of the first ("Go . . . and you shall be a blessing") and therefore should not be viewed as a command.[8]

In responding to these different views, we must first note that with sequential Hebrew imperatives, although the second imperative sometimes describes the result of the first, this is not always the case. DeYoung and Gilbert cite Gen 42:18 ("*Do* this and *you will live*") to support their argument, since the second imperative in this example is clearly the result of the first.[9] However, other examples may be adduced to support Wright's translation. For example, in Gen 17:1 God says to Abram, "I am God Almighty; *walk* before me, and *be blameless*." In this case, the second imperative is best understood not as a result of the first but as a coordinate command alongside it. Therefore grammar alone cannot determine how we should understand this part of the passage; context and content must also inform our interpretation.

The most immediate contextual element to consider when determining the function of the second imperative is its object, "a blessing" ($b^e r\bar{a}\underline{k}\hat{a}$). As Keith Grüneberg has demonstrated, elsewhere in the Old Testament, whenever the noun $b^e r\bar{a}\underline{k}\hat{a}$ refers to a person, it never describes that person as a source of blessing, but only as "a byword of blessing" or as "signally in receipt of blessing."[10] Stated another way, for someone to "be a blessing"

Announcements of Plot, 54; Humphreys, *Character of God*, 83; Alexander, *From Paradise to the Promised Land*, 152; Gentry and Wellum, *Kingdom through Covenant*, 230–34.

4. Wright, *Mission of God*, 221.
5. Wright, *Mission of God's People*, 68.
6. DeYoung and Gilbert, *What Is the Mission of the Church?*, 32.
7. DeYoung and Gilbert, *What Is the Mission of the Church?*, 31, quoting Wright, *Mission of God*, 201.
8. DeYoung and Gilbert, *What Is the Mission of the Church?*, 31–32.
9. DeYoung and Gilbert, *What Is the Mission of the Church?*, 32.
10. Grüneberg, *Abraham, Blessing and the Nations*, 119–21. See, e.g., Ps 37:26; Prov

never means that they are *blessing others*; such a concept is conveyed by the verb "bless" (e.g., Gen 14:19). Rather, to "*be* a blessing" always indicates that one is *a recognized recipient of blessing*. Illustrating this are the two other instances in the Old Testament where *bᵉrāḵâ* is the object of the verb "to be" (*hāyâ*): Isa 19:24-25 and Zech 8:13. As the closest grammatical parallels to our passage, these are the most informative examples to consider as we seek to understand the biblical meaning of "be a blessing."

In Isaiah 19 the prophet states that one day the Egyptians will receive God's protective deliverance (vv. 19-20), worship him in their own land (v. 21), receive his merciful healing (v. 22), and enjoy fellowship with the Assyrians as they together worship God (v. 23). Verses 24-25 then include Israel in this growing international fellowship and describe these three nations in terms recalling the Abrahamic promise:

> In that day Israel *will be* (*hāyâ*) the third with Egypt and Assyria, *a blessing* (*bᵉrāḵâ*) in the midst of the earth, whom the LORD of hosts has blessed, saying, "Blessed be Egypt my people, and Assyria the work of my hands, and Israel my inheritance."

Although Israel is the grammatical subject of the phrase "will be . . . a blessing," Egypt and Assyria are included contextually, since Israel is described as "the third" along with them. Verse 25 then immediately describes these three nations as those "whom the LORD of hosts *has blessed*." In context, therefore, these nations who are said to "be a blessing" are described as *recipients* of blessing. Although it is logically possible that verse 24 describes these nations as extending blessing, while verse 25 describes them as receiving blessing,[11] two considerations make it more likely that verse 24 portrays these nations as recognized recipients of blessing, while verse 25 identifies the LORD as the source of their blessedness.

First, the prepositional phrase following *bᵉrāḵâ* portrays these three nations as subjects of observation by the rest of the nations. Isaiah says that Israel, Egypt, and Assyria "will be . . . a blessing *in the midst of the earth* (*bᵉqereḇ hā'āreṣ*)." If verse 24 were describing these three nations as extending blessing to others, it would be more natural for the prepositional phrase following *bᵉrāḵâ* to introduce the object of their blessing (e.g., "will be . . . a blessing *to all the peoples of the earth*"). However, rather than specifying an object, the prepositional phrase identifies the *location* where Israel, Egypt, and Assyria will be a blessing: *in the midst of the earth*. "The earth" here is clearly metonymy for "all the nations/peoples of the earth" (cf. Pss 33:8;

10:7; Isa 19:24; Ezek 34:26; Zech 8:13.

11. As Wright interprets it (*Mission of God*, 236).

66:4), and therefore the picture here is of these three blessed nations being placed *in the midst* of the other nations so that the latter may clearly recognize their blessed status and, in turn, the source of their blessedness (v. 25). Second, that verse 24 portrays these nations as recipients of blessing is further supported by the LXX. Rather than using the noun "blessing" (*eulogia*) in verse 24, the Greek translators used a perfect passive participle, "blessed" (*eulogēmenos*), which reflects an understanding of these three nations as recipients rather than agents of blessing.

Even clearer in this respect is Zech 8:13. While describing Israel's restoration God says, "And as you have been a byword of cursing among the nations, O house of Judah and house of Israel, so will I save you, *and you shall be a blessing (wihyîtem bᵉrāḵâ)*." This verse contrasts Judah and Israel "being a blessing" with their past status of being "a byword of cursing among the nations." This suggests that the contrasting phrase, "and you shall be a blessing," is not describing Israel as an agent of blessing but as a byword of blessing among the nations.[12] Just as God's prior judgment against Israel resulted in the nations recognizing them as cursed, so will God's future blessing upon Israel result in the nations recognizing them as blessed. Therefore in these two other instances in the Old Testament where people are said to "be a blessing," this phrase describes them as a *recognized recipient of blessing*. This use of *bᵉrāḵâ* elsewhere with personal referents makes it improbable that the imperative in Gen 12:2 is functioning as a command, since it makes little sense to command someone to "be a recognized recipient of blessing."[13]

For this reason, it seems best to view the second imperative in Genesis 12 as introducing either a purpose or result clause[14] describing Abram as a recognized recipient of blessing. This also seems to be how the LXX translators understood this clause, since they render it with a future verb followed by an adjective ("and you will be *blessed* [*kai esē eulogētos*]") rather than an imperative followed by a noun ("and be a blessing [*kai isthi eulogian*]"). This understanding is also reflected in Ps 72:17, which alludes to Gen 12:3.[15] Concerning the Davidic king the psalmist says:

---

12. So also Petersen, *Haggai and Zechariah 1–8*, 308.

13. So also notes Lee, *Blessing of Abraham*, 71n43.

14. I agree with Wright that this section can be understood either as a purpose or result clause (*Mission of God*, 201), though I am inclined to view it as the former. Either way, God's response to Abram has the effect of making him a recognizable recipient of blessing.

15. For discussion of the allusive relationship between Ps 72:17 and Gen 12:3 see Lee, *Blessing of Abraham*, 102–5.

> May his name endure forever,
>> his fame continue as long as the sun!
> May all nations be blessed in him,
>> *all nations call him blessed!* (author's translation)

In this text, as the nations receive blessing through the Davidic king, *they recognize him as blessed.* Consequently Gen 12:2 should not be viewed as a command for Abram to "be a blessing"; in fact, it does not describe Abram extending blessing to others at all. Rather, it describes him as "signally in receipt of blessing" in such a way that others recognize that God has blessed him. Reflecting these conclusions, my own analysis of the structure of Gen 12:1–3 is as follows:

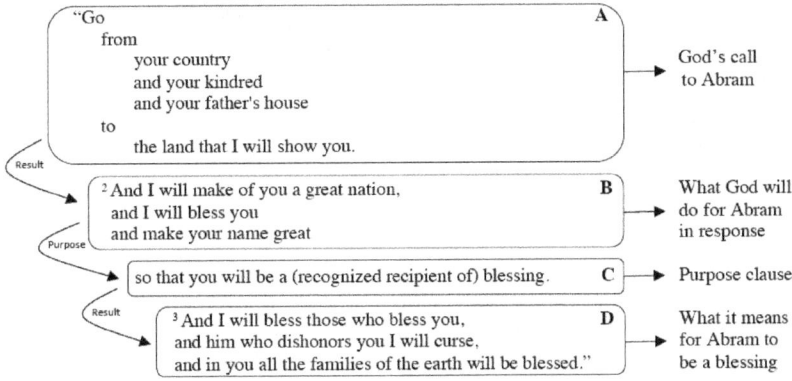

In the structure above, each box is distinguished based on the person of its main verbs: A (second person), B (first person), C (second person), and D (first person). Although the final clause of section D contains a third-person Niphal verb ($w^e nibr^e k\hat{u}$ ["will be blessed"]) with "all the families of the earth" as the subject (v. 3b), contextually this clause fits with the others in this section. Morphologically this last verb may be understood as a passive ("will be blessed"), a reflexive ("will bless themselves"), or a middle ("will find blessing"). However, since reflexive Niphals are rare in the Hebrew Bible and primarily limited to fientive verbs (whereas the Piel of *brk* is stative), and since the context presents God as the agent of blessing with Abram as the recipient of blessing (vv. 2a, 3a), it seems best to understand *brk* in verse 3b as a divine passive.[16] Viewed this way, this clause fits well in section D, where God is the subject of the first-person verbs.

---

16. With the Samaritan Pentateuch, Targumim, LXX, Vulgate, and Gal 3:8.

Later recollections of this promise in Genesis alternate between using the Niphal (18:18; 28:14) and Hithpael (22:18; 26:4) stems of *brk*. Although the Niphal is usually passive or middle in voice, the Hithpael is typically reflexive. Since *brk* is a stative verb, its reflexive use is best understood to have an "estimative-declarative" force in which the nations will "regard/consider/estimate themselves as blessed" on account of Abram's offspring.[17] On this reading, the Hithpael occurrences of *brk* overlap conceptually with the Niphal uses. That is, to "consider oneself blessed" (Hithpael, estimative-declarative) comports with the idea that one "is blessed" (Niphal, passive). Consequently, although the syntax varies between these different uses of *brk*, the promise remains consistent that Abram will function as the channel for God's blessing to extend among the nations.[18]

In terms of the content of the structure above, Section A records Abram's call, in which God commands him to "go." Section B then contains three cohortative verbs describing what God will do for Abram in response to his going. Section C provides a purpose clause that describes Abram becoming a recognized recipient of blessing, though the immediate context for this purpose clause is not Abram's going in section A but *God's response to Abram's going* in section B. That is, God will make Abram into a great nation, bless him, and make his name great *in order that* he will be a recognized recipient of blessing. Section D then explains the result of Abram being recognized this way.

Supporting this structure is another passage in Genesis where an imperative is followed by a cohortative in a result clause, which is followed by another imperative in a purpose clause. In Gen 45:17–18,[19] Pharaoh instructs Joseph how to bring his family from Canaan to Egypt:

---

17. Noonan, "Abraham, Blessing, and the Nations," 83; Lee, "Once Again," 279–96. For discussion of the various classifications of the Hithpael see Waltke and O'Connor, *Biblical Hebrew Syntax*, 429–31.

18. For another helpful discussion see Carroll, "Blessing the Nations," 23–24.

19. I was alerted to this parallel text by Grüneberg, *Abraham, Blessing and the Nations*, 143. I have adapted the ESV in Section C here to match more closely their rendering of Section C in Genesis 12, which is grammatically identical except for the number of the verb.

MISSION RESUMED 53

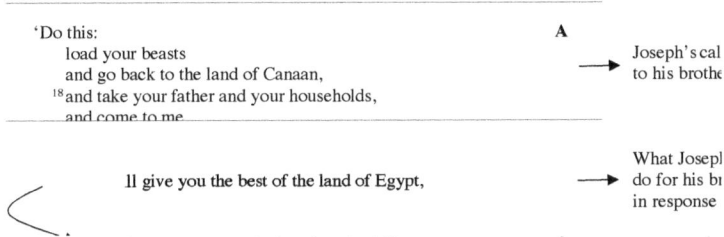

As in Gen 12:1–3, the sections of this passage alternate the person of the main verbs: A (second person), B (first person), and C (second person). In this case, section C is clearly the purpose of section B; Joseph will give his brothers "the best of the land" *in order that* they might "eat the fat of the land." The brothers are not being commanded to eat the fat of the land, nor will they eat the fat of the land simply because they relocate to Egypt (section A); rather, they will eat the fat of the land *because Joseph will give them the best of the land* (section B). Similarly, in Genesis 12 God promises to make Abram into a great nation, bless him, and make his name great *in order that* he might be recognized as a recipient of blessing. Abram is not commanded to be a blessing, nor will he be recognized as having been blessed simply because he goes (section A); rather, he will be recognized as blessed *because God will make him into a great nation, bless him, and make his name great* (section B).

We may therefore agree with DeYoung and Gilbert that the second imperative in Gen 12:1–3 is not a direct command. However, rather than being the result of the command for Abram to go in section A, this second imperative is best understood as the purpose of God's actions in section B; God will bless Abram *so that he will be recognized as divinely blessed*. As we will see below, the nations were to recognize Abram's blessed status and respond either by blessing or dishonoring him, which would reflect their disposition toward God and determine whether God would bless or curse them. A significant implication of this interpretation is that God is highlighted as the source of worldwide blessing. Abram is not commanded to "be a blessing" in the sense of going out and blessing others himself. Rather, this text focuses on God as the one who dispenses blessing, which points forward to the God-centered, gracious nature of the gospel to which the blessing of Abram points (see Gal 3:8). In the next section we will unpack further the significance of Abram's call as it relates to God's blessing going out to the nations.

THE SIGNIFICANCE OF ABRAM'S CALL

To explore the significance of Abram's call we will work our way through each of its constituent parts as outlined above. Section A portrays Abram's call as a movement *away* from one thing and *toward* another. That which Abram must leave is presented with increasing specificity, while his destination is described with conspicuous generality. Abram is called to leave his "country," which is the broadest term and refers to his geographical locale. He must also leave his "kindred," which refers to his extended family or kinship group. And finally, Abram must leave his "father's house," which denotes his immediate family. By presenting the first half of Abram's call in this reverse concentric manner, the text describes that which he must sacrifice with increasing intensity; aside from his barren wife, Abram must give up essentially everything in his life.[20] This specificity of what Abram must sacrifice is then contrasted by the opaqueness of where God calls him to go: "to the land that I will show you." Abram is not told where he is going, what it will be like, or how long it will take to get there. This lack of clarity concerning his destination shows that Abram's response to God's word must take the same shape as the responses positively portrayed in the Primeval History: faith expressing itself through action. As the writer of Hebrews says, "By faith Abraham obeyed when he was called to go out to a place that he was to receive as an inheritance. And he went out, not knowing where he was going" (Heb 11:8).

Section B presents God's response to Abram's faithful obedience: God will advance both the creation mandate and the *protoevangelium* through him. In order for Abram to become a "great nation," and especially in light of his wife's barrenness, God must make him fruitful and cause him to multiply. As we will see below, this creation mandate language will soon be applied to the proliferation of the Abrahamic line. In addition, we have already traced the line of the woman's offspring from Seth to Terah; in Gen 12:1–3 we see that among Terah's sons, Abram is the channel through which the *protoevangelium* will extend. Demonstrating this is the second part of God's response to Abram: "I will bless you." Although this promise of blessing likely includes both numerical increase (cf. Gen 26:24) and material provision (cf. Gen 24:1–2, 35; 26:12–13), because Abram's call comes on the heels of God's judgment at Babel, and because Abram is described as the channel through whom these same dispersed peoples will be "blessed" (v. 3), it appears that "blessing" in this context extends beyond numerical or material growth and includes a redemptive element. This is confirmed by the fact

---

20. Sarna, *Genesis*, 88. Walton notes that for Abram to leave his "father's household" means he is also leaving his inheritance behind (*Genesis*, 399).

that the New Testament consistently describes the blessing of Abram as fulfilled in the redemption secured by Jesus (Acts 3:25–26; Gal 3:8–9, 14). Finally, God promises to make Abram's "name great," which refers to elevating his status and making his influence widespread. This clause transitions the discourse from describing Abram as receiving God's blessings to making it known publicly that Abram has received these blessings.

This is what I argued for above concerning section C. This section provides the purpose of God's multiplication and blessing of Abram: that he might become a recognized recipient of blessing. God will multiply Abram's offspring, bless him, and make his name great so that people will look at him and recognize that God has blessed him. These onlookers may then respond to Abram in one of two ways, which are outlined in the final section.

Section D explains that in recognizing Abram as a recipient of divine blessing, people will either bless him or dishonor him. Those who bless Abram show that they esteem faithful relationship with God and therefore receive God's blessing ("I will bless those who bless you"). Contrasting this, the following clause states, "and him who dishonors you I will curse." The syntax of this clause indicates that cursing others is not God's objective in blessing Abram; that is, God does not bless Abram *in order to* curse others.[21] Nevertheless, those who dishonor Abram show no esteem for faithful relationship with God and therefore receive God's cursing rather than his blessing. In this way the spread of God's blessing through Abram is narrowed based on the disposition of those who observe him.

Verse 3bβ then broadens the scope of this blessing to include all the people groups of the world: "and in you all the families (*mišpᵉḥōṯ*) of the earth shall be blessed." The term *mišpᵉḥōṯ* denotes a variety of groups in the Old Testament, ranging from clans, which were subunits of tribes (e.g., Josh 7:16–17), all the way to entire nations (e.g., Jer 10:25). The term appears repeatedly in the Table of Nations (10:5, 18, 20, 31, 32), which aside from one description of the "families" of animals exiting the ark (8:19) accounts for every occurrence up to this point in Genesis. This suggests that the call of Abram is directed toward these various *mišpᵉḥōṯ* from the Table. Since the Table consistently uses *mišpᵉḥōṯ* distinctively from "nations" (*gôyim*; 10:5, 20, 31, 32), a term that refers to geopolitical entities, Gen 12:3 most likely uses *mišpᵉḥōṯ* similarly to denote smaller kinship units—something at either the tribe or clan level. Supporting this is the LXX's rendering of *mišpᵉḥōṯ* here as *phylai* ("tribes") as well as the New Testament's use of

---

21. The other clauses in this section all begin with *waw*-consecutive verbal forms, indicating logical succession, while verse 3aβ begins with a *waw* + substantival participle followed by a perfect verb, indicating disjunction. For a full discussion see Miller, "Syntax and Theology in Genesis XII 3a," 472–75.

patriai ("family related groups" [Acts 3:25]) and *ethnē* ("ethnic groups" [Gal 3:8]) when referring to this text.

Later recollections of this promise in Genesis use both *gôyim* ("nations"; Gen 18:18; 22:18; 26:4) and *mišpᵉḥōṯ* ("families"; Gen 28:14), though the substitution of the former term need not affect our understanding of Gen 12:3, since blessing all the *mišpᵉḥōṯ* logically includes blessing all the *gôyim*. Since the Table associates these *mišpᵉḥōṯ* with various languages (Gen 10:5, 20, 31; cf. 11:9), what we have here in Gen 12:3 is the first promise of God's redemptive blessing spreading to "every tribe and language and people and nation" (Rev 5:9). In short, the call of Abram envisions God's redemption—first promised in Gen 3:15—extending to every people group of the world.[22]

Furthermore, three of the four recollections of this promise in Genesis extend its instrumentation beyond Abram and include his offspring:

> Gen 22:18: "and *in your offspring* shall all the nations of the earth be blessed."
>
> Gen 26:4 (to Isaac): "And *in your offspring* all the nations of the earth shall be blessed."
>
> Gen 28:14 (to Jacob): "and *in you and your offspring* shall all the families of the earth be blessed."

Collectively these elaborations show that God's worldwide blessing will extend through *Abram's line*, not through Abram alone. This genealogical extension of the channel of blessing makes it quite natural for the New Testament writers to see this promise fulfilled in the saving work of Jesus, Abram's descendant (Matt 1:1).

THE CALL OF ABRAM, THE TABLE OF NATIONS, AND THE TOWER OF BABEL

Several additional factors portray God's call of Abram as his redemptive response to the sin at Babel that gave rise to the dispersed nations depicted in the Table. It is commonly recognized that, although the Table appears before the Babel account literarily, historically the monolingual rebellion at Babel (see 11:1) preceded the multilingual geographical spread outlined in the Table. By reversing the Table and tower accounts this way, the text directly juxtaposes the rebellion at Babel with the call of Abram and thereby highlights that the latter is God's gracious response to the former.

---

22. For a definition and discussion of "people groups," see chapter 11.

MISSION RESUMED 57

In terms of Abram's call addressing the nations portrayed in the Table, we noted above the lexical connection between *mišpᵉḥōṯ* in Abram's call and its prevalence in the Table. This term and several others are repeated in the Table's refrain, which occurs at the end of each of Noah's sons' genealogies and at the conclusion of the Table as a whole:

> From these the coastland *peoples* (*gôyim*) spread in their *lands* (*'arṣōṯ*), each with his own language, by their *clans* (*mišpᵉḥōṯ*), in their *nations* (*gôyim*) (10:5).
>
> These are the sons of Ham, by their *clans* (*mišpᵉḥōṯ*), their languages, their *lands* (*'arṣōṯ*), and their *nations* (*gôyim*) (10:20).
>
> These are the sons of Shem, by their *clans* (*mišpᵉḥōṯ*), their languages, their *lands* (*'arṣōṯ*), and their *nations* (*gôyim*) (10:31).
>
> These are the *clans* (*mišpᵉḥōṯ*) of the sons of Noah, according to their genealogies, in their *nations* (*gôyim*), and from these the *nations* (*gôyim*) spread abroad on the *earth* (*'ereṣ*) after the flood (10:32).

The obvious keywords in this refrain are "clans" (*mišpᵉḥōṯ*), "lands" (*'arṣōṯ*), and "nations" (*gôyim*). These keywords reappear together in God's call of Abram:

> Now the LORD said to Abram, "Go from your *country* (*'ereṣ*) and your kindred and your father's house to the *land* (*'ereṣ*) that I will show you. And I will make of you a great *nation* (*gôy*), and I will bless you and make your name great, so that you will be a (recognized recipient of) blessing. And I will bless those who bless you, and him who dishonors you I will curse, and in you all the *families* (*mišpᵉḥōṯ*) of the earth will be blessed." (author's translation)

This link between Abram's call and the Table's refrain reinforces the fact that God's promise to Abram is directed toward these distributed people groups presented in the Table. Since the Table describes genealogically the dispersal of the nations that the Babel account subsequently portrays, it is no surprise to find connections between the Babel story and Abram's call as well.

In the Babel account, the phrase *ḵol-hā'āreṣ* ("the whole earth" or "all the earth") occurs five times in nine verses,[23] emphasizing that this climactic rebellion against God is a worldwide epidemic. In response, God creates the various ethnolinguistic people groups of the world (11:7–9) that were previously portrayed in the Table (10:5; cf. vv. 20, 31). This desire of

---

23. Genesis 11:1, 4, 8, 9 (2x).

the whole earth to "settle" (11:1) and centralize contrasts with Abram's call to "go" (12:1). Moreover, while the people of Babel associate their plan to centralize with a desire to make a "name" for themselves (11:4), God says that if Abram will go he will make his "name" great (12:2). Therefore while the Babel builders attempt to make their name great through self-seeking rebellion against God, Abram's name will become great if he is willing self-sacrificially to obey God. Cumulatively, these literary connections show that God's call of Abram is his gracious response to the sin and judgment at Babel that gave rise to the world's people groups as outlined in the Table. Just as God promised redemption through the *protoevangelium* immediately after humanity first sinned, so he promises redemption of the world's people groups immediately after they are scattered because of their sin.[24] Abram's responsibility, as argued above, was to "go" so that *God* would do the work of extending his blessing across creation through him.

THE ROLE OF OBEDIENCE IN ABRAM'S CALL

This brings us to the role of obedience in Abram's call. Studies of the call of Abram often focus on Gen 12:1–3, and rightly so, since these verses contain the heart of God's promise to bless the nations. Yet we must not miss the significance of verse 4: "So Abram went, as the Lord had told him." Just as creation obeyed God in Genesis 1 and thereby reflected his kingship, so Abram treats God as King by obeying his word. Reinforcing the importance of this point, repetitions of this promise throughout Genesis emphasize the central role that Abram's obedience plays in its realization.

This promise that all nations will be blessed through Abram is repeated four times in Genesis, three of which highlight Abram's obedient posture toward God. In each passage below, I have italicized the repetition of God's promise from Gen 12:3 and underlined the stated rationale for why this promise will be realized:

> The Lord said, "Shall I hide from Abraham what I am about to do, seeing that Abraham shall surely become a great and mighty nation, and *all the nations of the earth shall be blessed in him*? <u>For I have chosen him, that he may command his children and his household after him to keep the way of the Lord</u> by doing righteousness and justice, <u>so that</u> the Lord may bring to Abraham *what he has promised him.*" (Gen 18:17–19)

---

24. In this latter case I am using the term "immediately" in the literary rather than historical sense.

> By myself I have sworn, declares the LORD, <u>because you have done this</u> and have not withheld your son, your only son, I will surely bless you, and I will surely multiply your offspring as the stars of heaven and as the sand that is on the seashore. And your offspring shall possess the gate of his enemies, and *in your offspring shall all the nations of the earth be blessed*, <u>because you have obeyed my voice</u>. (Gen 22:16–18)

> The LORD speaking to Isaac: "I will multiply your offspring as the stars of heaven and will give to your offspring all these lands. And *in your offspring all the nations of the earth shall be blessed*, <u>because Abraham obeyed my voice and kept my charge, my commandments, my statutes, and my laws</u>." (Gen 26:4–5)

In each case the text presents Abram's obedience as the reason that God's blessing will spread among the nations. Therefore inasmuch as the blessing itself comes from God, the catalyst that extends this blessing to the nations is Abram's faithful response to God.

Having observed this, we must also emphasize that human effort is not the ultimate cause of missional success. Abram was not to obey God in a legalistic or self-reliant manner. As we have already noted, the writer of Hebrews describes Abram's obedience as evidence of his faith (Heb 11:8). For this reason, we may conclude that Abram demonstrates his faith in God by obeying his word, and that *this is how God chooses to accomplish his mission.* James agrees,

> Do you want to be shown, you foolish person, that faith apart from works is useless? Was not Abraham our father justified by works when he offered up his son Isaac on the altar? You see that faith was active along with his works, and faith was completed by his works. (Jas 2:20–22)

In this passage James refers to the near-sacrifice of Isaac in Genesis 22, which is one of the passages quoted above that recalls God's promise to bless the nations and emphasizes Abram's obedience as catalytic for its realization. Here James makes explicit what Genesis leaves implicit: Abram obeys God because he has faith in him. As the writer of Hebrews summarizes: "By faith Abraham, when he was tested, offered up Isaac" (Heb 11:17).

THE CALL OF ABRAM AND THE CREATION MANDATE

The final aspect of Abram's call to consider is its relationship to the creation mandate. Several passages throughout the patriarchal narratives reveal that the call of Abram is a redemptive development of the creation mandate. At Babel, God confused the language of all humanity and dispersed them throughout the earth, thereby creating the various people groups of the world. Because of this dispersal humanity has now filled the earth, though they have done so as a result of God's judgment for their rebellion and thus do not represent his kingship rightly. By extending his redemptive blessing through Abram to all these families of the earth, God initiates what we might call a "redemptive version" of the creation mandate.[25] As we have seen, the nations receive God's blessing through Abram only by responding positively to him. By responding this way, the families of the earth realign their allegiance from the serpent to the true God and begin to represent his kingship rightly again—their function as God's image is restored. Consequently, from this point forward, the mission of God's people will be to fill the earth *with the blessing of Abram* and thereby fill the earth with God's redeemed representatives. In this way the call of Abram resumes the creation mandate and aligns it with the redemption promised in the *protoevangelium*.[26]

That the call of Abram resumes the creation mandate in this redemptive fashion is confirmed by the various reiterations of the mandate's language throughout the patriarchal narratives. The first reiteration occurs in Gen 17:1–7:

> When Abram was ninety-nine years old the LORD appeared to Abram and said to him, "I am God Almighty; walk before me, and be blameless, that I may make my covenant between me and you, and may multiply (*rabbâ*) you greatly." Then Abram fell on his face. And God said to him, "Behold, my covenant is with you, and *you shall be the father of a multitude of nations*. No longer shall your name be called Abram, but your name shall be Abraham, for *I have made you the father of a multitude of nations*. I will make you exceedingly fruitful (*pārâ*), and I will make you into nations, and kings shall come from you. And I will establish my covenant between me and you and your offspring after you throughout their generations for an everlasting covenant, to be God to you and to your offspring after you."

This passage records the final installment of God's covenant with Abram (hereafter referred to in Scripture as "Abraham"),[27] first introduced in chapter

---

25. So also Viands, *I Will Surely Multiply Your Offspring*, 56.

26. Contra Glasser et al., who view the creation mandate and God's purpose to redeem fallen humanity as distinct until Jesus inaugurates the kingdom at his first advent (*Announcing the Kingdom*, 39).

27. I will refer to the patriarch as "Abram" when describing his call or other events prior to Genesis 17 and as "Abraham" when referring to events in or after Genesis 17.

15. In this passage, the blessings of the covenant include God "multiplying" (*rabbâ*; v. 2) Abraham and making him exceedingly "fruitful" (*pārâ*; v. 6), language that alludes directly to the creation mandate. Moreover, the coordinate promise to make Abraham "the father of a multitude of nations" (vv. 4–5) recalls and elaborates upon God's original promise to make him into "a great nation" (12:2). All this suggests that God's promise to Abram in 12:1–3, which is ratified here by the covenant sign of circumcision, is a reiteration of the creation mandate previously given to Adam and Noah. However, two aspects of Genesis 17 show that this is not simply a reiteration but a development of the mandate. First, instead of being expressed as a command, the mandate language is now phrased as a promise that God will fulfill; God will *make* Abraham's line be fruitful and multiply.[28] Second, the context of this promise is God establishing a covenant with Abraham and his posterity (v. 7). This demonstrates that, whereas both the Adamic and Noachic lines could (and did) fail in their mission to fulfill the creation mandate, God will now ensure its fulfillment through his covenant faithfulness to Abraham's line.[29]

This covenantal context distinguishes God's multiplication of Abraham's promised offspring from the proliferation of humanity in general, including Abraham's other physical offspring. Concerning Ishmael God says, "I have blessed him and will make him fruitful and multiply him greatly" (17:20). This is subsequently contrasted with God's dealings with Isaac: "But I will establish my covenant with Isaac, whom Sarah shall bear to you at this time next year" (v. 21). Although humanity continues to multiply under God's general blessing, they do so as rebels against God's kingship and therefore do not fulfill the creation mandate. In contrast, God calls Abraham's covenantal descendants to channel his redemptive blessing to the rest of humanity by representing his kingship rightly through faithful obedience (cf. Gen 18:18–19).

This connection between the call of Abram and the creation mandate is further solidified by later allusions to the mandate in the patriarchal narratives. In each passage below, I have italicized the repetition of (or reference to) the promise of 12:3 and underlined the allusion to the creation mandate:

> The LORD speaking to Abraham: "I will surely bless you, and I will surely multiply (*rabbâ*) your offspring as the stars of heaven

---

28. Genesis 1:28 and 9:1, 7 use Qal imperatives to describe God *commanding* Adam and the Noachic males to proliferate, while Gen 17:2, 6 use Hiphil indicatives to describe God *causing* Abraham to proliferate.

29. See also Cohen, *Be Fertile and Increase*, 29; Kaminski, *From Noah to Israel*, 103–4; Viands, *I Will Surely Multiply Your Offspring*, 54.

and as the sand that is on the seashore. And your offspring shall possess the gate of his enemies, and *in your offspring shall all the nations of the earth be blessed.* (Gen 22:17–18a)

The LORD speaking to Isaac: "I will multiply (*rabbâ*) your offspring as the stars of heaven and will give to your offspring all these lands. And *in your offspring all the nations of the earth shall be blessed.*" (Gen 26:4)

Isaac speaking to Jacob: "God Almighty bless you and make you fruitful (*pārâ*) and multiply (*rabbâ*) you, that you may become a company of peoples. May he give *the blessing of Abraham* to you and to your offspring with you, that you may take possession of the land of your sojournings that God gave to Abraham." (Gen 28:3–4)

As in Gen 17:1–7, each of these passages rearticulates the creation mandate as a promise (or a petition) that God will fulfill through Abraham's line. Furthermore, each of these texts links this promised fulfillment to God's promise of blessing for the nations through Abraham and his offspring. The first two passages explicitly connect the fulfillment of the creation mandate with the promise of blessing by way of the land promise, evidencing a parallel progression of:

(1) Promise to fulfill the creation mandate (22:17a; 26:4aα).

(2) Promise of land (22:17b; 26:4aβ).

(3) Promise of international blessing (22:18a; 26:4b).

This threefold progression reveals God's plan for how Israel will serve as his representative people in the world. He will (1) cause them to be fruitful and multiply (Gen 47:27; Exod 1:7), (2) give them the promised land of Canaan, and (3) as Israel obeys God's word revealed in the Torah, they will serve as a witness to his kingship among the nations, who will then come to God to find his redemptive blessing.[30]

Concerning the third recollection (28:3–4), once we take the broader context into account, this same threefold progression is evident here as well. These verses contain the first two elements noted above (creation mandate fulfillment [v. 3] and promise of land [v. 4]), while the third element of international blessing is found in the subsequent scene at Bethel (28:10–22). In this later scene, God appears to Jacob and says,

---

30. For elaboration on Israel's witness among the nations see chapter 4.

I am the LORD, the God of Abraham your father and the God of Isaac. The land on which you lie I will give to you and to your offspring. Your offspring shall be like the dust of the earth, and you shall spread abroad to the west and to the east and to the north and to the south, *and in you and your offspring shall all the families of the earth be blessed.* (Gen 28:13–14)

This later scene connects the second element—the gift of the land—to the promise of blessing from 12:3, as was the case in both 22:17–18 and 26:4.[31] This results in the same threefold progression that we saw in the previous two passages:

Table 3. Creation Mandate, Land, and Blessing in the Patriarchal Narratives

	Gen 22:17–18	Gen 26:4	Gen 28:3–4, 13–15
Creation Mandate	"I will surely bless you, and I will surely multiply your offspring as the stars of heaven and as the sand that is on the seashore" (v. 17a)	"I will multiply your offspring as the stars of heaven" (v. 4aα)	"God Almighty bless you and make you fruitful and multiply you, that you may become a company of peoples" (v. 3)
Land	"And your offspring shall possess the gate of his enemies" (v. 17b)	"and will give to your offspring all these lands" (v. 4aβ)	"May he give the blessing of Abraham to you and to your offspring with you, that you may take possession of the land of your sojournings that God gave to Abraham" (v. 4) "The land on which you lie I will give to you and to your offspring" (v. 13)

31. The verb translated "spread abroad" in verse 14 (*pāraṣ*) does not denote "travel to other countries" but rather has the fundamental meaning of "breach" or "break through" (see Gen 38:29). This term will appear later to describe Israel's oppressed yet peaceful proliferation in Egypt—despite Pharaoh's campaign to curtail their growth, Israel "multiplies" (*rabbâ*) and "breaks through" (*pāraṣ*; Exod 1:12)—which indicates that this term does not necessarily carry a martial connotation. However, this verb is also used to describe God "breaking out" against his people in judgment (e.g., Exod 19:22, 24; 2 Sam 6:8) as well as the act of "breaching" in military incursions (e.g., 2 Sam 5:20; 2 Kgs 14:13), which suggests that in Gen 28:14 it refers to Israel's upcoming "breach" of the breadth of the land of Canaan.

International blessing	"and in your offspring shall all the nations of the earth be blessed" (v. 18a)	"And in your offspring all the nations of the earth shall be blessed" (v. 4b)	"and in you and your offspring shall all the families of the earth be blessed" (v. 14b).

As this table shows, in each passage the promissory (or petitionary) reiteration of the creation mandate is followed by the promise of land, which is then linked to the fulfillment of international blessing first articulated in 12:3. Along with 17:1–7, these passages reveal that the call of Abram is a redemptive reassertion of the creation mandate, with God presented as the covenantal guarantor of its success.

However, even though these texts shift the mandate's language to a promise, this does not preclude God from continuing to command his people to fulfill the mandate. In Gen 35:11 God says to Jacob, "I am God Almighty: *be fruitful and multiply*. A nation and a company of nations shall come from you, and kings shall come from your own body." This shift back to the imperative shows that God's covenantal guarantee does not exempt his people from obedient participation. Interestingly, however, when Jacob later recalls this encounter, he quotes God as *promising* the realization of the creation mandate through him:

> And Jacob said to Joseph, "God Almighty appeared to me at Luz[32] in the land of Canaan and blessed me, and said to me, 'Behold, *I will make you fruitful and multiply you*, and I will make of you a company of peoples and will give this land to your offspring after you for an everlasting possession.'" (Gen 48:3–4)

This alteration highlights that divine sovereignty and human responsibility are inextricably intertwined in the realization of the creation mandate. God both enables and requires his people to be fruitful and multiply. When all these data are considered, it is clear that God's people are still responsible to fulfill their mission of representing God's kingship to the ends of the earth. The center of gravity in these texts, however, has shifted the focus to God as the ultimate agent of mandate realization.

---

32. Luz was the original name of Bethel (cf. 28:19), where the encounter in chapter 35 took place (35:15).

SUMMARY

In this chapter we have seen that God does not call Abram to "be a blessing" in the sense of going out and blessing others, but rather to exercise faith by going to a land yet to be revealed to him. As Abram responds faithfully, God will bless and multiply him in such a way that the nations recognize his blessed status and respond by either blessing or dishonoring him. These responses will reveal the nations' esteem for faithful relationship with God, and based on these responses God will either bless or curse them. In this way God's redemptive blessing will extend to all the families of the earth. We then explored how Genesis presents God's call of Abram as his redemptive response to the sin at Babel that gave rise to the scattered nations of the world, and how Abram's obedient response to this call is catalytic for the extension of God's blessing among these nations. As God's blessing spreads to these rebellious nations and turns their allegiance back to him, they will begin to represent him rightly again and thereby fulfill the creation mandate. Although God's covenant with Abraham and his offspring ensures that the creation mandate will be fulfilled, the promissory nature of this covenant does not preclude God from requiring obedience on the part of Abraham's offspring. This role of obedience for missional living will be a significant element in God's call of Israel, which we will explore next chapter.

4 MISSION ORGANIZED
The Call of Israel

In the last chapter we saw how God promised to extend his redemptive blessing to every people group on earth through Abram. In this chapter we will see how God organizes this mission by delivering Abram's offspring from slavery in Egypt, communicating his Torah to them, giving them the land of Canaan, establishing the Davidic dynasty to lead them, and providing his abiding presence with them in the temple. Each of these elements is critical for Israel to display to the nations what it means to live in faithful relationship with God. Through these various means, like Adam and Abram before them, Israel is called to represent God's kingship to the ends of the earth.

THE FORMATION OF ISRAEL AND THE CREATION MANDATE

Initial Fulfillment in the Land of Egypt

In the closing chapters of Genesis all of Jacob's descendants migrate to Egypt to escape famine in the land of Canaan. While in Egypt, the people of Israel begin to fulfill the creation mandate: "Thus Israel settled in the land of Egypt, in the land of Goshen. And they gained possessions in it, and were *fruitful* (*pārâ*) and *multiplied* (*rabbâ*) greatly" (Gen 47:27). The book of Exodus opens by repeating this description, stating that "the people of Israel were *fruitful* (*pārâ*) and increased greatly; they *multiplied* (*rabbâ*) and grew exceedingly strong, so that the land was filled with them (Exod 1:7). These passages allude to the creation mandate, evidenced by the formulaic mandate language ("be fruitful" and "multiply") as well as the description in Exod 1:7 of the "land" (*'ereṣ*) being "filled," which recalls the mandate's charge to "fill the *earth* (*'ereṣ*)." Although *'ereṣ* refers to the whole "earth" in Gen 1:28, only the "land" of Goshen within Egypt is in view in Exod 1:7, making this latter passage a description of mandate fulfillment in microcosm.¹ A further connection between the creation mandate and Israel's proliferation in Egypt is the verb translated "increased greatly" (*šāraṣ*) in Exod 1:7. This verb occurs in the repetition of the mandate to Noah and his sons, where God says, "be fruitful and multiply, *increase greatly* (*šāraṣ*) on the earth and multiply in it" (Gen 9:7). Together these allusions portray Israel's growth in Egypt as an initial realization of God's design for humanity at creation. However, as we will see in the next section, this initial fulfillment of the creation mandate also leads to the Egyptian oppression of Israel, which is presented as an attempt to stifle the creation mandate.

Initial Fulfillment and Oppression in Egypt

In Exodus, immediately following the description of Israel's multiplication, the text introduces a problem:

> Now there arose a new king over Egypt, who did not know Joseph. And he said to his people, "Behold, the people of Israel are too *many* (*raḇ*) and too mighty for us. Come, let us deal shrewdly with them, lest they *multiply* (*rabbâ*), and, if war breaks out, they join our enemies and fight against us and escape from the land." (Exod 1:8–10)

This new Pharaoh notices that the Israelites are "many" (*raḇ*), which derives from the same root as the verb "multiply" (*rabbâ*; cf. v. 7), and responds by seeking to frustrate Israel's growth. In chapter 2 we saw that the central sins in the Primeval History were murder and centralization, which together are portrayed as a direct rejection of the creation mandate. Here we see that just as Israel's multiplication in Egypt is a microcosmic fulfillment of the creation mandate, so Pharaoh's attempt to frustrate this multiplication is a microcosmic reprise of humanity's primeval rebellion against the mandate.² This is underscored by the way Pharaoh articulates his plan to oppress Israel, which echoes the rebellious plans of the people of Babel as they sought to resist God's creation mandate:

---

1. Fretheim, *Exodus*, 25.
2. Enns similarly notes, "The very oppression of the Egyptians in wanting to reduce the number of Israelites is antithetical to the created order" (*Exodus*, 43).

Gen 11:4	Exod 1:10
"Come (*hāḇâ*),	"Come (*hāḇâ*),
let us build ourselves a city and a tower with its top in the heavens, and let us make a name for ourselves,	let us deal shrewdly with them,
lest (*pen*) we be dispersed over the face of the whole earth."	lest (*pen*) they *multiply* (*rabbâ*) . . ."

In both verses the speakers (1) begin communicating their plan with the imperative "Come" (*hāḇâ*), (2) describe the plan itself with a plural cohortative clause ("let us build ourselves a city"/"let us deal shrewdly with them"),[3] (3) introduce the reason for their plan with the conjunction "lest" (*pen*), and (4) provide a reason that is directly at odds with the creation mandate. The people of Babel resist God's command to "fill the earth" ("lest we be dispersed over the face of the whole earth"), while Pharaoh resists Israel's initial realization of the command to "be fruitful and multiply" ("lest they multiply").

Furthermore, just as the rebellious plans of the people of Babel were defeated by an ironic reversal, so are Pharaoh's rebellious plans. Pharaoh employs three strategies in attempting to stifle Israel's multiplication, each time meeting with an ironic reversal. First, Pharaoh and the Egyptians "set taskmasters over [the Israelites] to afflict them with heavy burdens" (Exod 1:11a). Forced labor conditions in antiquity were extremely harsh and thus slave mortality rates were often high. These "heavy burdens" were therefore likely designed to diminish Israel's numbers while simultaneously accomplishing Egyptian building campaigns (v. 11b).[4] In addition, the high degree of difficult labor depicted in the text[5] would have theoretically reduced the Israelites' time and energy for procreative activities, thereby curtailing their growth. However, verse 12 presents an ironic reversal: "But the more they were oppressed, the more they *multiplied* (*rabbâ*) and the more they spread abroad." Rather than halting Israel's multiplication, Pharaoh's plan has the opposite effect: his oppression increases it. In this way,

---

3. These are the only two places in the Pentateuch where the sequence *hāḇâ* + plural cohortative occurs (Gen 11:3, 4, 7; Exod 1:10). These are also the only two contexts in the Old Testament that mention "brick" and "mortar" together (Gen 11:3; Exod 1:14), further connecting these two passages. See also Hamilton, *Exodus*, 8.

4. Fretheim, *Exodus*, 28; Stuart, *Exodus*, 67.

5. Note the fivefold repetition of "work" in verses 13–14: "So they ruthlessly made the people of Israel *work* and made their lives bitter with hard *work*, in mortar and brick, and in all kinds of *work* in the field. In all their *work* they ruthlessly made them *work*" (author's translation).

this first ironic reversal depicts the Israelites as irrepressibly fruitful despite Pharaoh's efforts.

Pharaoh attempts to reduce Israel's population a second time by commanding the midwives to kill all the males at birth (vv. 15–16). However, rather than obeying Pharaoh, the midwives fear God and let the boys live. When Pharaoh interrogates them regarding their disobedience, they lie to him and claim they are unable to obey his command "because the Hebrew women are not like the Egyptian women, for they are vigorous and give birth before the midwife comes to them" (v. 19). Instead of decreasing Israel's numbers, the midwives deceptively portray the Israelites as unstoppably reproductive. Moreover, this deception has two further proliferative effects that counter Pharaoh's oppressive intent: (1) the Israelites are further able to multiply ("And the people *multiplied* (*rabbâ*) and grew very strong" [v. 20b]), and (2) the midwives themselves are enabled to multiply ("And because the midwives feared God, he gave them families" [v. 21]).[6] In these ways Pharaoh's second attempt to stop Israel's growth is ironically reversed.

In Pharaoh's third strategy he attempts to expand the scope of his murderous reach. Instead of enlisting only the midwives to kill the Hebrew boys, he commands "all his people," saying, "Every son that is born to the Hebrews you shall cast into the Nile" (v. 22). Chapter 2 follows this decree by narrating the birth of a Levite boy, and as rendered in the ESV, verse 2 notes that the baby's mother saw "that he was he was a fine child" (*ki-ṭôḇ hû'*). Translated woodenly this phrase simply says, "that he was good," recalling God's sixfold evaluation of creation, where he saw "that it was good" (*ki-ṭôḇ*).[7] In the midst of Pharaoh's attempts to stifle the realization of God's creation mandate through Israel, this baby boy is subtly portrayed as a reassertion of God's good creational intentions.

As the account continues, the baby's mother hides him and eventually places him in a basket in the Nile (v. 3). In perhaps the greatest irony so

---

6. This notice that the midwives multiplied supports the Masoretic vowel pointing in verse 15, which introduces the midwives as Hebrew (*lamyallᵉḏōṯ hāʿiḇriōṯ* = "to the Hebrew midwives" [v. 15]), as opposed to the LXX, which implies that they are Egyptian (*tais maiais tōn Ebraiōn* = "to the midwives of the Hebrews"). The LXX reading reflects only a single vowel difference in the Hebrew (*li* instead of *la*). However, a multiplication of *Hebrew* midwives as a result of Pharaoh's murderous decree adds to the consistent pattern of ironic reversal throughout this passage. A multiplication of Egyptian midwives contributes much less to the developing plot and therefore is less preferable from a narratological standpoint.

7. Gen 1:4, 10, 12, 18, 21, 25. Sarna, *Exodus*, 8; Dozeman, *Exodus*, 80–81. Genesis 1:31 provides a climactic seventh evaluative comment in a slightly varied grammatical form: "And God saw everything that he had made, and behold, *it was very good* (*ṭôḇ mᵉ'ōḏ*)."

far, Pharaoh's own daughter comes to the river, sees that he is a Hebrew child (v. 6), unwittingly employs his own mother to nurse him (vv. 7–9), and then adopts him as her own. She names the boy "Moses" (*mōšeh*), saying, "Because I *drew him out* (*māšâ*) of the water" (v. 10). The name "Moses" is ironic here for two reasons. First, this name reflects the fact that rather than obeying her father's command and casting this boy into the Nile, Pharaoh's daughter draws him out (*māšâ*). Second, the Hebrew name *mōšeh* seems to be related to the Egyptian word for "son" (*mōse*).[8] In Exod 1:22, Pharaoh had commanded his people to kill every "son" born to the Hebrews, but this Hebrew has now become the "son" of Pharaoh's own daughter! The birth of Moses, then, is the climactic reversal of Pharaoh's attempts to resist the fulfillment of God's creational purposes through his people. All this reveals that, in the exodus, God is not simply delivering Israel from slavery but repositioning them to fulfill their mission through the creation mandate.

THE CALL OF ISRAEL: COVENANT FAITHFULNESS FOR MISSIONAL PURPOSES

After Moses grows up, he flees to Midian for a season (Exod 2:11–22), during which time

> the king of Egypt died, and the people of Israel groaned because of their slavery and cried out for help. Their cry for rescue from slavery came up to God. And God heard their groaning, and God remembered his covenant with Abraham, with Isaac, and with Jacob. (vv. 23–24)

In response to Israel's oppression, God remembers his covenant with the patriarchs. As we have seen, in this covenant God promised to give Abraham land (12:1; 15:18) and offspring (12:2a; 17:2) in order to bless all the families of the earth through him (12:3; 18:18; 22:17–18). This shows that God's upcoming delivery of Israel is grounded in his covenant faithfulness and for the purpose of his redemptive mission. This covenantal and missional focus is then further reflected after the exodus when God calls Israel to serve as his representative people.

---

8. As reflected in the Egyptian names "Ah*mose*," "Thut*mose*," and "Ra*meses*." See the discussion in Hamilton, *Exodus*, 23–26.

Israel's Call to Covenant Faithfulness

After delivering Israel from Egypt, in Exod 19:3–6 God calls them to serve as his representative people. As Israel congregates at the foot of Mount Sinai, Moses ascends the mountain and receives this word from God:[9]

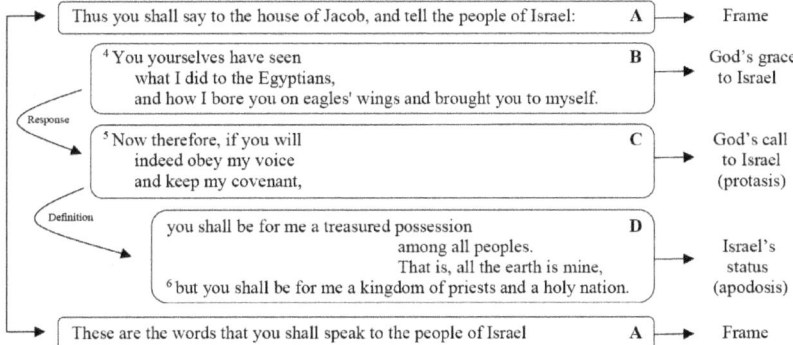

As the structure above shows, God's speech is framed by instructions for Moses to communicate the content of this discourse to Israel (sections A), which highlights the importance of these words for the life of God's people. The speech itself then begins in section B, where God recalls the grace he has shown Israel by saving them from Egypt. Two insights from this section are particularly important to note. First, it is significant that God reminds Israel of what he has done for them *before* giving them any requirements. Just as God graciously provided Adam with everything he needed in the garden before issuing commands, so he graciously delivers Israel from Egypt before specifying what he requires of them. By saying, "You yourselves have seen" (v. 4a), God is encouraging the Israelites to remember his grace as they consider his upcoming requirements. Second, this section highlights that the goal of the deliverance from Egypt is not simply to relieve Israel's suffering but to bring them into relationship with God ("and brought you *to myself*" [v. 4b]). The commands that follow, therefore, are not "law" in an abstract or detached sense, but rather parameters for living in proximity to and relationship with God.

The language in section C reinforces this relational component. God calls Israel to "indeed obey my voice" and thereby respond faithfully to the grace he has shown them. Just as creation and Abram obeyed God's voice,

---

9. Author's translation.

so Israel is called to obey and serve God as King. The means by which God communicates his kingly word to Israel is specified in the next clause: Israel must keep his covenant. While some argue that this description refers back to the Abrahamic covenant[10] and others suggest that it points forward to the Sinai covenant,[11] ultimately it seems unwise to distinguish sharply between the two. Just as God's covenant with Abraham required faithful allegiance that was demonstrated by obedience, so the upcoming Sinai covenant requires the same of Israel. Since Israel pledges to obey God's word immediately after Moses communicates this speech to them (Exod 19:7–8), it appears that the covenant most immediately in view here is the Abrahamic covenant, since this is the only covenant mentioned thus far in the book (Exod 2:24; 6:4–5). Nevertheless, immediately after this scene, chapter 20 begins by saying, "And God spoke all these words, saying" (v. 1), which is followed by the Decalogue (20:2–17) and the Book of the Covenant (20:22—23:33). This indicates that what God requires of Israel is not exhausted by the Abrahamic covenant but is spelled out in greater detail by the Sinai covenant.[12]

Sections C and D are structured as an "if/then" statement, with section C functioning as the protasis and section D as the apodosis. Although this construction is grammatically conditional, as Dale Patrick has persuasively argued, section D is not the conditional result of section C being previously met.[13] That is, it is not the case that if Israel first obeys God's voice and keeps his covenant, then as a result God will reward them by making them his treasured possession/kingdom of priests/holy nation.[14] On the contrary, every other time the Pentateuch describes Israel as God's "treasured possession" ($s^e gullâ$), the reason they receive this status is either because God has chosen them (Deut 7:6; 14:2) or promised it to them (Deut 26:18).[15] Therefore, rather than understanding section C as the precondition for section D being realized, it is better to understand section C as *defining* what section D entails. In other words, for Israel to be God's treasured possession/kingdom of priests/holy nation *involves* obeying God's voice and keeping

---

10. Enns, *Exodus*, 387; Köstenberger and O'Brien, *Salvation to the Ends of the Earth*, 33.

11. Sarna, *Exodus*, 103; Wright, *Mission of God's People*, 126; Okoye, *Israel and the Nations*, 58.

12. See also Enns, *Exodus*, 388.

13. Patrick, "Covenant Code Source," 148–49.

14. Contra Okoye, *Israel and the Nations*, 60.

15. See also Ps 135:4: "For the Lord has *chosen* Jacob for himself, Israel as his own possession ($s^e gullâ$)."

his covenant.[16] Section D thus explains that the actions of section C are those carried out by God's special people. This definitional use of the if/then construction may be illustrated by contrasting the following two examples.

Table 4. Conditional vs. Definitional If/Then Statements

	Example A: Conditional	Example B: Definitional
Protasis	If you move overseas and devote yourself to ministering the gospel in an unreached people group,	If you move overseas and devote yourself to ministering the gospel in an unreached people group,
Apodosis	then you will be invited to speak at missions conferences on the topic of cross-cultural evangelism.	then you will be a missionary.

In Example A, the protasis is a precondition of the apodosis, since being invited to speak about cross-cultural evangelism is contingent upon having previously served in that capacity. In Example B, however, the protasis is definitional for the apodosis, since being a missionary *involves* moving overseas and ministering the gospel. Exodus 19:5–6a functions in this latter way. God does not rescue Israel from Egypt and make them his treasured possession/kingdom of priests/holy nation because of any previous obedience on their part, but solely because of his covenant fidelity to their ancestors (cf. Deut 7:7–8). In Exodus 19 God is calling Israel to live out this privileged status by obeying his voice and keeping his covenant requirements.

In section D, the threefold description of Israel as God's treasured possession/kingdom of priests/holy nation supports our overall thesis that God's mission in the world is for his kingship to be represented to the ends of the earth. God first describes Israel as his "treasured possession" ($s^e gullâ$). This term refers to a king's personal treasure in distinction from his ownership of his kingdom overall (1 Chr 29:3; Eccl 2:8).[17] Therefore for Israel to be God's "treasured possession *among all peoples*" implies that, although God owns all peoples, Israel belongs to him in a special way. The remainder of section D further explains what it means for Israel to be God's treasured possession.

Translations vary in their renderings of the final clause of verse 5, which begins with the particle *ki*. This has been understood as a concessive clause ("*Although* the whole earth is mine" [NIV]), an asseverative clause

---

16. Patrick, "Covenant Code Source," 149; Moberly, *At the Mountain of God*, 226–27; Davies, *Royal Priesthood*, 43–44.

17. Sarna, *Exodus*, 104; Enns, *Exodus*, 388.

("*Indeed*, the whole earth is mine" [NRSV]), and most often as a causal clause ("*for* all the earth is mine" [KJV, NKJV, NASB, ESV; cf. NLT]). However, John Davies has argued convincingly that this should be viewed as an explanatory clause ("*That is*, all the earth is mine").[18] Two observations in particular support this reading. First, this view best fits the chiastic parallelism evident throughout section D as a whole:

> X: you shall be for me (*hāyâ* + *li*)
> a treasured possession
>
>> Y: among all peoples.
>> Y': That is (*ki*), all the earth is mine,
>
> X': but you (*wᵉʾattem*) shall be for me (*hāyâ* + *li*)
> a kingdom of priests and a holy nation

The X sections describe Israel's special status in relation to God, while the Y sections set this status in the context of humanity as a whole. An explanatory rendering of *ki* best supports this parallelism by viewing the X and Y sections as having parallel functions within the discourse. The second reason for viewing *ki* as explanatory is the fact that X' begins with *wᵉʾattem*, which as we noted in our discussion of Gen 9:6–7 is typically disjunctive ("but you").[19] This makes both the concessive and causal interpretations of *ki* unlikely, as a disjunction at X' does not make sense with either of those readings.[20] Although the asseverative reading makes sense with a disjunction at X' ("Indeed, the whole earth is mine, but you shall be for me . . ."), such an emphatic assertion concerning God's ownership of all creation shifts the focus away from Israel's status in relation to God, which seems to be more central to the context. In other words, the asseverative reading emphasizes Y', while the explanatory reading emphasizes X', which seems more appropriate given the passage's focus on Israel's status and responsibility before God. Consequently, although the asseverative interpretation cannot be disproven, the explanatory reading seems to cohere best with the overall flow of the discourse.

All this suggests that the second half of the chiasm further explicates the significance of the metaphorical imagery in the first half. Y' elaborates that "all peoples" mentioned in Y belong to God: "all the earth is mine." It is not that Israel is God's treasured possession but the rest of humanity does

---

18. Davies, *Royal Priesthood*, 55–60.

19. See chapter 3. So also notes Davies, *Royal Priesthood*, 61; Wells, *God's Holy People*, 44–45.

20. In line with this observation, none of the translations that render Y' concessively or causally translate *wᵉʾattem* disjunctively.

not belong to God or owe him allegiance. Rather, Israel is God's treasured possession amidst a realm populated by peoples who *do* belong to God and therefore *do* owe him their allegiance. Just as an earthly king owns his entire realm and yet owns his personal treasure in a special way, so God owns the whole world, yet he has a particular ownership of and relationship with Israel. The imagery in the first half of the chiasm implies this, but the second half makes it explicit. This parallel reading also suggests that X' further explains that being God's "treasured possession" means being "a kingdom of priests and a holy nation." We will explore the significance of this latter phrase in the next section.

Israel's Call for Missional Purposes

Whereas the *requirement* of Israel's call is covenant faithfulness, the *purpose* of Israel's call is international mission. This is made explicit in the description of Israel as "a kingdom of priests and a holy nation" (X'). Most interpret the former phrase as God's assigning Israel a priestly role among the nations; just as priests mediated between God and the people, so Israel is to function as a corporate priest, mediating between God and the nations.[21] On this reading, this passage portrays Israel as having an international missional calling.

DeYoung and Gilbert disagree with this approach and offer a series of arguments against interpreting this passage with a missional focus. They argue that (1) priests mediated primarily by means of sacrifice to remove wrath, not by representing God's presence; (2) "kingdom of priests" refers to Israel being set apart for God, not providing an incarnational presence among the nations; (3) the law at Sinai did not command Israel to go out to the nations in a missional fashion; (4) Israel's interactions with the nations primarily involved military conquest rather than mediation of blessing; and (5) the prophets never faulted Israel for neglecting a missionary mandate.[22] For these reasons, DeYoung and Gilbert do not view Exodus 19 as providing Israel with a missional charge.

However, several observations should lead us to reject DeYoung and Gilbert's arguments and affirm that Exod 19:3-6 does indeed portray Israel with a missional calling. Regarding their first argument, it is not at all clear that sacrifice was the primary means by which priests mediated in ancient Israel. Since Deut 33:8-11 mentions sacrifice *last* in a list of priestly activities,

---

21. E.g., Van Zyl, "Exodus 19:3-6," 267; Fretheim, *Exodus*, 212; Stuart, *Exodus*, 423; Goheen, *Light to the Nations*, 37-38; Wright, *Mission of God's People*, 121.

22. DeYoung and Gilbert, *What Is the Mission of the Church?*, 35-36.

some have argued that sacrificial duties may have been *least* prominent among the priests' responsibilities.[23] Yet whether sacrifice was primary or tangential for priestly mediation, the important point is that priests did mediate by other means as well. In addition to sacrifice, priests mediated between God and the people by (1) carrying the ark of the covenant,[24] which represented God's presence,[25] (2) determining ritual cleanliness, which enabled people to enter God's presence,[26] (3) divination,[27] (4) blessing the people,[28] and (5) teaching God's commands.[29] As we will see below, this last means of priestly mediation is especially important background for understanding Israel's function as a kingdom of priests among the nations.

Regarding DeYoung and Gilbert's second argument, we may agree that "kingdom of priests" refers fundamentally to Israel being set apart for God. Several elements in Exodus 19 suggest that Israel's status as a corporate priesthood pertains first and foremost to their *proximity to God* rather than any sort of active, outgoing relationship with the nations. First, thus far this discourse has emphasized how God brought Israel *to himself* (v. 4) and that Israel is responsible to obey *God's voice* and keep his covenant (v. 5a), both of which pertain to proximity to God. Second, the phrase parallel to "kingdom of priests and a holy nation" is "treasured possession" (v. 5b), which as we saw above portrays Israel as God's personal property, which again focuses on proximity and relationship. Third, God specifies that the significance of Israel as a treasured possession/kingdom of priests/holy nation pertains to their relationship *with him* by repeatedly stating that Israel engages in these roles "for me" (*lî*; vv. 5b, 6a). Finally, as Davies points out, Exod 19:22 provides a contextual definition of the significance of priests, describing them as "those who come near to the Lord" (*hanniggāšim ʾel-yhwh*, author's translation),[30] again highlighting priestly proximity to God.[31]

---

23. Nelson, *Raising Up a Faithful Priest*, 39–40; Chalmers, *Exploring the Religion of Ancient Israel*, 25.

24. Deut 10:8; 31:9; Josh 3:3, 6, 8, 13–15, 17; 4:9–10, 16, 18, et al.

25. Num 10:35; 1 Sam 6:19–20; 1 Chr 16:1.

26. Lev 13–14.

27. I.e., discerning God's will by the Urim and Thummim (Num 27:21; Ezra 2:63; Neh 7:65) or the ephod (e.g., 1 Sam 23:6–12).

28. Num 6:22–27; Deut 10:8; 21:5.

29. Lev 10:10–11; 2 Kgs 17:27; 2 Chr 15:3; Ezra 7:11–12, 21; Jer 18:18; Ezek 7:26; 22:26; Mic 3:11; see also Neh 8:7–8. For further discussion on the different roles of priests, see Chalmers, *Exploring the Religion of Ancient Israel*, 24–32.

30. Davies, *Royal Priesthood*, 98.

31. This is further reinforced by the instructions in chapter 28, which repeatedly state that Aaron's priestly responsibility is to minister "before the Lord" (vv. 12, 29, 30,

For these reasons we may agree with DeYoung and Gilbert that the focus in this context suggests that Israel's role as "a kingdom of priests and a holy nation" refers primarily to their proximity to God and their responsibility to live in such a way that fosters this holy relationship.

However, having observed this, we must also note that *this is how* Israel is to function as a missional people. By living in proximity to God and obeying his kingly commands, Israel is to teach the nations by example what it means to live with God in faithful relationship.[32] This agrees with our observation above that section C is definitional for section D. There we saw that obeying God's voice and keeping his covenant *defines* what it means to be God's treasured possession/kingdom of priests/holy nation. As a corporate priest, Israel is to mediate knowledge of God's kingship to the surrounding nations by treating God as King and obeying his word. In so doing they engage in the priestly function of *teaching* the nations what God requires of them. This will become even clearer below when we explore the missional character of the Torah.

Consequently, although DeYoung and Gilbert are correct that "kingdom of priests" refers to Israel's holy relationship with God, they incorrectly conclude that this relationship does not have an international missional purpose. Furthermore, this recognition that the Torah itself has a missional character addresses DeYoung and Gilbert's third and fifth arguments as well. The fact that the Torah does not command Israel to go out in a missional fashion or that the prophets do not condemn Israel for failing to do so is not surprising once we realize that *keeping the Torah itself* is missional for Israel. The prophetic condemnation of Israel's failure to keep the Torah, therefore, is their condemnation of Israel's failure to serve as God's missional-representative people among the nations. We will address DeYoung and Gilbert's fourth argument—Israel's military engagement with the nations—when we examine the missional nature of the conquest below. Before engaging that topic, however, we must turn our attention to explore the place of the Torah in Israel's mission.

THE TORAH AND MISSION

Christians often view the Old Testament "law" as a moralistic set of rules that was a burden for Israel and that we in the church are thankfully (and allegedly!) not required to keep. However, when properly understood

35, 38).

32. So also Köstenberger and O'Brien, *Salvation to the Ends of the Earth,* 34; Goheen, *Light to the Nations,* 39.

within the storyline of God's mission, we see that the "law"—or better, the Torah[33]—is a playbook for Israel's mission.

The Torah and the Creation Mandate

The first way the Torah functions as a playbook for mission is that Israel's faithful adherence to it will result in the fulfillment of the creation mandate. This is most explicit in Leviticus 26, which describes the blessings and curses that follow from Israel's covenant faithfulness and disobedience respectively. God begins by saying, "If you walk in my statutes and observe my commandments and do them" (v. 3), and then outlines the various blessings that will follow. One of these blessings, God says, is that "I will turn to you and make you *fruitful* (*pārâ*) and *multiply* (*rabbâ*) you and will confirm my covenant with you" (v. 9). Although God has already shown himself faithful in fulfilling his promise to multiply Abraham's offspring, here we see that the continued realization of the mandate through Israel is contingent upon their obedience to his word.

Similar notions are found throughout the book of Deuteronomy. Moses begins by reminding Israel that "The Lord your God has *multiplied* (*rabbâ*) you, and behold, you are today as numerous as the stars of heaven" (Deut 1:10). Throughout the book Moses repeatedly exhorts Israel to obey God in order that they might continue to multiply:

> Hear therefore, O Israel, and be careful to do them, that it may go well with you, and that you may *multiply* (*rabbâ*) greatly, as the Lord, the God of your fathers, has promised you, in a land flowing with milk and honey. (Deut 6:3)

> And because you listen to these rules and keep and do them, the Lord your God will keep with you the covenant and the steadfast love that he swore to your fathers. He will love you, bless you, and *multiply* (*rabbâ*) you. (Deut 7:12–13a)

---

33. Throughout this discussion I will transliterate the Hebrew word *tôrâ* rather than using the common translation "law." The term "law" found its way into English versions due to the LXX's consistent translation of *tôrâ* as *nomos* ("law"), which was then followed by the New Testament. However, for most people, the English word "law" connotes requirements that are based on civic structures, whereas the *tôrâ* of the Old Testament describes requirements that are based on the *relationship* that God has initiated with Israel. This is reflected in the basic meaning of *tôrâ*, which is "teaching" or "instruction." For an informative discussion of this issue, see Modrzejewski, "Septuagint as *Nomos*," 183–99.

> The whole commandment that I command you today you shall be careful to do, that you may live and *multiply* (*rabbâ*), and go in and possess the land that the LORD swore to give to your fathers. (Deut 8:1)

> None of the devoted things shall stick to your hand, that the LORD may turn from the fierceness of his anger and show you mercy and have compassion on you and *multiply* (*rabbâ*) you, as he swore to your fathers, if you obey the voice of the LORD your God, keeping all his commandments that I am commanding you today, and doing what is right in the sight of the LORD your God. (Deut 13:17–18)

> If you obey the commandments of the LORD your God that I command you today, by loving the LORD your God, by walking in his ways, and by keeping his commandments and his statutes and his rules, then you shall live and *multiply* (*rabbâ*), and the LORD your God will bless you in the land that you are entering to take possession of it. (Deut 30:16)

In all these passages, Israel's future multiplication is contingent upon their obedience to God's commands, revealing that their proliferation as God's representative images requires adherence to his will. Just as Adam had to obey God's kingly word in order to fulfill the creation mandate, so Israel must do the same in order to fulfill their mission.

The Torah and the Abrahamic Formula

The second way the Torah functions as a playbook for mission is that Israel's faithful adherence to it will channel God's blessing to the nations. As we saw last chapter, God promised that if Abram obeyed him, he would bless him in such a way that the nations would recognize his blessed status and respond either by blessing or dishonoring him, which would lead God either to bless or curse them. This same pattern—what we may call the *Abrahamic formula* (faith → obedience → blessing → international recognition)—is evident in Israel's call to keep the Torah as well. Along with mandate fulfillment, Leviticus 26 says that as a result of Israel's faithful obedience, God will bless them by giving them ample provision of food (vv. 4–5, 10), peace and protection (v. 6), military victory (vv. 7–8), and, most significantly, his own presence in their midst (vv. 11–12). Deuteronomy 28 similarly states that Israel's obedience will result in God's blessing over every area of life: wherever a person may go (v. 3), upon human and animal fertility (vv. 4, 11), and over both domestic (v. 5) and vocational (v. 6) endeavors. It will also lead to military victory (v. 7), provision of food (v. 8), financial success (v. 12), and overall superiority for Israel (v. 13). Together, these passages show that, like Abram before them, if Israel will demonstrate their faith in God by obeying his word, God will bless them abundantly.

Moreover, just as God promised to bless Abram so that he would "be a blessing"—that is, a recognized recipient of blessing—so he will bless Israel for this same purpose: that the nations might recognize their blessed status. This theme appears at the beginning and ending of Moses' exposition of the Torah's stipulations in the book of Deuteronomy. In chapters 1–3 Moses recalls God's faithfulness in bringing Israel from Sinai to Moab, and in 4:1–43 he prefaces his exposition by exhorting Israel to obey God and give their allegiance to him alone, with the exposition itself beginning in verse 44 ("This is the Torah that Moses set before the people of Israel" [author's translation]). In this preface, Moses describes the effect that Israel's adherence to God's commands will have:

> See, I have taught you statutes and rules, as the LORD my God commanded me, that you should do them in the land that you are entering to take possession of it. Keep them and do them, for that will be your wisdom and your understanding in the sight of the peoples, who, when they hear all these statutes, will say, "Surely this great nation is a wise and understanding people." For what great nation is there that has a god so near to it as the LORD our God is to us, whenever we call upon him? And what great nation is there, that has statutes and rules so righteous as all this law that I set before you today? (Deut 4:5–8)

In this passage, Moses exhorts Israel to keep God's commands *because* this will demonstrate their wisdom to the peoples of the world (v. 6). Since wisdom was viewed as a blessing from God,[34] by acknowledging Israel's wisdom the nations would thereby recognize that Israel had been divinely blessed. Furthermore, in line with the emphasis we observed in Exod 19:3–6, this passage also emphasizes Israel's proximity to God (v. 7), which is further evidence of their blessed relationship with him. If the nations respond by blessing Israel and follow their lead by submitting to God and obeying his word, God would bless them and so fulfill the Abrahamic formula. Reinforcing this is the threefold reference in this section to Israel as a "great nation" (*gôy gādôl*, vv. 6b–8), which recalls God's promise to Abram that if he faithfully obeyed his word, God would make him into a "great nation"

---

34. See Gen 41:39; 1 Kgs 3:28; 4:29; 5:12; 10:24; Ezra 7:25; Prov 2:6; Eccl 2:26; Dan 2:23.

(*gôy gādôl*, Gen 12:2).³⁵ In Deuteronomy 4, Israel is depicted as this great nation, equipped to receive God's blessing and poised to show the nations what it means to relate to God faithfully.

At the end of this central Deuteronomic exposition, Moses concludes by communicating this same idea:

> This very day the LORD your God is commanding you to observe these statutes and ordinances; so observe them diligently with all your heart and with all your soul. Today you have obtained the LORD's agreement: to be your God; and for you to walk in his ways, to keep his statutes, his commandments, and his ordinances, and to obey him. Today the LORD has obtained your agreement: to be his *treasured people* (*ʿam sᵉgullâ*), as he promised you, and to keep his commandments; *for him to set you high above all nations that he has made*, in praise and in fame and in honor; and for you to be a people holy to the LORD your God, as he promised. (Deut 26:16–19, NRSV)

In this passage, Moses refers to Israel as God's "treasured people" (*ʿam sᵉgullâ*, v. 18), a phrase that recalls God's initial use of *sᵉgullâ* in Exod 19:5 and therefore Israel's priestly-missional status introduced in that context. Moses then tells Israel that in conjunction with their obedience, God will "set you high above all nations that he has made" (v. 19). This phrase most likely means that Israel will *be recognized as supremely blessed by all nations*. This is evident from chapter 28, which begins with a near verbatim repetition of this idea:

> A: And if you faithfully obey the voice of the LORD your God, being careful to do all his commandments that I command you today,
>
> B: *the LORD your God will set you high above all the nations of the earth.*
>
> B': And all these blessings shall come upon you and overtake you,
>
> A': if you obey the voice of the LORD your God. (vv. 1–2)

In these verses, being "set high above all the nations" (B) is parallel with Israel's reception of God's blessings (B'), which are together framed by the requirement of obeying God's voice (A, A'). In the list of blessings that follows, Moses specifies that a result of Israel receiving these blessings is that "all the peoples of the earth shall see that you are called by the name of the LORD"

---

35. Block, *Deuteronomy*, 118.

(Deut 28:10). Since Israel's reception of blessing results in this international recognition, and since this reception of blessing is also paralleled with their exaltation above the nations, it follows that being "set high above the nations" describes Israel being supremely blessed by God and recognized as such by the nations. Following the Abrahamic formula, the way in which the nations respond to Israel's blessedness will then reveal their disposition toward God, which will in turn determine whether they are divinely blessed or cursed. In this way, Israel's Torah faithfulness leads to the fulfillment of God's promise to bless all the nations of the earth.

Excursus: Torah Faithfulness as Repentant Obedience

At this point it is important to pause and note that when we talk about "Torah faithfulness" or "obeying God's word," we are not talking about flawless obedience. Many people mistakenly believe that God required Israel to obey the Torah with inflexible rigidity and no room for failure. However, the Torah itself presumes failure on Israel's part, evidenced by its provisions of sacrifice and atonement found primarily in the book of Leviticus. When we examine this sacrificial system, we see that what God requires of Israel is not perfect obedience but *repentant obedience*. According to the Torah, God is pleased to forgive those who repent of their sin and trust in his provision of atonement. In order to understand this aspect of Torah faithfulness, we will briefly explore the Torah's provisions of forgiveness for both unintentional and intentional sin.

Forgiveness for Unintentional Sin

The first way an Israelite could fail to keep the Torah perfectly and need God's forgiveness is through unintentional sin. In Leviticus 4, God communicates the means by which any person within the covenant community may receive forgiveness for sinning this way. The passage begins, "And the LORD spoke to Moses, saying, 'Speak to the people of Israel, saying, If anyone sins unintentionally in any of the LORD's commandments about things not to be done, and does any one of them'" (vv. 1–2). This introduction is then followed by four situations covering unintentional disobedience of God's commands:

1) "if it is the anointed priest who sins . . ." (v. 3)

2) "If the whole congregation of Israel sins . . ." (v. 13)

3) "When a leader sins . . ." (v. 22)

4) "If anyone of the common people sins . . ." (v. 27)

Following each of these introductions, God provides instructions for how to prepare a sin offering (vv. 4–12, 14–21, 23–26, 28–31), which results in forgiveness for the offender (vv. 20, 26, 31). In short, this passage describes provision of atonement for every possible person who might sin inadvertently, whether a religious leader (v. 3), a civic leader (v. 22), a regular person (v. 27), or the community as a whole (v. 13). The only requirement for forgiveness is that the sinner(s) demonstrate their trust in and dependence upon God by following his sacrificial instructions.

Forgiveness for Intentional Sin

Whereas Leviticus 4 addresses unintentional sin, Leviticus 5 discusses forgiveness for intentional sin. Verse 1 says, "If anyone sins in that he hears a public adjuration to testify, and though he is a witness, whether he has seen or come to know the matter, yet does not speak, he shall bear his iniquity." Unlike the sins in chapter 4, the person envisaged here is consciously sinning by refusing to testify. Verses 2–4 then describe sins that may or may not be considered intentional, followed by instructions for receiving forgiveness:

> When he realizes his guilt in any of these and confesses the sin he has committed, he shall bring to the LORD as his compensation for the sin that he has committed, a female from the flock, a lamb or a goat, for a sin offering. And the priest shall make atonement for him for his sin. (vv. 5–6)

When compared to Leviticus 4, an additional element in this formula is the need for the worshiper to confess his sin. Unintentional sin does not require confession because the sinner does not intend to violate God's word. Intentional sin, however, requires confession because the sinner needs to show that he is *repentant*.

This same repentant disposition also appears in the discussion of the guilt offering in Leviticus 6:

> The LORD spoke to Moses, saying, "If anyone sins and commits a breach of faith against the LORD by deceiving his neighbor in a matter of deposit or security, or through robbery, or if he has oppressed his neighbor or has found something lost and lied about it, swearing falsely—in any of all the things that people do and sin thereby— if he has sinned and has realized his guilt and

> will restore what he took by robbery or what he got by oppression or the deposit that was committed to him or the lost thing that he found or anything about which he has sworn falsely, he shall restore it in full and shall add a fifth to it, and give it to him to whom it belongs on the day he realizes his guilt. And he shall bring to the priest as his compensation to the Lord a ram without blemish out of the flock, or its equivalent for a guilt offering. And the priest shall make atonement for him before the Lord, and he shall be forgiven for any of the things that one may do and thereby become guilty." (vv. 1–7)

All the actions described in this passage are intentional sins (deception concerning a deposit, robbery, oppression, and lying about finding lost property). However, once the sinner has "realized his guilt" (v. 4a), demonstrated his repentance by making restitution (vv. 4b–5), and trusted in God's provision of atonement, he will be forgiven (vv. 6–7).

These passages correct a common misperception that Old Testament sacrificial regulations did not provide atonement for those who sinned intentionally. Numbers 15:28–31 has been cited as evidence that only unintentional sin could be forgiven:

> And the priest shall make atonement before the Lord for the person who makes a mistake, when he sins unintentionally, to make atonement for him, and he shall be forgiven. You shall have one law for him who does anything unintentionally, for him who is native among the people of Israel and for the stranger who sojourns among them. *But the person who does anything with a high hand*, whether he is native or a sojourner, reviles the Lord, and that person shall be cut off from among his people. Because he has despised the word of the Lord and has broken his commandment, that person shall be utterly cut off; his iniquity shall be on him.

Some conclude from this passage that sinning "with a high hand" (v. 30) denotes sinning intentionally, since forgiveness for unintentional sin precedes it.[36] However, in context with Leviticus 5–6, which clearly describes atonement for intentional sin, it is better to understand sinning "with a high hand" to mean *sinning unrepentantly*, that is, refusing to confess, make restitution, and seek God's forgiveness through sacrifice.[37]

Collectively these sacrificial passages reveal that Torah faithfulness did not require one to keep God's commands perfectly, but rather to seek to

---

36. See, e.g., De Vaux, *Ancient Israel*, 420.
37. So also Ashley, *Numbers*, 288; Cole, *Numbers*, 253.

obey him with a faithful and repentant heart. When an Israelite disobeyed God—whether intentionally or unintentionally—provision was available for them to display their repentance and thereby receive forgiveness.[38] It was this submissive posture before God and his word that would enable Israel to serve as a priestly-missional people, teaching the nations by example how to relate to God in a faithful way.

To sum up: rather than being a legalistic burden for Israel to follow in order to gain God's favor, the Torah is a missional playbook that Israel receives *because they have been favored by God*. By treating God as King and obeying his word with a faithful and repentant heart, Israel is to model for the nations the proper way to relate to God. As God blesses Israel both numerically and materially in response to this obedience, the nations will see the benefits of giving their allegiance to the true God, turn from their idolatrous ways, and submit to him. In this way, Israel is to represent God's kingship to the ends of the earth.

THE CONQUEST OF CANAAN AND MISSION

After God rescues Israel from Egypt and communicates his Torah to them, their first responsibility as God's priestly kingdom is to conquer the land of Canaan. As we will see, both the *purpose* of the conquest and Israel's *means of executing it* are missional in nature: they are to conquer Canaan in order to advance the creation mandate, and they are to do so by faithful adherence to the Torah.

The Conquest of Canaan and the Creation Mandate

Israel is to conquer Canaan because it has the same function for their mission as Eden did for Adam: it is the staging ground for their fulfillment of the creation mandate. Two observations in particular demonstrate this. First, just as Eden was the temple space where God dwelled on earth (Gen 3:8), so is Canaan the place where God will put his "name,"[39] which represents his presence and for which the Solomonic temple was built.[40]

---

38. Certain crimes such as intentional homicide (Exod 21:12; Lev 24:17; Num 35:16–21), kidnapping (Exod 21:16; Deut 24:7), and adultery (Lev 20:10; Deut 22:22) were capital offenses and thus resulted in the execution of the guilty. Nevertheless, those guilty of such crimes could still demonstrate their repentance by their broken spirit and contrite heart (cf. Ps 51:16–17).

39. Deut 12:5, 11, 21; 14:23–24; 16:2, 6; 26:1–2.

40. 1 Kgs 3:2; 5:3, 5; 8:16–20, 29, et al.

Second, Israel's charge to conquer Canaan parallels Adam's charge to "subdue" (*kabāš*) the "earth" (*'ereṣ*).[41] After appearing in the creation mandate, the verb *kabāš* occurs elsewhere in the Pentateuch only to describe Israel "subduing" the "land" (*'ereṣ*) of Canaan (Num 32:22, 29; cf. Josh 18:1). In chapter 2 we saw that Adam's priestly responsibility to "work" and "keep" the garden (Gen 2:15) was an initial outworking of this charge to "subdue" the earth by harnessing and developing it and having dominion over the creatures. Adam was to "keep" or "guard" the garden's holiness from unclean things the same way that priests were later to guard the holiness of the tabernacle/temple from uncleanness (Lev 10:10; 13:40–46). Similarly, when Israel enters the land of Canaan they are to destroy all its inhabitants *for purposes of holiness*. After commanding Israel to destroy the Canaanites and their idolatrous altars and images, Moses provides this reason: "For you are a people holy to the Lord your God" (Deut 7:6). After repeating this instruction in Deut 20:16–17, he states that this destruction is necessary "that they may not teach you to do according to all their abominable practices that they have done for their gods, and so you sin against the Lord your God" (v. 18). Israel is to subdue the land by eradicating its inhabitants in order to maintain their holiness as God's corporate priest as they live in God's temple presence.

These connections demonstrate that just as Adam was to begin fulfilling his mission in Eden, so Israel is to begin fulfilling their mission in Canaan. The conquest is the first step in this fulfillment, by which Israel is to secure this sacred space where God will bring his temple presence and from which they will engage in their mission. In this location, Israel is to serve as a priestly people by living in proximity to God and obeying his kingly word and thereby serve as a witness to God's kingship among the nations. For this reason, we must reject DeYoung and Gilbert's fourth argument against viewing Israel's call as missional—that Israel's interactions with the nations primarily involved military conquest rather than mediation of blessing. On the contrary, as the preceding analyses of the missional roles of the Torah and the conquest have shown, Israel's conquest of Canaan is designed to sanctify the land so they may live as God's holy people and thereby mediate his blessing to the nations.

The Conquest of Canaan and Torah Faithfulness

Just as Israel's life in the land is to be characterized by obedience to God's word, so is their conquest of the land. In Deuteronomy Moses teaches that

---

41. See also Schmutzer, *Be Fruitful and Multiply*, 100–105.

Israel's success in conquering the land depends upon their faithfulness to the Torah:

> For if you will be careful to do all this commandment that I command you to do, loving the LORD your God, walking in all his ways, and holding fast to him, then the LORD will drive out all these nations before you, and you will dispossess nations greater and mightier than you. Every place on which the sole of your foot treads shall be yours. Your territory shall be from the wilderness to the Lebanon and from the River, the river Euphrates, to the western sea. No one shall be able to stand against you. The LORD your God will lay the fear of you and the dread of you on all the land that you shall tread, as he promised you. (Deut 11:22–24)

Similarly, the book of Joshua opens with God instructing Joshua how to lead Israel as they engage the Canaanites in battle. In 1:6–9 God says:

> ⁶ **Be strong and courageous**, for you shall cause this people to inherit the land that I swore to their fathers to give them. — A

> ⁷ ***Only*** **be strong and *very* courageous**, being careful to do according to all the law that Moses my servant commanded you. Do not turn from it to the right hand or to the left, that you may have good success wherever you go. ⁸ This Book of the Law shall not depart from your mouth, but you shall meditate on it day and night, so that you may be careful to do according to all that is written in it. For then you will make your way prosperous, and then you will have good success. — B

> ⁹ Have I not commanded you? **Be strong and courageous**. Do not be frightened, and do not be dismayed, for the LORD your God is with you wherever you go (Josh 1:6–9). — C

As the layout above makes clear, God exhorts Joshua three times to "be strong and courageous" (sections A, B, and C). Amidst this repetition is a significant variation, however, which is a tool that biblical writers use to focus attention.[42] The exhortation in section B is substantially longer than the others and is modified by two adverbs, "*Only* be strong and *very* courageous" (v. 7). By this technique the writer is drawing attention to this central section and focusing on it as the key element in Joshua's commissioning. Rather than relying on tactical preparation or combat training, the primary way that Joshua is to "be strong and courageous" in battle is by faithfulness to the Torah.

---

42. For discussions of variation amidst repetition in biblical narrative see Sternberg, *Poetics of Biblical Narrative*, 390–93; Fokkelman, *Reading Biblical Narrative*, 112–22.

The practical effect of this battle strategy is evident by comparing Israel's first two battles against Jericho and Ai. The former account opens by depicting the city of Jericho as an impenetrable fortress: "Now Jericho was shut up inside and outside because of the people of Israel. None went out, and none came in" (Josh 6:1). Yet because Israel faithfully obeys God's instructions, the walls of Jericho miraculously fall and Israel destroys the city.[43] Conversely, as Israel prepares for their second battle at Ai, the Israelite scouts who spy out the city advise Joshua to send only a few thousand men, "for they are few" (Josh 7:3). Nevertheless, because Achan disobeys the Torah and keeps items from the Jericho siege that were devoted to destruction (vv. 20–21; cf. Deut 7:25–26), the men of Ai route the Israelites despite their numerical disadvantage (Josh 7:4–5). These narrative accounts reinforce Deuteronomy's instruction that Israel's responsibility is to treat God as King by obeying his word, both while conquering the land and while living in it. Only by this means will their mission be successful.

THE KING OF ISRAEL AND MISSION

The next element to consider in Israel's missional calling is the role of the king. Based on how the monarchy arose in Israel, some scholars have argued that the OT has a less-than-favorable view of human kingship. For example, Richard Bauckham claims that "the Old Testament is highly ambivalent about earthly kings" and that "the establishment of monarchy in Israel was no more than a divine concession to Israel's foolish desire to be like the other nations."[44] Similarly, according to David Filbeck,

> The establishment of a monarchy seemingly contradicted God's original plan for Israel. God planned for Israel to be a kingdom of priests and a blessing to the nations. God was to be their king. No man . . . was to be king over Israel. When the Israelites called for a king, therefore, they rejected God as their king (1 Sam. 8:7) and their appointed role among the nations of the earth. Yet, in the end, God (re)directed this demand for a king, making it a contribution in accomplishing his own desire to include the nations in his salvation.[45]

---

43. For a discussion of the portrayal of Joshua and the people as wholly obedient to God throughout this chapter, see Hall, *Conquering Character*, 91–100.

44. Bauckham, *Bible and Mission*, 42.

45. Filbeck, *Yes, God of the Gentiles, Too*, 83. See also Wright, *Mission of God*, 344.

Contrary to these views, although Israel's request for a king in 1 Samuel 8 is indeed grounded in their wrong desire to be like the nations (vv. 5, 19–20), it does not follow that the monarchy itself is concessive or unoriginal to God's missional plan for Israel. As we will see below, it is the people's *motive* for requesting a king in 1 Samuel that is foolish, not simply the *fact* that they request a king. To understand kingship in Israel properly, we must examine how human kings are discussed throughout the entirety of Israel's history.

Genesis: Human Kingship and the Creation Mandate

The concept of human kingship over God's people first appears in God's dealings with Abraham. When God confirms his covenant with Abraham and promises to fulfill the creation mandate through him, he also promises that kings will descend from him: "I will make you exceedingly fruitful (*pārâ*), and I will make you into nations, *and kings shall come from you*" (Gen 17:6). God later reiterates this promise both to Sarah (Gen 17:16) and Jacob (Gen 35:11); in the latter instance future kingship is again associated with the creation mandate: "And God said to [Jacob], 'I am God Almighty: be fruitful (*pārâ*) and multiply (*rabbâ*). A nation and a company of nations shall come from you, *and kings shall come from your own body*.'" These texts connect human kingship to the creation mandate, hinting that the former will play a part in the fulfillment of the latter. Supporting this, when Jacob later blesses his sons, a connection between kingship and mission appears once again:

> The scepter shall not depart from Judah,
>   nor the ruler's staff from between his feet,
> until tribute comes to him;
>   *and to him shall be the obedience of the peoples.* (Gen 49:10)

This verse communicates at least two new developments in Genesis' incipient theology of kingship: Israel's king is to (1) come from the tribe of Judah, and (2) receive international submission. Therefore, before Israel is organized into a geopolitical entity we see that kingship over God's people has an international, missional function.[46]

---

46. This image of kingly international dominion is further reinforced by Balaam's final oracle, in which he sees a "scepter" rising out of Israel and possessing various peoples surrounding them (Num 24:17–19).

Deuteronomy: The King as Chief Keeper of Torah

The next major development in a biblical theology of human kingship comes in the book of Deuteronomy. As Moses explicates the Torah to Israel, one of the topics he addresses is how Israel's king is to function. In Deut 17:14–20 Moses presents a vision of kingship that is vastly different from the royal ideologies that prevailed during that time. Whereas most ancient Near Eastern monarchs were powerful warlords who established their authority through large armies, foreign marriage alliances, and huge quantities of wealth, the Torah forbids Israel's king from engaging in each of these practices. According to Moses, Israel's king may not "acquire many horses" (v. 16), "acquire many wives for himself" (v. 17a),[47] or "acquire for himself excessive silver and gold" (v. 17b). In short, Israel's king may not rule the way that kings typically ruled at that time. Instead, the responsibility of Israel's king is to lead the people in living faithfully before God.

After specifying that the king must be a fellow Israelite whom God will choose (v. 15), Moses describes the king essentially as a chief keeper of Torah:

> And when he sits on the throne of his kingdom, he shall write for himself in a book a copy of this law, approved by the Levitical priests. And it shall be with him, and he shall read in it all the days of his life, that he may learn to fear the LORD his God by keeping all the words of this law and these statutes, and doing them, that his heart may not be lifted up above his brothers, and that he may not turn aside from the commandment, either to the right hand or to the left, so that he may continue long in his kingdom, he and his children, in Israel. (vv. 18–20)

According to this passage, rather than being a warlord, Israel's king is to be a *student* and a *spiritual leader*. He is to study the Torah so he will fear the LORD (v. 19), be humble with respect to his fellow Israelites (v. 20a), and live according to God's word (v. 20b). We have seen that as God's priestly kingdom Israel is to represent his kingship to the ends of the earth by keeping the Torah with repentant obedience. Here we see that Israel's king is to lead the charge in this missional lifestyle.

---

47. This most likely refers to foreign wives, since the explanatory clause says, "lest his heart turn away." This turning away would come as the king's foreign wives influenced him toward worshiping their foreign gods, which is precisely what happened to Solomon (1 Kgs 11:3).

Judges: Everyone Did What Was Right In His Own Eyes

The book of Judges reinforces this connection between human kingship and Torah faithfulness. During the first centuries of Israel's life in the land they are depicted as consistently declining in their adherence to the Torah and in need of a faithful king to lead them in obedience. The prologue of Judges (1:1—3:6) presents Israel as failing to acknowledge God's work on their behalf (2:10) and therefore turning away from God and engaging in idolatry (2:11-13). In response to this rebellion, God hands them over to their enemies (2:14-15), as he had warned in the Torah (Lev 26:17; Deut 28:25), but also graciously raises up judges to deliver them (2:16). According to 2:17, these judges are to lead the people in living faithfully before God, though the people refuse to listen: "Yet they did not listen to their judges, for they whored after other gods and bowed down to them."[48] The prologue ends by noting that God allows other nations to remain in Canaan alongside his people "for the testing of Israel, to know whether Israel would obey the commandments of the LORD, which he commanded their fathers by the hand of Moses" (3:4). Since obedience to God's commands is the means by which Israel is to engage in their mission, this testing period under the leadership of the judges may be understood as a missional probation for the people of God.

This testing period proves to be nothing short of disastrous. As the book progresses through its accounts of the judges (3:7—16:31) and into the epilogue (17:1—21:25), a steady decline in Torah faithfulness is evident. This decline reaches its low point at the end of the book in the story of the Levite and his concubine (chs. 19-21), where the Benjaminites are portrayed like Sodomites (cf. Genesis 19). In light of this moral anarchy, the fourfold refrain in the epilogue crystallizes the message that has been building throughout the book: "In those days there was no king in Israel. Everyone did what was right in his own eyes" (17:6; see also 18:1; 19:1; 21:25). That is, without a faithful, covenant-keeping king to lead them, Israel is failing to keep the Torah and therefore failing to fulfill their mission. Rather than representing God to the nations, they are beginning to look just like the nations.[49]

---

48. See also Chisholm, *Judges and Ruth*, 23.

49. In line with this, Block sees the central theme of the book as "the Canaanization of Israel" (*Judges, Ruth*, 71).

Saul: A King "Like All the Nations"

Following the sporadic leadership of the judges, the books of Samuel narrate the establishment of Israel's monarchy. Despite experiencing God's powerful deliverance from the Philistines (1 Sam 7:3–14), the elders of Israel ask Samuel to "appoint for us a king to judge us like all the nations" (1 Sam 8:5). As God explains to Samuel, this request reveals that the people have rejected him as King (v. 7). However, it is important to recognize that Israel is not requesting the type of king that Deuteronomy 17 envisions. Rather than asking for a spiritual leader who will guide them in living faithfully before God—*and thereby treat God as King*—Israel is requesting a typical ancient Near Eastern warlord king. This is apparent from the nature of Samuel's warning that follows, which outlines the various exploitative practices of worldly monarchs at that time (vv. 10–18).[50] This is also evident from the people's response to this warning: "But the people refused to obey the voice of Samuel. And they said, 'No! But there shall be a king over us, *that we also may be like all the nations, and that our king may judge us and go out before us and fight our battles*'" (vv. 19–20). Rather than desiring to be a holy nation that represents God's kingship to the nations by following a Torah-keeping king and trusting in God's ability to deliver, Israel desires a king who will make them look and operate just like the nations around them.

In response, God gives them Saul, who is introduced as "a handsome young man. There was not a man among the people of Israel more handsome than he. From his shoulders upward he was taller than any of the people" (1 Sam 9:2). This description portrays Saul as an ideal king according to the standards of the surrounding nations, who placed great value on the physique and appearance of their rulers.[51] Conspicuously absent from this description is any spiritual qualification in Saul, which is of foremost importance in the Torah's instruction for Israel's king.

The narrative goes on to emphasize how Saul demonstrates his lack of faith in God by failing to obey, which is ultimately the reason for his rejection. First, contrary to God's word, Saul fails to wait for Samuel to arrive in Gilgal and offers unlawful sacrifices on his own (1 Sam 13:8–9). In response, Samuel tells Saul that his dynasty will not endure "because you have not kept what the LORD commanded you" (v. 14). After this, Saul disobeys God's command to annihilate the Amalekites, which leads God to reject him as king altogether, saying, "he has turned back from following me and has not performed my commandments" (1 Sam 15:11). After Samuel confronts Saul

---

50. Tsumura, *First Book of Samuel*, 255.
51. See the examples provided by Long, "1 and 2 Samuel," 311.

with this news, he eventually admits that he sinned because he "feared the people and obeyed their voice" (v. 24). Whereas the primary responsibility of Israel's king was to lead the people in fearing God and to obey *his* voice (Deut 17:18–19), Saul disobeys God because he fears the people and obeys *their* voice. Saul's actions, therefore, are not simply "minimal mistakes," as Walter Dietrich suggests.[52] Rather, they represent the very opposite of what the Torah calls Israel's king to do. For this reason, in addition to discontinuing Saul's dynasty, God declares that he will remove the kingship from him and give it to another (1 Sam 15:28).

David: A King "According to God's Heart"

When Saul first disobeys God in 1 Samuel 13, Samuel informs him that "the LORD has sought for himself *a man according to his heart* (ʾiš kilbābô)" (v. 14, author's translation). This latter phrase is ambiguous and may describe either (1) God's particular choice of this man ("a man of God's choosing"),[53] or (2) this man's disposition as aligned with God's heart ("a man who lives according to God's will").[54] Although these readings are different exegetically, ultimately they refer to the same type of person, since Deut 17:14–20 describes God's choice of a king as one who lives according to his will.[55] Paul seems to understand the phrase in the latter sense, paraphrasing God's choice of David as follows: "I have found in David the son of Jesse a man after my heart, *who will do all my will*" (Acts 13:22). Inasmuch as God rejects Saul for his failure to obey, he chooses David for his willingness to obey.

Some scholars object to this characterization of David based on his pattern of disobedience in the narratives that follow. For example, Tony Cartledge says,

> David schemes constantly; he kills without just cause; he commits adultery; he sanctions the murder of the innocent; he takes many wives; he refuses to be reconciled with his troublesome son. These actions are hardly modeled "after God's heart."[56]

However, once we remember that faithfulness to God involves repentant obedience rather than perfect obedience, we see that David, though far from

52. Dietrich, *Early Monarchy in Israel*, 100.
53. E.g., McCarter, *1 Samuel*, 229; Bodner, *1 Samuel*, 123.
54. E.g., Youngblood, "1, 2 Samuel," 657; Chisholm, *1 & 2 Samuel*, 83.
55. For a good discussion of the exegetical issues and a balanced conclusion, see DeRouchie, "Heart of YHWH," 467–89.
56. Cartledge, *1 & 2 Samuel*, 175.

perfect, is portrayed as having a faithful disposition before God.[57] For this reason, later texts describe David as walking "with integrity of heart and uprightness" (1 Kgs 9:4) and as "wholly true to the LORD his God" (1 Kgs 11:4; 15:3), and God says that he has "kept my commandments and followed me with all his heart, doing only that which was right in my eyes" (1 Kgs 14:8; cf. 11:34). These descriptions are not ignorant of David's failures, but instead highlight his willingness to repent from such failure and maintain a faithful and penitent relationship with God. This is the type of king Israel needs: one who will rely on God and lead the people in expressing their faith in him through repentant obedience that leads to missional effectiveness.

The Davidic Covenant: An Everlasting Kingdom

After David's kingship is established, he expresses a desire to build God a "house" (i.e., a temple; 2 Sam 7:2, 5), but God responds by saying that he will build David a "house" (i.e., a dynasty; v. 11). God informs David that his descendant will build his temple (vv. 12–13), promising that "your house and your kingdom shall be made sure forever before me. Your throne shall be established forever" (v. 16). This passage introduces the Davidic covenant, and though the term "covenant" does not appear in 2 Samuel 7, it does appear in the poetic recollection of this event in Ps 89:3–4:

> You have said, "I have made a covenant with my chosen one;
>   I have sworn to David my servant:
> 'I will establish your offspring forever,
>   and build your throne for all generations.'"

In this covenant God promises David that his dynasty will endure forever. Although God specifies that if any of David's descendants forsake his commands he will discipline them (2 Sam 7:14; Ps 89:30–32), he promises that he will never remove his steadfast love from them the way he did from Saul (2 Sam 7:15; Ps 89:33–34). In other words, the success of any particular Davidic king will depend on that king's faithfulness, though the success of the Davidic dynasty as a whole is forever secure because of God's covenantal promise.

The implications of this covenant for a theology of mission are tremendous. If God's mission in the world is for his kingship to be represented to the ends of the earth, and if this mission is fulfilled as Israel faithfully obeys God's word through the Torah, and if such obedience requires a faithful,

---

57. See, e.g., David's repentant spirit after Nathan confronts him concerning the Bathsheba/Uriah affair (2 Sam 12:13–23; Ps 51).

Torah-keeping king to lead the people, then this covenantal promise of an everlasting dynasty founded with a king "according to God's heart" is a critical element in Israel's missional identity. As the Davidic king leads the people in obeying God as their ultimate King, the Abrahamic formula will ensue, resulting in the nations coming to know God's redemptive blessing and submitting to him as King.

Psalm 72: A Worldwide Kingdom

This vision of the Davidic king leading the people in Torah faithfulness as a witness to the nations is vividly portrayed in Psalm 72. This psalm is a prayer that God would enable the Davidic king[58] to rule with justice and righteousness, especially as defender of the poor and needy (vv. 1–4). As he does so, the people will fear God ("May they fear *you* while the sun endures" [v. 5]), which will allow the righteous to flourish and peace to abound (v. 7). The psalmist then turns his attention to the international landscape and prays for all nations to submit to the Davidic king:

> May he have dominion from sea to sea,
>   and from the River to the ends of the earth!
> May desert tribes bow down before him,
>   and his enemies lick the dust!
> May the kings of Tarshish and of the coastlands
>   render him tribute;
> may the kings of Sheba and Seba
>   bring gifts!
> May all kings fall down before him,
>   all nations serve him! (vv. 8–11)

This prayer for the king's dominion to stretch "from sea to sea" and "from the River to the ends of the earth" refers to his rule extending over the whole world. However, the text does not indicate that this worldwide reign will be achieved through military domination. Rather, the reason these foreign kings are called to submit to the Davidic king is because of his righteous, Torah-directed rule:

---

58. The superscription to this Psalm reads *lišlōmō*, "of/by/for/concerning Solomon." Although this prepositional phrase may reflect authorship (cf. Hab 3:1), it is notoriously flexible and thus may indicate instead that the psalm is *dedicated to* Solomon or *about* him. This latter interpretation is supported by the colophon at the end of the psalm, "The prayers of David, the son of Jesse, are ended" (v. 20). This seems to suggest that David is the author of the psalm and is praying for the reign of his successor Solomon (see also Mays, *Lord Reigns*, 104; Alter, *Book of Psalms*, 248).

> For he delivers the needy when he calls,
>   the poor and him who has no helper.
> He has pity on the weak and the needy,
>   and saves the lives of the needy.
> From oppression and violence he redeems their life,
>   and precious is their blood in his sight. (vv. 12–14)

Because the king defends the cause of the poor and needy, which leads his people to fear God and flourish, the nations are called to come and submit to him. This logic follows the Abrahamic formula: Israel is to live righteously according to God's Torah (in this case, as led by the Davidic king), which will lead God to bless them, which will cause the nations to esteem their blessed status and thereby receive God's blessings themselves. Significantly, the text of Psalm 72 goes on to make this connection to the Abrahamic blessing explicit.

After petitioning God for "abundance of grain in the land" and asking that "people blossom in the cities" (v. 16)—two major manifestations of divine blessing—the psalmist says of the king,

> May his name endure forever,
>   his fame continue as long as the sun!
> May all nations be blessed in him,
>   all nations call him blessed! (v. 17, author's translation)

In a clear allusion to Gen 12:3, this verse calls for blessing upon all nations through Israel's king. The third line is elliptical ("May [all nations] be blessed in him"); the text does not explicitly identify the subject who is to receive blessing. However, since the subject of the parallel line is "all nations" (*kol-gôyim*), this is most likely the intended subject of the first line as well (see NRSV). Consequently, whereas God told Abram that "in *you* all the families of the earth shall be blessed" (Gen 12:3), here we see that this promise, though executed through Abram's offspring as a whole, is funneled through the righteous leadership of Israel's king in particular. As the king rules righteously according to the Torah, the nation as a whole will live faithfully before God, and as they receive God's blessing for their faithfulness they will draw the attention of the surrounding nations. In response, the nations will come and submit themselves to Israel's king, which is demonstrated by their offering of tribute (vv. 10, 15), and in so doing they will be submitting to Israel's God. As Richard Clifford summarizes it, "The tribute acknowledges that [the nations] and their patron gods are subordinate to the Lord and to his lieutenant, the Davidic king."[59] This is reinforced by the closing doxology

---

59. Clifford, *Psalms 1–72*, 333.

of Psalm 72, in which it is *God's glory* that is lifted up rather than the glory of the Davidic king:

> Blessed be the Lord, the God of Israel,
>   who alone does wondrous things.
> Blessed be his glorious name forever;
>   *may the whole earth be filled with his glory*!
> Amen and Amen! (vv. 18–19)

As the nations turn from their deities and submit to God by submitting to the Davidic king, the whole earth will be filled with *God's glory* as his formerly rebellious images turn their allegiance back to him.

THE TEMPLE AND MISSION

The last item to consider in Israel's missional organization is the role of the temple. The temple is the location where God places his "name" and thereby establishes his presence with his people (Deut 12:5; 1 Kgs 8:20). When Solomon completes the temple and brings the ark of the covenant into the Most Holy Place, God fills the temple with his glory cloud (1 Kgs 8:10–11). Solomon then offers a dedicatory prayer that identifies this temple as the rallying point for the nations to respond when they acknowledge the supremacy of Israel's God. After recalling God's covenant faithfulness to David and outlining various situations in which Israel may turn toward this temple in prayer, Solomon foresees people from other nations hearing about God's reputation and coming to the temple:

> Likewise, when a foreigner, who is not of your people Israel, comes from a far country for your name's sake (for they shall hear of your great name and your mighty hand, and of your outstretched arm), when he comes and prays toward this house, hear in heaven your dwelling place and do according to all for which the foreigner calls to you, in order that all the peoples of the earth may know your name, that they may fear you as do your people Israel, and that they may know that this house that I have built is called by your name. (1 Kgs 8:41–43, author's translation)

In this passage Solomon foresees foreigners being drawn to Israel's temple because they hear of God's "great name," his "mighty hand," and his "outstretched arm" (v. 42). Prior to this prayer, the phrases "mighty hand" and "outstretched arm" have appeared together only in the book of Deuteronomy to describe the powerful means by which God rescued Israel from Egypt.[60] This suggests that God's "great name" that foreigners will hear about is his reputation as a faithful deity who has proven himself powerful to deliver his people.

Solomon then describes the foreigner as coming and praying toward the temple, and asks God to respond to the foreigner's petition "in order that all the peoples of the earth may know your name" (v. 43b). By responding to the requests of foreigners, God will show that he is faithful not only to Israel but to all peoples who come and seek him. This faithful response to foreigners will then further publicize God's reputation among the nations, all of whom will eventually come to "know" his name. To "know" God's name in this context does not mean simply to have cognitive awareness of his label but to *acknowledge* who he is and what he has done. Therefore, God's good reputation, which began with his redemption of Israel, will eventually spread among all nations as he graciously receives foreigners who come to him.

This international acknowledgment of God's name is then described as having a twofold purpose: (1) that the nations might "fear" God (v. 43bα), and (2) that they might "know" that the temple is called by his name (v. 43bβ).[61] Regarding the first purpose, to "fear" God involves reverently submitting to him and responding to him with obedience (see, e.g., Deut 10:12–13). When the nations hear about God's redemptive work on Israel's behalf and observe him responding positively to the petitions of foreigners, their acknowledgement of this good reputation will lead them to submit to him and seek to do his will. In short, they will begin to treat God as King.

Regarding the second purpose, this acknowledgement of God's reputation will also lead the nations to recognize Israel's temple as the center of relationship with him. This is the place where the nations are to come and demonstrate their submission to God's kingship and worship him (cf. Deut 12:4–7). Such an influx of foreigners to the temple is later portrayed at various points in the prophetic literature. For example, in Isa 56:6–7 the prophet says,

> And the foreigners who join themselves to the LORD,
>   to minister to him, to love the name of the LORD,
>   and to be his servants,
> everyone who keeps the Sabbath and does not profane it,

---

60. Deut 4:34; 5:15; 7:19; 11:2–4; 26:8.

61. In verse 43 the MT has a disjunctive accent (*rebia*) after "your name," which is followed by two clauses, each of which begins with an infinitive of purpose: "that they may fear . . ." (*lᵉyirʾâ ʾōṯᵉḵā*) and "that they may know . . ." (*wᵉlāḏaʿaṯ*).

> and holds fast my covenant—
> these I will bring to my holy mountain,
> and make them joyful in my house of prayer;
> their burnt offerings and their sacrifices
> will be accepted on my altar;
> for my house shall be called a house of prayer
> for all peoples.

Collectively, all of this reinforces the idea that God's kingship is to extend over every nation of the world, and it identifies the temple as the geographical location to which the nations are to come and submit to him.

Further highlighting this missional focus of the temple is Solomon's closing supplication and exhortation. After recalling God's faithfulness to Israel and exhorting the people to be faithful to God, Solomon summarizes his dedicatory prayer in 1 Kgs 8:59–61:

> Let these words of mine, with which I have pleaded before the LORD, be near to the LORD our God day and night, and may he maintain the cause of his servant and the cause of his people Israel, as each day requires, *that all the peoples of the earth may know that the LORD is God*; there is no other. Let your heart therefore be wholly true to the LORD our God, walking in his statutes and keeping his commandments, as at this day.

The purpose clause of verse 60 indicates that worldwide recognition of Israel's God as the only true deity is the goal of Israel's life in the land. Israel's pursuit of Torah faithfulness and commitment to repentance at the temple are designed to witness to God's kingship among the nations. With the temple in place and the Davidic monarchy responsible for leading the people in Torah faithfulness, Israel is now positioned to serve as God's covenantal witness and represent his kingship to the ends of the earth.

SUMMARY

In this chapter we have seen that Israel's initial fulfillment of the creation mandate in Egypt is what led to their enslavement and that God rescues them in order that they might represent his kingship among the nations. After delivering Israel from slavery, God calls them to be a kingdom of priests and a holy nation by obeying his voice and keeping his covenant. As Israel faithfully adheres to the Torah through repentant obedience, God will fulfill the creation mandate through them and bless the nations by means of the Abrahamic formula. The conquest of Canaan is the initial installment of Israel's mission, whereby Israel is to subdue the promised land that they might dwell as God's holy people in his presence. Israel's king is responsible to lead the people in keeping God's word, and as God blesses his people in the sight of the nations, the temple is the place where foreigners may come to worship God and demonstrate their allegiance to him. If Israel had been faithful and obeyed God, they would have succeeded in this mission and God's kingship would have been represented to the ends of the earth. As we will see in the next chapter, however, like Adam before them, Israel fails to treat God as king and therefore fails to execute their mission.

5 MISSION FAILED
The Fall of Israel

Last chapter we saw how God organized his mission by calling Israel to himself and equipping them to witness to his kingship among the nations. In this chapter we will explore how Israel fails in this mission. After briefly looking at an early hint of mission failure during the exodus generation, we will examine how the Torah outlines the missional failure that will follow if Israel unrepentantly disobeys God's word. Then we will survey Israel's history in the promised land and see that it is characterized by such unrepentant disobedience. As a result, Israel fails in their mission; they receive covenant curses rather than blessings and therefore do not represent God's kingship among the nations. We will then see how, in the midst of this judgment, God promises to restore his people that they might engage in their mission once again. The postexilic books record God fulfilling this promise and restoring Israel to the land, though they also portray Israel as struggling with the same sinful inclinations that led to their downfall in the preexilic era. This reveals that, at the close of the Old Testament period, although Israel has been restored to the land geographically, they are still waiting for the fuller spiritual restoration that God promised through the prophets. It is only this latter, holistic restoration that will enable them to succeed in their mission.

AN EARLY HINT OF MISSION FAILURE

Early in Israel's history we see a hint of the mission failure that will eventually occur. Shortly after communicating the Torah to Israel, God leads them from Mount Sinai to the southern border of Canaan and commissions twelve scouts to spy out the promised land (Num 13:2). Despite God's past deliverance from Egypt and promised provision of Canaan, all the scouts except Joshua and Caleb conclude that they cannot conquer the land due to the powerful people who live there (vv. 30–33). They spread a bad report among the people who, rather than trusting God and obeying his word, believe this bad report and grumble against Moses and Aaron (14:1–4). In response, God threatens to destroy the people and start a new nation with Moses (vv. 11–12), but Moses intercedes and pleads with God not to annihilate them. At the height of this intercession Moses says, "Now if you kill this people as one man, then the nations who have heard your fame will say, 'It is because the LORD was not able to bring this people into the land that he swore to give to them that he has killed them in the wilderness'" (vv. 15–16). Moses contends that God should not destroy Israel because the surrounding nations will wrongly conclude that he is impotent to fulfill his promises.

This passage provides an early hint of mission failure by showing how Israel's rebellion against God will lead to a bad witness among the nations. By not obeying God and therefore not treating him as King, Israel will receive God's judgment rather than his blessing. According to Moses, the nations will misinterpret this judgment as reflecting *God's inability* to establish his people in Canaan, which would not reflect the true nature of his sovereignty over creation. The result of Israel's rebellion, then, is that God's kingship will *not* be rightly represented among the nations. Although God relents from bringing judgment against Israel on this occasion and shows himself patient during many subsequent rebellions, eventually his holiness will demand that he execute judgment against his people for their prolonged and unrepentant disobedience.

THE TORAH AND MISSION FAILURE

Just as the Torah teaches that Israel's obedience will result in missional success, so it specifies that their disobedience will warrant covenant curses and thereby result in failure to represent God to the nations. When we explored the fall of humanity in Genesis we saw that humanity's rebellion against God resulted in both relational separation from God and a frustrated ability to engage in mission. Similarly, if Israel follows Adam's example and rejects God's kingship, like Adam they will experience both relational separation from God and frustration in their mission. The relational separation will come from being scattered among the nations in exile away from God's presence (Lev 26:33; Deut 4:27; 28:64). The missional frustration will come through the opposite of the two major missional initiatives we have explored so far: Israel will be made *few in number* (the opposite of the creation mandate) and become a *recognized recipient of cursing* (the opposite of the Abrahamic blessing).

The Torah and Creation Mandate Failure

Just as Israel's adherence to the Torah will result in their fulfilling the creation mandate, so their disobedience will result in its reversal. In Leviticus 26, after outlining the blessings that follow covenant faithfulness (vv. 1–13), God says, "But if you will not listen to me and carry out all these commands, and if you reject my decrees and abhor my laws and fail to carry out all my commands and so violate my covenant, then I will do this to you" (vv. 14–16a), after which he lists a series of judgments that will follow. One of these judgments is that God will "make you few in number, so that your roads shall be deserted" (v. 22). Rather than making Israel fruitful and multiplying them (v. 9), God will reduce their numbers, thereby reversing the creation mandate.

This concept is also present in Deuteronomy's description of covenant curses. In describing the results of covenant unfaithfulness, Moses says,

> Whereas you were as numerous as the stars of heaven, you shall be left few in number, because you did not obey the voice of the LORD your God. And as the LORD took delight in doing you good and multiplying you, so the LORD will take delight in bringing ruin upon you and destroying you. And you shall be plucked off the land that you are entering to take possession of it. (Deut 28:62–63)

Moses contrasts God's proliferation of Israel in response to their faithfulness with his decimation of them in response to their disobedience.[1] Just as humanity's primeval rebellion was characterized by the opposite of the creation mandate, here we see this same reality manifested in God's judgment of Israel for their rebellion: he will reduce their numbers.

The Torah and Cursing Among the Nations

In addition to failing to fulfill the creation mandate, Israel's rebellion will result in failure to fulfill the Abrahamic formula. Rather than receiving blessings for their obedience, being recognized as blessed by the nations, and thereby modeling faithful relationship with God, Israel's disobedience will merit God's judgment, revealing that they did not treat him as King and

---

1. See also the discussion in Viands, *I Will Surely Multiply Your Offspring*, 74.

profaning his name among the nations. Leviticus 26 states that Israel's rebellion will result in disease (v. 16a), futility (v. 16b), military defeat (vv. 17, 25, 37–39), famine (vv. 20, 26, 29), destruction (vv. 30–32), and exile (v. 33). These curses are presented as the opposites of the blessings listed in verses 1–13[2] and thus have the reverse effect: rather than providing evidence of faithful relationship with God and drawing the nations to him, they will make Israel "a curse and a taunt among all the nations of the earth" (Jer 44:8).

The catalog of covenant curses in Deuteronomy 28 includes these same judgments and more. Moses says that Israel's disobedience will result in cursing wherever a person may go (vv. 16, 19), upon domestic labors (vv. 17, 38–40), and upon both human and animal fertility (v. 18). It will also include pestilence (v. 21), disease (vv. 22, 27, 35), military defeat (v. 25), oppression (vv. 28–29, 32–34), futility (vv. 30–31), subordination (vv. 43–44), and exile (vv. 36, 41). Most significant for our purposes, Moses specifies that such cursing will result in Israel serving as a bad witness among the nations:

> And you shall be a horror to all the kingdoms of the earth. (v. 25)

> And you shall become a horror, a proverb, and a byword among all the peoples where the LORD will lead you away. (v. 37)

Just as Israel's reception of blessing is to serve a public purpose, making them a recognized recipient of blessing, so their reception of cursing will be publicly recognized by the surrounding nations. Whereas the former situation would serve as a magnet to attract the nations to God, the latter will serve as a repellent, causing the nations to disdain Israel and by extension the God whom they claim to serve.

In both of these chapters—Leviticus 26 and Deuteronomy 28—the curses that follow from Israel's disobedience climax in the judgment of exile (Lev 26:33; Deut 28:36). However, just as God promised to forgive a Torah violator if they demonstrated repentance by faithfully following sacrificial protocol, so he promises to bring Israel back from exile and fulfill the creation mandate through them if they penitently turn to him. Moses tells Israel that upon such repentance, "the LORD your God will bring you into the land that your fathers possessed, that you may possess it. And he will make you more prosperous and *numerous* (lit. 'multiplied' [*rabbâ*]) than your fathers" (Deut 30:5). Moreover, not only does Deuteronomy envision this future mandate fulfillment upon Israel's restoration from exile, it also

---

2. Specifically, verses 16–17 reverse verses 7–8; verses 18–20 reverse verse 4; verses 21–22 reverse verses 6a, 9; verses 23–26 reverse verses 5, 6b, 10. See Milgrom, *Leviticus: A Book of Ritual and Ethics*, 319–22.

speaks of an internal heart transformation that will accompany it: "And the LORD your God will circumcise your heart and the heart of your offspring, so that you will love the LORD your God with all your heart and with all your soul, that you may live" (v. 6). It is important to observe here that the Hebrew verb "love" (*'āhab*) does not emphasize the popular contemporary focus on intimate feeling or deep affection. Rather, the covenantal context of Deuteronomy suggests that it carries the same emphasis as its common use in other ancient Near Eastern covenantal contexts: action that reflects allegiance and faithfulness to one's covenant partner.[3] Consequently, despite the judgment and bad witness that Israel's unfaithfulness will cause, one day God will transform their hearts and enable them to live in faithful relationship with him, thereby enabling them to fulfill the mission he has given them.

A HISTORY OF MISSION FAILURE

Turning our attention to the narratives that portray Israel's life in the land, we essentially read a history of mission failure. By failing to live in repentant obedience to the Torah, Israel continually falls short of representing God's kingship to the nations. This trend begins as early as Israel's conquest of the land and continues throughout their time in the land until God's patience finally reaches its end and the nation is exiled to live in a foreign land.

Mission Failure When Conquering the Land

Last chapter we observed that the conquest is presented as an outworking of the creation mandate and that Israel's success in subduing the land is contingent upon their adherence to the Torah. The portrayal of the conquest in Judges begins by describing Judah's annexation of their tribal allotment in the southern region of Canaan. After several brief accounts of military victory, a significant juxtaposition appears: "And the LORD was with Judah, and he took possession of the hill country, but he could not drive out the inhabitants of the plain because they had chariots of iron" (Judg 1:19). Despite God's presence, Judah fails to purge the lowland territory of its inhabitants, supposedly because of the advanced material of their opponents' chariotry. However, given the descriptions of divine warfare in preceding battle accounts, in which God has no difficulty destroying enemy chariotry[4] or

---

3. Moran, "Ancient Near Eastern Background," 77–87; Block, *Deuteronomy*, 698.
4. See Exod 14, especially verses 26–29; Josh 11:1–9.

even fortified cities,[5] it is clear that God's ability to overcome the Canaanite chariots is not the issue here. Rather, since Deut 20:1–3 presumes that a large enemy chariotry will instill fear in Israel's hearts, it is most likely that Judah's failure to conquer the lowlands is due to their fear of their enemies' iron chariots. As Jeffery Stevenson summarizes, "They must have felt that the chariots were too difficult to tackle, so they did not. They '*could* not' because they *would* not, therefore they *did* not."[6] Rather than proceeding by faith and trusting in God's promise to deliver the land despite formidable opposition (cf. Deut 7:17–19; 20:4; Josh 17:17–18), Judah's apparent fear disables them from fully securing the land.

After this subtle portrayal of Israel being guided by fear rather than faith, the remainder of Judges 1 reports a veritable landslide of conquest failure, mentioning the shortcomings of almost every tribe west of the Jordan (Judg 1:21–36). In each case, although Israel takes control of the land, they do not fully dispossess the indigenous inhabitants. In the Torah God had prohibited Israel from allowing the Canaanites to remain in the land because of their inevitable idolatrous influence (Exod 23:33; 34:12–16; Deut 7:16). Now, because of Israel's lack of faithful obedience, God declares that these inhabitants will remain in the land and that their gods will become a snare to Israel (Judg 2:1–3). It is this idolatrous Canaanite influence that will subsequently lead Israel astray throughout Judges 3–16 and require the deliverance of the judges (see Judg 2:11–23).[7] Collectively, these accounts show that Israel's entry into the land is marked by failure to keep the Torah and therefore failure to fulfill their mission.

Mission Failure When Living in the Land

Not only is Israel's entry into the land characterized by mission failure, so is their life in the land. As we saw last chapter, the message of Judges is that Israel needs a covenant-keeping king rather than warlord judges to lead them in fulfilling their mission. However, even though God chooses David and promises to give him an everlasting dynasty, the narrative of Israel's history in the land portrays the Davidic dynasty as leading the people in sinning against God rather than obeying him.

---

5. See Josh 6, especially verses 16, 27.
6. Stevenson, "Judah's Successes and Failures in Holy War," 50 (emphasis original).
7. These verses summarize the pattern presented in the ensuing narratives of chapters 3–16. Here it is specified that Israel's idolatry is the "evil" mentioned throughout the subsequent cycles (2:11–13, 19). See also McCann, *Judges*, 35.

This motif begins in the second generation of Davidic leadership under the reign of Solomon. After reporting that Solomon married a multitude of foreign women contrary to the stipulations of the Torah (1 Kgs 11:1–3; cf. Deut 7:1–4; 23:3), the narrator of Kings says, "when Solomon was old his wives turned away his heart after other gods, and his heart was not wholly true to the LORD his God, as was the heart of David his father" (1 Kgs 11:4). Solomon's unfaithfulness is then described as doing "what was evil in the sight of the LORD" (v. 6), which leads God to tear most of the nation away from his descendants, resulting in the divided kingdoms of Israel and Judah.

As the narrative progresses through the reigns of the various kings, many are similarly described as doing "what was/is evil in the sight of the LORD."[8] Rather than leading the people in Torah faithfulness, Israel's and Judah's kings lead them in idolatry, injustice, and sin. Echoing the situation portrayed immediately prior to the Noachic flood (Gen 6:5), through the prophet Hosea God summarizes this period of the divided monarchy: "The more they *increased* (*rābab*), the more they sinned against me" (Hos 4:7). This unfaithfulness eventually causes God to actualize the judgments of the Torah by sending foreign nations to destroy and exile his people. The most elaborate commentary on the rationale for the exile is found in 2 Kings 17. Instead of responding to God's grace by faithfully serving him and representing his kingship among the nations, Israel "walked in the customs of the nations" (v. 8) and therefore became indistinguishable from them. As a result, Israel receives God's judgment (vv. 9–18), which Judah also receives shortly thereafter (2 Kgs 24:10–17). Just as God exiled Adam and Eve from his presence in the garden because they refused to obey him, so he exiles Israel and Judah from his presence in the promised land for this same reason. In both cases God's people refuse to treat him as King, which disables them from representing his kingship and fulfilling their mission.

Mission Failure When Exiled from the Land

In addition to serving as judgment for Israel's disobedience, the Babylonian exile further forfeits Israel's witness among the nations. Jeremiah and Ezekiel state that God's exile of Israel makes them a "horror," a "curse," and a "reproach" among the nations.[9] This represents the opposite of Israel's calling as envisioned in the Abrahamic formula. Instead of attracting the nations to God by their faithful and blessed relationship with him, Israel's

---

8. 1 Kgs 15:26, 34; 16:7, 19, 25, 30; 21:20, 25; 22:52; 2 Kgs 3:2; 8:18, 27; 13:2, 11; 14:24; 15:9, 18, 24, 28; 17:2, 17; 21:2, 6, 9, 16, 20; 23:32, 37; 24:9, 19.

9. Jer 18:15–17; 19:8; 25:9, 18; 29:18; Ezek 5:15; 22:4; 23:32–34.

defeat and exile makes them a horror in the sight of the nations and thereby invalidates their witness to God's kingship. Rather than desiring to be like Israel and join in their blessed relationship with God, the nations come to despise them.

We saw above that in the wilderness Moses argued that the nations would misinterpret God's judgment upon Israel as reflecting his impotence to fulfill his promises. In a similar way, during the exile the nations draw false conclusions about God because of Israel's rejected status. In Ezekiel, God says of Israel:

> I scattered them among the nations, and they were dispersed through the countries. In accordance with their ways and their deeds I judged them. But when they came to the nations, wherever they came, they profaned my holy name, in that people said of them, "These are the people of the LORD, and yet they had to go out of his land." (Ezek 36:19–20)

In this passage the profanation of God's name follows from what the nations say *about God's people*. In antiquity the fate of nations on earth was viewed as corresponding to the fate of their gods in heaven. One nation's conquest over another was understood as reflecting the superior strength of that conquering nation's deity. In light of this background, Block summarizes the missional predicament that resulted from Israel's exilic judgment this way:

> Outsiders were left to conclude that either Yahweh had willingly abandoned his people, or that he was incapable of defending them against the superior might of Marduk, the god of Babylon. The first option challenges Yahweh's credibility and integrity; the second, his sovereignty. In either case, his reputation has been profaned among the nations.[10]

The nations look upon Israel's fate in exile, conclude that God is either unfaithful or impotent, and have no desire to serve or worship him. This is the reason God delayed bringing judgment upon his people in previous generations, that his name might not be profaned among the nations (Ezek 20:9, 14, 22). However, after centuries of unrepentant disobedience, God's holiness finally demands that his people be judged.

---

10. Block, *Ezekiel 25–48*, 348.

Summary

Throughout this section we have seen that Israel failed in their missional calling when entering the land, when living in the land, and when exiled from the land. Despite God's provision of the Torah to guide them in righteous living, the people of Israel and their kings consistently fail to obey God as King and therefore forfeit their mission among the nations. After humanity's exile from Eden in Genesis 3, this exile from Canaan is the next major low point in the Old Testament story. Once again God's people have failed in their mission and received God's judgment for their sin. However, just as God issued a word of hope at humanity's fall (Gen 3:15), so is the fall of Israel punctuated by prophetic declarations of future restoration. As we will see in the next section, in the midst of judgment God promises to restore his people in order that they might accomplish the mission he has given them.

RESTORED FOR THE SAKE OF MISSION

When we explore the prophetic outlook on Israel's restoration we see that relational reparation between God and his people is always for the purpose of missional mobilization. That is, God will redeem his people from their state of judgment in order that his kingship might be represented to the ends of the earth. We see this particularly in how God restores Israel (1) for the sake of his name, (2) in order to realize the Abrahamic formula, (3) in order that they might be a light for the nations, and (4) in order to fulfill the creation mandate.

Restored for the Sake of God's Name

Above we saw how Ezekiel presents the profanation of God's name as the result of Israel's exile from the land (Ezek 36:19–20). Immediately after this, God declares his resolve to preserve the honor of his name: "But I had concern for my holy name, which the house of Israel had profaned among the nations to which they came" (v. 21). This reveals that God's first priority as he considers Israel's exilic predicament is not Israel's welfare but his own reputation. Thomas Renz therefore does not overstate the case when he says, "V. 21, as a premise to the following oracles, states that Yahweh's honour is to be regarded as the beginning and end of Israel's restoration."[11]

---

11. Renz, *Rhetorical Function*, 111.

Indeed, in the oracle that follows, God states explicitly that Israel's welfare is not his driving concern in the redemption he is planning:

> Therefore say to the house of Israel, Thus says the Lord God: It is not for your sake, O house of Israel, that I am about to act, but for the sake of my holy name, which you have profaned among the nations to which you came. And I will vindicate the holiness of my great name, which has been profaned among the nations, and which you have profaned among them. And the nations will know that I am the Lord, declares the Lord God, when through you I vindicate my holiness before their eyes. I will take you from the nations and gather you from all the countries and bring you into your own land. I will sprinkle clean water on you, and you shall be clean from all your uncleannesses, and from all your idols I will cleanse you. And I will give you a new heart, and a new spirit I will put within you. And I will remove the heart of stone from your flesh and give you a heart of flesh. And I will put my Spirit within you, and cause you to walk in my statutes and be careful to obey my rules. You shall dwell in the land that I gave to your fathers, and you shall be my people, and I will be your God. And I will deliver you from all your uncleannesses. (Ezek 36:22–29a)

In this passage God says that his upcoming redemption will be (1) not for Israel's sake (v. 22a), but (2) for the sake of vindicating his name among the nations (vv. 22b–23a), so that (3) the nations will "know" that he is the Lord (v. 23b). This last phrase is commonly referred to as the "recognition formula" and pertains not simply to the nations *knowing about* Israel's God but *acknowledging* him for who he is: the supreme deity who sovereignly and faithfully maintains covenant loyalty to his people.[12] God's upcoming redemption, therefore, is simultaneously theocentric and missional.

In the verses that follow God describes precisely how he will bring this redemption about. He will restore Israel geographically (v. 24), forgive their idolatry (v. 25),[13] transplant living hearts of flesh in place of their hard hearts of stone (v. 26), and infuse his Spirit within them, enabling them to

---

12. See, e.g., Martens, "Ezekiel's Contribution," 77–79; Lapsley, *Can These Bones Live?*, 124.

13. Although the "cleansing" language used repeatedly in verse 25 is reminiscent of various rituals that established ceremonial cleanliness (e.g., Exod 29:4; Num 8:7; Lev 16:4), in the present context this cleansing seems to go beyond ceremonial externals and actually bridge the relational gap that existed between God and his people—that harmonious reality to which ceremonial purification pointed. In short, not only does God restore Israel from exile, he also restores their relationship with him by forgiving them of their idolatry. See the discussion of Block, *Ezekiel 25–48*, 354–55.

obey him (v. 27). As a result, Israel will dwell with God in faithful, covenant relationship (v. 28) with no further uncleanness to jeopardize their standing (v. 29a). Since Israel's covenant relationship with God is designed to serve as a missional magnet for the nations, this redemptive process serves simultaneously to restore God's people to him and reinstate their missional function among the nations. God will vindicate the holiness of his name by rescuing his people from exile, thereby showing that he has neither abandoned them nor been defeated, and he will then mobilize them for mission by softening their hearts and enabling them to obey him by the power of his Spirit.

Restored to Realize the Abrahamic Formula

In addition to describing Israel's restoration as a vindication of God's name, the prophets portray this restoration as resulting in the realization of the Abrahamic formula. Isaiah prophesies that upon Israel's release from exile,

> Their offspring shall be known among the nations,
>   and their descendants in the midst of the peoples;
> all who see them shall acknowledge them,
>   that they are an offspring the LORD has blessed. (Isa 61:9)

Just as God promised to bless Abram so that he would be a recognized recipient of blessing, so he will restore Israel from exile so the nations will recognize their blessed status.[14] In Jeremiah God describes the effects of this restoration in a similar fashion:

> I will restore the fortunes of Judah and the fortunes of Israel, and rebuild them as they were at first. I will cleanse them from all the guilt of their sin against me, and I will forgive all the guilt of their sin and rebellion against me. And this city shall be to me a name of joy, a praise and a glory before all the nations of the earth who shall hear of all the good that I do for them. They shall fear and tremble because of all the good and all the prosperity I provide for it. (Jer 33:7–9)

As was the case in Isaiah, here in Jeremiah the result of God restoring and blessing his people with "good" and "prosperity" (*šālôm*) is international recognition. In recognizing these blessings of God upon his people, the nations will fear God, which is precisely the process outlined in the Abrahamic formula.

---

14. See also Oswalt, *Isaiah 40–66*, 573–74.

In line with this, Jeremiah earlier specifies that such a witness among the nations will only come about when Israel repents of their sin and turns to God:

> If you return, O Israel, declares the LORD,
>   to me you should return.
> If you remove your detestable things from my presence,
>   and do not waver,
> and if you swear, "As the LORD lives,"
>   in truth, in justice, and in righteousness,
> *then nations shall consider themselves blessed in him,*
>   and in him shall they glory. (Jer 4:1–2, author's translation)[15]

In examining the role of the Torah in Israel's mission we saw that Torah faithfulness—and thus missional success—involved not perfect obedience but repentant obedience. Similarly, in this passage Jeremiah presents Israel's repentance from their unfaithfulness as the mechanism that will trigger the Abrahamic formula: "then the nations shall consider themselves blessed in him" (v. 2). This phrase alludes to the Abrahamic promise of Gen 12:3 with one major alteration: rather than receiving blessing through Abraham (Gen 12:3; 18:18) or his offspring (Gen 22:18; 26:4; 28:14), upon Israel's repentance the nations will consider themselves blessed "in *him*," that is, "the LORD" (v. 2). As J. A. Thompson says, the nations "will discern in the example of Israel that the source of true blessing lies in Yahweh and that he dispenses his blessings to those who are obedient to his covenant."[16] Applying Jeremiah's exhortation to Israel's subsequent exilic situation, it becomes clear that Israel's restoration for missional purposes must be accompanied by repentance on their part, which will then lead the nations to consider themselves blessed by God as they follow Israel's example.

This restorative process is portrayed similarly in Ezekiel. After God declares that he will transform Israel spiritually and repair covenant relationship with them (Ezek 36:22–29a), he goes on to say,

> And I will summon the grain and make it abundant and lay no famine upon you. I will make the fruit of the tree and the increase of the field abundant, that you may never again suffer the

---

15. I have departed from the ESV here and translated the italicized phrase with an estimative-declarative nuance. The verb "bless" occurs in the Hithpael stem (which the ESV translates reflexively ["shall bless themselves"]), whereas in Gen 12:3 it occurs in the Niphal (which the ESV translates passively ["shall be blessed"]). As noted in chapter 3, the Hithpael of this verb in this context most likely carries an estimative-declarative force, whereby the nations "regard/consider/estimate themselves as blessed," which coheres conceptually with the nations as passive recipients of blessing.

16. Thompson, *Jeremiah*, 213. See also Hwang, "*Missio Dei*," 490.

> disgrace of famine among the nations. Then you will remember your evil ways, and your deeds that were not good, and you will loathe yourselves for your iniquities and your abominations. It is not for your sake that I will act, declares the Lord God; let that be known to you. Be ashamed and confounded for your ways, O house of Israel. Thus says the Lord God: On the day that I cleanse you from all your iniquities, I will cause the cities to be inhabited, and the waste places shall be rebuilt. And the land that was desolate shall be tilled, instead of being the desolation that it was in the sight of all who passed by. And they will say, "This land that was desolate has become like the garden of Eden, and the waste and desolate and ruined cities are now fortified and inhabited." Then the nations that are left all around you shall know that I am the Lord; I have rebuilt the ruined places and replanted that which was desolate. I am the Lord; I have spoken, and I will do it. (Ezek 36:29b–36)

Although the specific language of Gen 12:1–3 does not occur here, the concept of the Abrahamic formula is clearly present. God will (1) restore blessing upon his people (vv. 29b–30, 33–34), which will (2) lead them to repent (v. 31), (3) lead the nations to recognize them as divinely blessed (v. 35), which will (4) lead the nations to acknowledge God for who he is (v. 36).

After Ezekiel's generation passes away and Israel spends their allotted time in exile, God shows himself faithful and restores his people to the land (2 Chr 36:22–23; Ezra 1:1–4). As Israel struggles to reestablish themselves in the postexilic period, God sends word through Zechariah and assures them that "as you have been a byword of cursing among the nations, O house of Judah and house of Israel, so will I save you, and you shall be a blessing" (Zech 8:13), that is, *a recognized recipient of blessing.*[17] In context God has just promised to bless Israel through abundant agriculture and precipitation (v. 12). This shows that God's missional purposes for Israel through the Abrahamic formula are still active in the postexilic period.

Restored to Be a Light for the Nations

One significant way that Isaiah expresses this realization of the Abrahamic formula is by describing Israel as "a light for the nations" (Isa 42:6; 49:6). This phrase occurs twice in Isaiah in the context of the so-called "servant songs."[18] This figure of the "servant" in Isaiah 40–55 is well known for hav-

---

17. See chapter 3 for an explanation of this interpretation.
18. Isa 42:1–4; 49:1–6; 50:4–9; 52:13—53:12.

ing a multifaceted identity.[19] Initially the servant is identified with Israel (Isa 41:8–9), who is given the task of bringing "justice" (*mišpāṭ*) to the nations (42:1, 3, 4). In contrast to the futility produced by idolatry that is critiqued in the previous section (41:21–29), in this opening servant song the term *mišpāṭ* refers to "that life-giving order which exists when the creation is functioning in accordance with the design of its Lord."[20] That is, as God's servant, Israel is called to mediate God's standards for just and righteous living to the nations (cf. Gen 18:18–19).

This idea is reinforced in Isa 42:4, where the "coastlands wait for his law (*tôrâ*)." In this context, the servant is then described as "a light for the nations" (v. 6), and as the next verse elaborates, this indicates that he is "to open the eyes that are blind, to bring out the prisoners from the dungeon, from the prison those who sit in darkness" (v. 7). That this describes the servant bringing light fundamentally to those in spiritual darkness is suggested by the following verse: "I am the LORD; that is my name; *my glory I give to no other, nor my praise to carved idols*" (v. 8).[21] Whereas the nations are languishing in the darkness and blindness of idolatry, Israel has been called as God's servant to enlighten them concerning the justice of God's reign.

Although this was Israel's calling, the oracle goes on to describe how the servant has shown himself to be just as blind as the nations whom he was called to enlighten:

> Who is blind but my servant,
>   or deaf as my messenger whom I send?
> Who is blind as my dedicated one,
>   or blind as the servant of the LORD? (42:19)

Despite God's gracious deliverance of Israel from Egypt and provision of the Torah to guide them, Israel's spiritual blindness has prohibited them from succeeding in their mission. Rather, as a result of their rebellion they have been conquered and plundered and therefore have not enlightened the nations concerning God's sovereign and just kingship. As Isaiah says,

> The LORD was pleased, for his righteousness' sake,
>   to magnify his law and make it glorious.

---

19. See the excellent and concise discussion of Lessing, "Isaiah's Servants," 130–34.

20. Oswalt, *Isaiah 40–66*, 110; see also Childs, *Isaiah*, 324–25; Okoye, *Israel and the Nations*, 137. It seems neither necessary nor appropriate to distinguish sharply between the spiritual and political components of *mišpāṭ* here, as Kaiser does, leading him to render it as "religion" (*Mission in the Old Testament*, 59–60). Rather, the political justice envisaged in this passage is inextricably intertwined with spiritual transformation (see especially 42:1).

21. See also Smith, *Isaiah 40–66*, 168–69.

> But this is a people plundered and looted;
>> they are all of them trapped in holes
>> and hidden in prisons;
> they have become plunder with none to rescue,
>> spoil with none to say, "Restore!" (42:21–22)

In further references to the "servant" God states that he will restore Israel from this conquered state (43:1–7), that they are still his "servant" (43:10), that he will pour out his blessing on their descendants (44:1–5), that he has blotted out their transgressions (44:21–22), that he has ordained Cyrus to liberate them (45:1–7), and that they are to flee Babylon (48:20).

After thus outlining God's restorative intentions, the second servant song (49:1–6) introduces an identity shift in the servant. In this passage the servant is once again identified as Israel ("You are my servant, Israel, in whom I will be glorified" [v. 3]), but then receives the task of *restoring Israel*. The servant says that God "formed me from the womb to be his servant, to bring Jacob back to him; and that Israel might be gathered to him" (v. 5). In one sense, therefore, the servant is still Israel, and yet in another sense he is distinct from corporate Israel and called to restore them. As Brevard Childs concludes, this servant of Isaiah 49 is therefore best understood as "a faithful embodiment of the nation Israel who has not performed its chosen role."[22] God then gives this "redemptive servant" the same task previously assigned to Israel in 42:6:

> It is too light a thing that you should be my servant
>> to raise up the tribes of Jacob
>> and to bring back the preserved of Israel;
> I will make you as a light for the nations,
>> that my salvation may reach to the end of the earth. (49:6)

This redemptive servant is responsible not only to restore Israel but also to take up Israel's task as "a light for the nations." Yet whereas chapter 42 described this international enlightenment in terms of God's just order, chapter 49 describes it in terms of God's salvation. Putting all this together, as God's salvation reaches across the earth, the nations will submit to God's just reign and thereby join Israel in submitting to his kingship. This connection between God's *salvation* extending to the nations and his *Torah-directed justice* extending among the nations is made explicit in Isa 51:4–5, where God says that "a law (*tôrâ*) will go out from me, and I will set my justice for a light to the peoples. My righteousness draws near, and my arms will judge the peoples; my salvation has gone out, the coastlands hope for

---

22. Childs, *Isaiah*, 385.

me, and for my arm they wait." Here in one breath God speaks of his Torah, justice, and salvation going out to the nations of the earth.

The final two servant songs fill out this picture by portraying this redemptive servant as performing his restorative service in the midst of suffering (50:6; 53:3, 7). Specifically, God's servant will suffer as he bears the sins and iniquities of the people (53:4–6, 12), and through his suffering the people will be considered righteous (53:11). This redemptive language of the fourth servant song casts a vision for Israel to expect a "suffering servant," one who will achieve forgiveness for the nation by way of personal affliction and thereby mobilize them to fulfill their missional role as a light for the nations.

Excursus: Centripetal or Centrifugal Mission for the Servant?

At this point we must pause and note that some scholars see a centrifugal mission for Israel presented here in the servant songs. According to Walter Kaiser, Isa 42:1–4 suggests that, as God's servant, corporate Israel "will engage in active mission work on behalf of all the nations."[23] Roger Hedlund considers Isa 49:6 to be "The Old Testament rendering of the Great Commission . . . wherein the servant is commissioned to go to the Gentiles with God's salvation."[24] Elmer Martens concludes similarly, arguing that Paul's use of Isa 49:6 in Acts 13:47 suggests this reading and that Isa 52:15 clarifies such a centrifugal interpretation.[25] Okoye concurs, stating that "The full meaning of 'light to the nations,' when interpreted in relation to Isaiah 60:1–3 . . . is that of missionary evangelization among the nations."[26] Since I have argued that the Abrahamic promise and Israel's missional organization were to be centripetal in nature, it is necessary to detour briefly and address these differing views.

First we must observe that, although Isa 42:1 states that the servant "will bring forth (*yôṣi'*) justice to the nations," contrary to Kaiser's conclusion, such a description does not necessitate centrifugal missionary activity. The Hiphil verb *yôṣi'* is causative, literally meaning "cause to go out." Although the Hiphil of this root may describe the activity of "bringing" or "carrying" an object (e.g., Gen 14:18), it may also connote "sending out" or "spreading" something. For example, when the scouts in Moses'

---

23. Kaiser, *Mission in the Old Testament*, 60. So also Blauw, *Missionary Nature of the Church*, 39.
24. Hedlund, *Mission of the Church in the World*, 114.
25. Martens, "Impulses to Mission in Isaiah," 227–29.
26. Okoye, *Israel and the Nations*, 139–40.

generation returned from spying out the land of Canaan, "they *caused to go out (wayyôṣi'û)* to the Israelites a bad report concerning the land they had spied out" (Num 13:32, author's translation). Although the scouts were certainly active in the dissemination of this report to "all the congregation" (14:1), they surely did not "bring" this report to each individual Israelite themselves. Rather, the picture here is of the bad report beginning with the scouts and then "spreading" throughout the Israelite camp (see, e.g., NIV). Similarly, it is most consistent with the preceding biblical material regarding Israel's mission to understand the servant not as "going out to the nations and bringing justice with him" but as "causing justice to go out to the nations" by his faithful obedience to God. As we have seen, this is precisely the way the Abrahamic blessing was to spread among the nations.

Concerning Isa 49:6, contrary to Hedlund, the servant is not "commissioned" to go out to the nations. Rather, he is simply "given" (*nātan*) as "a light for the nations, that [God's] salvation may reach to the end of the earth."[27] A light (i.e., a lamp) illumines a space by emitting light (i.e., luminous energy) from a single location; it is therefore unnecessary to read a centrifugal mission into this statement. Rather, Isa 49:6 may just as naturally be understood as portraying the servant as the lamp and God's salvation as the luminous energy that emits from the lamp.

Although Martens is correct that Paul cites this verse as support for his Gentile mission in Acts 13:47, that this verse is used to *support* centrifugal mission in the New Testament does not mean that it *describes* centrifugal mission in the Old Testament. The image of God's salvation going out to the

---

27. It is grammatically possible that "my salvation" is the object of the verb *lihyôṯ* in the latter half of verse 6, which would result in a translation like that of Peskett and Ramachandra: "I have set you for a light to nations [sic], to be *my salvation* to the ends of the earth" (*Message of Mission*, 143, emphasis mine). However, it is more probable that "my salvation" is the subject of the verb (so ESV, NASB, NRSV, NIV [2011]). Elsewhere in Isaiah, the preposition *lamed* marks the object of the infinitive construct *lihyôṯ* (Isa 56:6), whereas a noun immediately following *lihyôṯ* functions as the subject (Isa 10:2), the latter which is the case here in 49:6. Moreover, elsewhere in Isaiah the noun "salvation" (*yᵉšûʿâ*) is most often identified with God (Isa 12:2 [2x]; 33:2, 6) or directly associated with him (Isa 25:9; 26:1; 49:8; 51:6, 8; 52:10; 56:1; 59:17); it is never identified or associated with the servant. The same is true with the abbreviated noun *yēšaʿ* ("salvation"; Isa 17:10; 45:8; 51:5; 61:10; 62:11) and the various verbal forms of the root *yšaʿ* ("save"; Isa 25:9; 33:22; 35:4; 37:20, 35; 38:20; 43:12; 45:17, 22; 49:25; 59:1, 16; 63:1, 5, 9). These data reflect the significance of Isaiah's name itself, which means, "*Yahweh* is salvation" (*yᵉšaʿyāhû*). However, whether one opts for a subjective or objective understanding of "my salvation" here, the means by which this salvation will reach the ends of the earth remains unstated in this text. Although the 1984 NIV rendered this clause with a centrifugal interpretation ("that you may bring my salvation to the ends of the earth"), the 2011 NIV update wisely revised this ("that my salvation may reach to the ends of the earth").

ends of the earth fits with both centripetal and centrifugal missional frameworks. As we have seen, in the Old Testament God's salvation was to reach the ends of the earth as Israel obeyed God, received his bountiful blessing, and the nations responded positively to this publicized blessing. In the New Testament era, God's salvation is to reach the ends of the earth as the church proclaims the good news of Jesus' life, death, and resurrection among the nations. Since Isa 49:6 does not specify the means by which God's salvation will reach the ends of the earth, it may legitimately be used to support both of these missional frameworks. Consequently, Paul's application of this text to his New Testament mission should not be used to dictate how it functioned within the missional framework of the Old Testament.

Martens further argues that Isa 52:15 supports a centrifugal understanding of the servant's mission. In that text Isaiah says,

> so shall he [my servant] sprinkle many nations;
>   kings shall shut their mouths because of him;
> for that which has not been told them they see,
>   and that which they have not heard they understand.

Concerning this verse Martens writes, "The nations will be told. Someone will tell them of the redemptive work of the servant. Isaiah sees missionizing activity as part of the servant's work."[28] However, this text does not say that someone will "tell" the nations; it simply says, "that which has not been told them *they see*, and that which they have not heard *they understand*." Rather than explicitly depicting an outgoing proclamation to the nations, Isaiah only describes the nations *acquiring* sight and understanding. As was the case with Isa 49:6, the means by which this sight and understanding will spread among the nations is left unstated, leaving room for both centripetal and centrifugal applications. Therefore, that Paul uses this verse to support his centrifugal mission in Rom 15:21 does not support Martens' conclusion that "Isaiah's fourth servant passage is to be interpreted as warranting aggressive proclamation, even hinting at proselytizing."[29] Although this passage certainly *supports* Paul's centrifugal missionary work, like Isa 49:6 its ambiguity leaves room for a legitimate centripetal interpretation in the Old Testament period.

Lastly, Okoye's argument that Isa 60:1–3 supports a centrifugal reading of the phrase "light for the nations" does not seem to follow. In these verses Isaiah says to Israel,

---

28. Martens, "Impulses to Mission in Isaiah," 229.
29. Martens, "Impulses to Mission in Isaiah," 229.

> Arise, shine, for your light has come,
>   and the glory of the LORD has risen upon you.
> For behold, darkness shall cover the earth,
>   and thick darkness the peoples;
> but the LORD will arise upon you,
>   and his glory will be seen upon you.
> And nations shall come to your light,
>   and kings to the brightness of your rising.

Rather than depicting a centrifugal mission of Israel bringing light to the nations, these verses portray a centripetal pilgrimage of the nations to the light that has come upon Israel. Isaiah says that "his glory *will be seen* upon you" (v. 2) and that the "nations *shall come* to your light" (v. 3). Instead of intimating a "missionary evangelization among the nations," as Okoye suggests, these verses support our earlier conclusion that the servant/Israel, as a light for the nations, is to be like a lamp emitting luminous energy, which would enlighten the nations concerning God's just order and salvation. As Isa 60:1–3 says, when God blesses Israel with his light, the nations will notice, and the Abrahamic formula will ensue.

In sum, although the Isaianic servant songs do not *require* a centrifugal missional interpretation, they do legitimately *support* the centrifugal missionary activity of the New Testament church. Paul did not violate the integrity of these texts by using them to substantiate his mission work among the Gentiles, though his use of these texts for this purpose does not mean that Israel in the Old Testament period had a centrifugal mission. Rather, the ambiguity of these passages leaves room for both centripetal and centrifugal applications. Since Israel's missional calling up to this point has been centripetal in nature, it is best to understand the missional import of these servant songs in their Old Testament context to be centripetal as well.

Restored to Fulfill the Creation Mandate

The last relationship to consider is that between Israel's restoration and their fulfillment of the creation mandate. The mandate verbs "be fruitful" (*pārâ*) and "multiply" (*rabbâ*) occur together only three times in the prophetic literature, each time in the context of Israel's future restoration. In Jeremiah 3, God calls the exiled northern kingdom to repent and return to him (vv. 13–14a), declares that he will bring them back to Zion (v. 14b), and then issues a series of promises that will accompany this restoration:

> And I will give you shepherds according to my heart, who will
> feed you with knowledge and understanding. And when you

have *multiplied* (*rabbâ*) and *been fruitful* (*pārâ*) in the land in those days, declares the Lord, they shall no more say, "The ark of the covenant of the Lord." It shall not come to mind or be remembered or missed; it shall not be made again. At that time Jerusalem shall be called the throne of the Lord, and all nations shall gather to it, to the presence of the Lord in Jerusalem, and they shall no more stubbornly follow their own evil heart. (vv. 15–17, author's translation)

In this passage God states that he will give his people "shepherds"—that is, rulers—"according to my heart" (*kᵉlibbi*; v. 15a). This phrase recalls God's choosing of David as a man "according to his heart" (*kilḇāḇô*; 1 Sam 13:14), and as we saw last chapter, this idiom describes a ruler who will live according to God's will. However, in contrast to previous Davidic kings who failed to live this way, when God restores his people he will provide them with faithful Davidic leadership "who fill feed [them] with knowledge and understanding" (Jer 3:15b), which is precisely the type of kingship prescribed in Deut 17:14–20. Upon being restored, and in conjunction with this faithful leadership, God's people will then fulfill the creation mandate: "And when you have *multiplied* and *been fruitful* in the land in those days . . ." (v. 16a).

This future realization of the creation mandate will contribute to the fulfillment of humanity's original mission, which is hinted at by the subsequent imagery of verses 16b–17. Rather than the ark of the covenant being rebuilt as a representative symbol of God's presence, Jerusalem itself will become the throne of God, "and all nations shall gather to it, to the presence of the Lord in Jerusalem" (v. 17a). That these nations will submit to God's kingship is then indicated by verse 17b: "and they shall no more stubbornly follow their own evil heart." Therefore, the picture painted in Jer 3:15–17 is that upon Israel's restoration God will (1) provide them with faithful leadership, who will (2) enable them to fulfill the creation mandate, which will (3) correspond with the nations gathering and submitting to God's kingship. Although the relationship between (2) and (3) is not made explicit here, this passage clearly associates the creational proliferation of God's people with his kingship being recognized by the nations. It is *when* Israel is fruitful and multiplies that all nations will gather to the throne of God.[30] As nations from all over the world turn their allegiance to God, his kingship will be represented to the ends of the earth.

Similar imagery is present in Jeremiah 23. In chapters 21–22 Jeremiah brings a series of judgment oracles against the Davidic kings, condemning

---

30. Viands notes that the collocation *wᵉhāyâ ki* that begins verse 16 consistently introduces a temporal clause in Jeremiah (*I Will Surely Multiply Your Offspring*, 179).

them for failing to rule justly. These oracles climax with God rejecting Jehoiachin,[31] who is compared to a "signet ring" being removed from God's hand (Jer 22:24), thus signifying his removal from Israel's throne and exile to Babylon (vv. 25–26). As chapter 23 opens, God declares his intent to replace these unfaithful "shepherds" with faithful ones:

> "Woe to the shepherds who destroy and scatter the sheep of my pasture!" declares the LORD. Therefore thus says the LORD, the God of Israel, concerning the shepherds who care for my people: "You have scattered my flock and have driven them away, and you have not attended to them. Behold, I will attend to you for your evil deeds, declares the LORD. Then I will gather the remnant of my flock out of all the countries where I have driven them, and I will bring them back to their fold, and they shall *be fruitful (pārâ)* and *multiply (rabbâ)*. I will set shepherds over them who will care for them, and they shall fear no more, nor be dismayed, neither shall any be missing, declares the LORD. Behold, the days are coming, declares the LORD, when I will raise up for David a righteous Branch, and he shall reign as king and deal wisely, and shall execute justice and righteousness in the land. In his days Judah will be saved, and Israel will dwell securely. And this is the name by which he will be called: 'The LORD is our righteousness.'" (vv. 1–6)

In this section God holds the Davidic "shepherds" responsible for scattering his people into exile (vv. 1–2a) and says he will judge them accordingly (v. 2b). God then declares that he will restore his people, that "they shall be fruitful and multiply" (v. 3), and that he will "set shepherds over them who will care for them" (v. 4). As was the case in Jer 3:15–17, a direct correlation exists here between faithful shepherds leading Israel and the fulfillment of the creation mandate. Just as unfaithful kings led the nation to decimation and defeat, so faithful kings will lead them to proliferation and blessing. However, this passage introduces an additional element not present in chapter 3: God specifies that he will raise up a singular Davidic king—"a righteous Branch" (v. 5)—who will embody this faithful rule that Israel needs to fulfill their mission. Specifically, this righteous Branch, who will "execute justice and righteousness in the land," will be called, "The LORD is our righteousness" (v. 6). This suggests an exceptionally close relationship between this Davidic king and God himself; the latter's righteous divine reign will be

---

31. Referred to in this passage as "Coniah."

indistinguishable from and executed through the former's righteous human reign.[32]

The third and final use of creation mandate language in the prophetic literature appears in Ezek 36:8–15:

> But you, O mountains of Israel, shall shoot forth your branches and yield your fruit to my people Israel, for they will soon come home. For behold, I am for you, and I will turn to you, and you shall be tilled and sown. And I will *multiply* (*rabbâ*) people on you, the whole house of Israel, all of it. The cities shall be inhabited and the waste places rebuilt. And I will *multiply* (*rabbâ*) on you man and beast, and they shall *multiply* (*rabbâ*) and *be fruitful* (*pārâ*). And I will cause you to be inhabited as in your former times, and will do more good to you than ever before. Then you will know that I am the Lord. I will let people walk on you, even my people Israel. And they shall possess you, and you shall be their inheritance, and you shall no longer bereave them of children. Thus says the Lord God: Because they say to you, "You devour people, and you bereave your nation of children," therefore you shall no longer devour people and no longer bereave your nation of children, declares the Lord God. And I will not let you hear anymore the reproach of the nations, and you shall no longer bear the disgrace of the peoples and no longer cause your nation to stumble, declares the Lord God.

Here God addresses the "mountains of Israel"—a synecdoche for the land as a whole—and states that his people will soon be restored to them. God then foretells the people's proliferation in the land using the language of the creation mandate, declaring that he will "multiply" them and that "they shall multiply and be fruitful" (vv. 10–11). As a result of this multiplication, the mountains of Israel will acknowledge God for who he is and will no longer have to listen to the reproach of the nations (v. 15). That the personified mountains have heard the nations' disdainful comments due to Israel's exilic judgment reflects the fact that Israel has been a recognized recipient of cursing. However, upon Israel's restoration and subsequent fulfillment of the creation mandate they will cease to be viewed this way. Rather, by fulfilling the creation mandate, they will be recognized as recipients of blessing and thereby fulfill the Abrahamic formula.

---

32. See also Jer 33:14–16, where the contours and language of this oracle are reiterated.

RESTORED BY THE COMING OF THE "SON OF MAN"

According to the book of Daniel, the event that will accompany this restoration of God's people and its concomitant missional success is the coming of the "son of man." Daniel lived and served in the Babylonian royal court during the Babylonian exile. After the narratives of Daniel 1–6 highlight the faithfulness of Daniel and his friends amidst the harsh spiritual environment of the exile, Daniel 7–12 provides a series of apocalyptic visions designed to encourage perseverance among God's people as they wait for their full restoration. In the first of these visions, Daniel sees four great beasts rising out of the sea (7:1–8), which are interpreted as four earthly kings who will rise to power (v. 17). These kings, in turn, stand for four kingdoms, the last of which will acquire unprecedented power over the whole world (v. 23). In contrast to these worldly powers, verses 9–10 depict God as "the Ancient of Days," a glorious King sitting upon his throne, ruling over the multitudes, and executing judgment from his heavenly realm.[33] As part of this judgment, the fourth and most powerful beast is destroyed (v. 11) and the dominion of the remaining beasts is removed (v. 12).

Concurrent with this judgment, verses 13–14 describe the coming of "one like a son of man." The Aramaic phrase "son of man" (*bar ʾenāš*) corresponds to the Hebrew phrase *ben-ʾāḏām* (cf. Dan 8:17) and simply refers to a human being.[34] In Daniel's visionary experience, therefore, this figure has a human-like appearance, in contrast to the Ancient of Days with his supernatural and resplendent glory. As the worldly kingdoms are judged, this human-like figure ascends to the Ancient of Days and receives a worldwide kingdom that will never be destroyed:

> I saw in the night visions,
>   and behold, with the clouds of heaven
> there came one like a son of man,
>   and he came to the Ancient of Days
>   and was presented before him.
>
> And to him was given dominion
>   and glory and a kingdom,
>   that all peoples, nations, and languages
>   should serve him;
> his dominion is an everlasting dominion,

---

33. The title "Ancient of Days" is best understood as "an idiom for the eternality of God and in context contrasts the eternal God and his eternal kingdom with all temporary earthly kingdoms" (Hill, "Daniel," 137).

34. The Hebrew phrase is the standard way that God addresses Ezekiel in his prophecy (e.g., 2:1, 3, 6, 8; 3:1, 3, 4, 10, 17, 25; 4:1, 16; 5:1; 6:2; et al.).

>   which shall not pass away,
> and his kingdom one
>   that shall not be destroyed. (Dan 7:13–14)

This passage reveals that the ascension of this son of man accompanies the cessation of Israel's exile and the fulfillment of their mission. First, in verse 12 the beasts lose their "dominion" (šolṭān), while in verse 14 the son of man receives "dominion" (šolṭān). In light of Daniel's exilic context in which Israel lived under the dominion of foreign powers, this removal of dominion from earthly kingdoms and acquisition of such by the son of man suggests that the son of man's coming is the point at which Israel's exile will end.

Second, that the son of man receives a "kingdom" in which "all peoples, nations, and languages should serve him" (v. 14) indicates that his coming will also catalyze the fulfillment of Israel's mission. As we have seen, Israel's mission was to mediate knowledge of God's kingship to the nations, with the goal that all nations would submit to God as King. In this vision, the son of man receives a kingdom that encompasses all nations, thereby aligning his reign with the fulfillment of that mission.

Reinforcing this conclusion is the divine portrayal of the son of man in this passage. Although this figure is given an anthropological title, other indicators reveal that he is also depicted as divine. The son of man is described as coming "with the clouds of heaven" (v. 13), a description that elsewhere in the Old Testament is only used with reference to God (e.g., Ps 104:3; Isa 19:1). Moreover, the nations are said to "serve" (plḥ) the son man; elsewhere this Aramaic verb refers exclusively to worshipful allegiance to deity.[35] Additional indicators exist,[36] though these two observations alone demonstrate sufficiently that this figure is no ordinary human; rather, the son of man shares attributes with God himself. Since this divinely-portrayed man receives an everlasting dominion that includes the worshipful allegiance of every nation on earth, his ascension to the Ancient of Days marks not only the fulfillment of Israel's mission, but the fulfillment of the mission of God. With the coming of the son of man, God's kingship will be represented to the ends of the earth.[37]

---

35. Dan 3:12, 14, 17–18, 28; 6:16, 21

36. See Zehnder, "Why the Danielic 'Son of Man' Is a Divine Being," 331–47.

37. Beale sees Dan 7:13–14 as alluding to Gen 22:18, and through the latter passage's allusion to the creation mandate and its accompanying themes he interprets Dan 7:13–14 as portraying the son of man as an eschatological Adam figure (*New Testament Biblical Theology*, 36; 51n60; 83–84). If this interpretation is valid it would comport well with the thesis of the present study. However, although I view the son of man in Dan 7:13–14 as a significant element in the prophetic hope of Israel's restoration and

MISSIONAL FAILURE AND POSTEXILIC HOPE

The prophetic oracles surveyed above cast a hopeful vision for Israel's missional success upon their return from exile. However, although Israel's postexilic life begins well, soon they begin unrepentantly committing the same sins as their forefathers and thereby forfeit their witness among the nations. Nevertheless, God continues to communicate hope that one day he will provide a faithful shepherd who will lead his people in missional obedience.

Initial Success, Overall Failure

The book of Ezra begins by painting a positive picture of Israel's return from exile, stating that within the first year of Cyrus's edict they had "built the altar of the God of Israel, to offer burnt offerings on it, *as it is written in the Law of Moses* the man of God" (Ezra 3:2). They also

> kept the Feast of Booths, *as it is written*, and offered the daily burnt offerings by number *according to the rule*, as each day required, and after that the regular burnt offerings, the offerings at the new moon and at all the appointed feasts of the LORD, and the offerings of everyone who made a freewill offering to the LORD. (vv. 4–5)

This initial faithfulness is followed by the successful groundbreaking of the second temple, which begins in the second year of Israel's return (v. 8). As we have seen, both Torah and temple are significant elements for Israel's international witness, and therefore this depiction of Israel's early postexilic life is very positive.

Not long after this rebuilding project begins, however, regional opposition from the Samarians results in Israel ceasing temple construction for more than a decade (Ezra 4:1–5, 24). At the end of this period, through the prophet Haggai God condemns this failure to rebuild the temple as covenant disobedience. God rebukes Israel for enjoying security in their own houses while leaving his house a ruin (Hag 1:3–4) and points out that the hardships they are experiencing have come from him. Specifically, God highlights that the returnees' recent experience of futility (vv. 6, 9) is due to his ordaining a drought that has affected their sustenance, labor, and resources (vv. 10–11). As we saw above, the Torah describes such agricultural

---

corresponding missional success, I am not persuaded that there is a clear textual allusion to the creation mandate.

and economic futility as part of God's covenant curses for Israel's unrepentance.[38] Although Israel responds to Haggai's oracle by faithfully resuming temple construction (Hag 1:12–15) and completing the work in about four and half years (Ezra 6:14–15),[39] the postexilic narratives and prophecies that follow continue to characterize God's people as generally unfaithful and disobedient.

In order to facilitate faithfulness among the returnees, Ezra travels from Babylon to Jerusalem to teach the Torah (Ezra 7). The book of Nehemiah portrays Ezra's Torah ministry in an especially positive light, with Ezra reading the Torah to the people (ch. 8) and the people confessing their sins (ch. 9) and committing themselves to God's commands (ch. 10). As was the case before the exile, if the people respond faithfully to God's word, God will bless them in such a way that the Abrahamic formula ensues. As Malachi tells his postexilic audience,

> Bring the full tithe into the storehouse, that there may be food in my house. And thereby put me to the test, says the LORD of hosts, if I will not open the windows of heaven for you and pour down for you a blessing until there is no more need. I will rebuke the devourer for you, so that it will not destroy the fruits of your soil, and your vine in the field shall not fail to bear, says the LORD of hosts. *Then all nations will call you blessed, for you will be a land of delight*, says the LORD of hosts. (Mal 3:10–12)

This makes clear that God's postexilic mission for Israel is the same as their preexilic calling: faithful obedience that leads to internationally recognized blessing.

However, despite Ezra's Torah instruction and the people's commitment to follow, as time passes the postexilic community shows itself to be generally unfaithful. They repeatedly engage in foreign marriages (Ezra 9; Neh 13:13–31; Mal 2:10–12) and wrongly divorce their Israelite wives (Mal 2:13–16).[40] The priests are unfaithful in their sacrificial responsibilities (Mal 1:6–14) and in teaching the Torah (Mal 2:1–9), and the people are unfaithful by exacting interest from one another (Neh 5:1–19), not giving

---

38. E.g., Lev 26:20, 26; Deut 28:17–18, 30, 38–40. So also Verhoef, *Haggai and Malachi*, 63.

39. According to Hag 1:15, Israel resumes temple construction on "the twenty-fourth day of the month, in the sixth month, in the second year of Darius the king" (Sept 21, 520 B.C.), and according to Ezra 6:14–15 they finish the temple on "the third day of the month of Adar, in the sixth year of the reign of Darius the king" (Mar 12, 515 B.C.).

40. For a persuasive argument that these verses are condemning Israelite men for divorcing *Israelite* wives, see Zehnder, "Fresh Look at Malachi II 13–16," 229–36.

God their tithes (Neh 13:10; Mal 3:6–9), and profaning the Sabbath (Neh 13:15–22). Nehemiah observes that such Torah unfaithfulness will result in the opposite of the Abrahamic formula, chastising the returnees by saying, "The thing that you are doing is not good. Ought you not to walk in the fear of our God *to prevent the taunts of the nations our enemies*?" (Neh 5:9). Furthermore, in the last historical account of the Old Testament, Nehemiah emphasizes that the postexilic community's sins are essentially the same as those of their forefathers that brought about the exile:

> Did not your fathers act in this way, and did not our God bring all this disaster on us and on this city? Now you are bringing more wrath on Israel by profaning the Sabbath. (Neh 13:18)

> Did not Solomon king of Israel sin on account of such women? Among the many nations there was no king like him, and he was beloved by his God, and God made him king over all Israel. Nevertheless, foreign women made even him to sin. Shall we then listen to you and do all this great evil and act treacherously against our God by marrying foreign women? (Neh 13:26–27)

These narrative and prophetic texts depict a dire situation for restored Israel. Despite being delivered by God from their foreign oppressors again, Israel continues to fail in their calling to represent God's kingship through faithful international witness.

Future Hope for Missional Success

Although Israel is unable to fulfill their mission after the exile, the postexilic writers reiterate earlier prophetic hope in God's promise of faithful leadership for his people. Early in the postexilic period God reaffirms his commitment to the Davidic dynasty by referring to Zerubbabel, David's descendant, as a "signet ring" that he has chosen (Hag 2:23). As noted above, earlier God described Jehoiachin as a signet ring removed and cast away, symbolizing his rejected status. By choosing Zerubbabel with this same imagery God is reversing this previous rejection and reaffirming the leadership of the Davidic line. This election of Zerubbabel is then further highlighted in Zech 4:1–10, where God declares that his spirit will enable Zerubbabel to lead the people in completing the temple reconstruction. Nevertheless, despite being chosen and enabled by God to lead in this endeavor, neither Zerubbabel nor his postexilic descendants accede to the Davidic throne. God's people continue to be subject to foreign domination and do not experience the full realization of prior restoration prophecies. This reflects the fact that, although they have returned to the land geographically, functionally they remain in exile.[41]

This lack of a restored Davidic monarchy with its attendant missional success is balanced during this period by accompanying prophecies of a future messianic figure who will faithfully lead God's people. Recalling Jeremiah's prophecy of a future righteous ruler (Jer 23:5), Zechariah reiterates the coming of "the Branch" (Zech 3:8) who "shall bear royal honor, and shall sit and rule on his throne" (Zech 6:13). As Wolter Rose summarizes, "what we have here is a second stage in which the fulfilment of the *ṣemaḥ* ['Branch'] oracle of Jer. 23.5 is pushed even further into the future."[42] Coordinate with this, Zechariah also speaks of a figure who will be "pierced" in the context of Israel's salvation (12:10; cf. vv.7–9) and a "shepherd" who will be stricken, resulting in a refined covenant relationship between the LORD and his people (13:7–9). Collectively these images build upon Isaiah's fourth servant song and perpetuate the expectation of a future ruler who will suffer on behalf of the people and thereby reconcile them with God.[43] As has been apparent from the preceding analysis, it is this restored *relationship with God*—and not simply restoration to the land—that is prerequisite for Israel's missional success among the nations.

Upon this reconciliation with God, Israel could expect to receive the blessings that previous prophets stated would attend their restoration but had not yet come to pass. Specifically, Moses described a heart circumcision (Deut 30:6) and Ezekiel a heart transplant/Spirit infusion (Ezek 36:26–27) that would follow Israel's restoration, both of which would enable Israel to live according to God's commands. Since Israel's obedience to God is necessary for their missional success, it follows that in achieving forgiveness for God's people, this future, suffering, Davidic king would simultaneously enable them to fulfill their mission as God's priestly kingdom. In other words, this prophesied Messiah, who would be pierced and stricken for God's people, would thereby equip them to represent God's kingship to the ends of the earth.

This missional concern at the close of the Old Testament is further reflected in the postexilic preoccupation with God's kingship being universally acknowledged among the nations. Zechariah declares that "the LORD will be king over all the earth" (Zech 14:9), and in a startling description of universal submission states that "everyone who survives of all the nations

---

41. For discussion of the question of exile persisting beyond the Persian resettlement, see McComiskey, "Exile and Restoration from Exile," 673–96.

42. Rose, *Zemah and Zerubbabel*, 135.

43. See also the comments of Klein, *Zechariah*, 387–88.

that have come against Jerusalem shall go up year after year to worship the King, the Lord of hosts, and to keep the Feast of Booths" (v. 16). Similarly, Malachi proclaims God's international reign by exclaiming, "Great is the Lord beyond the border of Israel!" (Mal 1:5). Subsequently God himself twice reiterates this future, universal recognition of his kingship:

> For from the rising of the sun to its setting my name will be great among the nations, and in every place incense will be offered to my name, and a pure offering. For my name will be great among the nations, says the Lord of hosts. (Mal 1:11)

> For I am a great King, says the Lord of hosts, and my name will be feared among the nations. (Mal 1:14)

These statements reflect God's creational intent that his kingship be represented to the ends of the earth. Therefore, although the Old Testament ends with Israel restored to the land while suffering from missional ineptitude, it provides future hope that God's people will one day be reconciled to him so they may succeed in their mission. This sets the stage for us to approach the New Testament with an expectation that God will send this suffering servant to acquire forgiveness for his people, and that such forgiveness will be the catalyst that moves God's people from missional failure to missional success.

SUMMARY

In this chapter we have explored Israel's failure to fulfill their mission of representing God's kingship to the ends of the earth. The Torah describes the missional failure that will ensue if Israel disobeys God's word, and the historical books preserve the account of Israel failing in their mission precisely because of such unrepentant disobedience. However, despite Israel's rebellion, God extends mercy by restoring them from exile in order to fulfill his mission through them. Although Israel in the postexilic period demonstrates the same sinful tendencies as their preexilic ancestors, God promises that in the future he will provide a righteous Davidic ruler who will suffer to bring forgiveness for the people and thereby enable their missional success.

6 MISSION INTEGRATED
Tying the Old Testament Threads Together

Having surveyed the landscape of mission in the Old Testament, in this chapter I will attempt to tie up the loose ends by discussing a few remaining elements within the Old Testament's missional witness. First, in light of the conclusion that Israel's mission was centripetal rather than centrifugal, in this chapter we will explore how the books of Jonah and Psalms fit within this interpretive framework. Since many view Jonah as the prime example of Old Testament centrifugal mission, and the Psalter has been characterized as having "themes of cross-cultural outreach,"[1] a careful reading of each of these books is necessary to substantiate this study's conclusion regarding the centripetal nature of Israel's mission. Second, since the preceding discussion has traced the theme of mission primarily through Old Testament redemptive history, this chapter will address how the oft-neglected corpus of the Wisdom literature relates to the mission of God's people. Finally, having argued for the centripetal character of Israel's mission, this chapter will close by considering the Old Testament's eschatological vision for centrifugal mission that will be realized in the New Testament.

CENTRIPETAL MISSION, JONAH, AND THE PSALTER

As the foregoing analysis has sought to demonstrate, at creation God gives Adam a mission to multiply the divine image, fill the earth, and thereby represent God's kingship to the ends of the earth. After the fall and the dispersion at Babel, God resumes this mission by calling Abram and Israel, entering into a covenant relationship with them, and commissioning them to represent his kingship to the ends of the earth through faithful obedience in

---

1. Marlowe, "Music of Missions," 445–56.

the sight of the nations. The missions of Adam and Israel therefore contain elements reflecting both continuity and discontinuity. They are continuous in that they both have the same objective: to represent God's kingship to the ends of the earth. They are discontinuous in their methods of achieving this objective. Adam receives a centrifugal mission to spread out to the ends of the earth, while Israel receives a centripetal mission to draw the attention of the nations that are scattered across the face of the earth. Israel's mission is therefore a redemptive-historical development of Adam's mission that is significantly different in design. For this reason, we must disagree with those who view Israel's mission as centrifugal in nature. For example, Walter Kaiser states, "Centrifugal witnessing . . . is the role assigned to Israel as it was to share actively with others the Man of Promise who was to come."[2] Similarly, David Filbeck argues that "the overall purpose of the Old Testament is to take God's message of salvation to the ends of the earth."[3] Such conclusions go beyond the evidence and ascribe to Israel a missionary responsibility that is not mandated until the New Testament. However, having argued this point, we must also note that it does not follow, as Kaiser maintains, that such a centripetal understanding of Israel's calling gives them "only a passive role" in God's missional economy.[4] On the contrary, Israel's call to Torah faithfulness is presented as an active responsibility that is intended to witness to God's supreme kingship among the nations. To support this conclusion further we now turn our attention to the books of Jonah and Psalms to see how they cohere within this understanding of Israel's centripetal mission.

MISSION AND JONAH

Some interpreters have argued that Jonah's call to preach against the Ninevites provides definitive evidence that Israel was to engage in centrifugal mission among the nations. For example, Hedlund states, "The Book of Jonah is truly a missionary tract establishing the divine prerogative of centrifugal mission, that is, going out to the nations, in the Old Testament period."[5] In a similar manner, Kaiser sees the last two verses of the book as clarifying the

---

2. Kaiser, *Mission in the Old Testament*, xiii–xiv. By "Man of Promise" Kaiser is referring to the redemptive figure first mentioned in the *protoevangelium* of Gen 3:15.

3. Filbeck, *Yes, God of the Gentiles, Too*, 37. Others who see centrifugal missionary activity for Israel include Okoye, *Israel and the Nations*, 139–43 and Hedlund, *Mission of the Church in the World*, 114–17.

4. Kaiser, *Mission in the Old Testament*, xiii.

5. Hedlund, *Mission of the Church in the World*, 126.

purpose of the whole and concludes, "All expostulations against Jonah being a missionary book are vain in light of the force of the questions that come at the end of the book."[6] Although such a view of Jonah's call seems plausible at first, several observations argue against this conclusion and show that the book of Jonah coheres with our understanding of the centripetal mission of Israel.

Centrifugal Mission as Jonah's Calling, Not Israel's

When considering the relationship between the book of Jonah and Israel's mission, we must first acknowledge that God's commissioning of Jonah to communicate his word to a foreign nation clearly locates Jonah's call within the sphere of centrifugal mission. Moreover, although Jonah is called to preach only judgment against Nineveh ("Yet forty days, and Nineveh shall be overthrown!" [Jonah 3:4 cf. 1:2; 3:2]), implied in such judgment oracles are provisions for divine forgiveness if the hearers repent (see Jer 18:7–8).[7] Therefore it is entirely appropriate to summarize Jonah's prophetic calling as a centrifugal mission to preach God's word to a foreign nation.

However, the fact that *Jonah the prophet* is given this mission does not indicate that *Israel the nation* is also assigned this task. Several Old Testament prophets are called to engage in a variety of activities that are clearly not to be repeated by God's people as a whole. Hosea is called to take "a wife of whoredom and have children of whoredom" (Hos 1:2); Isaiah is called to walk around naked and barefoot for three years (Isa 20:1–4); and Ezekiel is called to prepare food using excrement as fuel (Ezek 4:12–15). In none of these cases do we assume that simply because the prophet is called to engage in such activity, the nation as a whole is likewise called to do so.[8] Consequently, Kaiser's conclusion concerning the universality of God's call on Jonah seems unwarranted:

> Was Jonah's mission unique, then? Hardly. How could God have sent this one prophet abroad and never have thought it worthwhile to send any other prophets? How could the dominant note of Genesis 12:3 be smothered by nationalistic concerns to the

---

6. Kaiser, *Mission in the Old Testament*, 70.

7. For excellent analyses of this prophetic phenomenon see Pratt, "Historical Contingencies and Biblical Predictions," 180–203; Chisholm, "When Prophecy Appears to Fail," 561–77.

8. See also Timmer, "Jonah and Mission," 170.

detriment of the world at large? Had not God sent individuals in the past to do this very same thing?[9]

In the quotation above, Kaiser speculates about the existence of other Jonah-like prophets, something the biblical text does not record. Moreover, as we have already explored in detail, the missional framework of Gen 12:1–3 is centripetal in method and international in scope and therefore does not require centrifugal mission on Israel's part. Rather than relying on such speculative argumentation or simply assuming that Jonah's mission applies to Israel as a whole, our understanding of the missional import of Jonah's call must come by examining the message of the book as a whole.

The Message of the Book of Jonah

As with all prophetic books, the book of Jonah has a didactic function. It was written not simply to record the events and oracles contained within it but to communicate a particular message to its readership, the people of Israel. But what is the message of the book of Jonah? Those who claim that Jonah is a missionary tract view the book as exhorting Israel to engage in centrifugal cross-cultural mission. But as we have seen, a leap from prophetic calling to national calling without additional data to support such a move is not sustainable when applied to other prophetic texts. Moreover, our analysis of Old Testament mission thus far has not yielded any centrifugal requirements for Israel, which would make such a didactic function of the book improbable, since it would be criticizing Israel for failing to do something they had never been instructed to do.

Clarity comes, however, by attending carefully to the end of the book. Although Kaiser is correct that the final verses of Jonah shed light on the message of the whole, his conclusion that "this is a missionary appeal" puts the didactic focus in the wrong place.[10] After Jonah reluctantly preaches judgment against Nineveh (3:4), the Ninevites repent (3:5–9) and God mercifully relents of his declared judgment (3:10). Chapter 4 then records Jonah's unsavory response to this divine mercy and God's patient dealings with the ornery prophet. It is this entire chapter, and not simply the last two verses, that clarifies the didactic force of the book. This chapter is important for discerning the book's message because at this point Jonah's mission is complete. He has successfully, if reluctantly, communicated God's word to the Ninevites, the Ninevites have responded positively, and God has shown

---

9. Kaiser, *Mission in the Old Testament*, 74.
10. Kaiser, *Mission in the Old Testament*, 70.

mercy. With this central plot action behind us, chapter 4 explicates the theological significance of this event by contrasting God's and Jonah's responses to it. Specifically, chapter 4 shows us that the book of Jonah is fundamentally about *God's gracious and compassionate character*. This message is communicated by (1) an allusion to God's self-revelation of his character in Exod 34:6–7 (Jonah 4:1–4), and (2) the object lesson of the plant (Jonah 4:5–11).

Allusion to Exodus 34:6–7

Chapter 4 begins by noting that God's mercy to the Ninevites "displeased Jonah exceedingly" (lit. "it eviled a great evil to Jonah"; v. 1) and that Jonah prayed to God, complaining that he knew all along that God's merciful character would result in such forgiveness: "O LORD, is not this what I said when I was yet in my country? That is why I made haste to flee to Tarshish; for I knew that you are a gracious God and merciful, slow to anger and abounding in steadfast love, and relenting from disaster" (v. 2). Ironically, this complaint establishes the overall theme of this chapter and elucidates the didactic function of the book.

Jonah's complaint alludes to God's self-revelation of his merciful character to Moses on Mount Sinai after Israel's debacle with the golden calf (Exod 34:6–7). In that account, after Israel commits idolatry with the golden calf, God declares his intent to wipe them out and begin a new people with Moses (Exod 32:9–10). Moses responds by interceding for Israel, saying to God,

> Turn from your burning anger and relent from this disaster against your people. Remember Abraham, Isaac, and Israel, your servants, to whom you swore by your own self, and said to them, "I will multiply your offspring as the stars of heaven, and all this land that I have promised I will give to your offspring, and they shall inherit it forever." (Exod 32:12b–13)

In a remarkable demonstration of mercy, God responds positively to this petition and "relented of the disaster that he had said he would do to his people" (v. 14, author's translation). In the wake of this mercy God then communicates his name to Moses, saying,

> The LORD, the LORD, a God merciful and gracious, slow to anger, and abounding in steadfast love and faithfulness, keeping steadfast love for thousands, forgiving iniquity and transgression and sin, but who will by no means clear the guilty, visiting

the iniquity of the fathers on the children and the children's children, to the third and the fourth generation. (Exod 34:6–7)

Jonah's allusion to this passage recounts God's self-revelation of his gracious and compassionate character in a situation in which Israel deserved judgment but did not receive it.

This background sheds great light on the situation portrayed in the book of Jonah. After the king of Nineveh hears Jonah's message of judgment, he immediately puts on sackcloth, sits in ashes, and commands his entire kingdom to mourn, fast, and repent, saying, "Who knows? God may turn and relent and turn from his burning anger, so that we may not perish" (Jonah 3:9, author's translation). This statement alludes to Moses' intercession after the golden calf incident noted above, where he asks God to forgive Israel for their idolatry:[11]

Moses (Exod 32:12b)	King of Nineveh (Jonah 3:9)
Turn (šûḇ)	God may turn (yāšûḇ)
from your burning anger (meḥᵃrôn ʾappekā)	and relent (wᵉniḥam)
and relent (wᵉhinnāḥem)	and turn (wᵉšāḇ)
from this disaster against your people.	from his burning anger (meḥᵃrôn ʾappô),
	so that we may not perish.

By this allusion the author of Jonah is portraying the king of Nineveh as responding to God's impending judgment the same way that Moses did. Following this, in both contexts the narrator describes God relenting in virtually identical language:

Exod 32:14	Jonah 3:10
	When God saw what they did, how they turned from their evil way,
And the LORD relented (wayyinnāḥem yhwh)	God relented (wayyinnāḥem hāʾᵉlōhîm)
of the disaster (ʿal-hārāʿâ)	of the disaster (ʿal-hārāʿâ)
that he had said he would do (ʾᵃšer dibber laʿᵃśôṯ)	that he had said he would do (ʾᵃšer-dibber laʿᵃśôṯ)

---

11. These are the only two passages in the Old Testament that use the collocation "turn from his/your burning anger" (šûḇ meḥᵃrôn ʾappô/ʾappekā) and "relent" (niḥam) together. See also Dozeman, "Inner-Biblical Interpretation," 23.

| to his people (*lᵉʿammô*).¹² | to them (*lahem*), |
| | and he did not do it. |

As this comparison shows, God responds to Nineveh the same way he responds to Israel: by relenting of the disaster he intended to bring. A substantial difference between these accounts, however, is that while God relents from judging Nineveh based on citywide repentance (3:5), Israel's forgiveness is not engendered by any repentance on their part; God simply forgives them because of his gracious, covenant love that he promised to the patriarchs (Exod 32:13).

All of this reveals that Jonah's allusion to God's self-revelation in Exod 34:6–7 is the climax of a larger comparison between Israel and Nineveh in relation to God's forgiveness. The message conveyed through this comparison is clear: God is gracious and compassionate, so much so that he occasionally shows mercy to Israel without requiring repentance—how much more is he prone to show mercy to those who repent!

This theme of God extending mercy both to unrepentant Israelites and penitent foreigners also appears at the beginning of Jonah, evidenced most clearly by the contrasting responses to God by Jonah and the foreign sailors. Chapter 1 introduces Jonah as wholly disobedient to God's word; rather than obeying God and going to Nineveh, he flees in the opposite direction on a ship toward Tarshish (Jonah 1:1–3). After God brings a storm upon the sea, the foreign sailors are portrayed as fully responsive to the news that Jonah's God has ordained it. Three times the text says that the sailors "feared," the progression of which shows that their encounter with God and his power over the sea eventually leads them to put their faith in him:¹³

Table 5. The Foreign Sailors' Escalating Fear in Jonah

Verse	English Translation	Hebrew Transliteration
1:5a	The sailors feared.	*wayyîrᵉʾû hammallāḥîm*
1:10a	The men feared a great fear.	*wayyîrᵉʾû hāʾnāšîm yîrʾâ gedôlâ*
1:16a	The men feared a great fear, the LORD.	*wayyîrᵉʾû hāʾnāšîm yîrʾâ gedôlâ ʾet-yhwh*

12. I have modified the ESV here only to reflect their rendering of the same language as it appears in Jonah 3:10 in order to highlight the parallel between these verses.

13. For this table and much of the discussion that follows, I am indebted to the helpful analysis of Bosma, "Jonah 1:9," 79–89.

In 1:5a, the sailors' "fear" is a general fear of physical harm, since the narrator has just stated that "the ship threatened to break up" (v. 4b). However, it is also clear that the sailors understand this situation to arise from a deity, since in response to their fear "each cried out to his god" (v. 5a). This spiritual sensitivity by the sailors is then contrasted with Jonah's spiritual dullness. In a disjunctive clause the narrator notes that while the sailors are petitioning their deities for help, Jonah is napping in the hull of the ship (v. 5b).

When the sailors cast lots and discover that Jonah is the cause of their predicament, Jonah gives an orthodox confession of faith, using the keyword "fear": "I am a Hebrew, and I *fear* the LORD, the God of heaven, who made the sea and the dry land" (v. 9). The irony in this statement is that Jonah has done everything but "fear the LORD" on both the sea and the dry land. Rather than demonstrating a fear of God by obeying his word, Jonah has disobeyed and attempted to evade God's call. Nevertheless, after Jonah's confession, "The men feared a great fear" (v. 10a). This escalation in the sailors' fear is due to their newfound identification of the specific deity responsible for their plight, evidenced by their question to Jonah and the narratorial comment that follows: "'What is this that you have done!' For the men knew that he was fleeing from the presence of the LORD, because he had told them" (v. 10b). This comment shows that, although the sailors' escalated fear may still be situational in nature, at this point they clearly believe that Jonah's God controls the sea.

After the sailors reluctantly hurl Jonah into the sea and the storm subsides, the narrator provides the third and final description of their fear: "Then the men feared a great fear, the LORD, and they offered a sacrifice to the LORD and made vows" (v. 16a). In this statement, "the LORD" is the direct object of the sailors' fear, and their corresponding acts of offering sacrifices and making vows indicate that this is a worshipful "fear of the LORD." In short, this use of the keyword "fear" throughout this narrative shows that these foreign sailors have gone from being spiritually ignorant to full-fledged Yahwistic converts.[14] This faithful response to God by the sailors contrasts sharply with Jonah's disobedience, which has resulted in his being cast into the sea. Nevertheless, God extends mercy even to unrepentant Jonah by appointing the great fish to swallow him (1:17) and thereby save him (cf. 2:9). This juxtaposition of Jonah and the sailors introduces this theme that is repeated later by Jonah's ironic allusion to Exodus 34: God is gracious and compassionate, at times willing to show mercy to his

---

14. So also Limburg, *Jonah*, 57–58; Strawn, "Jonah's Sailors and Their Lot Casting," 72; Bosma, "Jonah 1:9," 88–89.

unrepentant people and thus not surprisingly willing to show mercy to foreigners who respond positively and penitently to his word.[15]

The Object Lesson of the Plant

The second major section of Jonah 4 that contributes to our understanding of the book's message is the object lesson of the plant. After complaining about God's merciful character, Jonah constructs a booth for himself, sits in its shade, and waits to see what will happen to Nineveh. God appoints a plant to provide further shade for Jonah, which makes Jonah "exceedingly glad" (lit. "Jonah rejoiced a great rejoicing"; v. 6), but God subsequently appoints a worm to destroy the plant (v. 7). As the sun rises the next day, it beats hard on Jonah's head to the point that he becomes angry and longs for death (v. 8). The narrative ends with God questioning the validity of Jonah's anger and arguing that his divine pity for Nineveh is more reasonable than Jonah's pity for the plant (vv. 9–11).

In order to understand the significance of this object lesson we must correctly identify how its elements correspond to the events surrounding Nineveh. The most central element in the lesson, of course, is the plant itself. Many conclude that this plant corresponds to Nineveh, since God closes the book by comparing Jonah's "pity" for the plant with his own "pity" for Nineveh (4:10–11). However, as John Walton observes, Jonah does not truly care about the plant; he only cares about *the effects* of the plant (i.e., its comfortable shade).[16] Consequently, Walton persuasively argues that rather than representing Nineveh, the plant represents *God's mercy* to Nineveh.[17] The primary textual datum supporting this interpretation is the parallel use of

---

15. Even Jonah's ministry as recorded in 2 Kgs 14:23–27 reinforces this message. This passage notes that Jeroboam II "did what was evil in the sight of the Lord. He did not depart from all the sins of Jeroboam the son of Nebat, which he made Israel to sin" (v. 24). The text then notes that Jeroboam "restored the border of Israel from Lebo-hamath as far as the Sea of the Arabah, according to the word of the Lord, the God of Israel, which he spoke by his servant Jonah the son of Amittai" (v. 25). In this passage Jonah is responsible for prophesying the restoration of Israel's borders under the reign of wicked Jeroboam, a prophecy that sees fulfillment despite the fact that neither Jeroboam nor the nation as a whole is described as repenting from their sin. The reason why this prophecy is fulfilled is then stated in verse 26: "For the Lord saw that the affliction of Israel was very bitter, for there was none left, bond or free, and there was none to help Israel." In short, God mercifully restores Israel's borders despite their wickedness and unrepentance.

16. Walton, "Object Lesson," 49.

17. Walton, "Object Lesson," 50. Walton describes the plant as representing "God's unmerited grace."

rāʿâ ("disaster") in the Nineveh account and the object lesson. Just as God's mercy kept the "disaster" (*rāʿâ*) of his judgment from coming upon Nineveh (3:10), so does the plant "deliver" (*lᵉhaṣṣil*) Jonah from the "disaster" (*rāʿâ*) of the sun (4:6).[18] By this parallel use of *rāʿâ*, along with the salvific verb *lᵉhaṣṣil* to describe the effects of the plant, the narrator reveals that rather than standing for Nineveh, the plant represents God's mercy to Nineveh.

Once this identification is established it becomes clear that Jonah represents Nineveh in the object lesson. As noted above, the plant removes *rāʿâ* from Jonah the same way that God's mercy removes *rāʿâ* from Nineveh. Furthermore, the use of divine names throughout the book reinforces this identification of Jonah with Nineveh. Up until this point, the narrator has consistently used the generic divine title *ʾelōhim* to refer to God whenever he interacts with foreigners, while the covenant name *yhwh* appears in contexts involving Jonah.[19] However, when God provides the plant in 4:6, the compound name *yhwh ʾelōhim* occurs, after which only *ʾelōhim* is used to describe God's interactions with Jonah. As Walton concludes, this shift in the use of divine names at this juncture suggests that Jonah is now being treated like a foreigner—specifically, like the people of Nineveh—and is experiencing in microcosm that which he wished God would do to them.[20] That is, by removing the plant God is allowing *rāʿâ* to fall on Jonah, which is precisely what Jonah wished God would do to Nineveh.

In another irony, Jonah's response to the plant—both when it is provided and when it is removed—directly contradicts his frustration with God's mercy to Nineveh. The narrator uses parallel grammatical constructions to describe Jonah's response to God's mercy to Nineveh and his response to God's provision of the plant:[21]

Jonah's response to God's mercy (4:1)	Jonah's response to the plant (4:6)
"It eviled a great evil to Jonah."	"Jonah rejoiced . . . a great rejoicing."
(*wayyeraʿ ʾel-yônâ rāʿâ gᵉdôlâ*)	(*wayyismaḥ yônâ . . . simḥâ gᵉdôlâ*)

When God removes *rāʿâ* from Nineveh, Jonah views it as "evil," but when God removes *rāʿâ* from Jonah, he "rejoices." Furthermore, when God removes the plant and Jonah experiences the *rāʿâ* of the sun, his response is

---

18. Most translations render *rāʿâ* in 4:6 as "discomfort" (e.g., NIV, NASB, NRSV, ESV), though I translate it here as "disaster" to highlight the parallel with 3:10.

19. Kidner, "Distribution of Divine Names in Jonah," 126.

20. Walton, "Object Lesson," 48–49.

21. Each employs a verb with a cognate accusative modified by the adjective *gādol* ("great").

identical to his reaction when God relents from bringing *rā'â* upon Nineveh: "It is better for me to die than to live" (v. 8; cf. v. 3).

These contrasts show that Jonah's understanding of God's mercy is inconsistent and insufficient. As long as God extends mercy to him, Jonah finds it acceptable, despite the fact that he has demonstrated a consistently hard heart throughout the narrative.[22] However, when God extends mercy to the Ninevites, Jonah finds it unacceptable despite the fact that they have responded positively and repentantly to God's word. In conjunction with the allusion to the golden calf incident and God's mercy to Israel in that context, this reveals that Jonah neither understands nor appreciates God's gracious and compassionate character; he only cares about himself.

The final three verses of the book drive this point home. God asks if it is right for Jonah to be angry about the plant, and Jonah stubbornly asserts that it is (v. 9). God then uses Jonah's rather silly "pity/compassion" (*ḥûs*) for the plant to argue from the lesser to the greater that he has much more reason to have "pity/compassion" (*ḥûs*) for Nineveh (vv. 10–11). This ends the book with a focus on God's gracious and compassionate character, not on any missionary appeal.

The Missional Import of the Book of Jonah

With this understanding of the message of the book of Jonah, what are we to conclude concerning its missional significance? As mentioned above, we may not argue that simply because Jonah is called to a centrifugal

---

22. We have already explored Jonah's disobedience in chapter 1. Although Jonah's hymn of thanksgiving in the belly of the fish in chapter 2 suggests a possible change of heart, Walter Moberly has argued that Jonah's prophetic proclamation in 3:4 ("Yet forty days, and Nineveh shall be overthrown!") reveals that his disposition toward his task continues to be reluctant and hardened even after his sojourn in the fish ("Preaching for a Response?," 156–68). Specifically, Jonah says that judgment will come to Nineveh in "forty days." As Moberly notes, "'forty days' is the Hebrew idiom for an indefinite long period of time" ("Preaching for a Response?," 165), and therefore Jonah's use of this timeframe in his oracle to Nineveh indicates that "Jonah does not want the Ninevites to repent. He proclaims a message of judgment, in line with his commission, but he does his best to subvert it by implying that there is no urgency, for judgment is still a good way off" ("Preaching for a Response?," 167). Supporting this is Jonah's angry posture at Nineveh's repentance and God's mercy in chapter 4; his effort to subvert his own message has failed. Considered together, all these data indicate that Jonah is portrayed throughout the book as resistant to God's call, reluctantly obedient when caught in his flight, eager to undermine the message he is called to proclaim, and selfishly angry when that message is heeded. For these reasons, Kaiser's assessment that "Jonah is an excellent example of cross-cultural missions" (*Mission in the Old Testament*, 36) seems to miss the mark.

international mission, Israel as a nation is called to the same. However, this does not mean that the book of Jonah has nothing to say about Israel's missional calling. As argued in chapter 4, Israel's mission was to obey God's voice and keep his covenant as a priestly kingdom in order to serve as a witness to God's kingship among the nations. The Torah was the standard that Israel was to keep in this endeavor, and as we saw, the Torah did not require perfect obedience but repentant obedience. Although the book of Jonah is fundamentally about God's gracious and compassionate character, it communicates this message by contrasting Jonah's unrepentant disposition with the foreign sailors' and Ninevites' penitent actions. The application for Israel's missional calling is therefore clear: if God extends grace and compassion even to foreigners upon their repentance, how much more will he show grace and compassion to Israel, his own people, upon their repentance?[23] Since Israel will only be successful in their mission by exercising such repentant obedience, the book of Jonah is missional insofar as it exhorts Israel to repent from their hardened and disobedient posture toward God's word and respond to him faithfully.

MISSION AND THE PSALTER

Like Jonah, the book of Psalms is often viewed as significantly missional in character. Creighton Marlowe focuses his study on what he deems "the more explicit expressions in the Book of Psalms that reflect God's concern that Israel reach out to the nations in fulfilling its privilege and purpose as a light to the nations."[24] Similarly, Daniel Timmer suggests that "there is sufficient material in the Psalms to make the book's centrifugal missionary element incontrovertible."[25] Given such views, as we did with Jonah, we need to engage in a careful analysis of the book of Psalms in order to maintain the thesis that Israel's missional calling was centripetal rather than centrifugal in nature. In proceeding, first I will summarize the various contexts in which the nations appear in the Psalter and interact with those who argue that these passages present a centrifugal missional dynamic. Second, I will provide a brief overview of the structure and message of the Psalter as a whole and argue that, in its final canonical arrangement, this collection of songs exalts God as King over the entire earth and therefore coheres with the present study's overall thesis concerning God's mission in the world.

23. See also Walton, "Object Lesson," 55–56; Waltke, *Old Testament Theology*, 834.
24. Marlowe, "Music of Missions," 446.
25. Timmer, "Jonah and Mission," 161.

The Nations in the Purview of the Psalter

In examining the role of the nations in the Psalms, we may divide the relevant texts into three categories: (1) passages that directly address or are directly about the nations, (2) passages concerning Israel's relationship with the nations, and (3) passages concerning God's relationship with the nations. Although these categories overlap to a certain degree and should not be viewed as rigidly distinct from one another, they are nevertheless helpful for summarizing the role that the nations play in the Psalter.

Passages that Directly Address or Are Directly About the Nations

Throughout the Psalms the nations are directly spoken to or about in a variety of ways. The pertinent texts may be divided into three subgroups: those containing *second-person calls* for the nations to praise, those containing *third-person calls* for the nations to praise, and *other passages* directly related to the nations.

Second-Person Calls for the Nations to Praise

At several points the psalmists address the nations directly, commanding them to praise, worship, and/or fear God.[26] For example, Psalm 117 begins with an imperative calling all nations to praise the Lord:

> Praise the Lord, all nations!
> Extol him, all peoples! (v. 1)

Concerning this psalm, both Kaiser and Marlowe argue that since the nations are called to praise the Lord, it may be concluded that someone has gone out and told them about him; therefore this command to praise presumes a prior centrifugal outreach.[27] However, this conclusion wrongly assumes that centrifugal mission is the only means by which the nations could acquire knowledge of the true God. As we have seen, if Israel had faithfully obeyed God as King, the Abrahamic formula would have caused knowledge of God to spread among the nations in a centripetal manner. For this reason, we may not assume that Israel has executed a centrifugal mission simply because foreign nations are called to praise God.

---

26. Pss 47:1; 66:1, 8; 68:32; 96:7–8; 98:4; 100:1; 117:1.
27. Kaiser, *Mission in the Old Testament*, 34; Marlowe, "Music of Missions," 451.

Supporting this, whenever verbs of motion occur in these psalms, they always describe the nations *coming toward* Israel rather than Israel going out to them:

> The princes of the peoples *gather*
> as the people of the God of Abraham. (47:9)

> Say to God, "How awesome are your deeds!
> So great is your power that your enemies *come* cringing to you." (66:3)

> *Come* and see what God has done:
> he is awesome in his deeds toward the children of man. (66:5)[28]

> *Come* and hear, all you who fear God,
> and I will tell what he has done for my soul. (66:16)

> Because of your temple at Jerusalem
> kings shall *bear gifts to you*. (68:29)

> Nobles shall *come* from Egypt;
> Cush shall *hasten* [lit. "run"] to stretch out her hands to God. (68:31)

> Ascribe to the LORD the glory due his name;
> *bring* an offering, and *come* into his courts! (96:8)

> Serve the LORD with gladness!
> *Come into his presence* with singing!
> *Enter his gates* with thanksgiving,
> and his courts with praise!
> Give thanks to him; bless his name! (100:2, 4)

All the italicized verbs in the passages above depict centripetal movement, which supports our understanding of Israel's missional paradigm. Also comporting with this interpretation are the two psalms in this category not mentioned above, both of which call the nations to praise God *because of what he has done for Israel*. Psalm 98 begins this way:

> Oh sing to the LORD a new song,
> for he has done marvelous things!
> His right hand and his holy arm

---

28. In context these "deeds" that God has done "toward the children of man" refer specifically to his redemption of Israel in the exodus, as the following verse says, "He turned the sea into dry land; they passed through the river on foot" (Ps 66:6).

> have worked salvation for him.
> The Lord has made known his salvation;
> > he has revealed his righteousness *in the sight of the nations.*
> He has remembered his steadfast love and faithfulness
> > to the house of Israel.
> All the ends of the earth *have seen*
> > the salvation of our God. (98:1–3)

In this passage, the nations[29] are called to sing because of the marvelous salvation they have seen God work for Israel. The nations are thus portrayed as outsiders looking in and observing the redemptive outworking of God's "steadfast love" (*ḥesed*) and "faithfulness" (*'emûnâ*) to Israel and thereby gaining knowledge of God's salvation (v. 3). Similarly, Psalm 117, which we explored above, says,

> Praise the Lord, all nations!
> > Extol him, all peoples!
> For great is his steadfast love (*ḥesed*) toward us,
> > and the faithfulness (*'ᵉmet*) of the Lord endures forever.
> Praise the Lord! (117:1–2)

Like Psalm 98, this psalm calls the nations to praise the Lord because of his "steadfast love" (*ḥesed*) and "faithfulness" (*'ᵉmet*). Although Marlowe concludes that the referent of "us" in verse 2 is all humanity,[30] it more likely refers to Israel in particular. Not only does Psalm 98 state that God's steadfast love and faithfulness *to Israel* is the reason the nations should praise him, elsewhere in the Psalter the combination of "steadfast love" (*ḥesed*) and "faithfulness" (*'ᵉmet*) is only used in contexts describing God's commitment to Israel.[31] Therefore concerning Psalm 117 John Goldingay rightly concludes, "As elsewhere, the reason the world should worship is Yhwh's strong commitment [i.e. *ḥesed*] and lasting truthfulness [i.e., *'ᵉmet*] toward Israel."[32] Consequently, both Psalms 98 and 117 call for a fulfillment of the Abrahamic formula: the nations are called to praise God because of his blessing upon Israel, which stems from his steadfast love and faithfulness to them as his covenant people.[33]

---

29. Although verses 1–3 do not specify the addressee as the nations, verse 4 follows by saying, "Make a joyful noise to the Lord, *all the earth*," indicating a universal audience.

30. Marlowe, "Music of Missions," 451–52.

31. Pss 25:10; 26:3; 40:10–11; 57:3, 10; 61:7; 69:13; 85:10; 86:15; 89:14; 108:4; 115:1; 138:2.

32. Goldingay, *Psalms 90–150*, 350 (brackets mine).

33. See also Ludwig, "Mission in the Psalms," 13.

MISSION INTEGRATED

In sum, all the psalms that directly call the nations to praise, worship, and/or fear God either portray them in centripetal movement toward Israel or present God's covenant faithfulness to Israel as the grounds for their praise. All of this reflects a centripetal missional methodology and therefore we must reject the conclusion that imperatives calling the nations to praise God imply a centrifugal witness on Israel's part.

Third-Person Calls for the Nations to Praise

In addition to second-person commands, the Psalter contains several third-person calls for the nations to praise, worship, and/or fear God.[34] For example, Ps 33:8 says,

> Let all the earth fear the LORD;
> let all the inhabitants of the world stand in awe of him!

Passages such as this are not addressed to the nations but are volitional statements about the nations. They indicate the psalmist's desire that the nations submit to God without expressing this desire directly to the nations. However, even though these psalms communicate a desire that the nations fear God, it does not follow, as Marlowe suggests, that they "indirectly or implicitly . . . refer to Israel's duty to declare Yahweh's grace among the nations."[35] As was the case with the second-person commands, these third-person calls occur in contexts that reflect centripetal rather than centrifugal witness. Psalm 67 is the clearest example:[36]

---

34. Pss 33:8; 67:3, 4a, 5; 99:1; 150:6. Psalm 148:11 seems to fit both second- and third-person categories. Verse 7 issues an imperative in the second person ("Praise the Lord from the earth"), which includes the subjects of verse 11 ("Kings of the earth and all peoples, princes and all rulers of the earth!"), though verse 13 follows this with a third-person jussive ("Let them praise the name of the Lord").

35. Marlowe, "Music of Missions," 455n32.

36. I have departed from the ESV in verse 7b and used the NIV instead, since the ESV renders verse 7b as an asyndetic jussive ("let all the ends of the earth fear him"), which does not include the conjunction "and" that begins verse 7b ($w^e y\hat{i}r^{e}\hat{u}$). Contextually, since section A states that the purpose of God's blessing of Israel (v. 1) is "that [his] way may be known on earth" (v. 2), it seems most likely that the corresponding section A' communicates a similar thought. God blesses Israel (vv. 6–7a) *so that* "all the ends of the earth will fear him" (v. 7b). This causal relationship in A' is implicit in the NIV, though the NASB makes it explicit: "God blesses us, *that* all the ends of the earth may fear Him."

> ¹ May God be gracious to us and bless us **A**
> and make his face to shine upon us,
> ² that your way may be known on earth,
> your saving power among all nations.

>> ³ Let the peoples praise you, O God; **B**
>> let all the peoples praise you!

>>> ⁴ Let the nations be glad and sing for joy, **C**
>>> for you judge the peoples with equity
>>> and guide the nations upon the earth.

>> ⁵ Let the peoples praise you, O God; **B'**
>> let all the peoples praise you!

> ⁶ The earth has yielded its increase; **A'**
> God, our God, shall bless us.
> ⁷ God shall bless us;
> and all the ends of the earth will fear him!

As this layout makes clear, this psalm is arranged as a chiasm. The A sections each discuss God's blessing upon Israel and its missional effect among the nations. Alluding to the Aaronic blessing of Num 6:24–26, the psalmist begins section A by petitioning God to bless Israel in order that "your way may be known on earth, your saving power among all nations" (v. 2).[37] The picture here is of the Abrahamic formula being enacted: God will bless his people in such a way that they become recognized recipients of blessing, which will then cause God's blessing to spread among the nations. I argued in chapter 3 that this international blessing in the Abrahamic formula includes a theologically redemptive element; here we see this element made explicit as God's "saving power" is recognized among the nations. While section A emphasizes this redemptive aspect of God's blessing, section A' puts the focus on the nations' faithful response to Israel's blessedness. As God pours out his blessing upon his people, "all the ends of the earth will

---

37. Kaiser incorrectly states that "the psalmist has directly applied *to all the peoples and nations on earth* what the high priest Aaron and his fellow priests bestowed on the nation Israel. It is from this theme of enlargement that we boldly announce that this is indeed a missionary psalm (*Mission in the Old Testament*, 29 [emphasis mine])." On the contrary, verse 1 asks for God's blessing to come upon "us" (i.e., Israel), while verse 2 articulates the *purpose* of this request: international acknowledgment of God's way and salvation. The relationship is explicitly centripetal.

fear him" (v. 7b). As we have seen, such a reverential response to God is the mechanism by which the nations are to receive God's blessing themselves.

It is within this context of centripetal mission in the A sections that the B sections issue identical third-person calls for the nations to praise God (vv. 3, 5). To suggest that these jussive calls presume or imply centrifugal mission for Israel ignores this centripetal frame in the A sections and introduces a missional responsibility for Israel that is elsewhere unattested.

Finally, at the center of the psalm is section C, which is another third-person call. In this section the psalmist indirectly calls the nations to be glad and sing for joy because of the "equity" (*mîšôr*) of God's reign (v. 4). That God rules the peoples with "equity" indicates that he administers his reign over Gentile nations the same way he rules over Israel.[38] That is, what God expects of the nations is what he expects of Israel: that they respond to him with faithful and repentant obedience. If they do, God will bless them abundantly just as he blesses Israel; they will experience what they observe Israel experiencing now, at least in the petitionary vision of the psalmist. In these ways, Psalm 67 is the clearest example of centripetal mission among the category of third-person international calls to praise.

Although the other psalms in this category are not as clear in this regard as Psalm 67, they nevertheless cohere with a centripetal missional framework. Psalm 33:6–9 cites God's work of creation as grounds for the nations' praise. Psalm 99:1–3 describes God's greatness in Zion as the reason for international praise. And finally, Psalm 148 combines God's majesty over creation and his care for his people as rationale for the nations to praise. After referring to "kings of the earth and all peoples, princes and all rulers of the earth" (Ps 148:11), the psalmist says,

> Let them praise the name of the LORD,
>   for his name alone is exalted;
>   his majesty is above earth and heaven.
> He has raised up a horn for his people,
>   praise for all his saints,
>   for the people of Israel who are near to him. (vv. 13–14)

In these verses the psalmist provides two reasons for the nations to praise: (1) God's name is exalted/his majesty is above creation (v. 13), and (2) he has raised up a "horn" for Israel (v. 14). Regardless of how one understands the referent of the horn,[39] it is clear that verse 14 presents God's work on behalf of Israel as grounds for the nations to praise.

---

38. See also deClaissé-Walford et al., *Book of Psalms*, 540.

39. For a survey of interpretations and an exegetical analysis of the "horn" in Psalm 148, see Schmutzer and Gauthier, "Identity of the 'Horn' in Psalm 148:14a," 161–83.

Other Passages Directly Related to the Nations

Aside from these second- and third-person calls to praise, the Psalter states that the nations see God's glory (97:6), that they worship/praise/submit to God (48:10; 66:4; 76:12), and that they *will* worship/praise/submit to God.[40] Significantly, none of these psalms describes Israel going out to the nations, though two explicitly describe a centripetal movement of the nations:

> All the nations you have made shall *come*
>   *and worship before you, O Lord,*
>   and shall glorify your name. (86:9)

> Let this be recorded for a generation to come,
>   so that a people yet to be created may praise the LORD:
> that he looked down from his holy height;
>   from heaven the LORD looked at the earth,
> to hear the groans of the prisoners,
>   to set free those who were doomed to die,
> that they may declare in Zion the name of the LORD,
>   and in Jerusalem his praise,
> *when peoples gather together,*
>   and kingdoms, to worship the LORD. (102:18–22)

Therefore we may conclude that the psalms dealing directly with the nations provide no evidence of centrifugal mission, but instead support our view concerning Israel's centripetal calling.

Passages Concerning Israel's Relationship with the Nations

The second major category to consider includes passages in the Psalter that discuss Israel's relationship with the nations. Within this category we may subdivide the pertinent texts into *second-person calls* for Israel to praise God among the nations, *first-person statements* expressing the psalmist's intent to praise God among the nations, and *other passages* related to Israel's relationship with the nations.

---

40. Pss 22:27; 45:17; 46:10; 86:9; 102:15, 22; 138:4.

MISSION INTEGRATED   149

SECOND-PERSON CALLS FOR ISRAEL TO PRAISE GOD AMONG
THE NATIONS

Most significant in this category are the two verses in the Psalter that instruct Israel to recount God's deeds among the nations: Psalms 9:11 and 105:1.[41] Psalm 9:11 says,

> Sing praises to the LORD, who sits enthroned in Zion!
> Tell among the peoples his deeds!

Although Kaiser describes this verse as "a call for an active witness (i.e., it was to be centrifugal in its effect, reaching out from the center to others) by Israel to the Gentiles,"[42] careful analysis reveals that this is not the case. In the second colon, the psalmist says, "Tell among the peoples his deeds (*haggîdû bāʿammîm ʿălîlôṯāyw*)!" Here the plural imperative of the verb *nagad* ("Tell") is followed by the preposition *beth* ("among"), whose object is *hāʿammîm* ("the peoples"), which is followed by the object of the verb *ʿălîlôṯāyw* ("his deeds"). In Kaiser's interpretation, the object of the preposition becomes the direct recipient of the communicative action. That is, according to Kaiser, the reader is being called to tell *the peoples* about God's deeds. However, whenever *nagad* uses a preposition to mark the recipient of communication it is almost always *lamed*.[43] When *beth* follows *nagad* it typically indicates the location of communication.[44] For example, in his oracle against Moab, Jeremiah says,

---

41. Kaiser claims that Pss 57:9; 119:46; 126:2; 145:11–12, 21 call for "active and centrifugal outreach on the part of Israel" (*Mission in the Old Testament*, 33; cf. 34), though none of these passages contain an imperative of any kind, let alone one that commands Israel to go out and preach to the nations. See below for a discussion of Psalm 96.

42. Kaiser, *Mission in the Old Testament*, 33 (emphasis original); see also Marlowe, "Music of Missions," 449. I admit to being slightly unclear what Kaiser means here when he says that such "active witness" is to be "centrifugal *in its effect*, reaching out from the center" (emphasis mine). This sounds like what I will advocate below (i.e., this psalm describes praise occurring *in Jerusalem* in the midst of the nations, who are intended to overhear [thus being centrifugal *in its effect*] and come to worship God in centripetal movement). However, since Kaiser clearly distinguishes centrifugal witness as active and centripetal witness as passive (xiii), I proceed here with the understanding that he views Psalm 9 as exhorting centrifugal *movement* on the part of Israel.

43. This is consistently the case elsewhere, including other imperative constructions (e.g., Gen 24:49 [2x]; 29:15; 37:16; Judg 16:6, 10, 13; 1 Sam 9:18; 10:15; 14:43; 2 Sam 17:16; Jer 38:25; Jonah 1:8; Ruth 4:4; Song 1:7). The only variation I have found is in 1 Sam 3:15, where the similar preposition *ʾel* marks the recipient of communication.

44. See 1 Sam 4:13; 2 Sam 1:20; 2 Kgs 9:15; Jer 4:5; 46:14; 48:20; 50:28. Jeremiah 36:20 follows this generally by using this construction to describe the medium of communication ("they *reported* [*wayyaggîdû*] all the words *in the ears* [*bᵉʾozne*] of the king"). Three passages are ambiguous in this respect (Isa 66:19; Jer 5:20; 31:10) and

> Moab is put to shame, for it is broken;
> wail and cry!
> *Tell it beside the Arnon* (*haggidû bᵉʾarnôn*),
> that Moab is laid waste. (Jer 48:20)

This verse is not commanding the "inhabitant of Aroer" (v. 19) to communicate Moab's fall *to* the Arnon River but to tell of it "at" or "beside" the Arnon. The river is not the recipient of communication but the *location* where this representative Moabite is to lament the nation's fall. Similarly, in Ps 9:11 the psalmist is not calling his readers to communicate God's deeds *to* the peoples in the sense of going out to them, but to tell of his deeds "among" or "in the midst of" the peoples. Grammatically, the multinational landscape is not the direct recipient of communication but the *location* where Israel is to recount God's works. The psalmist is therefore exhorting his readers to tell of God's deeds *in the midst of the nations*, which is precisely where Israel is situated geographically (cf. Deut 4:5–7; 26:16–19; 28:10). Consequently, as the environment or arena within which Israel is to praise God for his marvelous works, the nations are presented as the audience observing this proclamation, though the text does not portray Israel going out to them in a centrifugal manner.

Two other data within Psalm 9 support this conclusion. First, the parallelism of verse 11 suggests that the "telling" envisioned in the second colon occurs in Jerusalem, not abroad. Parallel with "Tell among the peoples his deeds" is "Sing praises to the Lord, *who sits enthroned in Zion.*" In poetic verse such as this, where the cola are semantically parallel, the second colon usually specifies, intensifies, or dramatizes the first.[45] Since the first colon of verse 11 calls Israel to praise God and locates him in Zion (i.e., Jerusalem), this location is established as the probable context for the action expressed in the second colon. In other words, the act of praising God in Jerusalem in colon A is further specified by colon B in terms of *environment* (this praise occurs "among the peoples") and *content* (this praise entails recounting God's deeds). Second, two verses later the psalmist expresses his own desire to praise God, not internationally, but *in Jerusalem*:

> Be gracious to me, O Lord!
> See my affliction from those who hate me,
> O you who lift me up from the gates of death,
> that I may recount all your praises,

---

one is analogous to Ps 9:11 (Jer 50:2), though none of these requires the object to be understood as the recipient of communication as opposed to the location. Concerning Isa 66:19 see the discussion below.

45. Alter, *Art of Biblical Poetry*, 20.

that in the gates of daughter Zion[46]
I may rejoice in your salvation. (Ps 9:13–14)

The phrase "daughter Zion" personifies Jerusalem, and therefore the psalmist is longing to rejoice in God's salvation in Israel's capital city. Although these verses do not prove this reading of verse 11, they do provide the only other description of the geography of praise in the psalm and therefore further establish Jerusalem as the place where it occurs.

A similar conclusion follows for Psalm 105. This psalm is clearly addressed to the people of Israel (v. 6) and begins this way,

Oh give thanks to the LORD; call upon his name;
make known among the peoples his deeds! (v. 1, author's translation)

The second colon of this verse contains the plural imperative *hôdîʿû* ("make known"; the Hiphil of *yada*, "to know") followed by the preposition *beth* ("among"), whose object is *hāʿammim* ("the peoples"), followed by the object of the verb *ʿalilôṯāyw* ("his deeds"). This passage instructs Israel to publicize news of God's deeds among the nations using nearly identical terminology to Ps 9:11:

Psalm 9:11b	Psalm 105:1b
Tell (*haggiḏû*)	Make known (*hôḏîʿû*)
among the peoples (*bāʿammim*)	among the peoples (*bāʿammim*)
his deeds (*ʿalilôṯāyw*)	his deeds (*ʿalilôṯāyw*)

Aside from using different verbs these cola are identical. Further linking them is the fact that these are the only two instances in the Psalms where the nouns "peoples" (*ʿammim*) and "deeds" (*ʿalilôṯ*) occur together. As was the case in 9:11, here in 105:1 Israel is not called to communicate God's deeds *to* the peoples but rather *in the midst of* the peoples. Moreover, similar to the verb *nagad*, the Hiphil stem of *yada* does not use the preposition *beth* to mark the recipient of communication. Most often the Hiphil of *yada* uses an object suffix to indicate the recipient,[47] though occasionally either

---

46. I have adapted the ESV here to read "daughter Zion" instead of "the daughter of Zion," since the referent is not "Zion's daughter" but Zion itself, which is being personified as a "daughter." Such a construction is known as an appositional genitive (Waltke and O'Connor, *Biblical Hebrew Syntax*, 226) and is a preferable translation here. See the discussion of Dearman, "Daughter Zion," 144–59.

47. Exod 33:13; Deut 8:3; 1 Sam 6:2; 28:15; Jer 11:18; Ezek 20:4; Pss 25:4, 14; 39:4; 143:8; Job 10:12; 37:19; 38:3; 40:7; 42:4; Prov 22:21.

the direct object marker[48] or the preposition *lamed*[49] is employed. This suggests that the anomalous use of *beth* in 105:1—and its appearance in identical phrases in 1 Chr 16:8 and Isa 12:4—does not introduce the recipient of communication. Rather, in line with its function in the same phrase in Ps 9:11, the *beth* presents the peoples as the environment or arena within which the communicative action occurs.

Furthermore, as was the case with Psalm 9, the context of Psalm 105 indicates that Jerusalem is the place where the reader is to "make known among the peoples his deeds." After calling Israel to thank God, sing to him, tell of his works, and glory in his name (vv. 1–3), the psalmist exhorts his readers to "seek his presence continually" (v. 4). Elsewhere in the Psalter, to "seek" God's "presence" (*baqqᵉšû pānāyw*) refers exclusively to approaching God at the temple (Pss 24:3–6; 27:4–8). Therefore, although Israel is not called here to "go out" to the nations and make known God's deeds in a centrifugal fashion, by their praise of God in Jerusalem they do make him known amidst the surrounding international environment.

Excursus: What About Psalm 96?

Having explored Pss 9:11 and 105:1, at this point we must pause briefly and consider Psalm 96, which several writers have lauded as a missional masterpiece exhorting Israel to centrifugal outreach. For example, Hedlund says that "the context of Psalm 96 is positively missionary."[50] Marlowe notes that this psalm is "often considered the great missionary Psalm."[51] Theodore Mascarenhas similarly concludes, "The psalmist entrusts a task to Israel to proclaim actively the salvation of God."[52] However, the reader will notice that I have already included this psalm in the preceding section when dealing with passages addressed to the nations. The reason for this is that the addressee of this psalm is not Israel but the whole earth:[53]

> Oh sing to the LORD a new song;
> sing to the LORD, all the earth! (v. 1)

48. Gen 41:39; 2 Sam 7:21; Ezek 16:2; 43:11.

49. Isa 64:2; Pss 78:5; 145:12; Prov 9:9; Neh 8:12. This syntactic arrangement is also evident in the equivalent Aramaic stem, the Haphel. When the verb *yada* occurs in the Haphel, the recipient of communication either appears as an object suffix (Dan 2:29) or is marked by the preposition *lamed* (Dan 2:15, 17, 28, 45; 5:8).

50. Hedlund, *Mission of the Church in the World*, 85.

51. Marlowe, "Music of Missions," 451.

52. Mascarenhas, *Missionary Function of Israel*, 187.

53. See also Foster, "Plea for New Songs," 287; Goldingay, *Psalms 90–150*, 101.

> Ascribe to the LORD, O families of the peoples,
> ascribe to the LORD glory and strength! (v. 7)

> Worship the LORD in the splendor of holiness;
> tremble before him, all the earth! (v. 9)

At no point does the psalmist specify an addressee other than this comprehensive, earth-wide audience. Consequently, verses 3 and 10, which are the most "missionary" in tone, must be interpreted within this broader communicative context:

> Declare his glory among the nations,
> his marvelous works among all the peoples! (v. 3)

> Say among the nations, "The LORD reigns!" (v. 10a)

These verses are often read as if they are instructing Israel to engage in international evangelism.[54] However, not only does the stated addressee preclude this interpretation, other factors suggest that these verses are directed specifically to the whole created order.

Above I listed the three verses in this psalm that identify a particular audience: verses 1 and 9 address "all the earth" and verse 7 addresses the "families of the peoples." Significantly, the imperatives of verses 3 and 10a appear in the two sections addressed to "all the earth." Although this phrase sometimes denotes "all *the peoples* of the earth" (e.g., Ps 33:8), it also refers several times in the Psalter to the whole created order (e.g., Pss 57:5, 7; 108:5). Three observations suggest that this latter referent is intended here. First, aside from verse 3, the only other place in the Psalter where God's "glory" (*kābôd*) is "declared" (*sāpar*) is in 19:1, which says, "The *heavens* declare the glory of God, and the sky above proclaims his handiwork." This provides precedent within the Psalter that the created order engages in the specific activity commanded in 96:3. Second, Ps 96:11 calls "the heavens" to be glad and "the earth" to rejoice, which provides immediate contextual evidence that the created order is in view.

Third, the synoptic appearance of this psalm in 1 Chronicles 16 further supports the view that verse 10 addresses all creation. In that passage, David instructs Asaph and his brothers to sing a song of thanksgiving that includes portions of Psalms 96, 105, and 106. The rendition of Psalm 96

---

54. See, e.g., Klein, "Psalms in Chronicles," 268; Okoye, *Israel and the Nations*, 103–4; Mascarenhas, *Missionary Function of Israel*, 169; Schnabel, *Early Christian Mission*, 1:75n42.

in this passage follows the language of the Psalter very closely,[55] though a significant change occurs at Ps 96:10:

	Psalm 96:9–11		**1 Chronicles 16:29b–32a**
A	[9] Worship the LORD in the splendor of holiness; tremble before him, all the earth!	A	[29b] Worship the LORD in the splendor of holiness; [30] tremble before him, all the earth;
B	[10] Say among the nations, "The LORD reigns!	C	yes, the world is established; it shall never be moved.
C	Yes, the world is established; it shall never be moved;	E	[31] Let the heavens be glad, and let the earth rejoice,
D	he will judge the peoples with equity."		
E	[11] Let the heavens be glad, and let the earth rejoice;	B	and let them say among the nations, "The LORD reigns!"
F	let the sea roar, and all that fills it;	F	[32] Let the sea roar, and all that fills it;

As this comparison shows, the Chronicler's account (1) does not include line D, (2) places line B after line E, and (3) contains a third-person jussive in line B ("let them say among the nations") rather than the second-person imperative found in Ps 96:10 ("Say among the nations"). Since B now follows E and contains this third-person plural verb, it follows that "the heavens" and "the earth" from line E are the subject of line B in 1 Chronicles 16. In Chronicles, then, it is explicitly *the created order* that exclaims among the nations, "The LORD reigns!" This clarity in the synoptic version supports the view that the addressee of the imperative in Ps 96:10, "all the earth," refers to the whole created order as well.[56]

Collectively the preceding observations show that Israel is not the addressee of Psalm 96. Of course, as a song in Israel's Psalter this psalm is intended for Israel's instruction and benefit, but we must not confuse this broader didactic function with the psalm's internal communicative trajectory, which is a call for all creation and the peoples of the earth to praise and worship God.

---

55. The Chronicler's version only lacks Pss 96:1a, 2a, 10b, and 13b. Aside from this, the only differences are a few fuller spellings and constructions (vv. 30, 32, 33), the use of an independent preposition instead of its inseparable equivalent (v. 23), the inclusion of two direct object markers (vv. 24, 33) and one definite article (v. 33), and two subtle veilings of temple imagery. First Chronicles 16:27 says "strength and joy are in his *place*" where Ps 96:6 says "strength and beauty in his *sanctuary*," and 1 Chr 16:29 says "and come *before him*" where Ps 96:8 says "and come *into his courts*."

56. Contra Bosma, "Missional Reading of Psalms 67 and 96," 167–69.

First-Person Statements of Intent to Praise God Among the Nations

Returning to the psalms that do discuss Israel's relationship with the nations, the next category to consider consists of passages in which the psalmist states his intent to praise God among the nations. Three psalms fall into this group:

> For this I will give thanks to you, O LORD, among the nations,
>   and sing to your name. (Ps 18:49)[57]

> I will give thanks to you, O Lord, among the peoples;
>   I will sing praises to you among the nations. (Ps 57:9)

> I will give thanks to you, O LORD, among the peoples;
>   I will sing praises to you among the nations. (Ps 108:3)

These verses all have the same structure in the first colon ("I will give thanks to you [*'ôdᵉkā*], O LORD/Lord [*yhwh/'ᵃdōnāy*], among the nations/peoples [*baggôyim/bāʿammim*]"), and the latter two are identical in the second colon. Since *bāʿammim* ("among the peoples") elsewhere describes the nations as the arena within which God's deeds are recounted *in Jerusalem* (Pss 9:11; 105:1), this phrase most likely carries a similar force in these psalms as well. Supporting this is Psalm 77, which contains the only other occurrence of *bāʿammim* in the Psalter outside the verses we have considered so far. Verses 14–15 of that psalm say,

> You are the God who works wonders;
>   you have made known your might *among the peoples* (*bāʿammim*).
> You with your arm redeemed your people,
>   the children of Jacob and Joseph.

The remainder of the psalm identifies the redemption mentioned here as God's deliverance of Israel at the Red Sea (vv. 16–20). According to this passage, therefore, it is *through redeeming his people* that God has made known his might "among the peoples." It is not that God traveled around from nation to nation in a centrifugal manner and demonstrated his might in each locale. Rather, the picture here is of the nations *seeing or hearing about* God's deliverance of Israel and thereby learning of his supreme might.[58]

---

57. I have altered the ESV's "I will praise you" to "I will give thanks to you" to match the identical vocabulary found in Pss 57:9 and 108:3.

58. See, e.g., Lev 26:45, where God says that he "brought [Israel] out of the land of Egypt *in the sight of the nations*." See also Rahab's faithful confession in Josh 2:8–11, where she mentions that the people of Canaan have "heard how the Lord dried up the water of the Red Sea before you when you came out of Egypt" (v. 10). Similarly, the

This reinforces our understanding of *bāʿammim* in the psalms above as portraying the nations as the overall arena within which praise occurs in a central location. The psalmist will praise God in the midst of the nations (i.e., in Israel), and the nations will observe this praise and thereby become acquainted with God and his ways.

The other prepositional phrases in Psalms 18, 57, and 108 neither clearly confirm nor deny this understanding of the location of praise. Psalm 18:49a uses *baggôyîm* ("among the nations"), which functions elsewhere in a variety of ways and thus may or may not describe the nations as the arena of praise. Psalms 57:9b and 108:3b each use *bal-ʾummim* ("among the nations"), which is a rare collocation that only appears twice elsewhere in the Old Testament (Pss 44:14; 149:7), and in neither case does it function adverbially as it does in these two instances. Given this interpretive uncertainty concerning these other prepositional phrases, it seems best to understand these less clear expressions in light of the clearer evidence of *bāʿammim*. For these reasons, the passages that reveal the psalmists' desire to praise God among the nations should not be viewed as describing centrifugal outreach or as calling Israel to such outreach.[59] Rather, in line with our observations above, these texts describe the psalmists' intent to praise God in a central location in the midst of the nations, which are portrayed as the surrounding arena that observes this praise. This praise is missional in the sense that it is designed to teach the nations about God's glory, though there is no indication that the psalmists intended to go out to the nations in order to execute this mission.[60]

Gibeonites "heard" about the destructions of Jericho and Ai (Josh 9:3) and therefore acted cunningly to save their lives, offering a confession of faith very similar to Rahab's (vv. 24–25).

59. Contra Kaiser, *Mission in the Old Testament*, 33–34.

60. Due to its lack of clarity I am not including Ps 119:46 in this section, which says, "I will also speak of your testimonies before kings and shall not be put to shame." It seems probable that foreign kings are in view here, though the text is not explicit. Moreover, even if foreign kings are in view, this text provides no hint of centrifugal movement. The act of speaking before kings could just as logically occur as those kings come to Jerusalem, as was the case with Solomon and the Queen of Sheba (1 Kgs 10:1–13; 2 Chr 9:1–12).

Other Passages Related to Israel's Relationship with the Nations

Other psalms that describe Israel's relationship with the nations state that God has made or will make the Davidic king head over the nations,[61] that the nations will submit to the Davidic king (72:10–11), that the nations will be blessed through the Davidic king (72:17), and that Israel will execute judgment on the nations (149:6–7). None of these passages implies any sort of centrifugal outreach. Rather, as noted in chapter 4, Psalm 72 portrays a centripetal movement of foreign kings bringing tribute (vv. 10, 15) and other nations recognizing the blessed status of the Davidic king (v. 17). Consequently, as was the case with psalms directly related to the nations, this second category of psalms comports with our overall thesis concerning Israel's missional responsibility.

Passages Concerning God's Relationship with the Nations

The third and final category includes psalms describing God's relationship with the nations. Within this group are statements or calls for God to judge/rule over the nations,[62] descriptions of God as king or ruler over the whole earth,[63] and descriptions of God acting in the sight of the nations.[64] As was the case in the previous categories, none of these passages describes God's people going out to the nations, though several either depict a centripetal movement of the nations to God or identify the temple as the location of worship:

> Let the assembly of the peoples *be gathered about you*;
>   over it return on high. (7:7)

> Praise is due to you, O God, *in Zion*,
>   and to you shall vows be performed.
> O you who hear prayer,
>   to you shall all flesh *come*. (65:1–2)

> Exalt the LORD our God;
>   *worship at his footstool*!
> Holy is he! (99:5)

---

61. Pss 2:8; 18:43, 47; 72:8; 110:2–3; 144:2.

62. Pss 7:7–8; 9:5, 8, 19–20; 10:16; 22:28; 33:10; 45:5; 56:7; 59:5, 13; 79:6, 10; 82:8; 83; 96:13; 98:9; 110:5–6.

63. Pss 47:2, 7–9; 66:7; 67:4b; 99:2; 113:4.

64. Pss 65:5–8; 77:14; 98:2–3; 126:1–2.

> Exalt the LORD our God,
>   and *worship at his holy mountain*;
>   for the LORD our God is holy! (99:9)[65]

These texts confirm what the previous data have also shown: in the purview of the Psalter the nations are not portrayed as the objects of centrifugal mission. Rather, when the nations are described in motion they are depicted as *coming to* God in order to worship him in Jerusalem. Collectively these observations concerning the nations in the Psalter reinforce our view that Israel's missional calling was centripetal in nature.

The Structure and Message of the Psalter

Having explored the various ways in which the Psalter describes the nations, at this point it is instructive to pan out from looking at individual psalms and analyze the structure and message of the Psalter as a whole. Although the book of Psalms is often read as a series of independent songs that are largely disconnected from one another, recent scholarship has demonstrated that this collection has been edited and arranged into a meaningful whole that communicates a message at the macro level.[66] Although an exhaustive analysis of this topic is beyond the scope of this study, a broad survey will suffice to show that the overall message of the Psalter coheres with our understanding of God's mission.

Structurally, Psalms 1–2 introduce the Psalter, the remainder of which is divided into five books (chs. 3–41; 42–72; 73–89; 90–106; 107–150). These five books are each marked by a closing doxology (Pss 41:13; 72:19; 89:52; 106:48; 146–150), with the climactic fivefold call to praise in Psalms 146–150 functioning as a conclusion both to Book 5 and the Psalter as a whole. Both this introduction and the movement of these five books have a distinct focus on exalting God as King. Psalm 1 opens the Psalter by extolling the blessings and benefits of orienting one's life around the Torah. As we have seen, the Torah is the standard by which Israel is to obey God as King in the sight of the nations, and therefore inasmuch as the Torah is missional, Psalm 1 begins the Psalter on a missional note.

Psalm 2, however, notes that this recognition of God's kingship is not a reality on the international landscape. Verses 1–3 present the nations as

---

65. Pss 47:9 and 66:3 could also be included on this list, though I have already explored these verses above when highlighting the centripetal motion present in psalms with second-person calls for the nations to praise.

66. The seminal study in this regard is Wilson, *Editing of the Hebrew Psalter*. For a more recent analysis see Robertson, *Flow of the Psalms*.

vainly plotting and planning on how they might resist God's rule over them. Verse 4 then describes God as "sitting" in the heavens, which in this context is best understood as sitting *enthroned* (cf. NIV).[67] In the remainder of the psalm, God responds to this international rebellion by promising to extend his sovereignty over the nations by giving worldwide dominion to the Davidic king (vv. 5–9), a promise that the psalmist uses to exhort the nations to submit to God and his messiah (vv. 10–12). Read together, these two introductory psalms highlight that (1) adherence to the Torah is the means by which one may live in blessed submission to God as King, and (2) God will extend his kingship to the ends of the earth through the international reign of the Davidic king.[68]

This twofold introduction establishes the context within which to read the rest of the Psalms. As Gerald Wilson has argued, royal psalms found at the seams of the Psalter reveal a narrative framework that recounts the history of the Davidic monarchy and emphasizes that trust in God's kingship is Israel's ultimate hope for the future.[69] Books 1–2 take the reader from the glorious promises of Psalm 2 to the apex of Psalm 72, where these promises are envisioned as a reality for David's successor. Book 3 then brings us back down to a low point in Psalm 89, where the psalmist looks back upon the destruction of Jerusalem (vv. 38–45) and asks, "Lord, where is your steadfast love of old, which by your faithfulness you swore to David?" (v. 49). In light of the exile, by the end of Book 3, God's covenant promises concerning David's worldwide kingdom seem to have faded into the distance.

Book 4, however, opens by refocusing attention back on Moses, evidenced by the superscription of Psalm 90: "A Prayer of Moses, the man of God." This takes the reader back to a time before there was a Davidic dynasty or a temple in Jerusalem, and begins by saying, "Lord, you have been our dwelling place in all generations" (90:1). Ultimately Israel's hope should not be in the institutions of temple and monarchy but in God himself. This concept then reaches its zenith in the constellation of songs known as the *YHWH malak* psalms (93; 95–99). Each of these psalms explicitly describes God as King, with several using the phrase *YHWH malak*, or "The LORD reigns." This statement both answers the uncertainties raised by Israel's exile

---

67. See also Ross, *Psalms: Volume 1 (1–41)*, 205.

68. That Psalms 1–2 should be interpreted together this way is supported by the *inclusio* that appears when they are read side-by-side ("*Blessed* [ʾašre] is the man who walks not in the counsel of the wicked" [1:1]; "*Blessed* [ʾašre] are all who take refuge in him" [2:12]) as well as the contrast between the one who "meditates" (*hāgâ*) on the Torah (1:2) with those who vainly "plot" (*hāgâ*) their rebellion against God (2:1).

69. For a summary of his arguments, see Wilson, "Use of Royal Psalms," 85–94; Wilson, "Structure of the Psalter," 229–46.

and serves as the key theological affirmation of the entire Psalter. Although Israel has been exiled and the Davidic dynasty is without a ruler, God is still on his throne and therefore hope should be directed to him as Israel's true King. The emphasis at this juncture leads Wilson to call Book 4 "the editorial 'center' of the final form of the Hebrew Psalter."[70] For these reasons, many rightly conclude that the exaltation of God as King is the central message of the Psalter as a whole.[71]

Although the Psalter's primary rhetorical function is to turn Israel's focus back to God as their King, such a function does not indicate that God has abandoned his promises concerning the Davidic dynasty. Book 5 holds out hope that God will restore his reign through a Davidic ruler, evidenced most clearly in Psalms 110 and 132. Consequently, the Psalms do not advocate the reign of God at the expense of hope in the Davidic line, but rather bring Israel's messianic expectation to a more mature state—grounded upon the ultimate kingship of God.[72] This overall message of the Psalter agrees with the thesis of the present study, that God's mission in the world is for his kingship to be represented to the ends of the earth.

MISSION AND THE WISDOM LITERATURE

While Jonah and the Psalter are typically viewed as highly missional in character, the Wisdom literature tends to be the most neglected corpus in missional discussions. Analyses of mission usually focus on God's purposes and actions in redemptive history, but the Wisdom literature is notoriously unconcerned with redemptive history. The Hebrew sages make no mention of God's call of Abram, the exodus from Egypt, the covenant at Sinai, the conquest of Canaan, or any other major event in Israel's history. For this reason, many do not have a viable missional category within which to fit the Wisdom literature. When studies of mission do address this corpus, the focus is often on its "international character" or how it is useful for cross-cultural missional engagement.[73] However, although we may agree that these writings have many parallels with extrabiblical wisdom literature and may be helpful in certain evangelistic situations, these observations merely identify aspects of this literature's style and usefulness; they do

---

70. Wilson, *Editing of the Hebrew Psalter*, 215.

71. See, e.g., McCann, *Theological Introduction to the Book of Psalms*, 41–50; Mays, *Lord Reigns*, 12–22; Futato, *Interpreting the Psalms*, 72–95.

72. See also Robertson, *Flow of the Psalms*, 147–48.

73. See, e.g., Verkuyl, *Contemporary Missiology*, 95; Hedlund, *Mission of the Church in the World*, 139; Wright, *Mission of God*, 443, 448.

not incorporate this material into a biblical-theological understanding of mission.

A way forward in this regard is to recognize the relationship between Torah faithfulness and the "fear of the Lord." In the preceding analysis we have seen that the central mechanism for Israel's missional success is their adherence to the Torah. By repentantly obeying God's commands, Israel is to make visible their blessed relationship with God and thereby witness to his kingship among the nations. Significantly, the Old Testament repeatedly associates this outward act of Torah faithfulness with the inward disposition of the "fear of the Lord."[74] For example, in Deuteronomy 31 Moses instructs the priests to read the Torah before all Israel at each Sabbatical celebration of the Feast of Booths. He describes the intended effect of this reading as follows:

> Assemble the people, men, women, and little ones, and the sojourner within your towns, that they may hear and learn to fear the Lord your God, and be careful to do all the words of this law, and that their children, who have not known it, may hear and learn to fear the Lord your God, as long as you live in the land that you are going over the Jordan to possess. (vv. 12–13)

Twice Moses says that "hearing" the Torah will enable one to "learn to fear the Lord." This suggests that the "fear of the Lord" is expressed through Torah faithfulness,[75] and since Torah faithfulness is the means by which Israel is to execute their mission in the world, it follows that the "fear of the Lord" is the underlying disposition that leads to such missional living. In other words, the "fear of the Lord" describes Israel's missional *attitude*, while Torah faithfulness describes the *actions* that flow from this attitude.[76]

With this background in place it becomes clear how the Wisdom literature contributes to a biblical theology of mission. All three Wisdom books (Proverbs, Job, and Ecclesiastes) present the "fear of the Lord" as the basic principle for wise living. The preamble to Proverbs outlines the book's purpose, climaxing with the famous dictum: "The fear of the Lord is the beginning of knowledge; fools despise wisdom and instruction" (Prov 1:7). The remainder of the book divides into two main parts: the prologue

---

74. The most explicit examples of this connection are in Deut 4:10; 5:29; 6:1–2, 24; 8:6; 10:12–13; 13:4; 17:19; 28:58; 31:12–13; Josh 24:14–26; 1 Sam 12:14; Pss 19:7–9; 86:11; 112:1; 119:63; 128:1. See also the study of Cate, "Fear of the Lord in the Old Testament," 41–55.

75. For a discussion of the relationship between the fear of the Lord and the Torah, see Bullock, "Wisdom, the 'Amen' of Torah," 5–18.

76. For this juxtaposition of "attitude and action" in relation to fearing the Lord and keeping his Torah, I am indebted to Block, *Deuteronomy*, 270.

(1:8—9:18) and the proverbs proper (chs. 10–31). This theme of the "fear of the LORD" reappears several times throughout the book,[77] though its occurrence at the end of each of these two major sections highlights its prominence on a structural level:

> The fear of the LORD is the beginning of wisdom,
>   and the knowledge of the Holy One is insight. (9:10)

> Charm is deceitful, and beauty is vain,
>   but a woman who fears the LORD is to be praised. (31:30)

By this means, the "fear of the LORD" serves as a double *inclusio*, bracketing both the prologue and the book of Proverbs as whole.[78] Taken together, these data highlight that the wisdom outlined throughout the book of Proverbs is founded upon the fear of the LORD.

The book of Job also has a distinct focus on the fear of the LORD. Broadly structured, the book of Job is bracketed by a prologue (chs. 1–2) and an epilogue (42:7–17), between which are three cycles of dialogue (chs. 3–27) and a series of three monologues (chs. 29–41).[79] Falling at the structural center of the book is chapter 28, which is a poem asking where wisdom may be found.[80] This poem notes that although humanity is able to mine the depths of the earth for precious metals (vv. 1–12), wisdom is found nowhere on the earth and is not comparable with any of its riches (vv. 13–20); rather, only God knows where wisdom may be found (vv. 21–27). The poem then closes by revealing how humanity may find wisdom:

> And [God] said to man,
> "Behold, the fear of the Lord, that is wisdom,
>   and to turn away from evil is understanding." (v. 28)

According to this central poem, wisdom is not found in the created order, but only through fearful submission to the Creator himself.

---

77. Prov 1:29; 2:5; 3:7; 8:13; 10:27; 14:2, 26–27; 15:16, 33; 16:6; 19:23; 22:4; 23:17; 24:21.

78. See also Blocher, "Fear of the Lord," 4–5.

79. The divine monologue of chapters 38–41 is punctuated by two responses from Job (40:3–5; 42:1–6), though these responses are basically confessions that Job has no suitable answer to give in light of God's sovereignty. The overall character of these divine speeches is therefore that of a monologue.

80. Parsons describes this poem as "a kind of interlude which marks the transition between the two major parts of the poetic body—the previous dialogue between Job and his friends, and the forthcoming long discourses by Job (chaps. 29–31), Elihu (chaps. 32–37), and God (chaps. 38–41)" ("Structure and Purpose of the Book of Job," 141). Similarly, Steinmann observes that "This wisdom poem stands at the center of the book" ("Structure and Message of the Book of Job," 98).

This focus of the wisdom poem is illustrated by the plotline of the book of Job as a whole. The theme of the fear of the LORD first appears in the opening characterization of Job, who is portrayed as "blameless and upright, one who feared God and turned away from evil" (Job 1:1; cf. 1:8; 2:3). Satan then calls Job's fear of God into question, claiming that if his blessings are taken away (1:9–11) and his body afflicted (2:4–6), rather than fearing God he will curse him. This sets Job's subsequent affliction in the context of determining whether or not he will continue to fear God in the midst of suffering. Throughout the dialogue cycles that follow, Job's friends essentially assert that his suffering reveals that he has not feared God, though from the prologue we know this not to be the case. Ultimately, Job demonstrates his fear of the LORD in the midst of suffering when he responds to God's climactic monologue at the end of the book. When God asserts his sovereignty in the face of Job's questioning, Job shuts his mouth (40:3–5) and confesses his finitude in light of God's grandeur (42:1–6). Although the fear of the LORD is not mentioned explicitly at the end of the book, it is nevertheless portrayed through Job's submissive response to God's power and authority.[81] In this way, the highpoint of the wisdom poem's teaching is forcefully depicted by Job's closing encounter with God.

Finally, the book of Ecclesiastes similarly places a structural emphasis on the fear of the LORD. This book is bracketed by a narratorial superscription (1:1) and epilogue (12:9–14), within which we find the teaching of "the Preacher" (1:2—12:8), often referred to by the transliteration "Qoheleth" (Heb. *qōhelet*). An inner bracket conveys Qoheleth's teaching in the third person through the narrator (1:2–11; 12:8), while the central portion of the book presents Qoheleth's teaching in the first person (1:12—12:7). After recording Qoheleth's teaching in this concentric fashion, the narrator ends the book by saying:

> The end of the matter; all has been heard. Fear God and keep his commandments, for this is the whole duty of man. For God will bring every deed into judgment, with every secret thing, whether good or evil. (Eccl 12:13–14)

This conclusion shows that the narrator's fundamental concern is that readers leave the book with an understanding of the centrality of the fear of the LORD. These verses not only round out our survey of the pivotal role that the "fear of the LORD" plays in the Wisdom literature, but they bring us full circle and explicitly connect this fear of God with keeping his commands.

---

81. Here I disagree with Wilson, who concludes that because the *terminology* of the "fear of the Lord" is absent from the end of the book, the *concept* is therefore not part of the book's solution to Job's situation ("Book of Job and the Fear of God," 74–75).

Since keeping God's commands is the means by which Israel is to fulfill their mission, and since the "fear of the LORD" is the underlying disposition that enables one to keep God's commands, it follows that the Wisdom literature's focus on the "fear of the LORD" establishes it as a missional corpus. To live wisely is to live in fearful recognition of God's supremacy and to respond to his word accordingly.

CENTRIFUGAL MISSION AS ESCHATOLOGICAL VISION

In the preceding discussion I have surveyed the books of Jonah, Psalms, and the Wisdom literature and argued that Israel's mission was centripetal in nature. One passage in the Old Testament, however, envisions a centrifugal witness for God's people in the post-Adamic period. In the final chapter of Isaiah, the prophet looks forward to a time when God will bring judgment against idolaters, gather the nations to himself, and reclaim his dispersed people from faraway lands. According to Isa 66:18aβ–19:[82]

> [T]he time is coming to gather all nations and tongues.
> And they shall come and shall see my glory,
> and I will set a sign among them.
>
> *And from them I will send survivors to the nations,*
>   to Tarshish, Pul, and Lud, who draw the bow,
>   to Tubal and Javan, to the coastlands far away,
>
> that have not heard my fame
>   or seen my glory.
>   *And they shall declare my glory among the nations.*

Since God states his intent to send representatives to proclaim his glory among nations that are ignorant of his fame (v. 19), this oracle clearly describes a centrifugal witness for God's people. The language used here ("And they shall declare my glory among the nations" [*wᵉhiggîdû ʾet-kᵉbôdî baggôyîm*]) recalls constructions we explored above when looking at Pss 9:11, 18:49, 57:9, 105:1, and 108:3. There I argued that the verb *nagad* uses the preposition *beth* not to mark the recipient of communication but to indicate the location of proclamation. Whereas the Psalms portray this proclamation as occurring in Jerusalem with the nations depicted as the surrounding arena observing this proclamation, this Isaianic oracle describes God sending his people out to the nations. The centrifugal nature of this mission,

---

82. For the structural reasoning behind dividing the passage between verse 18aα and 18aβ, see Webster, "Rhetorical Study of Isaiah 66," 93–108.

therefore, derives fundamentally from verse 19a ("I will send survivors to the nations") rather than 19b ("And they shall declare my glory among the nations"). Like the Psalter, in verse 19b this oracle portrays the nations as the arena within which God's people are to declare his glory, though now the centralized proclamation in Jerusalem has given way to a dispersed proclamation throughout the earth. As Claus Westermann has stated, "This is the first sure and certain mention of mission as we today employ the term—the sending of individuals to distant peoples in order to proclaim God's glory among them."[83]

The "survivors" whom God sends in verse 19a are best understood as Israelites who have endured God's judgment of exile and are now mobilized to serve as his representatives.[84] However, from the viewpoint of Isaiah this centrifugal witness is presented not as a prescription for the present but as a vision for the future. The closing oracles in this chapter all have an eschatological setting, anticipating the time when Israel will be released from exile and God will execute his judgment and salvation on all creation. In verses 10-14 God declares his plan to comfort Jerusalem from her suffering and judgment. In verses 15-18aα God outlines his intent to judge those who commit abominations. In verses 20-21 those representatives sent to the nations in verses 18aβ-19 will bring dispersed Israelites ("your brothers") from those nations back to Jerusalem as an offering to God. And finally, verses 22-24 describe this restoration program as a new creation in which all people will worship God, while those who have rebelled will be fully and finally judged. Each of these sections reflects a future, eschatological setting:

- "Behold, I will extend peace to her like a river" (v. 12)
- "For behold, the LORD will come in fire" (v. 15)
- "[T]he time is coming to gather all nations and tongues" (v. 18aβ)
- "And they shall bring all your brothers from all the nations as an offering to the LORD" (v. 20)
- "And they shall go out and look on the dead bodies of the men who have rebelled against me" (v. 24)

In light of this language, the oracle foretelling the sending of representatives in verses 18aβ-19 is best understood as a mission to be executed by God's people upon their restoration from exile.

Although restoration from exile began when Cyrus issued his decree in 539 BC, as we saw in chapter 5, the postexilic community did not

---

83. Westermann, *Isaiah 40-66*, 425. So also Wright, *Mission of God*, 503.
84. Oswalt, *Isaiah 40-66*, 688.

experience the full realization of God's restoration promises during the second temple period. Israel continued to live as slaves in their own land (Neh 9:36) and grew in their anticipation of the day when God would send a Davidic messiah to free them and shepherd them in righteousness. After God's people spend many centuries waiting, Jesus appears in the synagogue of Nazareth in Luke 4 and reads from the scroll of Isa 61:1–2:

> The Spirit of the Lord is upon me,
>   because he has anointed me
>   to proclaim good news to the poor.
> He has sent me to proclaim liberty to the captives
>   and recovering of sight to the blind,
>   to set at liberty those who are oppressed,
>   to proclaim the year of the Lord's favor. (Luke 4:18–19)

In this text, Isaiah describes an anointed prophetic figure who proclaims Israel's return from exile.[85] After Jesus reads these verses, he declares to those listening, "Today this Scripture has been fulfilled in your hearing" (Luke 4:21). With the coming of Jesus, the exile of God's people has reached the beginning of the end. The eschaton has dawned, the age to come has broken in, and God's promises of restoration have begun their final realization. This establishes the New Testament period as the time when Isaiah's eschatological vision of centrifugal mission will become a reality for God's people. As we turn our attention to the New Testament, we will see that this is precisely what Jesus does. After atoning for sin and rising in power, Jesus commissions his followers to engage in the centrifugal mission of declaring his kingship among the nations.

---

85. For an excellent discussion of Isa 61:1–3 and its fulfillment in Luke 4, see Abernethy, *Book of Isaiah and God's Kingdom*, 160–68.

7 MISSION REDEEMED
Jesus and the Missional Roles of the Old Testament

In the preceding chapters we have seen that both Adam and Israel were charged to represent God's kingship to the ends of the earth, failed to accomplish this mission because of their sin, and were exiled from God's presence in Eden/Canaan. Although God was faithful to bring Israel back to the land, the Old Testament ends with Israel still functionally in exile. God's promises of widespread heart transformation and a worldwide kingdom ruled by a righteous, Davidic king have not come to pass. Instead, God's people continue to struggle under foreign domination and await the coming of a righteous Branch, a suffering servant who will be stricken in order to pay for their sins and restore their broken relationship with God. Once this restoration occurs, God's people will be repositioned as righteous images and enabled by God's Spirit to obey his word and fulfill their mission.

It is within this context that God becomes human in the person of Jesus Christ. The New Testament presents Jesus as faithfully fulfilling the key missional roles of the Old Testament and thereby redeeming the mission of God's people. Jesus is depicted as both the last Adam and true Israel, acquiring righteousness for his people through his faithful and obedient life. Jesus is also depicted as the suffering servant who dies to secure forgiveness for his people, the Davidic king who rules them in righteousness, the Danielic Son of Man who catalyzes their mission, and the eschatological temple to which the nations may come and worship God. In this chapter we will explore these six interrelated ways that Jesus is portrayed as the Redeemer of God's people and their mission: (1) Jesus as last Adam, (2) Jesus as true Israel, (3) Jesus as suffering servant, (4) Jesus as righteous Davidic King, (5) Jesus as Danielic Son of Man, and (6) Jesus as eschatological temple.

JESUS AS LAST ADAM

In chapter 2 we saw that through his disobedience the first Adam brought sin into the world, which frustrated the mission of God's people. The New Testament presents Jesus as a latter-day Adam, one who obeys where the first Adam failed and thereby inaugurates a new humanity who will fulfill the mission that God has given us.

The Gospels: Jesus as Last Adam by Implication

The Gospels of Matthew, Luke, and John each begin by drawing connections between the story of Jesus and the creation account, implying that Jesus is fulfilling a role parallel to that of Adam.[1] The Gospel of Matthew begins, "The book of the genealogy of Jesus Christ, the son of David, the son of Abraham" (1:1). The phrase "The book of the genealogy" (*biblos geneseōs*) occurs twice in the LXX, both times in the early chapters of Genesis (2:4; 5:1). Significantly, these two verses introduce the first two *tôlᵉḏōṯ* of the book of Genesis, which pertain to creation and Adam respectively:

> "This is the book of the generations (*biblos geneseōs*) of heaven and earth." (2:4)

> "This is the book of the generations (*biblos geneseōs*) of humanity." (5:1)[2]

As Beale observes, since Matthew uses this phrase at the beginning of a genealogy, it is probable that he is alluding most directly to Genesis 5, which provides the genealogy of Adam.[3] By this allusion, Matthew points our attention back to the creation story and especially to the account of Adam, implying that what follows is a *new creation story* about a *new Adam*.

Luke begins his Gospel with narratives surrounding Jesus' birth and early life (1:1—2:52) and John the Baptist's preparatory ministry (3:1-22),

---

1. Some view the beginning of Mark as similarly alluding to the creation account. In his opening line Mark writes, "The *beginning* (*archē*) of the gospel of Jesus Christ, the Son of God" (1:1). Some see this as recalling the LXX of Gen 1:1: "In the *beginning* (*archē*), God created the heavens and the earth" (see, e.g., Witherington, *Gospel of Mark*, 69; Boring, *Mark*, 31). However, since this proposed connection is based solely on a single word (*archē*), and since this word appears in syntactically distinct constructions (in Genesis it is the object of the preposition *en*, whereas in Mark it is modified by the genitive phrase *tou euaggeliou Iēsou Christou*), a direct allusion to Gen 1:1 seems improbable. Whereas John explicitly recalls creation through his use of *en archē*, it seems most likely that Mark is using *archē* simply to introduce his gospel. For further discussion see France, *Gospel of Mark*, 51–52.

2. Both verses are my translation of the LXX.

3. Beale, *New Testament Biblical Theology*, 388–89.

after which he also provides a genealogy (3:23–38). In this genealogy, Luke portrays Jesus in an Adam-like manner by beginning with Jesus and extending all the way back to Adam. The genealogy ends by identifying Adam as "the son of God" (v. 38), which contributes to Luke's focus on Jesus' divine sonship in this early portion of his Gospel. In the preceding baptism scene, God the Father says to Jesus, "You are my beloved Son; with you I am well pleased" (v. 22). At the beginning of the genealogy Luke provides an explanatory remark, noting that Joseph was *not* Jesus' true father (v. 23). In the immediately subsequent scene Satan twice questions whether or not Jesus is truly "the son of God" (4:3, 9). This broader contextual concern of establishing Jesus' divine sonship suggests that the phrase "the son of God" is the key element in Luke's genealogy. Just as the first Adam was "the son of God," so is Jesus, the last Adam, also "the son of God."[4]

John similarly begins his Gospel with creation overtones: "*In the beginning (en archē)* was the Word, and the Word was with God, and the Word was God" (1:1). This opening alludes to Gen 1:1: "*In the beginning (en archē)* God created the heavens and the earth" (Gen 1:1). Not only does this allusion recall the first creation account and thereby present John's Gospel as a new creation account, it does so by identifying Jesus as the agent of creation. Concerning "the Word," John tells us that "all things were made through him" (v. 3) and that "the Word became flesh and dwelt among us" (v. 14). In the creation account of Genesis, God creates humanity and commissions them to carry out his mission; in this new creation account, God himself becomes human in order to redeem his people and their mission. In this way, in the new creation era Jesus fulfills the role that Adam was called to fulfill in the old creation era.[5]

The Epistles: Jesus as Last Adam by Explication

While the Gospel writers teach implicitly about Jesus' Adamic identity, the apostle Paul makes it explicit. In Romans 5 Paul begins by rejoicing in the divine reconciliation that believers receive through the atoning death of Jesus (vv. 1–11). He then provides a series of contrasts between the judgment that Adam's disobedience brought for all humanity and the gracious gift of

---

4. Robert O'Toole does not see the genealogical focus on Jesus as "the son of God" as supporting an Adam-like depiction here (*Luke's Presentation of Jesus*, 10). Yet because Adam is introduced as "the son of God" (3:38), and Jesus is similarly portrayed as "the son of God" (3:22; 4:3–4, 9–12), this focus on Jesus' divine sonship naturally presents him as an Adam-like figure.

5. Space prohibits further discussion of the various ways the Gospel writers portray Jesus in Adamic terms. For a full-length study see Crowe, *Last Adam*.

righteousness that Jesus' obedience brings. Paul says that "sin came into the world through one man, and death through sin, and so death spread to all men because all sinned" (v. 12). This "one man," of course, was Adam, whom Paul later names and describes as "a type of the one who was to come" (v. 14), that is, Jesus. The following verses then systematically contrast these two representative figures and the results of their respective actions:

¹⁵ But the free gift is not like the trespass.
  For
    if many died through one man's trespass,
   much more have
    the grace of God
    and *the free gift*
      by the grace of that one man Jesus Christ
      abounded for many.
¹⁶ And the free gift is not like the result of that one man's sin.
  For
    the judgment following one trespass brought condemnation,
   but *the free gift* following many trespasses brought **justification**.
¹⁷ For
    if, because of one man's trespass, death reigned through that one man,
   much more will those who receive
     the abundance of grace
     and *the free gift* of **righteousness**
   reign in life through the one man Jesus Christ.
¹⁸ Therefore,
   as one trespass led to condemnation for all men,
   so one act of righteousness leads to **justification** and life for all men.
¹⁹ For
    as by the one man's disobedience the many were made sinners,
   so by the one man's obedience the many will be made **righteous**.

As this layout makes clear, Paul uses Adam's disobedience and its deathly consequences five times (the dotted boxes) as a base against which to contrast Jesus' obedience and its justifying effects (the solid boxes). As federal head of all humanity Adam brought condemnation to all his posterity (vv. 16, 18), since in him we were all regarded as sinners (v. 19). Yet, as federal head of a new humanity, Jesus obeys and in so doing acquires righteousness for all his posterity. In four of these five contrasts Paul uses some form of "righteous(ness) / justification" to describe the free gift of Christ as he takes the representative role formerly held by Adam.[6] Because of Jesus' obedience, those who are "in him" are counted as righteous.

---

6. "Justification" (*dikaiōma*; vv. 16, 18); "righteousness" (*dikaiosynē*; vv. 17, 21); and "righteous" (*dikaios*; v. 19).

In 1 Corinthians 15 Paul makes a similar contrast with a different focus. In Romans 5 Paul contrasts the death brought by Adam with the *justification* brought by Jesus. In 1 Corinthians 15 he contrasts the death brought by Adam with the *resurrection* brought by Jesus. In verses 1–11 Paul catalogues those to whom Jesus appeared after he was raised from the dead, and in verses 12–19 he exposes the theological conundrum that arises for those who claim that the dead cannot be raised. In verse 20 he argues that Christ has indeed been raised as the firstfruits of the general resurrection, and then in verses 21–22 he supports this claim by contrasting Christ with Adam: "For as by a man came death, by a man has come also the resurrection of the dead. For as in Adam all die, so also in Christ shall all be made alive." As was the case in Romans 5, here Paul uses Adam as a foil to highlight Christ's success. Due to these parallel roles that Adam and Christ play, it is natural for Paul to refer to Jesus as "the last Adam" (v. 45).

This brief analysis reveals that both the Gospels and the Epistles present Jesus as fulfilling the role that God called Adam to fulfill. However, whereas Adam disobeyed and forfeited his role as God's representative on the earth, Jesus succeeds through faithful obedience and thereby brings righteousness and final resurrection for those who identify with him through faith.

JESUS AS TRUE ISRAEL

In addition to depicting Jesus as the last Adam, the New Testament presents him as the faithful embodiment of Old Testament Israel. This is most apparent in the Gospel of Matthew, which through a variety of ways in its opening chapters portrays Jesus as reliving the formative period of Israel's history.

First, after alluding to Genesis in his opening clause, Matthew introduces Jesus as "the son of David, the son of Abraham" (1:1). The genealogy that follows begins with Abraham and traces his lineage all the way down to Jesus, thereby demonstrating Jesus' Israelite heritage. This introduction paves the way for Jesus to be portrayed as the faithful descendant of Abraham, the role that Israel was supposed to fulfill but failed to execute.

Second, like Israel, Jesus is taken into and out of Egypt. In Matthew 2, after the magi come to visit Jesus, an angel warns Joseph about Herod's plot to kill Jesus and tells him to take his family down to Egypt (v. 13). Joseph complies and stays in Egypt until Herod dies (vv. 14–15a), a course of events to which Matthew ascribes biblical-theological significance: "This was to fulfill what the Lord had spoken by the prophet, 'Out of Egypt I called my son'" (v. 15b). Here Matthew quotes Hos 11:1, which is not a predictive prophecy but a historical recollection of Israel's exodus from Egypt during the time of Moses:

> When Israel was a child, I loved him,
> and out of Egypt I called my son.

The fact that Matthew claims that Jesus' exodus "fulfills" this passage has created no shortage of objections from scholars who argue that Matthew violates Hosea's apparent lack of prospective focus here.[7] However, a simple and explicit "prediction-fulfillment" schema is not the only manner by which Old Testament phenomena are fulfilled in the New Testament. As we have just seen, Jesus fulfills the role that Adam was given, even though no Old Testament writer predicted a "new Adam," and no New Testament writer explicitly uses the verb "fulfill" to describe Jesus' Adamic role. As noted above, Paul says that Adam was "a type (*typos*) of the one who was to come" (Rom 5:15); that is, Adam provided a *pattern* that Jesus fulfills.[8] Since Israel had the same royal-priestly representative role that Adam had, it is unsurprising that Jesus is portrayed as fulfilling Israel's role in such a "typical" or "patterning" manner as well. Therefore, even if Hosea were only referencing Israel in the past,[9] by fulfilling Israel's pattern Jesus legitimately fulfills Hos 11:1, not as a prediction but as a historical reference. That is, Hosea refers to Israel's exodus from Egypt in the past, a pattern that Jesus fulfills as the true embodiment of Israel.

Reinforcing this understanding is the third major element in Matthew's depiction of Jesus: his baptism. After coming up from Egypt and relocating to Galilee (Matt 2:19–23), Jesus is portrayed next as a grown man coming to be baptized by John. Initially John refuses, but Jesus responds by saying, "Let it be so now, for thus it is fitting for us to fulfill all righteousness" (Matt 3:15). Just as Jesus' exodus from Egypt was designed to "fulfill" (*plēroō*) the word of Hosea, so his baptism is to "fulfill (*plēroō*) all righteousness." But whose righteousness is Jesus fulfilling? Elsewhere Matthew uses the verb *plēroō* almost exclusively to describe Jesus "fulfilling" various aspects of the Old Testament.[10] In the present context, therefore, it seems best to under-

---

7. For example, Enns writes, "It would take a tremendous amount of mental energy to argue that Matthew is respecting the historical context of Hosea's words, that is, that there is actually something predictive in Hosea 11" (*Inspiration and Incarnation*, 133).

8. See the NIV at Rom 5:14, which says that Adam "was a *pattern* of the one to come."

9. For a compelling argument that the broader context of Hosea allows for a future fulfillment of Hos 11:1, see Beale, "Use of Hosea 11:1 in Matthew 2:15," 697–715.

10. Matt 1:22; 2:15, 17, 23; 4:14; 5:17; 8:17; 12:17; 13:35; 21:4; 26:54, 56; 27:9. The only exceptions are 13:48 and 23:32, which both use *plēroō* in the sense of "fill up," not

stand Jesus as fulfilling the righteousness that Israel was called to pursue but failed to achieve.

Supporting this is the fact that (1) in the previous chapter Matthew has just compared Jesus' exodus to Israel's exodus; (2) immediately after this baptism the divine voice from heaven describes Jesus as his "son" (3:17), which corresponds to Israel's identity as God's "son" during the exodus (Exod 4:22–23), a connection that Matthew has also just made (2:15; cf. Hos 11:1); and (3) in the next scene Jesus will continue to identify with Israel as he faces temptation in the wilderness (4:1–11). Indeed, since this baptism falls between Jesus' leaving Egypt and spending forty days in the wilderness, the closest Old Testament narrative parallel to this watery event is Israel's passing through the Red Sea.[11] Further reinforcing this is Paul's description of the Red Sea crossing as a "baptism": "For I do not want you to be unaware, brothers, that our fathers were all under the cloud, and all passed through the sea, and all were *baptized* into Moses in the cloud and *in the sea*" (1 Cor 10:1–2). Therefore both Israel and Jesus are brought out of Egypt as a "son," pass through the waters of a "baptism," after which they each spend a season in the wilderness measured by the number "forty"— forty years for Israel and forty days for Jesus.

However, as Paul goes on to say concerning Israel, "Nevertheless, with most of them God was not *pleased* (*eudokeō*), for they were overthrown in the wilderness" (v. 5). This divine disapproval of Israel contrasts sharply with God's positive assessment of Jesus after his baptism: "This is my beloved Son, with whom I am well *pleased* (*eudokeō*)" (Matt 3:17). Due to Israel's unrepentant sin and rebellion, God was not pleased with them; yet because of Jesus' commitment to faithful obedience and righteousness, God is pleased with him.

Fourth, as already mentioned, after passing through the waters of baptism, like Israel, Jesus is taken into the wilderness (Matt 4:1–11). It is clear that Jesus' "forty days" in the wilderness are a compressed reenactment of Israel's "forty years" in the wilderness.[12] Yet while Israel was repeatedly unfaithful during their wilderness wanderings, Jesus is perfectly faithful. This is underscored by comparing Jesus' temptations to the corresponding events in Israel's history. For each of Jesus' three wilderness trials, the following tables provide (1) Satan's temptation, (2) Jesus' Deuteronomic response, (3) the quoted passage in Deuteronomy, and (4) the event in Israel's history to

---

"fulfill."

11. So also McDonnell, *Baptism of Jesus*, 74; Beale, *New Testament Biblical Theology*, 412.

12. See, e.g., France, *Matthew*, 128; Turner, *Matthew*, 126; Hare, *Matthew*, 24.

which the Deuteronomic passage refers. In each case I have italicized Jesus' quotation of Deuteronomy and the corresponding Deuteronomic source text, and I have underlined the historical recollection in that Deuteronomic passage as well as the corresponding reference in Israel's historical account.

Table 6. Jesus' First Temptation (Matt 4:3–4)

Satan's Temptation	Jesus' Response
"And the tempter came and said to him, 'If you are the Son of God, command these stones to become loaves of bread'" (Matt 4:3).	"But he answered, 'It is written, "*Man shall not live by bread alone, but by every word that comes from the mouth of God*"'" (Matt 4:4).
Israel's Corresponding Event	**Deuteronomy's Recollection**
"From Mount Hor they set out by the way to the Red Sea, to go around the land of Edom. And the people became impatient on the way. And the people spoke against God and against Moses, 'Why have you brought us up out of Egypt to die in the wilderness? <u>For there is no food and no water, and we loathe this worthless food</u> [i.e., manna]'" (Num 21:4–5).	"And you shall remember the whole way that the LORD your God has led you these forty years in the wilderness, that he might humble you, testing you to know what was in your heart, whether you would keep his commandments or not. <u>And he humbled you and let you hunger and fed you with manna</u>, which you did not know, nor did your fathers know, that he might make you know that *man does not live by bread alone, but man lives by every word that comes from the mouth of the LORD*" (8:2–3).

Table 7. Jesus' Second Temptation (Matt 4:5–7)

Satan's Temptation	Jesus' Response
"Then the devil took him to the holy city and set him on the pinnacle of the temple and said to him, 'If you are the Son of God, throw yourself down, for it is written, "He will command his angels concerning you," and "On their hands they will bear you up, lest you strike your foot against a stone"'" (Matt 4:5–6).	"Jesus said to him, 'Again it is written, "*You shall not put the Lord your God to the test*" (Matt 4:7).

Israel's Corresponding Event	Deuteronomy's Recollection
"All the congregation of the people of Israel moved on from the wilderness of Sin by stages, according to the commandment of the LORD, and camped at Rephidim, but there was no water for the people to drink. Therefore the people quarreled with Moses and said, 'Give us water to drink.' And Moses said to them, 'Why do you quarrel with me? Why do you test the LORD?' . . . And he called the name of the place Massah and Meribah because of the quarreling of the people of Israel, and because they tested the LORD by saying, 'Is the LORD among us or not?'" (Exod 17:1–2, 7).	"*You shall not put the LORD your God to the test*, as you tested him at Massah" (6:16).

Table 8. Jesus' Third Temptation (Matt 4:8–10)

Satan's Temptation	Jesus' Response
"Again, the devil took him to a very high mountain and showed him all the kingdoms of the world and their glory. And he said to him, 'All these I will give you, if you will fall down and worship me'" (Matt 4:8–9).	"Then Jesus said to him, 'Be gone, Satan! For it is written, *"You shall worship the Lord your God and him only shall you serve"*'" (Matt 4:10).
Israel's Corresponding Event	**Deuteronomy's Recollection**
"While Israel lived in Shittim, the people began to whore with the daughters of Moab. These invited the people to the sacrifices of their gods, and the people ate and bowed down to their gods. So Israel yoked himself to Baal of Peor. And the anger of the LORD was kindled against Israel" (Num 25 1–3).	"*It is the LORD your God you shall fear. Him you shall serve* and by his name you shall swear. You shall not go after other gods, the gods of the peoples who are around you—for the LORD your God in your midst is a jealous God—lest the anger of the LORD your God be kindled against you, and he destroy you from off the face of the earth" (6:13–15).

When we examined the fall of humanity, we saw that both the serpent and Eve misquoted God's word. In contrast, in each of these temptations Jesus responds to Satan by quoting God's word accurately. In each case, the passage in Deuteronomy that Jesus quotes either clearly refers or alludes to a failure on Israel's part to live faithfully before God. As the true embodiment of Israel, however, Jesus lives faithfully before God and therefore passes the test that Israel failed. In so doing, Jesus demonstrates the righteousness that he declared necessary at his baptism.[13]

Collectively, this sequence of narratives in the opening chapters of Matthew portrays Jesus as reliving the formative period of Israel's life. Yet in contrast to Israel, who was unfaithful to God and therefore ineffective in their mission, Jesus proves to be faithful, which will enable him to rule as King over God's people.

JESUS AS SUFFERING SERVANT

In order to rule over God's people, Jesus must first fulfill the role of the suffering servant and die on their behalf. In the Old Testament, both Adam and Israel failed to fulfill their mission because of their sin. This pattern of sin and missional failure reveals that for the mission of God's people to be successful, God himself must intervene and enable his people to obey. In Ezekiel God promised to do just that: to pour out his Spirit in a way that would enable his people to obey his word (Ezek 36:27). Yet just as Moses had to make atonement by a burnt offering (Exod 40:29) before God's glory entered the tabernacle (Exod 40:34–38), so Jesus must make atonement for God's people before the Spirit will fill them with power so they may accomplish their mission. Jesus does this by fulfilling Isaiah's prophecy of the suffering servant.

In the opening of Matthew's Gospel, an angel appears to Joseph and tells him to name Mary's son "Jesus, for he will save his people from their sins" (Matt 1:21). At various points the New Testament writers identify this saving ministry of Jesus as a fulfillment of Isaiah's fourth servant song. After Jesus drives out demons and heals the sick, Matthew says, "This was to fulfill what was spoken by the prophet Isaiah: 'He took our illnesses and bore our diseases'" (Matt 8:17; cf. Isa 53:4). In anticipation of his upcoming passion, Jesus quotes Isa 53:12 and declares that it finds fulfillment in him: "And he was numbered with the transgressors" (Luke 22:37). After Jesus' resurrection, as the Ethiopian eunuch is reading Isa 53:7–8, Philip starts with that text and explains the good news of Jesus to him (Acts 8:32–35). In a somewhat different use, Peter uses Jesus' role as the suffering servant as a model to exhort his readers toward appropriate ethics in the face of mistreatment (1 Pet 2:21–25).[14]

---

13. Leim, *Matthew's Theological Grammar*, 69.

14. Jobes observes that the emphasis in Peter's use of Isaiah 53 is on Jesus' appropriate speech in the face of trial (*1 Peter*, 196).

These references to Isaiah's suffering servant have various applications in their different contexts, though all of them have one thing in common: they all identify Jesus as the climactic fulfillment of this prophecy.[15] As we saw in chapter 5, originally the servant was Israel, who was called to be "a light for the nations" (Isa 42:6). However, because of Israel's blindness and sin, God needed to raise up another servant to restore them (Isa 49:5). This redemptive servant would also receive the charge to serve as "a light for the nations" (v. 6), and as the fourth servant song makes clear, this latter servant would restore Israel through suffering. All of this indicates that Jesus' restoration of God's people through his suffering is for the purpose of mobilizing them for mission. When exploring the fall of humanity in chapter 2, we saw that humanity's sin resulted in a frustrated ability to carry out our mission. This set the context for redemption to be viewed not simply as reconciliation with God but also as a restoration of our ability to execute our mission. In Jesus we see this reconciliation and missional restoration become a reality.

In line with this, one other allusion to Isaiah's servant songs explicitly connects Jesus' work of salvation with his mobilizing his people for mission. Shortly after Jesus' birth, Joseph and Mary bring him to the temple to redeem him as their firstborn son according to the Torah (Luke 2:22–24). The Holy Spirit had revealed to a man named Simeon that he would not die before he saw the messiah. When Simeon sees Jesus at the temple, he takes him and blesses God, saying,

> Lord, now you are letting your servant depart in peace,
>   according to your word;
> for my eyes have seen
>   *your salvation*
>   that you have prepared in the presence of all peoples,
>   *a light for revelation to the Gentiles,*
>   and for glory to your people Israel. (vv. 29–32)

The phrase "a light for revelation to the Gentiles" (*phōs eis apokalypsin ethnōn*; v. 32) alludes to Isa 42:6 and 49:6, where the servant is said to be "a light for the nations" (*phōs ethnōn*).[16] Syntactically this allusive phrase is in apposition with the phrase "your salvation" in verse 30,[17] and therefore the

---

15. Beyond these explicit references that I have surveyed, the New Testament refers to Isaiah's suffering servant in other contexts and through more subtle allusions. For several more references see Chisholm, "Christological Fulfillment of Isaiah's Servant Songs," 392.

16. Evans, "Light to the Nations," 96.

17. Green, *Gospel of Luke*, 148.

salvation that Jesus brings is further explained here in terms of the servant's international mission in Isaiah. Salvation and mission are so intertwined that they can be described in terms of one another. As suffering servant, Jesus will "raise up the tribes of Jacob" and "bring back the preserved of Israel" (Isa 49:6) in order that they might take up their calling as "a light for the nations" (Isa 42:6). This underscores what the preceding analysis has revealed at several points: the reconciliation that Jesus' sacrifice achieves is not an end in itself; rather, it is the means that God uses to recall rebellious images and reconstitute them as his missional representatives.

JESUS AS RIGHTEOUS DAVIDIC KING

After atoning for the sins of his people and rising from the grave, Jesus is exalted as their righteous Davidic King. In chapter 4 we explored God's covenant promise to David of an everlasting dynasty and worldwide kingdom. In chapter 5 we saw how later Davidic kings did not lead God's people faithfully, which resulted in missional failure. We then surveyed how the prophets anticipated a time when God would provide faithful Davidic leadership for his people. This leadership would enable God's people to engage in their mission effectively, which would result in the fulfillment of the creation mandate (see Jer 3:15–17; 23:1–6). The New Testament presents Jesus as this faithful, righteous heir of God's covenant promises to David, the one who will fully and finally lead God's people in fulfilling their mission.

From the outset, the New Testament emphasizes Jesus' Davidic lineage. In his genealogy Matthew identifies Jesus as "the son of David, the son of Abraham" (Matt 1:1). In his opening narratives Luke mentions twice that Jesus' earthly father, Joseph, is of the house of David (Luke 1:27; 2:4). Before Jesus is conceived, the angel Gabriel tells Mary, "the Lord God will give to him the throne of his father David, and he will reign over the house of Jacob forever, and of his kingdom there will be no end" (Luke 1:32–33). Throughout his earthly ministry Jesus is repeatedly referred to as the "son of David,"[18] and later New Testament books refer to him as "descended from David according to the flesh" (Rom 1:3), "the offspring of David" (2 Tim 2:8), "the Root of David" (Rev 5:5), and "the root and descendant of David" (Rev 22:16). These references make it clear that Jesus has the right ancestry for taking up God's kingdom promises to David.

But when does Jesus actually begin to reign as the righteous Davidic King? During his earthly ministry Jesus consistently refers to his reign as a future reality. It is "in the new world, when the Son of Man will sit on

---

18. Matt 9:27; 12:23; 15:22; 20:30; 21:9, 15; Mark 10:47; Luke 18:36.

his glorious throne" (Matt 19:28). It is "when the Son of Man comes in his glory" that "he will sit on his glorious throne" (Matt 25:31). In all three synoptic Gospels, during his trial Jesus declares his imminent ascension to the "right hand of power" (Matt 26:64, Mark 14:62, Luke 22:69). These texts all anticipate Jesus' resurrection and ascension, which is the pivotal point at which he begins to reign as the righteous Davidic King.

This connection between Jesus' resurrection and his ascension to the throne of David is made explicit in the book of Acts. In his Pentecost sermon, Peter quotes Ps 16:8–11 to support the biblical legitimacy of Jesus' death and resurrection (Acts 2:22–28). Peter goes on to state that David was

> a prophet, and knowing that God had sworn with an oath to him that he would set one of his descendants on his throne, he foresaw and spoke about the resurrection of the Christ, that he was not abandoned to Hades, nor did his flesh see corruption. (vv. 30–31)

Peter directly correlates the promise that one of David's descendants would accede to his throne with Jesus' resurrection from the dead. It is at this point, after Jesus has died and risen, that "God has made him both Lord *and Christ*" (v. 36); that is, the anointed Davidic King.[19]

While preaching in Pisidian Antioch, the apostle Paul similarly connects Jesus' resurrection with his coronation as the Davidic King. After recalling Jesus' death and resurrection, Paul says,

> And we bring you the good news that what God promised to the fathers, this he has fulfilled to us their children by raising Jesus, as also it is written in the second Psalm,
> "You are my Son,
>   today I have begotten you."
> And as for the fact that he raised him from the dead, no more to return to corruption, he has spoken in this way,
> "I will give you the holy and sure blessings of David."
> Therefore he says also in another psalm,
> "You will not let your Holy One see corruption." (Acts 13:32–35)

Paul unleashes this constellation of Old Testament quotations to demonstrate the biblical validity of Jesus' resurrection. He accomplishes this by appealing to three texts that relate directly to David's kingship. The first quotation is taken from Ps 2:7, which is a coronation psalm celebrating the establishment of the Davidic dynasty. God's decree to David, "You are

---

19. For further discussion on this allusion, see Bock, *Acts*, 127–29.

my Son; today I have begotten you," recalls his promise concerning David's descendant in 2 Sam 7:14: "I will be to him a father, and he shall be to me a son."[20] In the context of 2 Samuel 7, this filial language is followed by God's promise to David that "your house and your kingdom shall be made sure forever before me. Your throne shall be established forever" (v. 16). The similar filial language of Psalm 2 is followed by God's promise to deliver "the nations" and "the ends of the earth" to the Davidic king as a heritage and possession (vv. 8–9). Taken together, the imagery in these texts that describe the relationship between God and the Davidic king emphasizes both the *everlasting nature* and *worldwide scope* of the latter's reign. Significantly, Paul identifies the fulfillment of this filial declaration of Ps 2:7 in Jesus' resurrection. When Jesus is raised from the dead, he receives these coronation promises given to David precisely because his resurrection functions as his coronation to the eschatological Davidic throne.

Paul's second quotation, "I will give you the holy and sure blessings of David" (Acts 13:34), comes from the LXX of Isa 55:3.[21] In Isaiah, these "blessings" are grammatically parallel to God's offer to make "an everlasting covenant" with Israel should they turn back to him.[22] This description therefore recalls God's promise to David of an everlasting and worldwide dynasty. Once again, Paul locates the fulfillment of this promise in Jesus' resurrection. By rising from the dead as the righteous descendant of David, Jesus inherits "the holy and sure blessings of David": a kingdom that will encompass the entire world and will never end.[23]

Finally, like Peter, Paul quotes Ps 16:10 to bolster his case for Jesus' resurrection. As we saw above, Peter understood David's description of God preserving the Holy One from corruption to refer to Jesus' resurrection and accession to the Davidic throne. This earlier apostolic interpretation, as well as Paul's immediate association of Ps 16:10 with Isa 55:3, suggests that this understanding of Jesus' resurrection is present here as well.

In line with these sermons in Acts, the writer of Hebrews connects Jesus' resurrection and ascension with his inaugurated reign as Davidic king. The writer opens by lauding Jesus as God's latter-day prophet who created and sustains the world (Heb 1:1–3a). He then says:

---

20. As we will see below, the writer of Hebrews directly correlates Ps 2:7 with 2 Sam 7:14 (Heb 1:5). See also Ross, *Psalms: Volume 1*, 207.

21. Isaiah 55:3 (LXX): "*ta hosia Dauid ta pista*"; Acts 13:34: "*dōsō hymin ta hosia Dauid ta pista.*"

22. Paul, *Isaiah 40–66*, 434–35.

23. See also Schnabel, *Paul the Missionary*, 160.

After making purification for sins, he sat down at the right hand of the Majesty on high, having become as much superior to angels as the name he has inherited is more excellent than theirs.

For to which of the angels did God ever say,
> "You are my Son,
>> today I have begotten you"?

Or again,
> "I will be to him a father,
>> and he shall be to me a son"? (vv. 3b–5)

This passage describes the two-step process we have seen throughout the current and previous sections of this study. First, Jesus makes purification for sins through his death as the suffering servant. Second, after making this purification, Jesus sits down at the right hand of the Majesty on high through his resurrection and ascension. The writer then emphasizes Jesus' superiority over the angels by quoting Ps 2:7 and 2 Sam 7:14. As we have already seen, these two texts describe the coronation of the Davidic king and God's covenantal promise of his everlasting and worldwide reign.

This survey of texts shows that Jesus' resurrection functions as his coronation to the throne of David with its attendant promises of eternal and earth-wide dominion. Since the prophetic outlook on Israel's restoration foresaw that the rise of faithful Davidic leadership would enable God's people to fulfill the creation mandate, upon Jesus' enthronement we should expect to see a renewed missional vision and faithful execution of that mission by God's people. As we will see next chapter, the New Testament depicts the mission of the church in precisely these terms.

JESUS AS THE DANIELIC "SON OF MAN"

In addition to the righteous Davidic king, the Gospels present Jesus as the Danielic "Son of Man" who will receive the worshipful allegiance of all nations. In chapter 5 we saw how Dan 7:13–14 presents a divine-human "son of man" as "coming on the clouds of heaven" to the Ancient of Days and receiving eternal and earth-wide dominion over all nations. This ascension of the son of man is portrayed as the time when Israel's exile will come to an end and their mission will be fulfilled. Throughout the Gospels, Jesus consistently refers to himself as the "Son of Man,"[24] and although this phrase occurs in various contexts throughout the Old Testament, it is widely

---

24. E.g., Matt 8:20; 9:6; 10:23; 11:19; 12:8, 32, 40; 13:37, 41; 16:13, 27; 17:9, 12, 22; 19:28; 20:18, 28; 24:27, 30, 37, 39, 44; 25:31; 26:2, 24, 45, 64; Mark 2:10, 28; 8:31, 38; 9:9, 12, 31; 10:33, 45; 13:26; 14:21, 41, 62; et al.

accepted that Jesus' use alludes most directly to this apocalyptic figure in Dan 7:13–14.[25] The clearest evidence for this is found in Jesus' two references to the Son of Man "coming on/in/with the clouds (of heaven)," since Dan 7:13–14 is the only place in the Old Testament where this language occurs.

In all three synoptic accounts of the Olivet Discourse, Jesus describes an upcoming judgment in which the heavenly bodies will fail to produce their light, at which time the Son of Man will come on the clouds of heaven:

> Immediately after the tribulation of those days the sun will be darkened, and the moon will not give its light, and the stars will fall from heaven, and the powers of the heavens will be shaken. Then will appear in heaven the sign of the Son of Man, and then all the tribes of the earth will mourn, and they will see the Son of Man coming on the clouds of heaven with power and great glory. (Matt 24:29–30 [= Mark 13:24–25; Luke 21:25–27])

In popular interpretation, many assume that Jesus' "coming" in this passage refers to his second coming to earth at the final judgment. The prophetic imagery in this discourse, however, indicates that Jesus is referring to his "coming" to God at his ascension and the first-century destruction of Jerusalem. The description in verse 29 of the sun becoming darkened, the moon not giving its light, and the stars falling from heaven is standard Old Testament language used to describe God bringing judgment against a wicked nation.[26] In light of the initial conversation between Jesus and the disciples that gives rise to this discourse (Matt 24:1–3), the most natural referent for this cosmic imagery is the upcoming invasion of Jerusalem by the Romans that would result in the destruction of the temple.[27] At that time, Jesus says, "they will see the Son of Man coming on the clouds of heaven with power and great glory" (Matt 24:30 [= Mark 13:26; Luke 21:27]). Since Dan 7:13 clearly presents this "coming of the son of man" as a coming *to* the Ancient of Days in the heavenly realm, Jesus' use of this uniquely Danielic phrase is best understood as referring to his coming *to* God the Father at his ascension. Of course, Jesus' ascension occurred decades prior to Jerusalem's destruction in 70 AD, but this judgment on the city that crucified him would provide public vindication of his prophetic word and thereby enable his

---

25. For an examination of this issue, see Moloney, "*Constructing Jesus* and the Son of Man," 719–38.

26. Isaiah 13:9–10; 34:4–5; Ezek 32:7–8; Amos 8:9; Joel 2:10–11, 30–31; 3:14–16. See France, *Matthew*, 921–22.

27. See especially Luke's description, in which he specifies, "But when you see Jerusalem surrounded by armies, then know that its desolation has come near" (21:20).

followers to recognize more fully his status as the ascended Danielic Son of Man.

Furthermore, as the Danielic Son of Man, Jesus receives "dominion and glory and a kingdom" (Dan 7:13), which the Gospel writers describe as "power and great glory." And just as Daniel describes the son of man receiving a kingdom "that all peoples, nations, and languages should serve him" (Dan 7:14), in both Matthew and Mark, Jesus states that after the Son of Man receives his power and glory "he will send out his angels with a loud trumpet call, and they will gather his elect from the four winds, from one end of heaven to the other" (Matt 24:31 [= Mark 13:27]). This gathering of the elect from the four winds corresponds to Daniel's description of international submission to the Son of Man, and therefore upon Jesus' ascension the mission of Israel begins fulfillment as this divine-human king executes his worldwide dominion from his heavenly throne.

Similarly, in both Matthew and Mark's accounts of Jesus' trial, when the high priest asks Jesus if he is the Messiah and the Son of God, Jesus replies, "You have said so. But I tell you, from now on you will see the Son of Man seated at the right hand of Power and coming on the clouds of heaven" (Matt 26:64 [= Mark 14:62]; cf. Luke 22:69). Here Jesus associates his "coming on the clouds of heaven" with his being "seated at the right hand of Power," which, like the imagery in the Olivet Discourse, agrees with Daniel's vision of the Son of Man coming "with the clouds of heaven" and receiving "dominion and glory and a kingdom that all peoples, nations, and languages should serve him" (Dan 7:13). Since Daniel depicts the Son of Man as a divine-human figure, it is no surprise that the unbelieving high priest interprets Jesus' answer as blasphemy and the whole council renders a judgment of capital punishment against him (Matt 26:65–66; Mark 14:63–64).[28]

These texts sufficiently demonstrate the Danielic character of Jesus' use of "Son of Man" to refer to himself. As the Son of Man, Jesus' ascension marks the end of Israel's exile and the inaugurated fulfillment of Israel's mission among the nations. As a divine-human king, Jesus rightfully deserves the worshipful allegiance of the nations, to whom he will send his followers to make disciples after his resurrection. Moreover, the eternal and worldwide nature of the Son of Man's reign coheres with the portrayal of Jesus as the eschatological Davidic king who inherits God's promises of an eternal and worldwide dominion. Upon his resurrection and ascension, therefore, Jesus fulfills the roles of both the righteous Davidic king and the Danielic Son of Man, both of which are depicted as prerequisites to the successful execution of the mission of God's people.

28. See also the discussion of Leim, "In the Glory of His Father," 228–31.

JESUS AS ESCHATOLOGICAL TEMPLE

The final aspect of Old Testament mission that Jesus fulfills is the temple. As we have seen, in Israel's missional economy the temple was designed to function as the rallying point for the nations to come, submit to God, and worship him as King. Solomon prayed that God would respond positively to foreigners who sought him at the temple, and the prophets looked forward to a time when the nations would come, bring sacrifices, and be accepted by God there. In a variety of ways, the New Testament presents Jesus as the eschatological temple—the latter-day presence of God on earth—and therefore portrays him as fulfilling the missional role of the temple.

First, in the prologue of the Fourth Gospel, John introduces Jesus as "the Word" (1:1), a term that Greek philosophers used to describe the rational principle that undergirds all reality and from which they believed humans receive reason. Yet as Carson points out, in light of John's heavy reliance upon the Old Testament throughout his Gospel, the phrase "the word of the LORD" in the Hebrew Scriptures is a better place to begin for understanding the significance of John's use.[29] In the Old Testament, among other functions, "the word of the LORD" is presented as the means by which God created (e.g., Ps 33:6; cf. Genesis 1). This understanding of "the word" as the agent of creation was prevalent in contemporary Jewish targumim[30] and appears immediately in John's narrative as well (1:2–3). However, John's depiction of the Word differs from this Hebrew background in one important respect: he describes this creative Word not only as divine ("the Word was God" [v. 1]) but also as human ("the Word became flesh" [v. 14]). Moreover, in describing the incarnation of this divine Word, John uses temple imagery, stating that the Word "tabernacled among us" (*eskēnōsen en hēmin*; v. 14 [author's translation]).[31] Since the temple was the place where God's heavenly presence intersected with creation, John is presenting Jesus as a living temple.[32]

Second, when Jesus and his disciples pull heads of grain to eat on the Sabbath, the Pharisees rebuke them (Matt 12:1–2). In response, Jesus notes that both David and the priests engaged in analogous activity at the

---

29. Carson, *John*, 115. Indeed, that John's very first clause ("In the beginning") alludes to Gen 1:1 provides immediate contextual rationale for looking to the Old Testament to understand Jesus as "the Word."

30. Coloe, *God Dwells With Us*, 21–23.

31. The verb *skēnoō* is related to the noun *skēnōma*, which means "tent" or "dwelling," and at points in the LXX refers to both the tabernacle (e.g., 1 Kgs 2:28; Ps 84:1 [LXX 83:2]) and the temple (e.g., Ps 132:5 [LXX 131:5]; Lam 2:6).

32. For further discussion see Kerr, *Temple of Jesus' Body*, 122–23.

tabernacle/temple (vv. 3–5), and then makes the startling claim: "I tell you, 'something greater than the temple is here'" (v. 6). Although Jesus' assertion is somewhat veiled at this point (he says, "some*thing* greater than the temple" rather than "some*one* greater"), his subsequent statement—"something greater than Jonah is here" (v. 41)—is uttered after explicitly comparing his upcoming three-day sojourn in the grave with Jonah's three-day sojourn in the fish (v. 40).[33] The clarity of this parallel statement provides contextual evidence that Jesus understands himself to be the "something" that is greater than the temple in verse 6. Consequently, through this claim Jesus implies that he embodies that which the Old Testament temple signified: God's special presence on earth.

Third, all four Gospels provide an account of Jesus cleansing the temple due to misuse.[34] In each case, Jesus enters the temple, sees it functioning as a marketplace rather than a house of worship, and turns over tables and drives out moneychangers. As Beale notes, this cleansing may foreshadow Jesus' replacement of the old temple with the new temple of his body.[35] Supporting this is what Jesus says at the end of the cleansing account in John. After Jesus ruins the temple commerce, the Jews ask him, "What sign do you show us for doing these things?" (John 2:18). Jesus replies, "Destroy this temple, and in three days I will raise it up" (v. 19). Although no one understands the significance of this statement at the time, two verses later John tells us that "he was speaking about the temple of his body" (v. 21). As the eschatological temple of God on earth, Jesus rightfully rebukes the misuse and abuse of the penultimate temple.

Furthermore, the Synoptic Gospels each portray Jesus as supporting this temple cleansing by appealing to Isa 56:7 and Jer 7:11:

> It is written, "My house shall be called a house of prayer," but you make it a den of robbers. (Matt 21:12)

> Is it not written, "My house shall be called a house of prayer for all the nations"? But you have made it a den of robbers. (Mark 11:17)

> It is written, "My house shall be a house of prayer," but you have made it a den of robbers. (Luke 19:45)

In all three accounts, Jesus uses Isa 56:7 to describe the proper function of the temple. In chapter 4 we examined the larger passage within which this

---

33. See also Jesus' claim in verse 42 that "something greater than Solomon is here," though as was the case in verse 6, that Jesus himself is the referent here is only implied.

34. Matt 21:12–13; Mark 11:15–17; Luke 19:45–46; John 2:14–21.

35. Beale, *Temple and the Church's Mission*, 179.

verse occurs as an example of the missional intention of the temple. According to Isaiah, God will draw those foreigners who love his name to his temple and will accept their prayer and worship there (Isa 56:6–7). Yet instead of using the temple this way—as a headquarters for the nations to come and worship—Israel has made it into a "den of robbers," a phrase that alludes to Jeremiah's condemnation of Israel's misuse of the temple just prior to the Babylonian exile. All of this shows that Jesus understood the international, missional design of the temple, and therefore when the temple of his body is destroyed and raised, he will fulfill this design of the temple in himself.

Finally, all three Synoptic Gospels describe the curtain of the temple tearing in two as Jesus breathes his last (Matt 27:50–51; Mark 15:37–38; Luke 23:45–46).[36] As a central element in the temple, the torn curtain foreshadows the destruction of the temple that will occur only a few decades later (cf. Matt 24:1–2). Supporting this is the cosmic significance of the temple vis-à-vis the cosmic upheaval that occurs during the tearing of the curtain. As Beale has highlighted, the architecture, vessels, and artwork of the temple portray it as a miniature version of the entire cosmos.[37] Therefore the upcoming destruction of the temple points forward to the eventual destruction of the world that will occur at the eschaton (2 Pet 3:10). At the same time, Matthew and Luke describe the tearing of the curtain as accompanied by an earthquake, rock-splitting, midday darkness, and bodily resurrections (Matt 27:51b–53; Luke 23:44–45a). This cosmic upheaval, which portrays both de-creation and re-creation, foreshadows the cosmic upheaval that will occur at the eschaton, which will also include both de-creation and re-creation.[38] Consequently, both the destruction of the temple and the cataclysmic events that accompany the curtain tearing point forward to the eschatological destruction and renewal of all things. For this reason, the tearing of the curtain is best understood as a proleptic sign of the temple's upcoming destruction and therefore is a substantial step in the process of God's earthly presence ceasing representation through the edificial temple.[39]

36. For a discussion concerning why Luke positions the curtain tearing just before Jesus dies, as opposed to Matthew and Mark, who position the curtain tearing just afterward, see Sylva, "Temple Curtain and Jesus' Death," 239–50.

37. Beale, *Temple and the Church's Mission*, 31–45.

38. E.g., 2 Pet 3:11–13; Rev 8:5, 12; 11:19; 16:10, 18. See also Bauckham, "Eschatological Earthquake," 224–33; Keener, *Matthew*, 685–87.

39. Stein argues that the curtain tearing does not suggest this, since the early church continued to worship at the temple (*Luke*, 596). However, it may be better to suggest that Jesus' death inaugurated this final judgment on the edificial temple, which was finalized by its destruction in 70 AD. In the intervening period, his followers may still have participated in certain temple functions, yet the manifestation of God's earthly

Taken together, these various texts indicate that the New Testament depicts Jesus as the eschatological temple of God. In the Old Testament, God dwelled with his people through the temple, the place where sacrifice was carried out so that sinful people could receive forgiveness and live in relationship with a holy God. The temple was also the location where the nations were called to come, submit to God as King, and receive his mercy and blessing. In the New Testament, God dwells with his people by becoming human and sacrificing himself on their behalf so that sinful people can receive full and final forgiveness and live in eternal relationship with God. Moreover, just as the temple was the rallying point for the nations in the Old Testament, in the New Testament it is Jesus, the eschatological temple, who is the rallying point for the nations. Jesus is the one to whom the nations must come, submit, and receive mercy and blessing.

SUMMARY

In this chapter we have seen how Jesus fulfills the major missional roles of the Old Testament. As the last Adam and true Israel, Jesus obeys where God's people had previously failed and acquires righteousness for them. As the suffering servant, Jesus is punished for the sins of his people and thereby secures forgiveness for them. In this process of saving, Jesus also restores and repositions his people to fulfill their Old Testament missional calling as a light for the nations. Upon his resurrection and ascension, Jesus takes his throne as the righteous Davidic King and Danielic Son of Man, the one who will lead God's people in faithfully carrying out their mission and receive the worshipful allegiance of the nations. As the eschatological temple, Jesus both manifests God's presence on the earth and serves as the centerpoint for the nations to come and submit to God. In all of these ways, Jesus redeems the mission of God's people, and by his power and righteousness as King of kings will ensure its fulfillment. The means by which Jesus will fulfill this mission is once again God's covenant people, now gathered and organized as the church. In the next chapter we will explore how Jesus reinstates the mission of God's people by sending the church to proclaim the good news of his kingship to the ends of the earth.

---

presence was nevertheless shifting from the edifice.

8 MISSION REINSTATED
The Call and Equipping of the Church

After redeeming God's people through his life, death, and resurrection, Jesus reinstates the mission of God's people by commissioning his followers to represent his kingship to the ends of the earth. Although many discussions of the church's call to missions begin at this stage of redemptive history, Jesus' various post-resurrection commissions cannot be adequately understood without the missional-theological framework that the preceding biblical material has provided. In this chapter we will examine how Jesus calls the church to its mission through these post-resurrection commissions, noting their similarities as well as the unique emphases that each contributes. We will then explore how Jesus equips the church for mission by pouring out the Holy Spirit at Pentecost. As we will see, the singular theme that appears in all four post-resurrection commissions is Jesus' ongoing presence with his followers through the Holy Spirit. I will argue that this distribution of God's presence at Pentecost, made possible by Jesus' death and resurrection, is what transforms God's people into the temple of God and shifts the mission of God's people from the centripetal pull of Israel's calling to the centrifugal movement of the church's witness. By giving his followers clear instructions and equipping them with his empowering presence, Jesus reinstates the mission of God's people and enables the church to succeed where Adam and Israel failed.

JESUS CALLS THE CHURCH TO MISSION

The Gospels of Matthew, Luke, John, and the first chapter of Acts all provide narratives of Jesus appearing to his disciples after his resurrection.[1] In these

---

1. Mark 16:9–20 does not appear in certain early New Testament manuscripts and

narratives Jesus commissions his followers to serve as his representatives to the ends of the earth, incorporating converts into the covenant community by proclaiming the need for repentance and faith and teaching them to obey all that he requires of them. In this section we will examine each of these post-resurrection commissions, highlight their major themes, and see how they collectively contribute to our understanding of the mission of God's people in the new covenant era.

Matthew 28:18–20: The Church's Mission and Jesus' Authority

As mentioned in chapter 1, by far the most famous of Jesus' post-resurrection commissions is found at the end of the Gospel of Matthew. Traditionally referred to as "the Great Commission," this text is often viewed as *the* fundamental grounds for the church's call to missions. While this passage is certainly significant and speaks directly to the need for Jesus' followers to proclaim the gospel to all nations, within the biblical-theological trajectory of mission we have traced so far, the implications of this commission are neither novel nor unexpected. As we have seen, since the initial expression of the creation mandate the mission of God's people has been to fill the earth as God's representatives and thereby demonstrate that his kingship extends over the entire earth. The Gospels have presented Jesus as fulfilling the various missional roles of the Old Testament, including those of the righteous Davidic King and the Danielic Son of Man. Both of these figures are royal in nature and receive eternal and earth-wide dominion, with the Son of Man also portrayed as divine.[2] In light of this depiction, it is unsurprising that upon his resurrection—which is presented as his coronation as the eschatological Davidic King—Jesus would command his followers to represent his kingship to the ends of the earth. Perhaps the only unexpected element in Jesus' commission is the charge for his followers to go out to the nations, since Israel's mission was centripetal in nature. However, although first-century Jews may not have anticipated such a modification in missional methodology, as we will see, from a biblical-theological perspective such a change is not unexpected in light of Jesus' work of redemption on the cross.

Among Jesus' post-resurrection commissions, the special emphasis of Matt 28:18–20 lies in its presentation of Jesus' *authority* as both the grounds and the goal of the mission of the church:

---

therefore its reliability is questionable. For this reason I will not incorporate this account into our consideration of Jesus' post-resurrection instructions.

2. See the discussion in chapter 5.

190 FILL THE EARTH

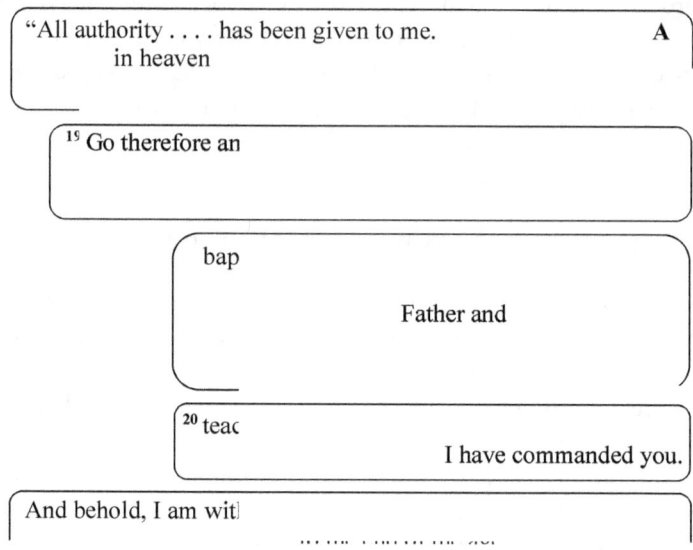

In section A, Jesus begins by explaining that he has received "all authority in heaven and on earth," and he does so by alluding to the reign of the Danielic Son of Man.[3] Jesus says that all "authority" (*exousia*) has "been given" (*edothē*) to him, and in section B he sends his followers to "all nations" (*panta ta ethnē*). Similarly, Dan 7:14 (LXX) says that "authority" (*exousia*) has "been given" (*edothē*) to the son of man in order that "all nations" (*panta ta ethnē*) should serve him. In Jesus' discourse, therefore, his authority over all creation as the Danielic Son of Man (section A) is presented as the grounds for his commissioning his followers to make disciples of all nations (section B). In chapter 1, I argued that a biblical motive for missions must be fundamentally theocentric rather than anthropocentric. Here in the most famous "missions" passage in the Bible, Jesus himself provides this theocentric grounding for the church's missionary call.[4] The church has a mission to all nations, not primarily because the nations are lost and destined for hell—though this is true and should be of great concern—but first and

---

3. Köstenberger and O'Brien, *Salvation to the Ends of the Earth*, 390.

4. I agree with Goheen's assessment that this commission is "not a *task* assigned to isolated *individuals*" but "an *identity* given to a *community*" (*Light to the Nations*, 115 [emphasis original]). For this reason, I refer to this commission as "the church's missionary call."

foremost because King Jesus has *authority* over all nations and therefore deserves their worship and allegiance.

This theme of authority also appears in Jesus' instructions for how his disciples are to carry out this mission. In section B, Jesus tells his followers to "go . . . and make disciples of all nations." It is occasionally suggested that since the English word "go" translates a Greek participle (*poreuthentes*), it could be rendered as "having gone" or "as you go."[5] On this reading, the act of "going" is incidental to the main imperative, "make disciples," and therefore some have concluded that Jesus is not actually commissioning his followers to "go" anywhere but to "make disciples" as they go about their daily lives.[6] Although the qualifying phrase "of all nations" would preserve the global scope of this commission, this reading removes the geographically proactive element of "going" in Jesus' command.

This interpretation, however, reflects a misunderstanding of the syntactic relationship between "go" (*poreuthentes*) and "make disciples" (*mathēteusate*). Although *poreuthentes* is a participle, the syntax of this clause suggests that it functions as a "participle of attendant circumstance," in which case the participle adopts the mood of the clause's finite verb. In other words, since the finite verb *mathēteusate* is an imperative, the participle *poreuthentes* receives an imperatival force as well. Daniel Wallace provides Matt 2:13 as an example of this participial function:[7]

> Now when they had departed, behold, an angel of the Lord appeared to Joseph in a dream and said, "Rise (*egertheis*), take (*paralabe*) the child and his mother, and flee to Egypt, and remain there until I tell you, for Herod is about to search for the child, to destroy him."

In this verse the angel first uses an aorist participle ("rise" [*egertheis*]), followed by an aorist imperative ("take" [*paralabe*]). Based on the context, the angel is clearly not telling Joseph to take Jesus and Mary to safety in Egypt "as he rises up." Rather, the angel is commanding Joseph to do two things: (1) rise, and (2) take Jesus and Mary to safety in Egypt. As a participle of attendant circumstance, *egertheis* assumes the imperative mood of the finite verb on which it depends. The primary action receiving focus in this syntactic arrangement is the finite verb, with the attendant participle functioning as a prerequisite to the main action (i.e., it is necessary for Joseph to "rise" before he "takes" the child to Egypt). Similarly, in Matt 28:19 an

---

5. See, e.g., Peters, *Biblical Theology of Missions*, 182–83; Wright, *Mission of God*, 354.

6. See, e.g., Hunter, *Who Broke My Church?*, 103.

7. Wallace, *Greek Grammar Beyond the Basics*, 641.

aorist participle of motion (*poreuthentes*) is in construction with an aorist imperative (*mathēteusate*), and therefore like Matt 2:13 it is best understood as a participle of attendant circumstance. According to Wallace, virtually all aorist participle + aorist imperative constructions in New Testament narrative function this way.[8] Consequently, in this commission Jesus is indeed commanding his followers both to "go" and "make disciples" of all nations,[9] though the command to "go" is viewed as logically prerequisite to the action of the finite verb, "make disciples."[10]

The next two sections explain what is involved in this disciple-making endeavor: it includes "baptizing them" (section C) and "teaching them" (section D). Trinitarian baptism is the sign and seal of membership in God's covenant community, and the teaching envisioned here is designed to equip these covenant members to acknowledge Jesus' kingship by submitting to his authority and "observing all that he has commanded."[11] In Matthew's articulation, therefore, the goal of the church's mission is to incorporate people from every ethnolinguistic group into God's covenant community and teach them to submit to Jesus' supreme authority by obeying his word.

As the preceding study has made clear, however, obedience to God's word has been a perennial struggle for God's people throughout the Bible. In chapter 2 we saw how Adam failed to obey God's word and therefore failed in his mission to represent God's kingship. In chapter 3 we examined how Genesis emphasizes the role that Abraham's obedience played in his reception of God's promise that the nations would be blessed through him. Similarly, in chapter 4 we explored how Israel's missional success depended on their obedience to God's word, and in chapter 5 we saw that, like Adam, Israel failed to obey God and therefore failed to fulfill their mission. In this post-resurrection commission, Jesus instructs his disciples to teach new followers to obey his word precisely because such obedience is necessary for the mission of God's people to succeed. However, in light of humanity's consistent failure to obey God throughout the Scriptural narrative, one may rightly wonder about the church's ability to execute this mission successfully. This concern illustrates the grand significance of Jesus' final statement

---

8. Wallace, *Greek Grammar Beyond the Basics*, 642n71.

9. I will discuss the signification of "all nations" (*panta ta ethnē*) below when considering Jesus' post-resurrection commission in Luke.

10. For further discussion of this grammar, see Köstenberger and O'Brien, *Salvation to the Ends of the Earth*, 103–4, especially 104n66.

11. At the end of Jesus' longest didactic discourse in this Gospel, Matthew explicitly associates Jesus' teaching with his *authority*: "And when Jesus finished these sayings, the crowds were astonished at his teaching, for he was teaching them as one who had authority, and not as their scribes" (Matt 7:28–29).

in this commission, in which he promises his followers that he will accompany them on their mission.

Jesus ends this commission in section E by saying, "And behold, I am with you always, to the end of the age." As R. T. France observes, "this assurance is focused not on the personal comfort of the individual disciple but on the successful completion of the mission entrusted to the community as a whole."[12] Although Matthew does not spell out specifically how Jesus will accompany his followers on their mission, subsequent post-resurrection commissions clarify that Jesus will accompany the church through the outpoured presence of the Holy Spirit.

Luke 24:44–49: The Church's Mission and the Proclamation of Repentance

Like Matthew, Luke closes his Gospel by recording a post-resurrection appearance of Jesus. In Luke's account, Jesus does not give his followers a missional command *per se*, but instead makes a missional observation based on a proper understanding of the Old Testament, and then commands his followers to *stay*:

[44] Then he said to them,

> "These are my words   A
>   that I spoke to you
>   while I was still with you,
>
>   that everything written about me ... must be fulfilled."
>   in the Law of Moses
>   and the Prophets
>   and the Psalms

[45] Then he opened their minds to understand the Scriptures, [46] and said to them,

> "Thus it is written,   B
>   that the Christ should suffer
>   and on the third day rise from the dead,
>   [47] and that repentance .... should be proclaimed
>   for the forgiveness of sins
>   in his name
>   to all nations,
>   beginning from Jerusalem.

> [48] You are witnesses of these things.   C

> [49] And behold, I am sending the promise of my Father upon you.   D
> But stay in the city until you are clothed with power from on high."

---

12. France, *Matthew*, 1119.

We examined this passage in chapter 1 when considering the missional character of the Old Testament. At this point it is instructive to make a few additional comments concerning this second post-resurrection commission. In section B, Jesus summarizes three elements in the Old Testament's witness: (1) the Christ will suffer; (2) the Christ will rise from the dead; and (3) repentance for the forgiveness of sins should be proclaimed. Whereas Matthew emphasizes baptism and teaching as core elements of the church's mission, Luke emphasizes the need for proclaiming *repentance* that leads to forgiveness.

To a certain degree, this emphasis on repentance is simply another facet of Matthew's emphasis on teaching. In chapter 4 we surveyed the critical role that the Torah played in Israel's mission. By faithfully obeying the Torah (i.e., God's *teaching*), Israel would receive God's blessing, the Abrahamic formula would ensue, and God's blessing would channel to the nations. In that discussion we observed that Torah faithfulness is not conceived as a rigid program of flawless obedience but rather as a repetitious lifestyle of repentant obedience. Israel was to endeavor to keep God's word, and when they failed to do so, they were to humble themselves, repent of their sin, and seek God's forgiveness through his provision of atonement in the sacrificial system. Israel's missional failure, therefore, was not due to their lack of perfection but rather to their protracted lack of repentance. Further, it must be emphasized that this requirement of repentance was *intrinsic* to the Torah. Avenues of atonement and forgiveness were built into the Torah precisely because failure on Israel's part was assumed. Therefore, to obey God's teaching in a faithful manner involved, among other things, acknowledging one's inability to obey him completely and one's need to repent and seek God's gracious forgiveness.[13]

In Luke's post-resurrection narrative, Jesus interprets the message of the Old Testament in precisely these terms, with it climaxing in the need to proclaim repentance that leads to forgiveness. However, now that the Christ has suffered and risen (v. 46) and atoned for sins completely, the forgiveness one receives upon repenting is no longer the temporary sort brought about by animal sacrifices but the permanent forgiveness achieved by the once-for-all sacrifice of Jesus. Of course, Old Testament believers were not ultimately justified on the basis of Levitical sacrifices but by the sacrifice of Christ to which those animal offerings pointed. Divine forgiveness in

---

13. For this reason, I am not persuaded by Harris's claim that "Matthew's mission is oriented towards incorporation into the Church's life, while Luke is more concerned with individual conversion" (*Mission in the Gospels*, 140). On the contrary, repentance is necessary not simply at the point of individual conversion but as a way of life for the covenant community as a whole.

the Old Testament was granted on the basis of the historically unrealized atonement of Christ, credited to those who exercised repentance and faith by virtue of God's forbearance in not punishing sin immediately (see Rom 3:25). But now that Jesus has come and provided final atonement for sin, his followers are to proclaim repentance for the forgiveness of sins "in his name, to all nations, beginning from Jerusalem" (v. 47).

That repentance should be proclaimed "in his name" indicates that this message is conveyed under Jesus' authority,[14] which coheres with Matthew's emphasis on Jesus' authority. Illustrating this, after Peter and John heal a crippled beggar at the temple in Acts 3, the Jewish leaders ask them, "By what power *or by what name* did you do this?" (Acts 4:7). By this question the leaders are asking by whose power *or authority* these seemingly ordinary men have acted in this extraordinary way.[15] In response, Peter declares that it is "by the name of Jesus Christ" that this man was healed (v. 10), and then goes on to connect this authority to heal with Jesus' authority to save: "there is salvation in no one else, for there is *no other name* under heaven given among men by which we must be saved" (v. 12). Since Jesus is the suffering servant who atoned for the sin of his people, the Davidic King who now leads them in righteousness, and the Danielic Son of Man who has received all authority, Jesus' name represents his authority to provide permanent forgiveness of sins to those who repent and submit to him.

That this repentance should be proclaimed "to all nations" reflects the international and worldwide scope of the church's mission. When surveying the call of Abram in chapter 3, we noted that God's promise to Abram—"in you all the *families* (*mišp^{e}ḥot̪*) of the earth shall be blessed" (Gen 12:3)—referred to God's redemptive blessing extending not simply to every geopolitical entity but to every ethnolinguistically distinct sub-group throughout the world. Similarly, the term Jesus uses in Matt 28:19 ("make disciples of all *nations* [*ethnē*]") and in Luke 24:47 ("to all *nations* [*ethnē*]") refers not to geopolitical entities but to "people groups" or "ethnic groups."[16] Just as the spread of the Abrahamic blessing to every tribe and tongue scattered at Babel was Israel's means of filling the earth and thus fulfilling the creation mandate, so the spread of the gospel to "to all *ethnē*" is the church's means of filling the earth and thus fulfilling that same mission. This connection between the spread of the gospel and the creation mandate will become explicit next chapter when we explore Luke's portrayal of the church's growth in the book of Acts.

---

14. Köstenberger and O'Brien, *Salvation to the Ends of the Earth*, 124n47.
15. So also Bock, *Acts*, 190.
16. See the excellent analysis in Piper, *Let the Nations Be Glad!*, 183–211.

Finally, that this repentance should be proclaimed "beginning from Jerusalem" reflects the centrifugal methodology that will characterize the mission of the church in the book of Acts. In chapter 4 we saw that Israel's temple in Jerusalem was the central location to which the nations were to come, submit to God, and receive his blessing. The narrative of Acts reveals that after Jesus ascends to heaven, he pours out his Spirit upon the church and thereby transforms the covenant community into the temple of God on earth.[17] No longer is God's earthly presence housed in an edificial structure; with the outpouring of the Holy Spirit his earthly presence now dwells amidst the ecclesial community (cf. 1 Cor 3:16). Therefore, after the Spirit is outpoured, the nations will no longer submit to God by coming to the edificial temple in Jerusalem; rather, beginning from Jerusalem the ecclesial temple will now go out to the nations.[18]

In section C, Jesus states that the disciples are "witnesses of these things," which in Luke's narrative typically refers to those who experienced Jesus in his risen state and therefore can offer firsthand testimony of his death and resurrection.[19] Jesus closes this commission in section D by commanding these witnesses to stay in Jerusalem, for he is "sending the promise of my Father upon you" so that "you are clothed with power from on high." As we will see in Acts 1, this promise that empowers these witnesses is the Holy Spirit, who will enable them to testify to Jesus' supreme kingship to the ends of the earth. This command to "stay," therefore, is prerequisite to the Matthean command to "go," since it is the outpoured Holy Spirit who will ensure the success of the church's mission. In Matthew, Jesus says that he will be with his followers to the end of the age, though precisely how he will accompany them is left unstated. Here in Luke we receive a hint concerning this promise of divine presence that will gain further clarity in the post-resurrection accounts in John and Acts.

---

17. See the discussion in chapter 9.

18. As Carroll says, "Jerusalem is no longer the center and goal of the nations' movement but the point of departure for a centrifugal mission to the whole world" (*Luke*, 403).

19. See, e.g., Acts 1:22; 2:32; 3:15; 5:30–32; 10:39–41; 13:30–31. See also Bock, *Acts*, 64. This term "witness" (*martys*) seems ultimately drawn from Isaiah, where Israel is summoned to serve as God's "witness," testifying to his unique status as savior (e.g., Isa 43:10–13). See Johnson, "Jesus Against the Idols," 347.

John 20:21–23: The Church's Mission as an Extension of Jesus' Mission

Although the post-resurrection narrative in John is longer than those in Matthew and Luke, Jesus' commission to his disciples is more abbreviated and less explicitly global in nature. Nevertheless, the distinct emphasis in John's account contributes an important element to our understanding of the mission of the church. After rising from the dead, Jesus appears first to Mary Magdalene and sends her to tell the disciples about this encounter (John 20:11–18). That evening Jesus appears to his disciples, shows them his scars, and gives them this third version of his post-resurrection commission:

²¹ Jesus said to them again,

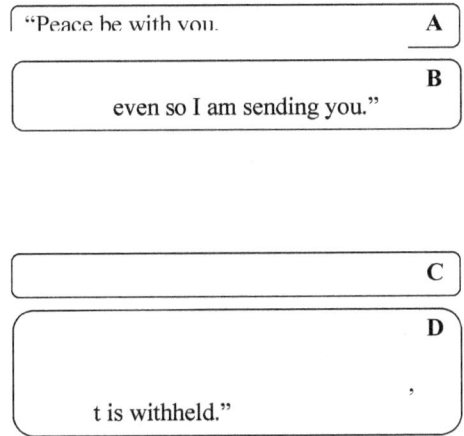

After greeting the disciples in section A, in section B Jesus compares his sending of the disciples to the Father's sending of him. This comparative language in section B has engendered all sorts of interpretations, some of which draw from it quite extensive conclusions concerning the nature of the church's mission. For example, based on this language Geoffrey Harris states, "The closest possible connection is drawn here: the disciples are to abide in the Son, to imbibe his teaching, to imitate his ways and then to impart all these things—along with his living presence—to others. That is the essence of mission."²⁰ Similarly, Henry Schriever concludes, "The disciples are to be like the Son: sent into the world out of love for the world to be as He was in the world, in the same relationship He has with the Father!"²¹

---

20. Harris, *Mission in the Gospels*, 177.
21. Schriever, "As the Father Has Sent Me," 16.

While certain aspects of these summaries are no doubt true theologically, the breadth and specificity of these conclusions seem to go beyond the rather brief and general nature of Jesus' statement.

In this passage Jesus does not say that his followers are to "imitate his ways" or that they will have "the same relationship He has with the Father." Rather, the focus in section B is on the *similarity of sentness* between Jesus and his followers. John's Gospel repeatedly emphasizes that the Father sent Jesus into the world,[22] and now Jesus declares that, in a similar way, he is sending his followers after him. The primary contribution of this statement, then, lies in its emphasis on the *continuity* between Jesus' mission and the church's mission.[23] Jesus' followers receive a mission that is an extension of Jesus' own mission because he, the one whom the Father sent, is now the one sending them.

Reinforcing this interpretation is the relationship between sections B and C in the discourse structure above. After Jesus describes his sending of the disciples in section B, John the narrator says, "And *when he had said* (*eipōn*) this, *he breathed* (*enephysēsen*) on them and said to them, 'Receive the Holy Spirit'" (v. 22). In this verse John uses an aorist participle (*eipōn*) to refer to Jesus' speech in section B, followed by an aorist indicative (*enephysēsen*) to describe Jesus breathing on the disciples. An aorist participle typically describes action that precedes the finite verb, though when an aorist participle is in construction with an aorist indicative, the participial action is often contemporaneous with that of the finite verb.[24] Consequently, while Jesus' speech in section B may have preceded his act of breathing, it is also possible that it coincided with it. Either way, but especially in the latter scenario, Jesus' comparative statement in section B is closely associated with this act of breathing. But this then raises a question: why does John record Jesus' "breathing" here?

This act of breathing is best viewed as an echo of God's breathing the breath of life into Adam at creation.[25] The verb John uses here (*emphysaō*) is used nowhere else in the New Testament and occurs only seven times in the LXX. Of these LXX occurrences, four describe an act of breathing life into someone (Gen 2:7; 1 Kgs 17:21; Wis 15:11; Ezek 37:9) and three

---

22. E.g., 4:34; 5:23–24, 30, 36–38; 6:29, 38–39, 44, 57; 7:16, 28–29, 33; 8:16, 18, 26, 29, 42, et al.

23. An observation that Harris also makes (*Mission in the Gospels*, 178). See also Carson, *John*, 648–49; Köstenberger and O'Brien, *Salvation to the Ends of the Earth*, 222.

24. Wallace, *Greek Grammar Beyond the Basics*, 624.

25. So also conclude Witherington, *John's Wisdom*, 342; Köstenberger, *John*, 575; Beale, *New Testament Biblical Theology*, 571.

occur in contexts of judgment (Job 4:21; Nah 2:1 [LXX 2:2]; Ezek 21:31 [LXX 21:36]). Since the context of John 20:22 is clearly not one of judgment, Jesus' act of breathing is best understood as his breathing life into the disciples. The foundational act of such breathing in the Old Testament is in the creation account, when "the LORD God formed the man of dust from the ground and *breathed (emphysaō)* into his nostrils the breath of life, and the man became a living creature" (Gen 2:7). Beale has argued persuasively that Ezek 37:9 alludes to this verse,[26] and the deuterocanonical book Wisdom of Solomon uses *emphysaō* explicitly to refer back to it (Wis 15:11). This trajectory of usage in the LXX suggests that by "breathing" on the disciples Jesus is giving them life in a manner similar to God giving life to Adam at creation. However, while these Old Testament acts of breathing depict the bestowal of physical life,[27] Jesus "breathes" in order to provide his followers with spiritual life, as section C makes clear.

Immediately after breathing on the disciples, in section C Jesus says, "Receive the Holy Spirit." In light of earlier statements in John's Gospel specifying that Jesus would not send the Spirit until after he ascends to the Father (e.g., 7:39; 16:7), we should not understand section C as the actual transference of the Spirit to the disciples. Rather, together with Jesus' act of breathing, this statement is best viewed as symbolically anticipating the future outpouring of the Spirit at Pentecost, which will bestow new spiritual life on the disciples.[28] According to John's Gospel, after Jesus ascends the Holy Spirit's role will be to teach and reiterate what Jesus has taught (14:26), bear witness about him (15:26), and convict the world concerning sin, righteousness, and judgment (16:8), doing all of this not on his own authority but with the goal of glorifying Jesus (16:13-14). This portrays the Spirit's ministry as an extension of Jesus' own ministry. Consequently, since Jesus' comparison of his mission with the disciples' mission is closely connected to his act of breathing, and since this breathing symbolizes a bestowal of life that is further characterized by the outpouring of the Holy Spirit, and since the Fourth Gospel presents the Spirit's ministry as an extension of Jesus' ministry, our conclusion concerning the significance of Jesus' language in section B seems warranted. That is, the mission of the church is an extension of Jesus' mission by virtue of the life-giving presence of the Holy Spirit who will be poured out after Jesus ascends to his heavenly throne.

26. Beale, *New Testament Biblical Theology*, 561-62.

27. The vision in Ezekiel 37 represents the giving of new spiritual life to Israel, though this message is conveyed through the imagery of dry bones receiving new physical life.

28. Carson, *John*, 653; Köstenberger, *John*, 574.

Jesus ends this commission in section D by noting that the disciples' extending or withholding forgiveness of sin reveals a person's true status as forgiven. At first this statement may seem to invest the disciples with an uncomfortable amount of authority, yet consideration of the broader context of the Gospel of John as a whole allays any concerns one may have. Although the language used in section D is uncharacteristic for John,[29] this Gospel has made it abundantly clear that forgiveness of sin comes only through belief in the Son,[30] and that anyone who does not believe in the Son is condemned.[31] According to 20:31, this is expressly why John has written this Gospel in the first place: "these are written so that you may *believe* that Jesus is the Christ, the Son of God, and that by believing you may have life in his name." Therefore, within the context of the Gospel of John as a whole, Jesus' statement in section D does not give the disciples autonomous jurisdiction over a person's eternal destination but rather authorizes them to determine a person's status based on the soteriological categories they have received from Jesus, namely, whether or not that person believes that Jesus is the Christ.[32] This authorization enables Jesus' followers to provide assurance of forgiveness to those to whom they minister, since they have been sent by the very one who has achieved that forgiveness. This emphasis at the end of this post-resurrection commission helps focus the otherwise broad nature of Jesus' comparison in section B by specifying that his followers' mission pertains fundamentally to the forgiveness of sins. This accords with Jesus' own mission, as he himself clearly says:

> And this is the will of him who sent me, that I should lose nothing of all that he has given me, but raise it up on the last day. For this is the will of my Father, that everyone who looks on the Son and believes in him should have eternal life, and I will raise him up on the last day. (John 6:39–40)

The Father has sent the Son to provide eternal life for all who would believe in him, and in continuity with that mission Jesus sends his followers in the power of the Holy Spirit to proclaim and provide assurance of forgiveness through the good news "that whoever believes in him should not perish but have eternal life" (3:16).[33]

---

29. In the Fourth Gospel, only 20:23 uses the verb *aphiēmi* to refer to the forgiveness of sins, and only this verse uses the verb *krateō* ("withhold").

30. E.g., 3:16, 18a, 36; 5:24a; 6:40, 47.

31. E.g., 3:18b; 5:24b; 8:24.

32. Hansen, "Forgiving and Retaining Sin," 24–32; Köstenberger and O'Brien, *Salvation to the Ends of the Earth*, 222.

33. For a superb analysis of this passage, see Johnson, "Church's Mission," 22–28.

Acts 1:6–8: The Church's Mission as a Witness to the Ends of the Earth

Jesus' final post-resurrection commission is found in the first chapter of the book of Acts. In line with the emphasis in John's commissioning narrative, Luke begins this book by intimating the continuity between Jesus' mission and his followers' mission, saying that in his first book (i.e., the Gospel of Luke) he has "dealt with all that Jesus *began* to do and teach" (Acts 1:1). This implies that the account that follows records what Jesus *continued* to do and teach, though since Jesus ascends to heaven in verse 9, it is clear that his continued mission will be executed through his followers. The account continues with Jesus reemphasizing what we saw in Luke 24:49, that the disciples must stay in Jerusalem until they receive "the promise of the Father" (Acts 1:4), after which he gives them this final post-resurrection commission:

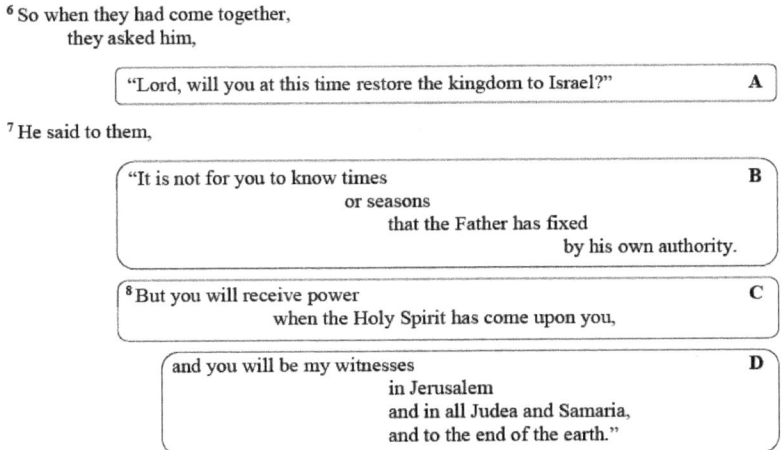

⁶ So when they had come together,
   they asked him,

> "Lord, will you at this time restore the kingdom to Israel?"   **A**

⁷ He said to them,

> "It is not for you to know times   **B**
>   or seasons
>   that the Father has fixed
>   by his own authority.

> ⁸ But you will receive power   **C**
>   when the Holy Spirit has come upon you,

> and you will be my witnesses   **D**
>   in Jerusalem
>   and in all Judea and Samaria,
>   and to the end of the earth."

This is the only post-resurrection commission that does not employ an imperative verb.[34] In Matthew Jesus commands his followers to "*make disciples* of all nations" (Matt 28:19); in Luke he instructs them to "*stay* in the city until you are clothed with power from on high" (Luke 24:49); and in John he tells them to "*receive* the Holy Spirit" (John 20:22). Significantly, only the first of these imperatives requires Jesus' followers to engage in any kind of activity; both the commands to "stay" and to "receive" portray the disciples as passive recipients of God's action of equipping them for their

---

34. Contra Peters, who states, "There are no imperative verbs in either Luke and [*sic*] John" (*Biblical Theology of Missions*, 175).

mission. In line with this, in Acts 1:6–8 Jesus does not command his followers to do anything; rather, he authoritatively describes *what they will receive* (section C) and *what they will become* (section D).

This grammatical observation reveals an important reality about the mission of the church. It is not simply the case that the church has been commanded to carry out a mission, but rather that the church *is a missional community* that has been equipped by Jesus to fulfill our very reason for existence. While it is true that Jesus gives his followers a "Great Commission" in Matthew, the majority of Jesus' post-resurrection commissioning discourse is indicative rather than imperative; that is, he is fundamentally describing *who we are* more so than commanding *what we should do*. However, rather than minimizing action on our part, this observation actually increases the responsibility of the church. By trusting in Jesus and submitting to his authority, his followers receive an entirely new identity, one that is designed to represent his kingship to the ends of the earth. Consequently, in this passage Jesus does not call his disciples to respond to a series of commands but instead promises to equip them in order that they might fulfill the purpose of their new identity.

In section A, after Jesus' forty-day teaching on the kingdom of God (1:3), the disciples ask him, "Lord, will you at this time restore the kingdom to Israel?" (v. 6). Although this question is occasionally viewed as misguidedly preoccupied with Israel in a nationalistic manner,[35] in light of our Old Testament analysis this inquiry seems entirely warranted from a missiological standpoint.[36] In fulfillment of the Abrahamic formula, Israel's mission of representing God's kingship to the nations would only be successful insofar as they obeyed God and received his blessing, which among other things would result in their superiority over the nations (Deut 28:1–2). Therefore this question concerning the restoration of the kingdom to Israel need not be understood as ethnocentric or unconcerned with the nations. Rather, according to the missiology of the Old Testament, a restored Israel free from external domination and exalted in her divinely bestowed blessings in the sight of the nations was the means by which God's kingship would be represented to the ends of the earth. Yet as we saw in chapter 7, in his life Jesus embodied the identity of true Israel and fulfilled all righteousness through his perfect obedience. In his death he inaugurated a new covenant in his blood (Luke 22:20), and now in his resurrected state he is organizing a new covenant community—a new Israel—founded upon these disciples

---

35. E.g., Johnson, "Jesus Against the Idols," 348.

36. So also conclude Peterson, *Acts of the Apostles*, 109; Köstenberger and O'Brien, *Salvation to the Ends of the Earth*, 129; Goheen, *Light to the Nations*, 125.

who have trusted in his blood sacrifice. This explains the significance of the disciples' first action after Jesus ascends: they fill the vacant position of Judas Iscariot with Matthias, thereby restoring their number to *twelve* (1:12–26). This apostolic company who will continue the mission of Jesus is the new covenant equivalent of the twelve tribes of Israel, and the kingdom is indeed being restored through them, though seemingly not in the way they expect.

Supporting this understanding of section A is Jesus' response to the disciples' question in section B. Jesus does not correct the disciples for any lack of faith or misunderstanding, something he was certainly willing to do even after his resurrection (e.g., Luke 24:25, 38). Rather, Jesus declares that the disciples are not to know the *timing* of the kingdom's restoration. This response suggests that the emphasis in the disciples' question is not, "Lord, will you at this time restore the kingdom *to Israel*?" but rather, "Lord, will you *at this time* (i.e., now) restore the kingdom to Israel?" The primary thrust of the question pertains not *to whom* the kingdom will be restored but rather *when* it will be restored. Jesus replies that this issue is not for his followers to know, and then in sections C and D he communicates that which he does want them to know.

The adversative conjunction that begins verse 8 (*alla*) indicates a sharp contrast between sections B and C; rather than receiving knowledge of the timing of kingdom restoration, Jesus' followers will receive the *means* of kingdom restoration. Jesus states that his followers will receive "power" (*dynamis*) when the Holy Spirit comes upon them. Luke uses *dynamis* to describe Jesus' reign at God's right hand (Luke 21:27; 22:69) as well as his followers' ability to bring healing (Acts 3:12; 4:7; cf. 10:38), offer testimony concerning Jesus' resurrection (4:33), perform signs and wonders (2:22; 6:8; 8:13; 19:11), and transmit the Holy Spirit to others (8:14–19). At Pentecost, Peter will associate Jesus' receiving the promise of the Holy Spirit with his exaltation to God's right hand (2:33), and after the outpouring of the Spirit at Pentecost, Luke repeatedly describes Jesus' followers as "filled with the Holy Spirit" when they speak boldly concerning him (4:8–12, 31; 13:9–12). All of this suggests that the *dynamis* that will accompany the coming of the Holy Spirit in section C will equip Jesus' followers to serve as his "witnesses" in section D.

As mentioned above when discussing Luke 24:48, a "witness" in Luke's narrative refers to one who had direct experience with Jesus after his resurrection and therefore can testify firsthand to his exalted status. Since Jesus' resurrection is his coronation as the eschatological Davidic King, to function as a witness in Acts is to testify concerning the reality of Jesus' eternal and earth-wide kingship. It is fitting, therefore, that in section D Jesus describes his followers as witnesses in an expanding ethnic and geographical manner.

Jesus says that "you will be my witnesses in Jerusalem and in all Judea and Samaria, and to the end of the earth." As many have observed, this statement introduces the threefold structure of the book of Acts.[37] Chapters 1–7 are set in Jerusalem; in chapters 8–12 the setting shifts to focus on the larger region of Judea and Samaria; and beginning in chapter 13 the narrative primarily follows Paul as he takes the gospel beyond the borders of Palestine all the way to Rome.

Of particular interest in this commission is the phrase "to the end of the earth" (*heōs eschatou tēs gēs*). In the LXX this phrase most generally denotes the furthest outskirts of creation,[38] often with Gentile nations immediately in view.[39] The only other time Luke uses this phrase is in Acts 13:47, where he quotes the LXX of Isa 49:6. In this Isaianic text, "to the end of the earth" describes the extent to which God's salvation will spread as the servant functions as "a light for the nations." For Isaiah, then, this comprehensive geographical description includes a multiethnic connotation; to reach "the nations" is to reach "the end of the earth." That Luke quotes Isa 49:6 in Acts 13:47 makes it probable that this same Isaianic allusion is present in 1:8 as well. This suggests that "to the end of the earth" in 1:8 similarly connotes not only comprehensive geographical coverage but also worldwide ethnic inclusion.[40] That is, Jesus' followers are to testify concerning his risen and exalted status not simply in faraway lands in general, but in *every* land and among *every* people group throughout the world.

Reinforcing this further is the language of Jesus' commission in Luke 24. Since Luke the writer is responsible for both the Gospel of Luke and the book of Acts, and since the end of Luke and the beginning of Acts each report a post-resurrection commission, it is natural for these twin commissions to provide a certain degree of mutual interpretation.[41] In each text Jesus describes his followers as "witnesses" who will receive "power" and will begin their ministry in "Jerusalem." However, while Jesus in Luke describes his followers' ministry extending from Jerusalem "to all nations" (v. 47), in Acts he describes them expanding from Jerusalem "to the end of the earth." This parallel coheres with the implication of the Isaianic allusion that this geographical description connotes all ethnicities throughout the world.

---

37. See, e.g., Senior and Stuhlmueller, *Biblical Foundations for Mission*, 269–71.

38. Deut 28:49; Ps 135:7 [LXX 134:7]; Isa 48:20; 62:11; Jer 10:13; 51:16 [LXX 28:16].

39. Isa 8:9; 45:22; 49:6; Jer 6:22; 16:19; 50:41 [LXX 27:41]; 25:32 [LXX 32:32]; 31:8 [LXX 38:8].

40. For discussion of Acts 1:8 describing both an ethnic and a geographical spread, see Moore, "To the End of the Earth," 389–99; Beers, *Followers of Jesus*, 131–33.

41. Moore, "To the End of the Earth," 394.

This point regarding the comprehensive geographical and ethnic scope of Acts 1:8 must be emphasized, since the global expansion depicted here has occasionally been lifted from its redemptive-historical context and relativized in order to serve a more immediate application. For example, in seeking to base a model of global discipleship on Acts 1:8, Aaron Wheeler has posited that, in any given context, "Jerusalem and Judea" include "everything that is done within the church and local outreach efforts," "Samaria" refers to "activities of the church that cross barriers within the local area of the church or activities outside the area of the local church on a short-term basis," and "the end of the earth" includes "activities of the church that are outside of the local church area."[42] In addition to the exegetical difficulty introduced by this division,[43] this application relativizes "the end of the earth" so that, according to Wheeler, "To the church in Rio de Janeiro, a church in Seoul is the ends of the earth and vice versa."[44] Based on the preceding analysis, there are at least two significant problems with this interpretation.

First, this interpretation views "the end of the earth" not as "*all* nations" but simply as "*other* nations." However, as we have seen, "the end of the earth" in Acts 1:8 connotes both comprehensive geographical coverage and complete ethnic inclusion. Jesus does not commission his followers simply to go *somewhere else* but rather to go *everywhere*, to every people group scattered throughout the world. This means that the true referent of "the end of the earth" is not any indiscriminate point that happens to be geographically distant from a relatively located subject, but rather those peoples throughout the world who do not recognize or submit to Jesus' kingship. To go "to the end of the earth" means to *fill the earth* with God's representatives, that is, with those who respond to the good news of Jesus' death and resurrection with repentance and faith and thereby treat him as King.

Second, by relativizing these locations, this interpretation does not take sufficient account of the biblical-theological significance that Jerusalem occupies in the mission of God's people. As we saw in our Old Testament analysis, the temple in Jerusalem was the central location where Israel was to praise God among the nations and to which the nations could come and submit to God. As we will see in the next section, Jerusalem is also the

---

42. Wheeler, "Commissioning of All Believers," 156.

43. In Acts 1:8, the phrase "all Judea and Samaria" uses a single definite article (*pasē tē Ioudaia kai Samareia*), which grammatically connects Judea with Samaria, not Jerusalem.

44. Wheeler, "Commissioning of All Believers," 160. Drawing a similar conclusion, Christopher Wright states, "The earth, of course, is a globe that has no 'ends'. From a missional perspective, the 'ends of the earth' are as likely to be found in your own street as far across the sea" (*Mission of God's People*, 286).

location where God will pour out his Spirit upon his followers. Jesus instructs his disciples to wait in Jerusalem in order that they might be clothed with power in order to execute their mission (Luke 24:49; Acts 1:4). Jerusalem, therefore, has substantial redemptive-historical and biblical-theological significance and cannot be relativized to refer to the local context of any given person. In sum, Jesus' commission in Acts 1:8 is not that we would minister first in our own situation and then look for ways to branch out. Rather, Jesus is promising to equip his church with power from on high and then send them from that location to serve as his witnesses throughout the world. Whereas Jerusalem was the destination of the nations' centripetal coming in the Old Testament, it is the starting point for the church's centrifugal going in the New Testament.

Taking all of this together, Jesus' commissioning statement in sections C and D may be summarized as follows. Rather than knowing the timing of the restoration of God's kingdom, the disciples will receive the means of kingdom restoration through the empowering presence of the Holy Spirit. The Spirit, in turn, will enable the disciples to serve as witnesses, testifying in word and deed concerning the resurrected reign of Jesus as the exalted Davidic King. Since God promised that David's kingdom would be both everlasting and worldwide in scope, Jesus' followers are not simply to testify concerning his kingship in Jerusalem where they receive their missional power but among every people group all across creation—to the end of the earth. By this means the kingdom will be restored and God's mission will be fulfilled.

Summary: What is the Mission of the Church?

These four post-resurrection commissions provide a full-orbed picture of the mission of the church. Having looked at each of them individually, at this point it is instructive to summarize their collective teaching.

First, according to Jesus' commissions, the mission of the church is fundamentally predicated upon Jesus' authority over all creation (Matt 28:18). Although compassion for the lost and a desire to see them saved is good and necessary, this concern must never supplant Jesus' kingly authority as both the grounds and the goal of the church's mission. Jesus' authority is the reason his followers are sent and that to which converts must submit.

Second, to this end, the church's mission involves not simply leading people to a decision but incorporating them into the covenant community by baptizing and teaching them to obey all of Jesus' authoritative commands (Matt 28:19–20). This means that Christian mission must necessarily be ecclesial in nature, executed with a view toward bringing converts into the fold of the church. It also means that Christian mission may not be limited to the evangelistic enterprise, but must include elements such as worship, discipleship, education, and outreach—the entire spectrum of ministries required for the church as a whole to obey all that Jesus has commanded.

Third, the mission of the church involves the proclamation of repentance that leads to forgiveness (Luke 24:47; cf. John 20:23). This is the only means by which a person may be incorporated into the covenant community, and this is the posture by which covenant members must continually live in relationship with God.

Fourth, the mission of the church is an extension of Jesus' own mission (John 20:21; cf. Acts 1:1). The Father sent the Son to restore the kingdom by acquiring forgiveness for sin on the cross, and now the Son sends the church to proclaim the good news of that kingdom and call people everywhere to enter it through repentance and faith.

Fifth, the mission of the church is executed by the power of Jesus' presence, now manifested through the Holy Spirit.[45] This is the only element that appears in all four post-resurrection commissions, and as the outpouring of the Spirit at Pentecost will show, the significance of this divine presence for the success of the church's mission cannot be overstated. Both Adam and Israel failed in their mission to represent God's kingship because of their sin, but because of Jesus' atoning work and the Spirit's indwelling presence, the church will succeed where those two failed.

Sixth, the mission of the church is not merely a task that Jesus' followers have been commanded to carry out, but rather reflects the new identity we have received through Jesus' atoning work (Luke 24:48; Acts 1:8). Based on the preponderance of Jesus' post-resurrection discourse, mission is fundamentally an outflow of *who we are* more than simply being something we should do.

Finally, the mission of the church has as its scope every people group of the world; it is comprehensive both geographically and ethnically (Matt 28:19; Luke 24:47; Acts 1:8). As we have seen, Matthew's emphasis on Jesus' authority reflects his status as the Danielic Son of Man, and Luke's focus on the disciples as witnesses of the resurrection highlights Jesus' role as the eschatological Davidic King. Since both of these Old Testament figures are depicted as receiving rule over an earth-wide kingdom, it is fitting that Jesus' followers fulfill their mission by going "to all nations," "to the end of the earth."

---

45. Matt 28:20; Luke 24:49; John 20:22; Acts 1:8.

Taken together, these commissioning narratives present Jesus as reinstating the mission of God's people. By going forth to all nations, declaring the reality of Jesus' resurrection, and calling people everywhere to repent, receive forgiveness, and submit to Jesus as King, the church will fill the earth with God's representatives and thereby demonstrate that his kingship extends over the entire earth.

JESUS EQUIPS THE CHURCH FOR MISSION

As we have noted, the single element that appears in all four post-resurrection commissions is the promise of Jesus' presence with his followers through the Holy Spirit. In Matthew, Jesus assures the disciples that he will be with them to the end of the age. In Luke he tells them that he will send the as-yet undefined "promise of my Father," which will clothe them with power from on high. In John he specifies the Holy Spirit as that which the disciples will receive, and in Acts these various threads come together into a clarified whole: the means by which Jesus will accompany his followers and equip them to execute their mission is his power distributed through the outpoured Holy Spirit. This equipping of the church takes place formally when Jesus ascends to heaven and pours out the Holy Spirit at Pentecost. In order to understand the significance of Pentecost for the mission of the church, we will first examine how the outpoured Spirit transforms the church into the eschatological temple of God. Then we will discuss how this universalization of God's temple presence shifts the mission of God's people from the centripetal pull of Israel's witness to the centrifugal spread of the church's witness. Finally, we will explore how the outpoured Spirit enables the church to obey God and thereby successfully execute our mission; by God's indwelling presence we are equipped to succeed where both Adam and Israel failed.

The Outpoured Spirit and the Church as the Temple of God

Space prohibits an extensive presentation of a biblical theology of the temple, though a brief summary will help orient our discussion.[46] Broadly defined, the "temple" is the place where God's special, heavenly presence intersects with the earth. Of course, God is omnipresent, so in a certain sense his presence on earth is everywhere; yet Scripture also portrays certain

---

46. For an exhaustive analysis of this topic, see Beale, *Temple and the Church's Mission*. For a condensed and easier-to-read study, see Beale and Kim, *God Dwells Among Us*.

locations and situations as containing a heightened presence of God that is distinct from his general omnipresence. The original manifestation of God's temple presence on earth was the garden of Eden. This was the place where God would walk "in the cool of the day" (Gen 3:8) and interact directly with humanity. After the fall, however, God barred humanity from his temple presence by casting them out and stationing cherubim to guard the entrance of the garden (Gen 3:24).

After establishing his covenants with Abraham and Israel, God brings his temple presence back to humanity through the tabernacle and subsequently the Solomonic temple. The descriptions of God descending upon and filling these structures highlight their function as the intersection of God's heavenly presence on earth (Exod 40:34–35; 1 Kgs 8:10–11). In particular, the furniture within the Most Holy Place depicts God as a King seated upon his heavenly throne, with the inner sanctuary serving as the earthly extension of his throne room. Inside this inner sanctuary was the ark of the covenant, upon which rested the mercy seat, over which two golden cherubim stood with outstretched wings (Exod 25:10–21; 26:34). Throughout the Old Testament, God is repeatedly described as "enthroned on/upon/above the cherubim."[47] Since cherubim were heavenly beings,[48] the furniture within the Most Holy Place portrays God as seated on his heavenly throne, symbolically situated above the golden cherubim. The ark of the covenant immediately beneath the cherubim is described as God's "footstool" (1 Chr 28:2; cf. Pss 99:5; 132:7), the place where he symbolically rests his feet as he sits on his heavenly throne. The image that emerges from this temple furniture therefore portrays God as sitting upon his throne in heaven and extending his feet to rest within the holiest portion of Israel's temple (cf. Isa 66:1). Consequently, Israel's tabernacle and temple were not simply the intersection of God's heavenly presence on earth; they represented God reigning as the heavenly King and extending his throne-room presence into the midst of his people. Significantly, the cherubim that were stationed outside the garden to guard God's presence from sinful humanity reappear here in the tabernacle/temple to separate God and humanity once again.

As we have already explored in depth, like Adam, Israel unrepentantly disobeyed God's word and therefore was exiled from his temple presence. The prophet Ezekiel observes an elaborate process by which God's Spirit departs the Solomonic temple and leaves Jerusalem prior to the Babylonian invasion (Ezekiel 10–11). However, Ezekiel also receives a vision of God returning to the temple (Ezek 43:1–5), and elsewhere the prophets describe

---

47. 1 Sam 4:4; 2 Sam 6:2; 2 Kgs 19:15; 1 Chr 13:6; Pss 80:1; 99:1; Isa 37:16.
48. Clements, *God and Temple*, 31.

this new temple as one to which the nations will gather and worship (e.g., Isa 2:1–5; Mic 4:1–5; Zech 6:9–15). Of particular significance, Jeremiah envisions a time when God's heavenly presence on earth will expand beyond the inner sanctuary of the temple and connects this expansion to the fulfillment of the creation mandate:

> And I will give you shepherds according to my heart, who will feed you with knowledge and understanding. And when you have *multiplied* (*rabbâ*) and *been fruitful* (*pārâ*) in the land in those days, declares the Lord, they shall no more say, "The ark of the covenant of the Lord." It shall not come to mind or be remembered or missed; it shall not be made again. At that time Jerusalem shall be called the throne of the Lord, and all nations shall gather to it, to the presence of the Lord in Jerusalem, and they shall no more stubbornly follow their own evil heart. (Jer 3:15–17, author's translation)

In this passage, as God provides his people with faithful leadership, they will simultaneously fulfill the creation mandate and no longer need the ark of the covenant. Instead of being separated and confined to the Most Holy Place, the earthly intersection of God's heavenly throne room will expand beyond the bounds of the edificial temple and encompass all of Jerusalem.[49]

Despite these grand prophecies, conspicuously absent in the Old Testament postexilic literature is any historical reference to God's Spirit returning to the second temple; the prophetic vision of a reestablished and expanded temple is never realized. However, in chapter 7 we saw that God finally brings his temple presence back to earth through Jesus' incarnation. Jesus is the eschatological temple—the true intersection of God's heavenly presence on earth—to whom the nations will gather and worship. After Jesus atones for sin on the cross, rises from the dead, and ascends to his heavenly throne, he extends his reign onto the earth by pouring his presence upon the church through the Holy Spirit, thereby transforming the covenant community into the temple of God. Although the apostle Paul explicitly refers to the corporate body of the church as God's temple (1 Cor 3:16–17),[50] precisely *when* the church becomes the temple has not been widely recognized. However, Beale has provided convincing evidence that the outpouring of the Spirit at Pentecost is the event that transforms Jesus' followers into the temple of God.[51] Relying on many of Beale's insights, here

---

49. See also Weinfeld, "Jeremiah and the Spiritual Metamorphosis of Israel," 24.
50. For further commentary on this text see the discussion in chapter 9.
51. Beale, "Descent of the Eschatological Temple: Part 1," 73–102; Beale, "Descent of the Eschatological Temple: Part 2," 63–90.

I summarize several observations that cumulatively indicate that Pentecost is the juncture at which the church becomes the temple.

First, as we have already seen, Jesus states that the Spirit cannot be poured onto the church until he ascends to heaven (John 16:7). Since the temple is the earthly extension of God's heavenly throne room, it is only logical that Jesus must first ascend to his heavenly throne before he can extend that throne-room presence onto the earth. Consequently, Jesus' insistence that his ascension must precede the Spirit's outpouring situates this latter event in a place analogous to the establishment of a temple; it extends Jesus' royal, heavenly presence onto the earth.

Second, this initial observation explains why Jesus requires his followers to wait *in Jerusalem* before they engage in their mission (Luke 24:49; Acts 1:4–5). God's temple presence on earth was formerly limited to the edificial structure in Jerusalem, which makes Jerusalem the logical place to establish this latter-day ecclesial temple. This outpouring of God's temple presence in Jerusalem not only directly fulfills Jeremiah's prophetic oracle noted above, but it also provides continuity between the old covenant edificial temple and the new covenant ecclesial temple.

Third, Pentecost is often rightly understood to be a reversal of the linguistic confusion that transpired at the tower of Babel.[52] At Babel God created the different languages of the world in order to confuse sinful humanity and judge their efforts to restrict his earthly representation. At Pentecost God miraculously communicates his word to Jews "from every nation (*ethnos*) under heaven" (Acts 2:5) in their various languages, thereby bringing understanding amidst this multilingual environment (v. 11). As we saw in chapter 2, the tower of Babel is depicted as a ziggurat, which was a staircase-type structure connecting a deity's heavenly abode with their earthly temple. Since Babel was designed to function in this temple-like manner, it makes sense that the reversal of this effort at Pentecost would also be portrayed in temple-like terms.[53]

Fourth, the language that begins the Pentecost event recalls Old Testament appearances of God, particularly the descent of God's presence at the tabernacle and temple. According to Luke, "And suddenly there came from heaven a sound like a mighty rushing wind, and *it filled the entire house (eplērōsen holon ton oikon)* where they were sitting" (Acts 2:2). This expression recalls God's original descent on the tabernacle, where "the glory of the LORD *filled the tabernacle (eplēsthē hē skēnē)*" (Exod 40:34), and alludes

---

52. See, e.g., Davis, "Acts 2 and the Old Testament," 45–46.
53. Beale, "Descent of the Eschatological Temple: Part 1," 75–76; Beale, *Temple and the Church's Mission*, 201–3.

even more directly to his descent on the Solomonic temple, where "a cloud *filled the house (eplēsen ton oikon)* of the LORD" (1 Kgs 8:10). Even clearer than these two passages is the synoptic account of God's temple descent in 2 Chronicles. In this text, after Solomon finishes his dedicatory prayer, *"fire came down from heaven and consumed the burnt offering and the sacrifices, and the glory of the LORD filled the temple (eplēsen ton oikon)"* (2 Chr 7:1). This fiery filling of the temple in the Old Testament corresponds to the fiery filling of this "house" in Acts 2:2.[54]

Fifth, this "house" that is "filled" in Acts 2:2 is most likely the temple in Jerusalem, making the connection between the edificial and ecclesial temples even stronger. "Pentecost" is a term used in the New Testament to describe the "Feast of Harvest," also known as the "Feast of Weeks." This was one of three annual festivals during which all Israelite males were to appear before God at the temple in Jerusalem (Exod 23:14–17; 34:18–23; Deut 16:16). This makes it probable that the setting of this event in Acts 2 is the temple, especially since Luke describes those in attendance that day as "devout men" (v. 5). This would also explain Luke's notice after Peter's sermon that about three thousand people were added to their number that day (v. 41). This figure is too large to have gathered in a private residence, though a temple setting explains well how this "multitude" could have gathered at the sound of the apostles' miraculous tongue-speaking (v. 6).[55] This outpouring of the Spirit, therefore, is best viewed as occurring at the edificial temple, which strengthens the depiction of this event as the establishment of an ecclesial temple.

Finally, when the crowd speculates that the apostles may be drunk, Peter responds by identifying this event as the fulfillment of Joel 2:28–32. When Peter quotes Joel, however, he replaces the beginning of Joel's prophecy ("after these things" [*meta tauta*]; Joel 2:28) with "in the latter days" (*en tais eschatais hēmerais*). The only place in the LXX where this latter phrase occurs is Isa 2:2, which describes the establishment of God's eschatological temple:

> It shall come to pass *in the latter days* (*en tais eschatais hēmerais*)
>   that the mountain of the house of the LORD
> shall be established as the highest of the mountains,
>   and shall be lifted up above the hills;
> and all the nations shall flow to it,
>   and many peoples shall come, and say:
> "Come, let us go up to the mountain of the LORD,

---

54. Beale, "Descent of the Eschatological Temple: Part 2," 64.
55. Beale, "Descent of the Eschatological Temple: Part 2," 65.

>   to the house of the God of Jacob,
>   that he may teach us his ways
>   and that we may walk in his paths."
> For out of Zion shall go forth the law,
>   and the word of the LORD from Jerusalem. (Isa 2:2–3)

This text envisions a new temple arising out of Jerusalem that will draw the devotion of the nations and teach them to obey God's word. By inserting this unique phrase into his quotation of Joel, Peter imports this Isaianic context into his response and thereby characterizes the outpouring of the Spirit as the establishment of God's eschatological temple.[56]

Taken together, these various data demonstrate that the outpouring of the Holy Spirit at Pentecost does not simply equip Jesus' followers with practical abilities useful for gospel proclamation. Rather, at Pentecost Jesus is extending the reach of his heavenly throne room to intersect with the earth through the church as the temple of God. This reveals that the church is equipped to carry out our mission, not primarily through tactical plans or practical capabilities, but first and foremost by virtue of our spiritual connection to Jesus who is reigning on his throne and directing us by his sovereign power.

The Outpoured Spirit and the Church's Centrifugal Mission

This distributed temple presence through the Holy Spirit enacts a major change in the missional methodology of God's people. Throughout this study I have argued that Adam's mission was centrifugal, Israel's mission was centripetal, and now we have seen that the church's mission is centrifugal as well. Israel was to draw the nations to God by their blessed relationship with him, but Jesus commissions his followers to "go and make disciples of all nations" and describes them as "witnesses . . . to the end of the earth." Discussions of a biblical theology of mission often highlight this methodological shift between the missions of Israel and the church, though the rationale for this change is rarely pursued beyond the general observation that Jesus has commanded his followers to "go."[57] However, I suggest that underlying Jesus' centrifugal commission at a more fundamental level is the distribution of God's temple presence through the outpoured Holy Spirit, which has

---

56. Beale, "Descent of the Eschatological Temple: Part 1," 94.

57. See, e.g., Stetzer, "Missional Church," 107; Goheen, *Light to the Nations*, 115. Peters refers to Pentecost as "the watershed of evangelical missions" (*Biblical Theology of Missions*, 134), but does not go into detail how the Spirit empowers the apostles beyond giving them boldness and bravery (*Biblical Theology of Missions*, 134–35, 144).

been made possible by Jesus' atoning work on the cross. This soteriological and pneumatological reality is the ultimate rationale behind the shift from a centripetal to a centrifugal missional methodology.[58]

The centrifugal-centripetal-centrifugal movement of the mission of God's people through Adam, Israel, and the church corresponds to the immediate-mediate-immediate proximity to God's temple presence that these three groups experience. In the garden Adam enjoyed immediate proximity to God's temple presence. Consequently, if Adam had faithfully fulfilled the creation mandate while simultaneously working and keeping the garden, God's temple presence would have spread along with humanity as they filled the earth.[59] However, as we have already explored in detail, humanity does not treat God as King and therefore God banishes them from his temple presence. After exiling humanity from the garden, God stations cherubim at the entrance, highlighting that humanity's immediate access to God's temple presence has been removed.

In the call of Israel, God graciously brings his presence back into the midst of his people through the tabernacle and subsequently the temple. However, the multiple layers of separation between God and his people built into these structures, culminating in the reappearance of the cherubim to guard God's heavenly throne room, reveal that God's temple presence will not extend beyond the bounds of the physical edifice. Because of humanity's sin, anyone who experiences God's immediate presence cannot live (Exod 33:20). This is underscored among other ways by the rare and elaborate process necessary for the high priest to enter the Most Holy Place (Leviticus 16; Heb 9:7). Only one man could enter God's temple presence once a year with great ceremonial care and precision, and even he was still separated from God's presence by the cherubim guards. God's presence with his people in the edificial temple was therefore *mediate*—that is, separated because of the people's sin—and thus Israel's mission was to attract the nations to God in his temple rather than expanding the bounds of his temple presence to reach them.[60]

---

58. Ott et al. rightly identify the decentralization of God's Spirit at Pentecost as catalytic for the church's centrifugal mission, though they do not flesh out in much detail this relationship between God's temple presence and the church's missional methodology (*Encountering Theology of Mission*, 27).

59. See also Beale, *Temple and the Church's Mission*, 81–82. As Beale notes, that the closing vision of Revelation depicts the new creation as a worldwide garden-temple (Rev 21:1—22:5) substantiates the view that God's original design was for the garden-temple of Eden to fill the earth.

60. Beale has marshalled much evidence suggesting that, to a certain degree, Israel had a vision of God's temple expanding beyond the boundaries of Zion and filling the earth (see especially *Temple and the Church's Mission*, 81–167). While this expectation

When Jesus comes and atones for sin fully and finally, the veil of the temple is torn in two, symbolizing the removal of the spiritual separation between God and his people (Matt 27:51; Mark 15:38; Luke 23:45). In line with this, the writer of Hebrews contrasts the repetitive Levitical sacrifices with Jesus' once-for-all sacrifice (Heb 10:11–14) and concludes that now "we have confidence to enter the holy places by the blood of Jesus, by the new and living way that he opened for us through the curtain" (vv. 19–20). As our great High Priest, Jesus continually intercedes before God on our behalf (vv. 21–22; cf. 7:23–28), and therefore we as God's redeemed people may once again enjoy immediate and continual access to God's temple presence. However, rather than simply allowing his people access to the inner sanctuary of the edificial temple, Jesus pours out his presence through the Spirit and thereby makes his people an ecclesial temple.

For this reason, like Adam, the church receives a centrifugal mission; God's temple presence can once again accompany his people as they fill the earth. This is the reason Jesus' command for his disciples to "stay" (Luke 24:49) logically precedes his command for them to "go" (Matt 28:19). Jesus' followers must first receive the outpouring of God's temple presence through the Spirit, only after which are they released to spread that temple presence as they go out into the world. As the church fills the earth by going and making disciples of all nations, the earthly extension of Jesus' throne room will spread all across creation, thereby representing his kingship to the ends of the earth.

The Outpoured Spirit and the Church's Missional Success

The final element in the church's equipping that we need to explore is the Spirit's work of enabling God's people to obey his word. Above we noted the more public ways in which the Spirit empowers Jesus' followers in Acts to bring healing, offer testimony, and perform signs and wonders as corroborating evidence of Jesus' resurrected reign. Yet these visible acts would carry no missional effectiveness if not accompanied by an internal heart disposition of repentant obedience. As we have seen, the principal problem throughout Scripture has been humanity's unrepentant sin and disobedience that has disabled them from fulfilling their mission. Consequently, in order for God's people to experience missional success they must attend

---

on Israel's part is plausible, in my view it is best understood eschatologically rather than historically. That is, Israel's historical mission was always to draw the nations to the temple, though their eschatological vision was that one day the temple would expand out and encompass the nations.

carefully to God's word, endeavor to obey it, and repent when they fail to do so. According to the Old Testament prophetic outlook, this corporate posture of repentant obedience would only become a reality upon the inauguration of the new covenant.

God communicates the well-known prophecy of the new covenant in Jer 31:31–34. According to these verses, a central characteristic that distinguishes the new covenant from the Sinai covenant is the writing of God's law on the hearts of his people. In verses 32–33, God declares that this new covenant is

> not like the covenant that I made with their fathers on the day when I took them by the hand to bring them out of the land of Egypt, my covenant that they broke, though I was their husband, declares the LORD. For this is the covenant that I will make with the house of Israel after those days, declares the LORD: I will put my law within them, and I will write it on their hearts. And I will be their God, and they shall be my people.

The problem with the Sinai covenant was not the covenant itself but *the people's inability to keep the covenant* ("my covenant that they broke" [v. 32]). This is confirmed by the writer of Hebrews' introduction to his quotation of these verses, where he says, "For if that first covenant had been faultless, there would have been no occasion to look for a second. For he finds fault with *them* (*autous*) when he says . . ." (Heb 8:7–8), and then he quotes Jer 31:31–34. The masculine plural pronoun *autous* cannot refer to the feminine singular *diathēkē* ("covenant"), but rather refers to the covenant partners with whom that earlier covenant was made. The problem with the Sinai covenant was that "they did not continue in my covenant" (Heb 8:9), and therefore a necessary element in the new covenant is the people's capability of keeping it.[61]

Jeremiah describes this capability of faithfulness in the new covenant era as the law being written on the heart, or cardionomography.[62] Although Jeremiah does not expressly connect this cardionomographic work to God's Spirit, Ezekiel describes this phenomenon in precisely these terms. A

---

61. Of course, from a broader canonical perspective we may conclude that the new covenant is better because of the final efficacy of Jesus' singular sacrifice to which the repetitive old covenant sacrifices pointed (Heb 9:1—10:18). However, while the new covenant prophecy hints at this reality (Jer 31:34), the Jeremianic context emphasizes the contrast with the people's failures under the old covenant administration (see especially Jer 31:27–30).

62. This long but helpful term, referring to the "law" (*nomos*) being "written" (*graphē*) on the "heart" (*cardia*), has recently been coined in the excellent analysis of Coxhead, "Cardionomographic Work of the Holy Spirit," 77–95.

comparison between Jer 31:33 and Ezek 36:27-28 reveals this connection between Jeremiah's new covenant and Ezekiel's vision of the eschatological work of the Spirit:[63]

	Jer 31:33	Ezek 36:27-28
A	I will put *my law* within them,	And I will put *my Spirit* within you,
B	and I will write it on their hearts.	and cause you to walk in my statutes and be careful to obey my rules ...
C	And I will be their God, and they shall be my people.	and you shall be my people, and I will be your God.

The tight parallels of theme and terminology between these two oracles indicate that Jeremiah and Ezekiel are describing the same eschatological phenomenon. In Jeremiah God says he will put his "law" (*tôrâ* = "teaching") within his people, while in Ezekiel he says he will put his "Spirit" within them (section A). This reveals that God's Spirit is the instrument by which God's teaching will be internalized by God's people in the new covenant era. Moreover, God's work of cardionomography in Jeremiah is described in Ezekiel as God's Spirit *causing* his people to live faithfully before him (section B). Both texts then describe this divine enabling of God's people to keep God's word as resulting in a stable covenant relationship between God and his people (section C). As we have seen, such a faithful covenant relationship is necessary for God's people to fulfill their mission.

Of course, during the Old Testament period the Holy Spirit was active in individual lives,[64] though his cardionomographic work was only present among a small, faithful remnant, not distributed across the covenant community at a corporate level.[65] This latter situation is precisely what Ezek 36:27-28 envisages; this passage does not describe individual regeneration but rather community revival based on the corporate dispersal of the Spirit.[66] This prophetic vision of corporate revival becomes a reality when Jesus inaugurates the new covenant through his death (Luke 22:20) and executes this cardionomography by rising, ascending, and pouring out the Holy Spirit at Pentecost. The Spirit is the one who circumcises the hearts of God's people (Rom 2:28-29) and thereby enables us to respond to his word with

---

63. For this comparison I am indebted to Block, "Prophet of the Spirit," 39.

64. E.g., Ps 51:11; Acts 1:16; 4:25; 2 Pet 1:21.

65. See also Coxhead, "Cardionomographic Work of the Holy Spirit," 88.

66. Notice that God says that he will put his Spirit "in the midst of *you all* (*bᵉqir-bᵉkem*)" (Ezek 36:27), which corresponds to the plural used in Jer 31:33: "I will put my law *in the midst of them* (*bᵉqirbām*)" (both translations mine). See also Block, "Prophet of the Spirit," 41.

repentant obedience (Deut 30:6). Therefore, this outpouring of the Spirit at Pentecost marks a turning point in the missional effectiveness of God's people. From this point forward, rather than being disabled by the pervasive presence of unrepentant sin, God's people will succeed in their mission by the power of the Holy Spirit as they respond to his word with repentance and faith.

SUMMARY

In this chapter we have explored how Jesus reinstates the mission of God's people. In his four post-resurrection commissions Jesus instructs his followers to go out in his authority to all nations, proclaim the need for repentance and forgiveness, baptize and teach people to obey all his commands, and to do so as an extension of his own mission. This instruction is not simply a set of commands to be obeyed but reflects the new identity we have received as God's redeemed people designed to represent his kingship. We then examined how Jesus equips his people for this mission by pouring out the Holy Spirit at Pentecost, thereby transforming the church into the temple of God. This spiritual distribution of God's temple presence establishes the church as the earthly extension of Jesus' heavenly kingdom, enacts a methodological shift from a centripetal to a centrifugal mission, and enables the church to respond to God's word with repentant obedience. As we will see in the next chapter, having received a reinstated mission through the work of Jesus and by the power of the Spirit, the early church begins to execute this mission through the leadership of Jesus' apostolic followers.

9 MISSION EXECUTED
The Expansion of the Church

As the New Testament makes clear, Jesus' post-resurrection commissions and outpouring of the Holy Spirit catapult the church into a geographical expansion that stretches from Jerusalem all the way to Rome, with Paul making plans to extend his ministry as far west as Spain. The book of Acts presents a narrative account of this expansion and the epistles record apostolic correspondence that addresses issues arising during the course of this mission. In this chapter we will first explore how the New Testament presents the church's mission as a geographical expansion that stretches further and further away from its staging ground in Jerusalem. Then we will examine how the New Testament depicts the church as fulfilling the major missional roles of the Old Testament as it carries out this expansionistic endeavor. Finally, we will explore how the theme of God's kingship is portrayed as a central element in the church's missional proclamation. Collectively these data will show that the church receives the same mission that Adam and Israel received: to fill the earth as God's representatives and thereby demonstrate that his kingship extends over the entire earth. However, while Adam and Israel both failed to carry out this mission because of their sin, the church is portrayed as successfully executing it by Jesus' sovereign power and the Spirit's indwelling presence.

THE CHURCH'S MISSION AS GEOGRAPHICAL EXPANSION

Geographical Expansion in Acts

In the previous chapter we observed that the geographical description in Acts 1:8—"you will be my witnesses in Jerusalem and in all Judea and

Samaria, and to the end of the earth"—provides a general summary of the movement of the gospel throughout the book. After Jesus ascends to heaven (1:9) and an angel assures the apostles that he will return in the same manner (vv. 10–11), Luke notes that the apostles "returned to Jerusalem from the mount called Olivet, which is near Jerusalem," even taking time to specify how long this travel takes: "a Sabbath's day journey" (v. 12). This emphasis on the apostles' return to Jerusalem inaugurates the first of the three sections of the book: gospel witness in Jerusalem. Initially, the apostles re-establish their covenantal number to twelve by replacing Judas with Matthias (1:13–26) and receive the empowering presence of the Holy Spirit (2:1–13), after which their witness begins with Peter's Pentecost sermon at the temple (2:14–41). At the end of this sermon Luke provides the first notice of the multiplication of God's people: "there were added that day about three thousand souls" (v. 41). The subsequent description of the earliest ecclesial community (2:42–47) similarly ends with a description of the church's proliferation: "And the Lord added to their number day by day those who were being saved" (v. 47).

Chapters 3–7 record further events in Jerusalem, with most of the narrative action taking place at the temple. Peter and John heal a lame beggar at the temple (ch. 3), a miracle that becomes "evident to all the inhabitants of Jerusalem" (4:16). The believers then gather at Solomon's Portico (5:12), with people coming to receive healing "from the towns around Jerusalem" (5:16). After a miraculous deliverance from prison, the apostles teach in the temple again (5:21), contrary to the decree of the Jewish leaders, who later claim that they have "filled Jerusalem" with their teaching (5:28). This practice of teaching in the temple and the surrounding houses is then described as continuing on a daily basis (5:42), reaching its climax with Stephen's speech (7:2–53), which is directly connected to the temple ("this holy place" [6:13]). Throughout this section Luke again notes that "more than ever believers were added to the Lord, multitudes of both men and women" (5:14) and that "the number of the disciples multiplied greatly in Jerusalem" (6:7).

After Stephen sees Jesus reigning as the Danielic Son of Man on his heavenly throne (7:56) and suffers martyrdom (7:59–60), a persecution scatters the church "throughout the regions of Judea and Samaria" (8:1), transitioning the narrative to this second missional phase. In chapters 8–12 the setting is primarily this larger geographical area as Philip goes and ministers in Samaria (8:5), converts the Ethiopian eunuch on the road from Jerusalem to Gaza (8:26), and then preaches from Azotus to Caesarea (8:40). Saul is converted on the way to Damascus (9:3) and preaches in both Damascus (9:20–25) and Jerusalem (9:26–31), resulting in the church experiencing peace throughout "all Judea and Galilee and Samaria" (9:31). After this Peter heals Aeneas in Lydda (9:32), raises Dorcas in Joppa (9:36), and converts Cornelius and his family in Caesarea (10:1–48). Peter defends this Gentile ministry in Jerusalem (11:1–18), after which the narrative shifts north to follow scattered Christians "as far as Phoenicia and Cyprus and Antioch" (11:19). After Peter is imprisoned and freed in Jerusalem, this section ends with Herod traveling to Caesarea where he is struck dead (12:19–23), and Barnabas and Saul returning to Antioch (12:25), from where they will be sent beyond the borders of Palestine to initiate the third and final section of the book. As was the case with the first section, this second section contains several notices of the church growing and increasing numerically as Jesus' followers spread geographically (9:31, 35, 42; 11:21, 24).

The third and final section of Acts (chs. 13–28) is traditionally divided by Paul's three missionary journeys (chs. 13–14, 15:36—18:22; 18:23—20:38), which are punctuated by the council of Jerusalem (15:1–35) and followed by Paul's arrest, public defenses, and transport to Rome (21–28).[1] The first missionary journey expands the church into various cities in Asia Minor, immediately to the west of the sending community in Antioch. The second missionary journey extends farther west across the Aegean Sea to include the cities of Philippi, Thessalonica, Berea, Athens, and Corinth. The third journey similarly includes travel across Asia Minor, Macedonia, and Greece, with Paul spending an extended period with the church in Ephesus. Continuing the pattern observed above, these missionary journeys are full of comments concerning the spread of the word of God and the numerical growth of the church:

- "the word of the Lord was spreading throughout the whole region" (13:49)
- "a great number of both Jews and Greeks believed" (14:1)
- in Derbe they "made many disciples" (14:21)
- "the churches were strengthened in the faith, and they increased in numbers daily" (16:5)
- concerning Corinth God declares, "I have many in this city who are my people" (18:10)
- "the word of the Lord continued to increase and prevail" (19:20)

After his extended Ephesian ministry Paul returns to Jerusalem, which brings his third missionary journey to a close and sets the stage for his arrest and final travel to Rome. As Porter and Westfall summarize, "These three

1. For an extended discussion of these sections see Köstenberger and O'Brien, *Salvation to the Ends of the Earth*, 137–57.

missionary trips of Paul reveal a pattern of increasing distance between the home base in Antioch and increasing penetration into the world further away from the eastern Mediterranean, including even Achaia."[2] As such, this geographical and numerical expansion of the early church in Acts fits the profile of the mission of God's people that we have observed so far: the church is being fruitful and multiplying and filling the earth with redeemed images of God as they preach the gospel in ever expanding geographical locales. Below we will we explore how Luke makes this connection between the church's expansion and the creation mandate explicit.

Geographical Expansion in the Epistles

Just as the book of Acts is largely preoccupied with Paul's expanding missionary ministry, the epistolary literature is predominately written by Paul during these missionary endeavors. At several points in his correspondence Paul reflects upon his calling as an apostle to the nations, the most important of which is Rom 15:14–29. In this passage Paul begins by affirming the Romans' knowledge of God and explains his need to instruct them further in order that they might be acceptable as an offering to God (vv. 14–16). He gives full credit to Christ for his work among the Gentiles (vv. 17–19a), after which he declares that "from Jerusalem and all the way around to Illyricum I have fulfilled the ministry of the gospel of Christ" (v. 19b). Although Paul's missionary career began in Antioch, as we observed above he also ministered in Jerusalem, which marks the southeastern edge of this geographical description. Illyricum was the Roman province beyond Macedonia on the eastern side of the Adriatic Sea, thus marking the northwestern limit of Paul's missionary activity to date.[3] This description therefore presents the total geography of Paul's ministry up until the writing of this epistle.

Within this considerably large area, which spans all of Palestine, Asia Minor, Greece, and Macedonia, Paul says that he has "fulfilled the ministry of the gospel of Christ." Such a claim obviously does not indicate that Paul has shared the gospel with every individual in this vast area, but rather that he has completed the work of planting churches that will serve as ongoing witnesses to the gospel in these regions.[4] This is why Luke can similarly

---

2. Porter and Westfall, "Cord of Three Strands," 122.

3. Although some have suggested that *mechri tou Illyrikou* ("to Illyricum") describes this region exclusively (i.e., "up to but not including Illyricum"), Allan Chapple makes a strong case for taking the phrase inclusively ("Paul and Illyricum," 24–25).

4. So also Moo, *Romans*, 896; Plummer, "Theological Basis for the Church's Mission," 262.

describe Paul and Barnabas as "fulfilling" the work to which they had been commended at the end of their first missionary journey (Acts 14:26), and why Paul says in verse 23, "I no longer have any room for work in these regions."[5] Paul's calling, as he states in verse 20, is to "to preach the gospel, not where Christ has already been named, lest I build on someone else's foundation," and thus his objective is to expand the borders of the church's presence into areas where no witness exists.

For this reason, Paul's next stated objective is to visit the Roman church on his way to minister the gospel further west in Spain (vv. 24, 28). From an eastern Mediterranean perspective, Spain was "the end of the earth," the farthest geographical locale before one encounters the Atlantic Ocean.[6] In this passage, therefore, the same expansionistic focus portrayed in the book of Acts comes to the fore: Jesus' followers, typified by Paul, are called to spread geographically in order to extend the witness of the church and thereby expand Jesus' representation across creation. According to Paul, this mission to the nations is the reason God saved him (Gal 1:15–16) and the reason why God sustains him through trials (2 Tim 4:17). As an apostle to the Gentiles, Paul's objective is to fill the earth with gospel-proclaiming churches that will testify to the good news of Jesus.

Having made this observation about Paul's calling and ministry, we must also affirm that not every person is called to engage personally in the type of frontier missionary work that Paul carried out. At several points in his writings Paul acknowledges that different people within the church will minister in different ways. In 1 Corinthians 12 he outlines various spiritual gifts (vv. 1–11), compares those who receive these gifts to different parts of the body (vv. 12–26), and implies that not every person will use the same gift as they minister (vv. 27–31). In Rom 12:4–8 and Eph 4:4–16 Paul uses this same physiological metaphor and draws the same conclusion concerning the diversity of function within the body of Christ. Regarding the planting of churches in particular, in 1 Corinthians 3 Paul uses an agricultural metaphor to describe different people engaging in different roles: "I planted, Apollos watered, but God gave the growth" (v. 6). After this he switches to an architectural metaphor, saying, "According to the grace of God given to me, like a skilled master builder I laid a foundation, and someone else is building upon it. Let each one take care how he builds upon it" (v. 10). Here Paul describes his frontier missionary work as "laying a foundation," with subsequent laborers receiving the calling to build upon it through ongoing

---

5. See further the discussion in Strauss, "Missions Theology," 462–63.
6. Das, "Paul of Tarshish," 61.

gospel ministry.[7] This indicates that, in Paul's view, not every Christian is called personally to engage in the frontier work of establishing churches in places where no gospel witness exists. Some may receive the calling to build upon a foundation laid by others. The gifts and callings of the members of the church are as varied in function as the different parts of the human body.

Nevertheless, the fact that (1) the book of Acts exhibits a narrative emphasis on Paul's expansionistic mission, (2) the bulk of the epistolary literature is set within this expansionistic mission, and (3) Paul explicitly describes his ministry ambition in expansionistic terms reveals that, on a canonical level, the geographical expansion of the church is of central importance within the New Testament's missional outlook. Although not every Christian will participate in this mission in the same way, the preponderance of post-ascension New Testament material indicates that the church is by definition a geographically-expanding community. Substantiating this conclusion is the observation that the New Testament locates the church's expansionistic mission within the trajectory of Old Testament missiology by depicting the church as fulfilling the major missional roles of the Old Testament.

THE CHURCH'S MISSION AND THE MISSIONAL ROLES OF THE OLD TESTAMENT

In chapters 1–4, I argued that the mission of God's people develops organically throughout the Old Testament: God's creation mandate to Adam goes through a redemptive reassertion in the call of Abram, which is later organized at a corporate level with the call of Israel. In chapter 7 we saw that Jesus fulfills the roles of both Adam and Israel (and therefore implicitly Abram), and in chapter 8 we saw that the church's mission is described as an extension of Jesus' mission. For this reason, it is entirely logical that the New Testament would portray the church as fulfilling the same Old Testament missional roles that Jesus did during his earthly ministry. In this section we will explore how the church is depicted as fulfilling the creation mandate, the call of Abram, the call of Israel, the Isaianic servant, and the eschatological temple.

---

7. Schnabel, "Paul's Missionary Strategy," 157.

The Church's Mission and the Creation Mandate

The Creation Mandate in Acts

As noted above, the book of Acts divides into three major sections that follow the expansion of the church from Jerusalem (chs. 1–7) through Judea and Samaria (chs. 8–12) and to the ends of the earth (chs. 13–28). At three significant junctures in this movement Luke provides summary statements of the spread of the gospel that allude to the creation mandate:

Table 9. The Creation Mandate and the Spread of the Word of God in Acts

Creation Mandate	Spread of the Word of God in Acts
	"And the word of God continued to increase (*auxanō*), and the number of the disciples multiplied (*plēthynō*) greatly in Jerusalem" (Acts 6:7).
"Be fruitful (*auxanō*) and multiply (*plēthynō*) and fill the earth" (Gen 1:28 [LXX]).	"But the word of God increased (*auxanō*) and multiplied (*plēthynō*)" (Acts 12:24).
	"So the word of the Lord continued to increase (*auxanō*) and prevail (*ischyō*) mightily" (Acts 19:20)

As this table shows, these verses in Acts each allude to the LXX of Gen 1:28 by using the mandate verbs in succession.[8] This is further apparent from the fact that Stephen uses these same verbs (*auxanō* and *plēthynō*) in Acts 7:17 to summarize Israel's growth prior to their Egyptian oppression in an obvious reference to Exod 1:7, which itself is an allusion to Gen 1:28.[9] Significant for a theology of mission is the observation that in each of these three allusions the subject of creation mandate action is "the word of God/ the Lord." Moreover, these three allusions occur in each of the three major sections of Acts, and each precedes a major development in the geographical expansion of the church.

The first allusion (Acts 6:7) occurs at the end of the appointment of the seven Hellenists who are chosen to ensure the right distribution of food among the Greek-speaking widows in Jerusalem. The apostles declare their need to maintain focus on prayer and the ministry of the word (6:2, 4), and

---

8. See below regarding the use of *ischyō* rather than *plēthynō* in Acts 19:20.

9. Both Exod 1:7–10 and Acts 7:17–19 describe (1) Israel's creation mandate proliferation followed by (2) the rise of a new Pharaoh who "deals shrewdly" (*katasophizomai*) with them.

after they lay hands on these seven Hellenists and pray for them, Luke says, "And the word of God continued to increase (*auxanō*), and the number of the disciples multiplied (*plēthynō*) greatly in Jerusalem" (v. 7). In light of the focus on the apostolic word ministry as distinct from the mercy ministry of the seven, the increase of the word of God here appears to refer most directly to the apostles' ministry, which the service of the seven is portrayed as enabling and supporting. In other words, even though the seven are appointed to tend to the physical needs of widows within the ecclesial community, their ministry complements and facilitates the outward-focused apostolic ministry of the word.[10]

Furthermore, it is significant to note that in this initial instance Luke provides two subjects to govern the mandate verbs: as "the word of God" increases (*auxanō*) the "number of the disciples" multiplies (*plēthynō*). In the book of Acts, "the word of God/the Lord" refers to the message about the life, death, and resurrection of Jesus.[11] In chapter 1 we saw that humanity's mission at creation was to be fruitful and multiply and fill the earth as God's images and thereby represent that his kingship extends over the entire earth. Here we see that in the post-ascension period this creation mandate is fulfilled as God's people proclaim the good news of Jesus and the number of his followers multiplies. Immediately after this first mandate allusion is the account of Stephen (6:8—8:1a), one of the seven, whose martyrdom catalyzes the second major phase of the book as persecuted believers are scattered throughout the broader region of Judea and Samaria (8:1b). The fulfillment of the creation mandate thus leads both to the numerical increase and geographical expansion of the church.

The second allusion to the creation mandate comes at the end of this second section of Acts (12:24). This account begins with Herod persecuting the church and imprisoning Peter (12:1–5), who is freed by the angel of the Lord (vv. 6–11) and returns to inform the believers who are praying for him (vv. 12–17). The account ends with Herod traveling to Caesarea and the angel of the Lord putting him to death when he fails to glorify God upon receiving ascriptions of deity (vv. 20–23), after which Luke provides the contrasting summary statement: "But the word of God increased (*auxanō*) and multiplied (*plēthynō*)" (v. 24). Peter's liberation and Herod's execution in this passage are the only two places in Acts where "the angel of the Lord" appears, and in both cases the angel "strikes" (*patassō*) these men; the angel "strikes" Peter to wake him up and free him (v. 7) and "strikes" Herod

---

10. However, as the ministries of Stephen and Philip will show, these seven were not limited to mercy ministry but engaged in powerful word ministry as well.

11. See, e.g., Acts 4:31; 8:14, 25; 11:1; 13:5, 7, 44, 46, 48; 16:32; 17:13; 18:11. See also Kodell, "Word of God Grew," 508.

dead (v. 23). This literary contrast between God's dealings with Peter and Herod highlights the divine instrumentation behind the creation mandate fulfillment portrayed in verse 24: just as God promised the patriarchs that he would "make them fruitful" and "cause them to multiply,"[12] so he sovereignly ensures the fulfillment of the creation mandate through the church's faithful proclamation of the word despite opposition and persecution. As was the case with the first allusion in relation to the first section of Acts, this second allusion closes this second section of the book and introduces an increased geographical expansion of the church. Immediately after this allusion, Luke describes Paul and Barnabas returning to Antioch (v. 25), from where they will begin their Gentile mission beyond the borders of Palestine (13:1–3).

The third creation mandate allusion comes toward the end of Paul's third missionary journey (19:20). After describing the power that Paul exercised by healing diseases and casting out demons (19:11–12), Luke introduces seven sons of Sceva who similarly attempt to use Jesus' name to exorcise demons but are overpowered (vv. 13–16). After this event Luke records several results that follow:

(1) "And this became known to all the residents of Ephesus, both Jews and Greeks" (v. 17a)

(2) "And fear fell upon them all" (v. 17bα)

(3) "and the name of the Lord Jesus was extolled" (v. 17bβ)

(4) "Also many of those who were now believers came, confessing and divulging their practices" (v. 18)

(5) "And a number of those who had practiced magic arts brought their books together and burned them in the sight of all" (v. 19a)

(6) "And they counted the value of them and found it came to fifty thousand pieces of silver" (v. 19b)

This list contains actions representing, generally speaking, faith (1–3) and repentance (4–6). The great power evident in Jesus' name has clarified the futility of the Ephesians' magical practices, leading them both to renounce their former ways and fearfully extol the name of Jesus. Following this description, Luke provides the third and final allusion to the creation mandate: "So (*houtōs*) the word of the Lord continued to increase (*auxanō*) and prevail (*ischyō*) mightily." The adverb *houtōs* ("so, in this way") indicates that the preceding description of repentance and faith is the manner by which

---

12. Gen 17:2, 6; 22:17; 26:4, 24; 48:4; cf. 28:3. See the discussion in chapter 3.

the word of the Lord continues to increase and prevail.[13] In other words, the creation mandate is fulfilled through the spread of the word of God as people repent of their sins and submit to the name of Jesus.

In this third allusion, the standard mandate verb *auxanō* is accompanied not by *plēthynō* (as in 6:7 and 12:24) but by *ischyō*, "to overpower or prevail." Although this verb does not occur in the creation mandate itself, a prefixed form of it appears in the LXX of Exod 1:7: "But the people of Israel were fruitful (*auxanō*) and increased (*plēthynō*) greatly; they multiplied and grew exceedingly strong (*katischyō*)." Since this verse alludes to Gen 1:28, within the broader contextual trajectory of Acts 6:7 and 12:24 it seems warranted to view the combination of *auxanō* and *ischyō* in 19:20 as similarly alluding to the creation mandate, perhaps by way of Exod 1:7.[14] Further explaining this shift from *plēthynō* to *ischyō* is the observation that Luke has just used this latter verb in verse 16 to describe the possessed man "overpowering" the seven sons of Sceva. Just as the possessed man "overpowered" (*ischyō*) the sons of Sceva, so the word of the Lord "overpowers" (*ischyō*) those who formerly adhered to the ways of the Ephesian worldview.[15] As these people repent and trust in Jesus, the creation mandate is fulfilled and God's mission advances. Furthermore, in line with the pattern set by the first two allusions, this third allusion is followed by a surge in the geographical expansion of the church: "Now after these events Paul resolved in the Spirit to pass through Macedonia and Achaia and go to Jerusalem, saying, 'After I have been there, I must also see Rome'" (v. 21). From this point on Paul sets his sights on the political and cultural heart of the empire, where he will eventually proclaim the good news of Jesus (28:23, 30–31). Just as Adam was charged to be abundantly fruitful and fill the earth, in Acts the word of the Lord is abundantly fruitful and the apostle Paul seeks to fill the earth as a preacher of that word by expanding beyond the borders of his previously charted territory.

The Creation Mandate in the Epistles

The clearest allusion to the creation mandate in the epistles is found in Colossians 1. After greeting the Colossians and giving thanks for their faith (vv. 1–5a), Paul attributes this faith to their hearing "the word of the truth, the gospel, which has come to you, as indeed in the whole world it is bearing fruit (*karpophoreō*) and increasing (*auxanō*)—as it also does among you"

13. So also Witherington, *Acts of the Apostles*, 583; Bock, *Acts*, 605.
14. Marshall, "Acts," 555.
15. Oschwald, "Word of the Lord Grew," 48.

(vv. 5b–6a). Although the term *karpophoreō* ("to bear fruit") does not appear in the LXX of Gen 1:28, its singular Old Testament use (Hab 3:17) translates the Hebrew verb *pāraḥ* ("to bud, sprout"), which is similar to the mandate verb *pārâ* ("to be fruitful"). Christopher Beetham makes a strong case that Paul has alluded directly to the Hebrew text here, since *karpophoreō* captures the botanical imagery of the Hebrew verb *pārâ* better than *plēthynō*.[16] Douglas Moo suggests that Paul may have chosen *karpophoreō* because it communicates more accurately than *plēthynō* the qualitative effects of the word of God in the life of the believer, which Paul emphasizes in this passage.[17] Therefore despite this deviation from the LXX, sufficient evidence exists to warrant the view that Paul is alluding to Gen 1:28.[18] The subject of mandate action in this text is "the gospel," which epexegetically modifies "the word of the truth" (v. 5) and thereby connects this passage to the creation mandate usages in Acts. Paul further notes that this proliferation of the gospel is occurring "in the whole world," which further aligns this text thematically with the creation mandate. The fruit that the gospel bears in this text is the Colossians' "hope" (v. 5), which has produced in them a "faith in Christ Jesus" and a "love ... for all the saints" (v. 4).

Coordinate with this emphasis, in verses 7–8 Paul recalls how the Colossians heard the gospel from Epaphras, and then he expresses how he and Timothy have continually prayed for them:

> And so, from the day we heard, we have not ceased to pray for you, asking that you may be filled with the knowledge of his will in all spiritual wisdom and understanding, so as to walk in a manner worthy of the Lord, fully pleasing to him, bearing fruit (*karpophoreō*) in every good work and increasing (*auxanō*) in the knowledge of God. (vv. 9–10)

Once again Paul alludes to the creation mandate using the same verbs as verse 6 in order to describe the Colossians' spiritual growth: "bearing fruit *in every good work* and increasing *in the knowledge of God*" (v. 10). Whereas the book of Acts portrays the word as expanding geographically and multiplying the number of disciples, Colossians portrays it as increasingly bearing the fruit of faith, hope, love, knowledge, and good works. The former describes the quantitative growth of the church, the latter the qualitative growth. The fact that verses 15–16 identify Jesus both as "the image of the invisible God" and the agent of creation further reinforces the creation mandate overtones that reverberate throughout this text.

16. Beetham, *Echoes of Scripture*, 52–55.
17. Moo, *Colossians and Philemon*, 88.
18. For further discussion see Beale, *Temple and the Church's Mission*, 263–68.

This analysis of Acts and Colossians reveals that the latter-day fulfillment of the creation mandate occurs fundamentally by means of the spread of the word of God through the church. The task of the original creation mandate was for God's images to fill the earth and represent God's kingship. This task is now executed as the church fills the earth and proclaims the word of God, which overpowers unbelieving worldviews and brings about faith, hope, love, knowledge, and good works in the lives of believers. As the church expands geographically and preaches the gospel, images of God who were formerly in sinful rebellion hear the word, repent of their sin, trust in Jesus, receive forgiveness, and are thereby restored to their original function of representing God's kingship. In this way, the geographical expansion of the church fulfills the original purpose for which humanity was created.

The Church's Mission and the Call of Abram

In addition to the creation mandate, the New Testament portrays the church as fulfilling the Abrahamic formula. The New Testament refers directly to God's promise to Abram in Genesis 12 at only two points: Acts 3:25 and Gal 3:8. In the former text, Peter and John have just miraculously healed a lame beggar (vv. 1–10), after which Peter addresses the astonished crowd. During this address, Peter attributes the man's healing to Jesus' power and emphasizes how the Jews handed Jesus over to be killed, but God raised him from the dead (vv. 11–16). Peter then calls upon the crowd to repent of their rejection of Jesus, identifies him as the prophet whom Moses foretold (cf. Deut 18:15, 19), and notes that the prophets after Moses have also foretold these days (vv. 17–24). Peter then says,

> You are the sons of the prophets and of the covenant that God made with your fathers, saying to Abraham, "And in your offspring shall all the families of the earth be blessed." God, having raised up his servant, sent him to you first, to bless you by turning every one of you from your wickedness. (vv. 25–26)

Peter quotes the final clause of the Abrahamic formula, which was originally given in Gen 12:3, though his wording here aligns more closely with the recollection found in Gen 22:18.[19] As we saw in chapter 3, in Gen 12:1–3 Abram's responsibility was to listen to God's voice and respond with faith and obedience. This would lead God to bless him in such a way that the

---

19. Both Acts 3:25 and Gen 22:18 specify Abraham as the recipient of this promise (as opposed to Gen 26:4 and 28:14, which are addressed to Isaac and Jacob, respectively), and state that it is "in your offspring" that the nations will be blessed. See further Léonas, "Note on Acts 3,25–26," 150; Bock, *Acts*, 180.

nations took notice, and based on how the nations' responded to Abram's relationship with God they would receive either blessing or cursing. In this way, Abram's relationship with God was designed to channel God's blessing to every people group of the world.

In this text, Peter identifies his Jewish audience as (1) sons of the prophets, and (2) sons of the Abrahamic covenant (v. 25). He then identifies Jesus as the one who fulfills the blessing promised in the Abrahamic covenant by bringing about repentance from wickedness (v. 26). As we saw in chapter 4, God's requirement for Torah faithfulness was not perfect obedience but repentant obedience, and as we saw in chapter 5, this repentance was precisely what Israel failed to exercise during the Old Testament period. Consequently, if these Jews in Peter's day would receive the good news of Jesus with repentance and faith, like Abram they too would be positioned to serve as a channel for God's blessing to extend to the nations. According to Peter, in this new covenant administration of the Abrahamic formula, Jesus not only requires repentance on the part of his representatives, he actually brings it about himself: "[God] sent [Jesus] first to you to bless you *by turning each of you from your wicked ways*" (v. 26). As we have seen, the material blessing promised in the original Abrahamic formula was designed to make Israel a recognized recipient of blessing in the sight of nations in order that God's redemptive blessing might extend to the ends of the earth. Here we see that the content of this blessing in the new covenant era is precisely what Israel lacked in the old covenant period: divinely enabled repentance. Consequently, rather than receiving material blessing as the mechanism to reach the nations, the church receives the spiritual blessing of repentance in order that we might channel that same blessing to the ends of the earth. Theologically this corresponds to the cardionomographic work of the Holy Spirit among the new covenant community that we explored last chapter.

In light of Peter's struggle to accept Cornelius the Gentile in chapter 10, John Polhill argues that Peter most likely did not have the "missionary imperative implicit in this promise to Abraham" in mind when he preached these words, but instead was focused more on his Jewish audience recognizing Jesus as the fulfillment of the Abrahamic covenant.[20] Although we may agree that Peter seemingly did not understand *how* God would incorporate the Gentiles into the new covenant community at this point, it seems to go against the evidence to suggest that he did not foresee the Gentiles being incorporated *at all*. Not only did Peter hear Jesus' statement in Acts 1:8 that the apostles would serve as witnesses "to the end of the earth," he ended his Pentecost sermon by telling the Jews that "the promise is for you and your

---

20. Polhill, *Acts*, 136–37. See also Léonas, "Note on Acts 3,25–26," 150.

children *and for all who are far off*" (2:39), the latter category most likely including Gentiles as well as diaspora Jews.[21] Moreover, the issue in the Cornelius episode is not whether Gentiles may join the covenant community, but whether they must be ceremonially clean through circumcision in order to do so (10:15, 34–35, 44–45). That Peter quotes only the last clause of Gen 12:3, which is wholly concerned with God's blessing extending to the nations, suggests that he does indeed have the missional character of the Abrahamic formula in mind. However, it seems that until Cornelius' conversion Peter viewed this mission as requiring Gentiles to express their repentance by undergoing circumcision and thereby becoming Jews.[22] What Cornelius' conversion reveals is that the blessing of repentance, which 3:26 identifies as the eschatological content of the Abrahamic covenant, is available directly to the Gentiles without the ceremonial mediation of Israel's law. Indeed, when Peter later explains his actions with Cornelius to the Jerusalem apostles, they conclude: "Then to the Gentiles also *God has granted repentance* that leads to life" (11:18). When any person—Jew or Gentile—repents from their sin and submits to Jesus as King, they are incorporated into the church and the Abrahamic formula is fulfilled.

This analysis is supported by the other New Testament reference to the Abrahamic formula, Gal 3:8. In this chapter Paul is continuing his discussion of justification by faith that begins in chapter 2. After arguing that no one is justified by works of the law (2:15–21), Paul asks twice whether the Galatians received the Spirit by works or by faith (3:2, 5), noting between these rhetorical questions the futility of attempting to proceed by means of the flesh (i.e., by works; vv. 3–4). With an implied answer of "faith,"[23] Paul notes that Abraham was similarly justified by faith (v. 6), argues that "it is those of faith who are the sons of Abraham" (v. 7), and supports this by quoting the final clause of Gen 12:3:

> And the Scripture,
>   foreseeing that God would justify the Gentiles by faith,
>   preached the gospel beforehand to Abraham,
>   saying, "In you shall all the nations be blessed."
> So then, those who are of faith are blessed along with Abraham,
>   the man of faith. (vv. 8–9)

---

21. Polhill himself acknowledges this (*Acts*, 117). See also Marshall, *Book of Acts*, 82.

22. A view with which Peter would struggle after the Cornelius episode as well (see Gal 2:11–12).

23. Silva notes that the grammar in verse 6 is elliptical; implied in the first half of the verse is the answer to the rhetorical questions of verses 2 and 5: "Surely of faith: and so it was with Abraham" ("Abraham, Faith, and Works," 253).

According to the logic of these verses, having foreseen that justification by faith would extend to the nations, the personified Scripture preached "the gospel" beforehand to Abraham, the content of which is identified as the final clause of the Abrahamic formula. A direct correlation exists therefore between (1) the nations being *justified by faith* (v. 8a), and (2) the nations being *blessed* (v. 8b). Paul confirms this association with his summary statement in verse 9 that "those who are of faith are *blessed* with Abraham." Since the argument of this larger section is that faith is the instrument by which one is justified (see also vv. 10–14), and since Paul states that those who have this faith receive the Abrahamic blessing, it follows that in these verses Paul is describing the content of the Abrahamic blessing as justification.[24]

This fits hand in glove with Peter's use of Gen 12:3 in Acts 3:25 to describe repentance, since repentance and faith together are the twin responses necessary for one to be justified. From these two uses of Gen 12:3 in the New Testament we may conclude that the mission of the church is clearly a fulfillment of the Abrahamic formula. The church has received the task of preaching the gospel to all nations and calling all people to repent, believe, and be justified in God's sight. Just as Abram was to showcase his right relationship with God to the nations by being a recognized recipient of blessing, so the church is to publicize our right relationship with God, now achieved through the justifying work of Jesus and demonstrated by our posture of repentance and faith.

The Church's Mission and the Call of Israel

As we explored in chapter 4, God's call of Israel in Exod 19:3–6 was an organized development of his prior call of Abram. Like Abram, Israel was to respond to God's word with faith and obedience, and in so doing they would serve as a kingdom of priests and a holy nation in the midst of the peoples, mediating and representing God's kingship to the ends of the earth. In 1 Peter 2 the apostle alludes to this passage when describing the nature of the church. After exhorting his readers to turn away from sin (v. 1) and exercise faith by coming to Jesus as the living stone (vv. 2–7), Peter notes that some stumble "because they disobey the word" (v. 8). In contrast to this disobedient posture, Peter says: "But you are a chosen race, a royal priesthood, a holy nation, a people for his own possession, that you may proclaim the excellencies of him who called you out of darkness into his marvelous light" (v. 9). The phrase "a chosen race" most closely resembles the final clause of

---

24. So also concludes Rhoads, "Children of Abraham, Children of God," 287; Lee, *Blessing of Abraham*, 40, 201.

Isa 43:20, while "a royal priesthood, a holy nation" alludes directly to the LXX of Exod 19:6, and "a people for his own possession" echoes both Exod 19:5 and Isa 43:21.[25]

Concerning this allusion to Exodus 19 two observations in particular are worth highlighting. First, as noted above, this passage contrasts the portrayal of the church in terms of Israel's call with those who disobey God's word in verse 8, suggesting that to function as God's "royal priesthood" and "holy nation" involves obeying his word.[26] This coheres with the interpretation of Exod 19:3–6 offered in chapter 4, where we saw that to be a kingdom of priests and a holy nation in the Old Testament involved obeying God's voice and keeping his covenant. Second, according to Peter, the purpose for which the church has been gathered as this royal priesthood and holy nation is missional in nature: "that (*hopōs*) you may proclaim the excellencies of him who called you out of darkness into his marvelous light." In light of the allusions to Isa 43:20–21 in the first half of this verse, the "excellencies" (*aretas*) that God's people are to proclaim likely correspond to the "praise" (Heb. *tᵉhillâ*; LXX: *aretas*) for which God formed his people in Isa 43:21.[27] Moreover, the description of God calling us "out of darkness into his marvelous light" fills out the nature of these excellencies that God's priestly people are to proclaim. God has saved us from darkness into light and made us a royal priesthood and holy nation in order that we would proclaim that life-giving and light-generating salvation to others. That verse 12 goes on to provide instruction concerning how God's people are to conduct themselves "among the Gentiles" connects this text thematically with the call of Israel even further; just as Israel was to represent God's kingship "among all peoples" by obeying his voice and keeping his covenant, so the church is to seek to obey God's word, declare the excellencies of our salvation, and conduct ourselves honorably among the nations, all for the sake of God's glory.

The Church's Mission and the Isaianic Servant

Having examined the ways in which the church fulfills the three major missional initiatives of the Old Testament, it is also instructive to explore additional ways that the New Testament portrays the church's mission in Old Testament terms. Although the servant in the book of Isaiah is not as prominent in the Old Testament metanarrative as Adam, Abram, or Israel,

---

25. Davids, *First Epistle of Peter*, 90–91; Jobes, *1 Peter*, 162.
26. The postpositive conjunction *de* is most naturally read adversatively here.
27. Schreiner, *1, 2 Peter, Jude*, 115.

this figure plays a critical role in the prophetic expectation that finds eventual realization in the saving work of Jesus. Since this Isaianic servant is tasked not only with suffering on behalf of God's people but also serving as a light for the nations, it makes sense that after Jesus suffers, rises, and ascends to heaven, the New Testament would depict him as continuing his work through the international ministry of his followers, thereby fulfilling this missional calling of the servant.

We have already explored how Jesus' programmatic statement in Acts 1:8 specifying that his followers would serve as his witnesses "to the end of the earth" alludes to the mission of the servant. Just as God makes the Isaianic servant as "a light for the nations, that my salvation may reach to the end of the earth" (Isa 49:6), so Jesus commissions his followers to serve as witnesses concerning his saving work "to the end of the earth." This servant theme is picked up again during the conversion of Saul, who will be the one to trailblaze the Gentile mission beyond the borders of Palestine toward the end of the earth. In Acts 9 the ascended Christ blinds Saul and sends him to wait in Damascus (vv. 1–9), after which he commissions Ananias to go and restore his sight (vv. 10–12). After Ananias expresses concern over Saul's antagonistic endeavors, Jesus says, "Go, for he is a chosen instrument of mine to carry my name before the Gentiles and kings and the children of Israel. For I will show him how much he must suffer for the sake of my name" (vv. 15–16). This language of Saul being "chosen" (*eklogē*) to represent God among "the Gentiles and kings and the children of Israel" (*ethnōn te kai basileōn huiōn te Israēl*) in the context of "suffering" (*paschō*) resembles Isaianic descriptions of the servant's ministry (42:1–4; 49:6–7; 52:15).[28] Furthermore, Ananias's assignment of restoring Saul's sight (*anablepō*; Acts 9:12) recalls the servant's task of bringing recovery of sight to the blind (*anablepō*; Isa 61:1 [LXX]; Luke 4:18; cf. Isa 42:7), a task that Jesus also assigns to Paul in the latter's recollection of this event before King Agrippa (26:18). Even the instruction for Ananias to locate Saul on "the street called Straight [*Eutheian*]" (Acts 9:11) perpetuates the Isaianic reverberations in this section ("make *straight* [*eutheias*] in the desert a highway for our God"; Isa 40:3–4; cf. Luke 3:4–5).[29] In these ways the general call of Jesus' followers to take up the servant's mantle in Acts 1:8 receives further elaboration in the calling of Saul.

This implicit portrayal of Saul/Paul in servant terms finds explicit corroboration in his ministry at Pisidian Antioch. After the Jews reject the gospel message and attempt to contradict it,

---

28. Beers, *Followers of Jesus*, 149–50; Lyons, "Paul and the Servant(s)," 354.

29. Beers, *Followers of Jesus*, 149.

> Paul and Barnabas spoke out boldly, saying, "It was necessary that the word of God be spoken first to you. Since you thrust it aside and judge yourselves unworthy of eternal life, behold, we are turning to the Gentiles. For so the Lord has commanded us, saying,
>
>> 'I have made you a light for the Gentiles,
>> that you may bring salvation to the ends of the earth.'" (Acts 13:46–47)

Here Paul and Barnabas quote God's speech to the Isaianic servant (Isa 49:6) to substantiate their call to preach the gospel to the nations. Interestingly, even though the Isaianic text contains an indicative statement addressed to the servant, Paul and Barnabas summarize this verse as a command addressed to them. This indicates that these first international missionaries developed their missional theology not simply from Old Testament imperatives or traditions stemming from Jesus' post-resurrection commands, but from a biblical-theological understanding of God's missional objectives conveyed within the Old Testament Scriptures.

In a similar manner, in Romans 10 Paul uses an Isaianic text bordering the fourth servant song to describe the work of gospel ministry:

> How then will they call on him in whom they have not believed? And how are they to believe in him of whom they have never heard? And how are they to hear without someone preaching? And how are they to preach unless they are sent? As it is written, "How beautiful are the feet of those who preach the good news!" (Rom 10:14–15)

In this passage Paul quotes Isa 52:7 to support the need to send ministers out to preach the gospel. However, whereas the Isaianic passage describes a singular messenger ("How beautiful upon the mountains are the feet *of him* who brings good news"), Paul alters this text to make it plural ("How beautiful are the feet *of those* who preach the good news").[30] This democratization of the Old Testament passage reflects the same interpretive method present in Acts 13:47 as well as Paul's subsequent use of a servant text that begins just a few verses later in Isaiah. After articulating his ambition to preach the gospel in uncharted territory (Rom 15:20), Paul supports this missional calling in verse 21 by quoting Isa 52:15:

> Those who have never been told of him will see,
> and those who have never heard will understand.

---

30. Wagner, *Heralds of the Good News*, 173–74.

This verse appears at the beginning of the fourth servant song, which Philip had earlier used to describe the saving work of Jesus (Acts 8:26–35), but which Paul now applies to his calling to extend the good news of Jesus to those who have never heard. In these various ways the church's mission of preaching the gospel to the ends of the earth is presented as an extension of Jesus' fulfillment of the Isaianic servant of the Lord.

The Church's Mission and the Eschatological Temple

The final Old Testament element in the church's missional identity that we will explore is the temple. So far in this study we have seen that (1) the temple played a critical role in Israel's missional economy, (2) Jesus embodied the temple during his earthly ministry, and (3) Jesus transformed the church into the temple through the outpouring of the Holy Spirit at Pentecost. As I argued last chapter, the church's establishment as the eschatological temple at Pentecost is the catalyst that transforms the mission of God's people from the centripetal pull of Israel's witness to the centrifugal expansion of the church. Within the context of this centrifugal expansion, as mentioned above, in 1 Cor 3:10–15 Paul uses an architectural metaphor to describe his frontier missionary work of establishing new churches in previously unchurched areas. In context, Paul is critiquing the Corinthians' schismatic divisions in which some were claiming to follow Apollos and others Paul (vv. 3–4). Paul responds by outlining the different missional roles that he and Apollos fulfilled (vv. 5–9) and describing his own pioneering ministry as laying a foundation upon which others are building (vv. 10–15). Continuing this architectural metaphor, Paul goes on to say concerning the church,

> Do you (pl.) not know that you (pl.) are God's temple (sg.) and that God's Spirit dwells in you (pl.)? If anyone destroys God's temple (sg.), God will destroy him. For God's temple (sg.) is holy, and you (pl.) are that temple (sg.). (vv. 16–17)

In these verses, the verbs and pronouns referring to the Corinthians are all plural, while "temple" is singular, indicating that Paul is describing the church as a whole as the temple of God. Paul's missionary work is an act of building and expanding the temple of God on earth, and his concern in this passage is to warn the Corinthian congregation not to "destroy God's temple" by their schismatic and disunifying behavior.

This description of the church as the temple reappears again in 1 Cor 6:12–20. In these verses Paul is addressing some within the Corinthian church who have downplayed the significance of one's physicality to the point of engaging the services of a prostitute.[31] After quoting and correcting some popular sayings used to support licentiousness (vv. 12–13a), Paul argues that the body is not meant for sexual immorality but for the Lord (v. 13b), and that by virtue of our union with Christ our bodies will be raised just as his was (vv. 14–15a); therefore we should not be united to a prostitute (vv. 15b–17). He then observes that sexual sin is unique in that by committing it Christians sin against their own bodies (v. 18), following this with another reference to the temple:

> Or do you (pl.) not know that your (pl.) body (sg.) is a temple (sg.) of the Holy Spirit within you (pl.), whom you (pl.) have from God? You (pl.) are not your own, for you (pl.) were bought with a price. So glorify God in your (pl.) body (sg.). (vv. 19–20)

As was the case in 1 Corinthians 3, the verbs and pronouns referring to the Corinthians here are plural, while "temple" (and in this case also "body") is singular. At first glance this seems to indicate that Paul is again describing the entire church as the body of Christ and as the temple of God. Yet the context shows that Paul's concern in this passage is to discuss the proper use of one's physical body in relation to sexual activity ("Do you [pl.] not know that *your bodies* [pl.] are members of Christ? Shall I then take the members of Christ and make them members of a prostitute? Never!" [v. 15]). For this reason, a purely ecclesial understanding of "your (pl.) body (sg.) is a temple" does not seem appropriate to Paul's argument here.

Elsewhere in the New Testament the singular noun "body" (*sōma*) is occasionally modified by a plural genitive pronoun that functions distributively, in which case the singular noun denotes multiple referents.[32] For example, in Rom 8:23 Paul describes believers as groaning inwardly and awaiting our adoption as sons, which he elaborates as "the redemption of our *body* (sg.)" (my translation). Most translations rightly render the singular "body" (*sōmatos*) as a plural here, since the plural pronoun "our" clearly functions distributively to describe the resurrection of each individual believer's body.[33] Similarly, given the context of Paul's argument in 1 Corinthians 6, the singular "body" in verse 19 is best understood as a plural, distributed referentially by the modifying plural pronoun "your." By utilizing this grammar Paul is able to address the problem at hand by teaching the sanctity of each individual believer's body, while also connecting back

---

31. Or possibly pagan temple prostitutes. See Rosner, "Temple Prostitution," 336–51.

32. Gupta, "Which 'Body' Is a Temple?" 522.

33. E.g., NRSV, ESV, NIV (1984, 2011), CSB, et al.

to his earlier teaching that the corporate body of Christ is the temple.[34] In so doing Paul underscores that the covenant community as a whole is the temple of God precisely because the individual members who constitute it experience the sanctifying, temple presence of God through the Holy Spirit.

Paul provides further clarity on this issue in 2 Corinthians 6 while again addressing the nature of relationships between believers and unbelievers. In 1 Corinthians 6 Paul proscribes sexual union with prostitutes; in 2 Corinthians 6 he prohibits marital union between Christians and non-Christians. In verses 14-15 Paul instructs the Corinthians not to be unequally yoked, supporting this with a series of rhetorical questions designed to show the utter incompatibility of believers and unbelievers. The last of these rhetorical questions shifts the discourse once again to the theme of the temple:

> What agreement has the temple of God with idols? For we are the temple of the living God; as God said,
>
> "I will make my dwelling among them and walk among them,
>   and I will be their God,
>   and they shall be my people.
> Therefore go out from their midst,
>   and be separate from them, says the Lord,
>   and touch no unclean thing;
>   then I will welcome you,
> and I will be a father to you,
>   and you shall be sons and daughters to me,
>   says the Lord Almighty." (vv. 16-18)

In verse 16a Paul includes the grammatically unnecessary first-person plural pronoun to emphasize that *"we* (i.e., the church) are the temple of the living God."[35] Buttressing this statement, Paul assembles a series of Old Testament quotations that connect the themes of (1) God dwelling with his people (v. 16b; cf. Lev 26:11-12; Ezek 37:27), (2) God bringing his people out of exile and charging them to be holy (v. 17; cf. Isa 52:11; Ezek 20:34), and (3) God's covenant commitment (v. 18; cf. 2 Sam 7:14).[36] Paul's immedi-

---

34. See also, e.g., Thiselton, *1 Corinthians*, 474.

35. Reflecting this emphasis, Harris renders the significance of this clause as follows: "It is we—yes, we Christians—who form the dwelling place of God" (*Second Epistle to the Corinthians*, 505).

36. The original contexts of these primary Old Testament citations each pertain to the temple in one way or another. Lev 26:11-12 is explicitly about the tabernacle/temple; Isa 52:11 is directed to the priests who transport the temple elements ("you who bear the vessels of the Lord"); and the promise of 2 Sam 7:14 is directed toward the one who will "build a house for my name" (v. 13).

ate goal in citing these texts is to support his argument that believers should not intermarry with unbelievers, yet it is insightful to note that the primary Old Testament texts to which Paul alludes here all resound with significant missional overtones in their original contexts.

In verse 16b Paul quotes Lev 26:11–12: "I will make my dwelling among you, and my soul shall not abhor you. And I will walk among you and will be your God, and you shall be my people." This promise of God's presence amidst his people is the culmination of God's covenant blessings for Israel if they would live faithfully before him according to the Torah. Immediately prior to this, God promises that upon Israel's faithful obedience he will fulfill the creation mandate through them: "I will turn to you and make you fruitful and multiply you and will confirm my covenant with you" (Lev 26:9). In the Levitical context, therefore, God's temple presence is closely associated with his fulfilling the creation mandate through his people.

In 2 Cor 6:17 Paul next quotes from Isa 52:11: "Depart, depart, go out from there; touch no unclean thing; go out from the midst of her; purify yourselves, you who bear the vessels of the LORD." This is a call for Israel's exiled priests to leave the domain of their captors and return to the promised land in holiness. In the Isaianic context, immediately preceding this call is a statement of the universal, international recognition of God's upcoming act of redemption ("all the ends of the earth shall see the salvation of our God" [v. 10]). Immediately following this call is the fourth servant song (52:13—53:12), which as we observed above provided Paul with Scriptural grounds for his call to preach the gospel among unreached people groups ("that which has not been told them they see, and that which they have not heard they understand" [v. 15; cf. Rom 15:21]). Therefore, like the Levitical context examined above, this Isaianic context exhibits a global undercurrent that adds missional significance to the passage that Paul quotes.

Paul's final major Old Testament quotation comes from 2 Sam 7:14: "I will be to him a father, and he shall be to me a son." This statement occurs in the midst of the establishment of the Davidic covenant, which as we saw in chapter 4 is of critical significance for a biblical theology of mission. God promised to give David's dynasty an everlasting and earth-wide dominion, and here Paul expands the language of this promise to include the covenant community as a whole: "I will be a father to *you* (pl.), and *you* (pl.) shall be *sons and daughters* to me" (2 Cor 6:18). Moreover, in the preceding verse of 2 Samuel 7 God states that the object of his covenant faithfulness—David's descendant—will "build a house for my name" (i.e., a temple; v. 13). In a similar way, as the eschatological temple of God the church is called to "build a house for God's name" by its multiplication and geographical expansion throughout the world. God's promise of covenant fidelity to the Davidic line thereby receives further application through his indwelling presence amidst the new covenant community, who is then called to extend that temple presence to the ends of the earth. This collection of Old Testament quotations in 2 Cor 6:16–18 thus underscores the missional nature of the new covenant community as the eschatological temple of God on earth.

The final New Testament text describing the church as the temple of God that we will explore is Ephesians 2. After outlining the gracious salvation that God extends to sinners through Jesus (vv. 1–10), Paul notes that the Gentiles who were formally separated from God's covenant people (vv. 11–12) have now been brought near (v. 13) and joined together with Jews in having access to God through the Spirit (vv. 14–18). Paul then portrays this Gentile inclusion with the Jews as the construction of a temple:

> So then you are no longer strangers and aliens, but you are fellow citizens with the saints and members of the household of God, built on the foundation of the apostles and prophets, Christ Jesus himself being the cornerstone, in whom the whole structure, being joined together, grows into a holy temple in the LORD. In him you also are being built together into a dwelling place for God by the Spirit. (vv. 19–22)

Several observations from this text contribute to our understanding of the church as the eschatological temple of God. First, Jesus is described as the "cornerstone" of this temple, which follows naturally from the Gospels' portrayal of Jesus as both the builder of the church (e.g., Matt 16:18) and as the eschatological temple himself. Second, the apostles and prophets are described as the "foundation" of this temple, which again follows naturally from the New Testament's depiction of the birth of the church.[37] Third, and most significant for our purposes, this passage indicates that the church as the eschatological temple is a work in progress.[38] In verse 21 Paul says that this household of God comprising Jews and Gentiles "grows (*auxanō*) into a holy temple." As we have repeatedly seen, *auxanō* is one of the two primary creation mandate verbs as rendered in the LXX. Therefore, as the word of God "increases" (*auxanō*; Acts 6:7; 12:24; 19:20) and the number of disciples multiplies, the eschatological temple of God "grows" (*auxanō*). As the church executes this mission and represents God's kingship to the ends of the earth, eventually this eschatological, ecclesial temple will fill the

---

37. E.g., Matt 28:18–20; Luke 24:44–49; John 20:21–23; Acts 1:8. See the discussion in chapter 8.

38. See also Fowl, *Ephesians*, 99; Beale, *Temple and the Church's Mission*, 263.

earth. As we will see next chapter, this is precisely the picture painted by the closing vision of the book of Revelation.

To summarize: in this section we have surveyed a variety of ways in which the New Testament depicts the church as fulfilling the missional roles of the Old Testament. The church is portrayed as fulfilling the creation mandate, the call of Abram, the call of Israel, as well as the roles of the Isaianic servant and the eschatological temple. This analysis reveals that the mission of the church is not distinct from the mission of Adam or Israel, but rather represents an eschatological development of that mission in light of the saving work of Jesus.

THE CHURCH'S MISSION AND THE PROCLAMATION OF THE KINGDOM OF GOD

Throughout this book I have argued that God's mission in the world is for his *kingship* to be represented to the ends of the earth. God's throne is in heaven, yet his intention is to manifest the supremacy of his reign over the earth through the allegiant obedience of his faithful, representative images. During the Old Testament period this reign of God was not well represented because of the pervasive power that sin held over all humanity. However, with the atoning work of Jesus and the outpoured presence of the Holy Spirit, the eschatological kingdom of God has dawned and God's people are now positioned to represent God's kingship faithfully. In line with this, when we examine the New Testament, we see that the proclamation of "the kingdom of God/heaven" is front and center both in Jesus' public ministry and in the ministries of his followers.

When John the Baptist comes to prepare the way for Jesus, his message is, "Repent, for the kingdom of heaven is at hand" (Matt 3:2). Jesus similarly comes and preaches about the kingdom of God throughout his ministry,[39] instructs his disciples to preach about the kingdom,[40] and entrusts them with both the "secrets" (Matt 13:11; Mark 4:11; Luke 8:10) and the "keys" (Matt 16:19) of the kingdom. According to Jesus, this kingdom has been prepared from the foundation of the world (Matt 25:34), has arrived subtly through his own coming (Luke 17:20–21), and is manifested through his work of casting out demons (Matt 12:28; Luke 11:20). Jesus declares that this kingdom is "not of this world" (John 18:36), that we must be born again to see it (John 3:3–5), that we must seek it first (Matt 6:33; Luke 12:31), that the Old Testament patriarchs entered it (Matt 8:11; Luke 13:28–29), and that

---

39. Matt 4:17, 23; 9:35; Mark 1:15; Luke 4:43; 8:1; 9:11; 16:16.
40. Matt 10:7; Luke 9:2, 60; 10:9.

he will enter it upon his ascension to heaven.[41] Those who respond to God's word with faith and obedience inherit this kingdom,[42] since it requires our fullest devotion (Luke 9:61–62), and those who enter it must produce fruit (Matt 21:43) and will ultimately receive a reward in the age to come (Luke 18:29–30). Greatness in this kingdom comes through exercising humility like that of a child[43] and poverty of spirit (Matt 5:3; cf. Luke 6:20), and the path to entering this kingdom involves suffering and persecution.[44] It is difficult for the rich to enter this kingdom,[45] and those who reject it will be judged (Luke 10:10–12). In light of this centrality of the kingdom, Jesus instructs his followers to pray for its coming (Matt 6:10; Luke 11:2).

In the epistles we learn that the kingdom is for those who are rich in faith and love (Jas 2:5), that salvation involves God transferring us into this kingdom (Col 1:13–14; 1 Thess 2:12), and that to advance this kingdom Jesus will destroy "every rule and every authority and power" (1 Cor 15:24). Paul describes his missionary work as "for the kingdom of God" (Col 4:11), states that the kingdom consists of "power" (1 Cor 4:20) and "righteousness, peace, and joy" (Rom 14:17), and held on to the promise that God would one day bring him into this kingdom (2 Tim 4:18). The kingdom of God cannot be shaken (Heb 12:28), and neither flesh and blood (1 Cor 15:50) nor those who live unrepentantly can inherit it.[46]

Most relevant for the present discussion is the observation that the New Testament portrays the proclamation of the gospel of the kingdom as a regular component in the execution of the mission of God's people. Several descriptions of Jesus' homiletic activity depict the preaching of the kingdom as a consistent element in his public ministry:

> *From that time Jesus began to preach*, saying, "Repent, for the kingdom of heaven is at hand." (Matt 4:17)

> And he went *throughout all Galilee*, teaching in their synagogues and proclaiming the gospel of the kingdom and healing every disease and every affliction among the people. (Matt 4:23)

> And Jesus went *throughout all the cities and villages*, teaching in their synagogues and proclaiming the gospel of the kingdom and healing every disease and every affliction. (Matt 9:35)

---

41. Matt 16:28; Mark 9:1; Luke 9:27; 21:31–32.
42. Matt 5:10, 19; 7:21; 21:31–32; Mark 9:47; 12:28–34; Luke 12:32; cf. 2 Pet 1:10–11.
43. Matt 18:3–4; 19:14; 20:20–28; Mark 10:14–15; Luke 18:16–17.
44. Acts 14:22; 2 Thess 1:5.
45. Matt 19:23–24; Mark 10:23–25; Luke 18:24–25.
46. 1 Cor 6:9–10; Gal 5:19–21; Eph 5:5.

244 FILL THE EARTH

> I must preach the good news of the kingdom of God *to the other towns as well*; for I was sent for this purpose. (Luke 4:43)
>
> Soon afterward he went on *through cities and villages*, proclaiming and bringing the good news of the kingdom of God. (Luke 8:1)
>
> The Law and the Prophets were until John; *since then* the good news of the kingdom of God is preached, and everyone forces his way into it. (Luke 16:16)

Each of these passages portrays the proclamation of the good news of the kingdom as an iterative endeavor that Jesus engages in throughout his travels. In a similar fashion, Luke summarizes the content of Jesus' post-resurrection teaching as pertaining to the kingdom: "He presented himself alive to them after his suffering by many proofs, appearing to them during forty days and speaking about *the kingdom of God*" (Acts 1:3). Following this example, Philip goes to Samaria and preaches "good news about the kingdom of God" (8:12). At the end of Paul and Barnabas' first missionary journey they retrace their steps throughout Asia Minor and visit several churches in order to encourage the people concerning "the kingdom of God" (Acts 14:22). Luke later describes Paul's ministry among the Jews in Ephesus in this manner as well: "And he entered the synagogue and for three months spoke boldly, reasoning and persuading them about *the kingdom of God*" (Acts 19:8).

Concerning this season in Ephesus, when Paul later gives his farewell speech to the Ephesian elders in Acts 20, he summarizes his extended ministry there in a way that provides further insight into the centrality of the kingdom of God:

> nor as precious to myself,

> I did not   k from   laring to you   ιe whole counsel of God

In section A, Paul describes the ministry he received from Jesus as a call "to testify to the gospel of the grace of God" (v. 24). In section B he summarizes his ministry among the Ephesians as "proclaiming the kingdom" (v. 25), and in section C he asserts his blood innocence on the grounds that he "did not shrink from declaring to you the whole counsel of God" (v. 27). Since section A records Paul's divine calling and sections B and C contain descriptions of his actual ministry—with the latter declaring Paul's innocence against any accusation that he failed to fulfill his calling—it follows that the bolded clauses in sections B and C correspond to the same phenomenon as the bolded clause in section A. That is, "to testify to the gospel of the grace of God" (A) is elaborated here as "proclaiming the kingdom" (B) and "declaring . . . the whole counsel of God" (C). This underscores the centrality of the kingdom of God for our understanding of Paul's specific calling as well as the very nature of the gospel itself.[47]

Continuing this focus, the book of Acts ends by emphasizing the fundamental role that the kingdom of God played in Paul's ministry in Rome. After arriving in Rome, Paul addresses the local leaders of the Jews who desire to hear the specifics of his beliefs (28:17–22). According to 28:23,

> When they had appointed a day for him, they came to him at his lodging in greater numbers. From morning till evening he expounded to them, *testifying to the kingdom of God* and trying to convince them about Jesus both from the Law of Moses and from the Prophets.

After certain Jews depart (vv. 24–27) and Paul notes that God's salvation is going to the nations (v. 28), the narrative of Acts ends with a final description of Paul's habitual practice of proclaiming the kingdom of God: "He lived there two whole years at his own expense, and welcomed all who came to him, *proclaiming the kingdom of God* and teaching about the Lord Jesus Christ with all boldness and without hindrance" (vv. 30–31). These various texts indicate that the proclamation of the kingdom of God was a central, fundamental element in Jesus' and the early church's gospel proclamation. The gospel is not simply the good news that individuals are forgiven by the shed blood of Jesus on their behalf, but rather that Jesus' life, death, resurrection, and ascension have inaugurated the eschatological kingdom of God on earth. In light of this inaugurated kingdom, God's people are to go to all nations and call them to repent, believe, receive forgiveness, and join in proclaiming the good news of this everlasting kingdom.

---

47. Kilgallen argues on rhetorical grounds that verse 25 is the structural crux of Paul's speech here ("Paul's Speech to the Ephesian Elders," 116).

One final element in the early church's proclamation points to the significance of the kingdom of God for a theology of mission: the focus on Jesus' *resurrection*. Although the modern evangelical church tends to emphasize Jesus' sacrificial death on the cross in the proclamation of the gospel, the singular theme that appears in every major apostolic speech in the book of Acts is not Jesus' death but his resurrection.[48] Within the book of Acts, eight speeches have been identified as "missionary speeches."[49] Of these eight speeches, the first six mention both Jesus' death[50] and his resurrection.[51] However, all six references to Jesus' death occur not as descriptions of his atoning work but as accusations against the Jews for killing him: "you crucified and killed" (2:23); "you killed the Author of life" (3:15); "whom you crucified" (4:10); "whom you killed" (5:30); "they put him to death" (10:39); "when they had carried out all that was written of him" (13:29; cf. vv. 27–28). The seventh so-called "missionary speech" (14:15–17) mentions neither Jesus' death nor his resurrection, though it is questionable whether this should be considered a "missionary speech" *per se* given the chaotic nature of the scene and Paul and Barnabas' immediate concern to stop the men of Lystra from sacrificing to them.[52] As Polhill suggests, this speech seems to be cut short, since not only do Paul and Barnabas not discuss Jesus' death or resurrection, they do not mention Jesus at all![53] Since the men of Lystra are non-Jewish polytheists who are attempting to worship Paul and Barnabas, it is unsurprising that the apostles do not advance beyond basic assertions of monotheism to include testimony concerning Jesus and his death and resurrection. Lastly, the final missionary speech in Acts is Paul's famous Areopagus address in 17:22–31. In contrast to the frenetic scene portrayed at Lystra, Paul delivers this address in a calm environment to listeners who are engaged and eager to hear new ideas (v. 21). Significantly, in this speech Paul does not mention Jesus' death, though his speech is both

---

48. In making this observation I do not intend to downplay the significance of Jesus' atoning work on the cross in any way. In his epistles Paul states that "we preach Christ crucified" (1 Cor 1:23), that he "decided to know nothing among you except Jesus Christ and him crucified" (1 Cor 2:2), and that his only boast was "in the cross of our Lord Jesus Christ" (Gal 6:14). Nevertheless, these epistolary statements addressed to existing churches do not alter the portrayal of the apostolic kerygma directed to unbelievers in the narrative of Acts, which is more preoccupied with proclaiming Jesus as *risen* than Jesus as *crucified*.

49. Acts 2:14–39; 3:12–26; 4:8–12, 19–20; 5:29–32; 10:34–43; 13:16–41; 14:15–17; 17:22–31. For a helpful summary see Strandenœs, "Missionary Speeches," 341–42.

50. Acts 2:23; 3:15; 4:10; 5:30; 10:39; 13:29.

51. Acts 2:24, 31; 3:15, 26; 4:10; 5:30; 10:40; 13:30, 33, 34, 37.

52. Bock, *Acts*, 478.

53. Polhill, *Acts*, 317.

precipitated by and climaxes in the proclamation of Jesus' resurrection (vv. 18, 31).

In line with this focus in the missionary speeches is the emphasis in Acts on the apostles as "witnesses." The noun *martys* ("witness") occurs thirteen times in the book of Acts, and aside from two references to witnesses who falsely accuse and stone Stephen (6:13; 7:58), every time it refers to Jesus' followers as "witnesses" of his resurrection. Jesus' commission in 1:8 describes the apostles as his "witnesses" without defining the specifics of what this task entails, though as the remaining uses of this term make clear, the apostles are called "witnesses" because they have observed Jesus in his resurrected state:

> beginning from the baptism of John until the day when he was taken up from us—one of these men must become with us *a witness to his resurrection*. (1:22)

> This Jesus *God raised up, and of that we all are witnesses.* (2:32)

> and you killed the Author of life, whom *God raised from the dead. To this we are witnesses.* (3:15)

> *The God of our fathers raised Jesus*, whom you killed by hanging him on a tree. *God exalted him at his right hand* as Leader and Savior, to give repentance to Israel and forgiveness of sins. *And we are witnesses to these things*, and so is the Holy Spirit, whom God has given to those who obey him. (5:30–32)

> And we are *witnesses* of all that he did both in the country of the Jews and in Jerusalem. They put him to death by hanging him on a tree, *but God raised him* on the third day *and made him to appear*, not to all the people but *to us who had been chosen by God as witnesses*, who ate and drank with him after he rose from the dead. (10:39–41)

> and for many days *he appeared to those who had come up with him from Galilee to Jerusalem, who are now his witnesses* to the people. (13:31)

> And he said, "The God of our fathers appointed you to know his will, *to see the Righteous One* and to hear a voice from his mouth; *for you will be a witness* for him to everyone of what you have seen and heard. (22:14–15)

> But rise and stand upon your feet, *for I have appeared to you for this purpose, to appoint you as a servant and witness* to the things

in which you have seen me and to those in which I will appear to you. (26:16)

All of these passages directly correlate the role of a "witness" with firsthand testimony concerning Jesus' resurrection. The only remaining use of *martys* in the book of Acts appears in 22:20, where Paul recalls his prayer in which he previously referred to "the blood of Stephen your witness." Although it is unclear if Stephen was among those who saw Jesus between his resurrection and ascension, the text of Acts is clear that during his trial Stephen sees Jesus standing at the right hand of God (7:55) and testifies to such (7:56), which establishes him as a witness to Jesus' resurrection. Since Jesus' resurrection functions as his coronation to the eschatological Davidic throne, it follows that the apostolic role of "witness" pertains directly to God's kingdom, since the resurrected Jesus now rules over this kingdom as both the divine and human king.

SUMMARY

In this chapter we have seen that the New Testament portrays the church as successfully executing the mission of God's people. Just as Adam was commanded to fill the earth, the New Testament presents the church as expanding geographically, beginning in Jerusalem and spreading further and further toward the end of the earth. The book of Acts presents a narrative depiction of this expansionistic mission, while the epistles provide practical and theological reflection from the apostles as they engage in this mission. We also saw how the New Testament portrays the church as fulfilling the missional roles of the Old Testament, particularly those of Adam, Abram, Israel, Isaiah's servant, and the temple. This Old Testament portrayal of the New Testament church reinforces the conclusion that the church receives the same mission as both Adam and Israel. Lastly, we saw that throughout the Gospels and Acts both Jesus and his followers regularly preach the good news of the kingdom, which reinforces the royal nature of God's supremacy and the church's mission. The gospel is the announcement that God has inaugurated his kingdom on earth through the life, death, and resurrection of Jesus, and that all people everywhere must turn and submit to Jesus as King through repentance and faith. In so doing, sinners turn their allegiance back to God, receive his forgiveness, and join God's people in proclaiming the good news of this kingdom to the ends of the earth.

10 MISSION FULFILLED
The New Creation

As we saw last chapter, the narrative of Acts presents the beginning of the successful execution of the mission of God's people. Jesus' followers proclaim the good news of his kingdom in increasingly distant locales from their starting point in Jerusalem, and the narrative ends with this mission still in process. It is only when we open the book of Revelation that we see the mission of God completed. In this chapter I will provide an overview of the structure and purpose of the book of Revelation, after which we will explore how Revelation portrays God, his people, and the new creation. In so doing we will see that this final book of the canon depicts the mission of God as fulfilled; God is presented as the great King, and his people are portrayed as an international priestly kingdom that has filled the earth.

THE STRUCTURE AND PURPOSE OF THE BOOK OF REVELATION

The structure of the book of Revelation has yet to receive scholarly consensus, though certain major literary divisions can plausibly be made.[1] The prologue (1:1–8) and epilogue (22:6–21) enclose the two major portions of the book, which may be described as the "letter section" (1:9—3:22) and the "visionary section" (4:1—22:5). Supporting this structure is the language of John being "in the spirit" (*en pneumati*), first occurring at 1:10 and recurring at 4:2, 17:3, and 21:10, thus beginning these two major sections and dividing the visionary section into three sub-sections (4:1—16:21;

---

1. More than forty years ago Collins commented: "There are almost as many outlines of the book as there are interpreters" (*Combat Myth*, 8). For a more recent assessment of the situation, see Tavo, "Structure of the Apocalypse," 47–68.

17:1—21:8; 21:9—22:5).[2] At the beginning of the visionary section John is lifted to heaven, sees the throne of God, and observes, "From the throne came flashes of lightning, and rumblings and peals of thunder" (4:5). This language of cosmic upheaval is repeated at the end of each of the three series of seven judgments in this sub-section (8:5; 11:19, 16:18), indicating both the divine origin of these judgments and that each series culminates with the same final judgment.[3] This suggests that rather than offering a linear presentation, these three series provide a cyclical portrayal of God judging the world from his heavenly throne. Although these cycles each reflect a progression toward the same final judgment, the literary depiction of this judgment increases in intensity each time, providing a sense of escalation as the reader progresses through the apocalyptic vision.[4]

Alongside this increased intensity of judgment, this sub-section of chapters 4–16 displays a progression of increased delay of judgment. Between both the sixth and seventh seals and trumpets are literary intercalations (7:1–17; 10:1—11:13) designed to demonstrate a delay of the seventh and final judgment in each series.[5] This is supported explicitly in the latter intercalation where the angel swears "that there would be no more delay, but that in the days of the trumpet call to be sounded by the seventh angel, the mystery of God would be fulfilled, just as he announced to his servants the prophets" (10:6b–7). By the time we reach the bowl cycle, however, there is no portrayal of delay as the vision moves immediately from the sixth to the seventh judgment. Chapters 12–14 fall between the seventh trumpet (11:15–19) and the introduction to the bowl cycle (15:1), thereby serving as an interlude that explicates in greater detail the material of the previous two intercalations and introduces vocabulary to be used in the following bowl cycle.[6] This material, having such affinities with the prior two intercala-

---

2. Bauckham, *Climax of Prophecy*, 3; Smith, "Structure of the Book of Revelation," 392; Filho, "Apocalypse of John," 215.

3. Boxall, *Revelation*, 86; Bauckham, *Climax of Prophecy*, 8.

4. In addition to the "flashes of lightning," "rumblings," and "peals of thunder" introduced at 4:5, 8:5 adds an "earthquake," 11:19 adds an "earthquake and heavy hail," and 16:18 describes "a great earthquake such as there had never been since man was on the earth, so great was that earthquake."

5. Bauckham notes that "such delay would be particularly felt in oral performance" (*Climax of Prophecy*, 12).

6. Bauckham (*Climax of Prophecy*, 16–17) lists both the material recounted from the prior intercalations (the 144,000 in 7:4 and 14:1; the apocalyptic period of the church's suffering and witness in 11:2–3 and 12:6, 14; 13:5; and the beast who makes war against and conquers the saints in 11:7 and 13:7) and the material introduced in chapters 12–14 that is incorporated into the bowl cycle (those with the beast's mark who worship its image [16:2]; the throne and the kingdom of the beast [16:10]; the

tions and standing between the trumpet and bowl cycles, can be thought of as a literary interlude that serves to delay the last and most intense depiction of final judgment in the bowl cycle.[7]

After these three cycles of judgment, the final two sub-sections of the book focus on the contrasting fates of Babylon the Harlot (17:1—21:8) and Jerusalem the Bride (21:9—22:5), which represent respectively God's enemies and his people. This division is marked not only by John's final two descriptions of being "in the spirit" (17:3; 21:10) but also by the parallel speech that precedes each of these descriptions, where the angel invites John to "come" and offers to show him the female figure in question (17:1-2; 21:9).[8] We may therefore summarize the visionary section of Revelation as follows: John beholds the power and majesty of God on his throne (chs. 4-5), after which he observes cycles of increased judgment and delay (chs. 6-16) followed by portrayals of those whom God judges and redeems (17:1—22:5).

The purpose of the book of Revelation is to exhort God's people to persevere as they experience hardship and opposition between Jesus' ascension and return.[9] This is evident first of all from John's self-introduction as "your brother and partner in the tribulation and the kingdom *and the patient endurance (hypomonē) that are in Jesus*" (1:9). John writes as one who is enduring hardship for the sake of the gospel and is exhorting his readers to persevere through hardship as well. Reflecting this further is Jesus' sevenfold promise of blessing to "the one who conquers" (*ho nikōn*) found in the letter section[10] as well as the reiteration of this promise to "the one who conquers" (*ho nikōn*) in the vision of the new creation (21:7). The only explanation in the book of what it means for God's people to "conquer" is found in 12:11, which says that "they have conquered (*nikaō*) him [Satan] by the blood of the Lamb and by the word of their testimony, for they loved not their lives even unto death." Those who persevere in faith even unto death "conquer" Satan despite his attempts to oppose them and therefore receive the reward of life in the new creation. Supporting all of this is the twofold call found in the literary interlude of chapters 12-14, in which John pauses amidst the visions to exhort his readers to endure:

---

dragon, the beast, and the false prophet [16:13]; and Babylon the great [16:19]).

7. Osborne, *Revelation*, 452. While the material is not an "intercalation" like the prior two that stand between judgments six and seven, it does stand between cycles two and three and thus performs an analogous function, hence the term "interlude."

8. "Come, I will show you the judgment of the great prostitute who is seated on many waters" (17:1); "Come, I will show you the Bride, the wife of the Lamb" (21:9).

9. See, e.g., Hurtado, *Lord Jesus Christ*, 590.

10. Rev 2:7, 11, 17, 26; 3:5, 12, 21.

> Here is a call for the endurance (*hypomonē*) and faith of the saints. (13:10)
>
> Here is a call for the endurance (*hypomonē*) of the saints, those who keep the commandments of God and their faith in Jesus. (14:12)

For these reasons, Revelation may be viewed as an exhortation to faithfulness cast in apocalyptic form. The means by which God's people are encouraged to persevere are (1) the revelation of the heavenly realm, which shows the reality of God on his throne despite the spiritual war that rages on earth, and (2) the revelation of the final judgment and new creation, which show respectively the destination of the unfaithful and the faithful at the consummation of history.

THE PORTRAYAL OF GOD IN THE BOOK OF REVELATION

Aligning with our analysis in previous chapters, within this apocalyptic text God is portrayed first and foremost as King. In the prologue John offers a benediction "from him who is and who was and who is to come, and from the seven spirits *who are before his throne*" (1:4). John then introduces Jesus as "the ruler of the kings on earth" (1:5) and describes him as "coming with the clouds" (1:7), a phrase that alludes to the heavenly ascension of the Danielic Son of Man who receives a kingdom over all nations (cf. Dan 7:13).[11] This Danielic depiction of Jesus continues in the letter section as John receives instructions from a voice and turns to see "one like a son of man" (1:13), which also alludes to Dan 7:13. When John describes this figure, however, the language he uses reflects Daniel's description of the Ancient of Days (Rev 1:13–15; cf. Dan 7:9–10).[12] Since both the Son of Man and the Ancient of Days are royal figures in Daniel, this opening depiction of Jesus presents him as the supreme, divine-human King.

This royal imagery continues in the visionary section as John is elevated to the heavenly realm, which is portrayed throughout Revelation as a throne room. The bulk of chapters 4–16 are set within this throne room, with virtually every object, entity, and event in the heavenly realm described in relation to the throne.[13] Throughout the visionary section this imagery of

---

11. Beale with Campbell, *Revelation*, 42.
12. Smith, "Identification of Jesus with YHWH," 75; Resseguie, *Revelation*, 76.
13. This includes (1) God (Rev 4:2, 9–10a; 5:1, 7, 13), (2) a rainbow (4:3), (3) twenty-four elders on their own thrones (4:4), (4) cosmic upheaval (4:5), (5) a sea of

God's throne occurs in a variety of contexts including judgment,[14] salvation (7:9-17; 14:3), Jesus' ascension (12:5), and the new creation (21:3, 5; 22:1, 3). In line with this, within the visionary section God is described as "King of the nations" (15:3) and Jesus is portrayed both as the Davidic King[15] and the Danielic Son of Man (14:14) who has inaugurated his kingdom by dying, rising, ascending, and ejecting Satan from his heavenly seat of accusation (12:10). Taken together, these various descriptions paint a picture of God as the supreme King reigning on his throne in heaven and exercising his rule through the Davidic/Danielic reign of Jesus.

According to the book of Revelation, this heavenly reign of God will become fully manifest on earth only at the final judgment. As mentioned above, the book provides cyclical portrayals of God's final judgment by means of cosmic upheaval that will occur at the eschaton, depicted literarily at the opening of the seventh seal (8:1-5), the sounding of the seventh trumpet (11:15-19), and the pouring of the seventh bowl (16:17-21). At each of these literary junctures, this final judgment against humanity is directly associated with God's reign as King. First, at the opening of the seventh seal, when the imagery of cosmic upheaval recurs for the first time, the angel who executes this final judgment does so by filling a censer with fire from an altar "before the throne" and throwing it upon the earth (8:5; cf. v. 3). As was the case with the throne room scene in chapter 4, this act connects God's rule as King with the angel's execution of this eschatological judgment. Second, at the sounding of the seventh trumpet, loud voices in heaven declare, "The kingdom of the world has become the kingdom of our Lord and of his Christ, and he shall reign forever and ever" (11:15). This is the clearest and most concise description of the consummative establishment of God's kingdom over the whole world, which is explicitly described in terms of Jesus' messianic rulership. Third, at the pouring of the seventh bowl, "a loud voice came out of the temple, *from the throne*, saying, 'It is done!'" (16:17). Once again God's judgment is associated with his kingship and is portrayed as final in its accomplishment.

Lastly, the vision of Babylon the Harlot portrays God's eschatological judgment twice: in chapter 19 Jesus executes judgment from a "white horse" (19:11) and in chapter 20 God executes judgment from a "white throne" (20:11). In the first scene Jesus is once again depicted as the eschatological Davidic King by means of an allusion to Ps 2:9 (Rev 19:15), after which he

---

glass (4:6a), (6) the four living creatures (4:6b), (7) the elders' casting their crowns (4:10b), (8) the Lamb (5:6), (9) the multitude of praising angels (5:11-12), and (10) the multitude from every tribe and tongue who offers praise (7:9-10).

14. Rev 6:16; 16:17; 19:4; 20:11-12.
15. Rev 5:5; 12:5; 19:15; 22:16.

receives the supreme and all-encompassing royal title, "King of kings and Lord of lords" (19:16). The second scene contains the last elaborate description of final judgment in the book of Revelation and explicitly connects this judgment to God sitting on his royal throne (20:11–15). From this brief survey, it is abundantly clear that among the many terms and images that Revelation uses to portray God, the description of God as the divine King is central.

THE PORTRAYAL OF GOD'S PEOPLE IN THE BOOK OF REVELATION

Along with this portrayal of God as King, the book of Revelation repeatedly depicts God's people as an international priestly kingdom. In the prologue, in the midst of describing Jesus as the Danielic ruler of the kings of the earth (1:5a, 7), John gives praise to Jesus by saying, "To him who loves us and has freed us from our sins by his blood *and made us a kingdom, priests to his God and Father,* to him be glory and dominion forever and ever" (1:5b–6). Accordingly, as mentioned above, John introduces himself a few verses later as "your brother and partner in the tribulation *and the kingdom* and the patient endurance that are in Jesus" (1:9). Continuing this theme, in the letter section Jesus exhorts the church at Thyatira to persevere using royal terminology:

> The one who conquers and who keeps my works until the end, to him I will give authority over the nations, *and he will rule them with a rod of iron, as when earthen pots are broken in pieces,* even as I myself have received authority from my Father. (2:26–27)

The italicized portion of this promise alludes to the LXX of Ps 2:9, where God promises to give David a worldwide kingdom with authority over the nations.[16] In Revelation it becomes clear that those who persevere in faith will inherit this promised Davidic kingdom because Jesus himself has inherited this kingdom as the eschatological Davidic King (see Rev 12:5; 19:15). Finally, in the millennial vision of chapter 20, God's people are again described with both royal (v. 4) and priestly (v. 6) language, solidifying their depiction as a priestly kingdom.

In addition to this royal-priestly portrayal, the book of Revelation describes God's people as comprising individuals from every "tribe" (*phylē*)

---

16. This allusion is nearly word-for-word: "*poimaneis autous en rhabdō sidēra, hōs skeuos kerameōs syntripseis autous*" (Ps 2:9 [LXX]); "*poimanei autous en rhabdō sidēra hōs ta skeuē ta keramika syntribetai*" (Rev 2:9).

MISSION FULFILLED 255

and "language" (*glōssa*) and "people" (*laos*) and "nation" (*ethnos*). This four-part description occurs five times throughout the book and denotes universality on an ethnolinguistic level.[17] It transcends the boundaries of geopolitical entities to include every tribal and linguistically-distinct subgroup of humanity. This phrase appears once in the introductory throne room vision (5:9–10) and four times in the literary intercalations and interlude that punctuate the cycles of divine judgment (7:9; 11:9; 13:7; 14:6). In the opening throne room vision, the four living creatures and twenty-four elders fall down before the slain Lamb and praise him, saying,

> Worthy are you to take the scroll
>   and to open its seals,
> for you were slain, and by your blood you ransomed people for God
>   from every tribe and language and people and nation,
> and you have made them a kingdom and priests to our God,
>   and they shall reign on the earth. (5:9–10)

Once again, the language of a priestly kingdom appears, and according to these verses Jesus has redeemed and brought into this priestly kingdom individuals from every people group of the world. This comprehensive people-group focus appears again in the first intercalation between the sixth and seventh seals, where John sees a great multitude with this same description standing "before the throne" and praising God for his salvation (7:9–10). In contrast to this, the remaining uses of this four-part phrase refer to the enemies of God's people: those who gaze upon the dead bodies of martyrs (11:9) and live under the rule of the beast (13:7), in contrast to those who follow the Lamb wherever he goes (14:6; cf. v. 4).[18] Consequently, this four-part phrase reveals that although those who rebel against God's kingship may be found among every people group of the world, God's people who constitute his priestly kingdom are also comprised in this ethnolinguistically comprehensive manner.

THE PORTRAYAL OF THE NEW CREATION IN THE BOOK OF REVELATION

This portrayal of God as King and his people as an international priestly kingdom receives final amplification in Revelation's closing vision of the

---

17. Two additional phrases approximate this expression, with 10:11 replacing *phylē* with *basileusin* ("kings") and 17:15 replacing it with *ochloi* ("multitudes"). See du Preez, "People and Nations," 50.

18. For a discussion concerning the unbelieving portrayal of those mentioned in 14:6, see especially Beale, *Revelation*, 747–50.

new creation. Although Rev 21:9 marks a shift in the book's literary structure, the final apocalyptic vision of the new creation begins just before this juncture and extends until the book's epilogue (21:1—22:5). This ultimate destination of God's people serves as a climactic contrast to the final depiction of God's eschatological judgment meted out against his enemies from the great white throne (20:11–15). When we explore this final vision of Revelation, we see the fullest and most elaborate picture of the mission of God fulfilled: God is depicted as King and his people have filled the earth as an international priestly kingdom.

The New Creation and God's Kingship

As was the case with the preceding visions, this final vision of Revelation depicts the new creation as the place where God reigns as King. This theme appears explicitly at both the beginning and the end of the vision as well as implicitly within it. At the beginning, after seeing both "a new heaven and a new earth" (21:1) and the "new Jerusalem" (v. 2), John hears "a loud voice from the throne saying, 'Behold, the dwelling place of God is with man. He will dwell with them, and they will be his people, and God himself will be with them as their God'" (v. 3). Verse 5 then relays the direct speech of the one "seated on the throne," who says, "Behold, I am making all things new." Both of these announcements issue from "the throne" and therefore establish a royal context for the vision that follows. The specification of God as the speaker in verse 5, as well as the shift from third-person to first-person speech, suggests that the speaker in verse 3 is not God but most likely one of his angels.[19] This angelic speech introduces this new creational vision as the consummate fulfillment of God's promise of covenantal presence first articulated in Lev 26:11–12:

Lev 26:11–12	Rev 21:3
I will make my dwelling among you, and my soul shall not abhor you. And I will walk among you and will be your God, and you shall be my people.	And I heard a loud voice from the throne saying, "Behold, the dwelling place of God is with man. He will dwell with them, and they will be his people, and God himself will be with them as their God."

As we saw last chapter, this promise of covenantal presence in Lev 26:11–12 refers to God's dwelling with his people through the temple in conjunction

---

19. Osborne, *Revelation*, 733.

with their fulfilling the creation mandate (Lev 26:9), and as we will see, Revelation 21 portrays the entire new creation as a temple. Since the temple is the intersection of God's heavenly throne room on earth, this angelic declaration of consummate covenantal presence introduces the new creation as the place where God will reign as King.[20] The divine speech in verse 5 sharpens this idea even further by specifying that this consummate covenantal presence will be achieved by a complete overhaul of creation. The establishment of God's eschatological reign will ultimately be accomplished by God's sovereign re-making of the entire cosmos.

Balancing this twofold mention of God's throne at the beginning of this vision is the twofold reference at the end. After John describes the details of the new Jerusalem (21:9–27), he sees "the river of the water of life, bright as crystal, flowing from the throne of God and of the Lamb" (22:1). He then specifies that this new creational city will no longer experience curse, but instead "the throne of God and of the Lamb will be in it, and his servants will worship him" (v. 3). In both of these verses the singular throne is occupied by both God and the Lamb, highlighting the divine and royal nature of the Lamb who has conquered. These texts also present the throne as the centerpiece of the new creation; it is the source of the life-giving water that flows through the city and the location where God and the Lamb receive everlasting worship. By bookending this vision with these dual references to God's throne, the text presents God's kingship as an overarching element; it is that which both initiates and centrally characterizes the new creation.

Between this explicitly royal imagery at the beginning and the end, the center of this vision reflects God's kingship implicitly by depicting the new creation as a worldwide temple. Although this vision begins by introducing "a new heaven and a new earth" (21:1), the description that follows is not of the earth in general but of a city in particular, "the holy city, new Jerusalem" (vv. 2, 9–27). As Beale argues, this juxtaposition indicates not that the new creation has a city on it but that it is being depicted *as a city*.[21] Among other pieces of supporting evidence is the fact that Rev 21:1–2 alludes to Isa 65:17–18, which explicitly identifies the new creation with the new Jerusalem:

---

20. Mathewson argues that Ezek 37:26b–27 is the more immediate text to which John is alluding here, but since Ezekiel is alluding to Leviticus in that passage, John may have both texts in mind (*New Heaven and a New Earth*, 50–51). Either way, since Leviticus and Ezekiel both have God's presence with his people through the temple in view, John's application of this formula in the vision of the new creation is the same no matter which text is in the forefront.

21. Beale, *Temple and the Church's Mission*, 23–25.

> *For behold, I create new heavens and a new earth,*
>   and the former things shall not be remembered or come into mind.
>   But be glad and rejoice forever in that which I create;
> *for behold, I create Jerusalem* to be a joy and her people to be a gladness.

As we will see in the next section, this metropolitan portrayal of the new creation does not refer to its architecture in a literalistic fashion but to its populous nature. For the present point, however, it is important to observe that since the new creation is presented as a city, to a certain degree the descriptions of this city are to be understood as descriptions of the new creation in general.

In light of this, John's language in 21:16 is most informative: "The city lies foursquare, its length the same as its width. And he measured the city with his rod, 12,000 stadia. Its length and width and height are equal." In this verse John describes the new Jerusalem as a cube with dimensions of 12,000 stadia, or approximately 1,400 miles. Since the city wall is only 144 cubits thick (v. 17)—or about 216 feet—if taken literally these dimensions would be architecturally unfeasible. This points to a symbolic meaning for these dimensions, and as many have concluded, by describing the new Jerusalem as a cube that is covered in gold (v. 18), John is portraying it like the Most Holy Place in Israel's temple, which is the only other biblical structure that is cubic and overlaid with gold (cf. 1 Kgs 6:20).[22] Since the new Jerusalem is depicted as this giant Most Holy Place, and since the new Jerusalem itself is a depiction of the new creation in general, it follows that the new creation *as a whole* is being portrayed as an earth-wide Most Holy Place. Since the Most Holy Place was the location where God's heavenly throne room extended to the earth, this final apocalyptic vision is depicting God's heavenly throne room as encompassing the entire new creation.

The New Creation and God's People

Complementing this depiction of God as King is the final vision's portrayal of God's people as an international priestly kingdom that has filled the earth. Several interrelated elements combine to provide this eschatological picture. First, in this apocalyptic presentation, the new Jerusalem is best understood not as the location where God's people will dwell eternally but *as God's people themselves.*[23] This is a city not fundamentally in terms of space and architecture but in terms of population. Supporting this are 21:2 and

---

22. E.g., Mathewson, *New Heaven and a New Earth*, 106–7; Mounce, *Revelation*, 392; Beale, *Revelation*, 1075–76; Keener, *Revelation*, 487.

23. For a lengthy defense of this view see Gundry, "New Jerusalem," 254–64.

21:9, both of which describe the new Jerusalem as a "bride," an image that is used elsewhere to refer to God's people (e.g., 2 Cor 11:2; Eph 5:22–30).[24] Accompanying this twofold reference to the "bride" is the twice-mentioned observation of this city "coming down out of heaven from God" (vv. 2, 10). It seems improbable that this describes a physical metropolis descending from heaven, though it is most plausible that it is portraying the return of God's people to the renovated creation. Supporting this is the angelic speech in verse 3 that alludes to Lev 26:11–12. As we saw above, this promise of covenantal presence finds initial fulfillment in Israel's edificial temple, which in turn finds later fulfillment in the Spirit-filled ecclesial temple. Since the New Testament presents the people of God as the temple of God, it is most probable that this final fulfillment of Lev 26:11–12, which in this context describes the descent of the new Jerusalem, refers to God's people.

Further supporting this understanding of the new Jerusalem as the people of God are the city's architectural descriptions. John observes that the city has "twelve gates" on which "the names of the twelve tribes of the sons of Israel" are written, and the city wall has "twelve foundations" on which "the twelve names of the twelve apostles of the Lamb" are written (21:12–14). That this city is thus characterized by the founding groups of both Old Testament Israel and the New Testament church reflects the unity of God's people across the canon.[25] Moreover, although it is possible that these gates and foundations portray this city as the home of God's unified people, it is more likely that they characterize the city as God's unified people. In Eph 2:20 Paul describes the apostles and prophets as the "foundation" (*themelios*) upon which the ecclesial temple is built. The architectural metaphor in this context describes the people, not simply the place where one finds the people. Similarly, in Rev 3:12 Jesus writes to the church in Philadelphia:

> The one who conquers, *I will make him a pillar in the temple of my God*. Never shall he go out of it, and I will write on him the name of my God, and the name of the city of my God, the new Jerusalem, which comes down from my God out of heaven, and my own new name.

This verse contains the only other reference to the new Jerusalem outside the vision of the new creation. Here we see that the one who "conquers" and endures faithfully through trials *will become a pillar in the temple of God*, which is directly associated with "the new Jerusalem." Once again, the

---

24. Keener, *Revelation*, 486.
25. Keener, *Revelation*, 492.

architectural metaphor describes the people, not the place where one finds the people. These texts provide further rationale for viewing the architectural metaphor in the closing vision of Revelation as signifying God's people and not simply the place where they will reside.

In addition to the gates and foundations, the measurements of the new Jerusalem point to its function as a metonym for God's covenant people. As we saw above, Rev 21:16 describes the cubic shape of the city and specifies its dimensions of 12,000 stadia. The only other passage in Revelation where the number 12,000 appears is the intercalation of chapter 7, where John hears the number of God's servants who receive the seal of God: 12,000 from each of the twelve tribes, making for a total of 144,000 (vv. 1–8). Immediately after hearing this act of numbering, John looks and sees "a great multitude *that no one could number*, from every nation, from all tribes and peoples and languages" (v. 9). One feature of Revelation's apocalyptic methodology is the audition-vision sequence in which John *hears* one thing but then *sees* something else that provides interpretive clarity to the phenomenon being revealed. For example, in chapter 5, after *hearing* about the "the Lion of the tribe of Judah" who has conquered (v. 5), John *sees* "a Lamb standing, as though it had been slain" (v. 6). Both animal images represent the same subject—Jesus—with the slain Lamb clarifying how the Lion has conquered. Similarly, in Revelation 7 John *hears* the roll call of 144,000 of God's servants listed in groups of 12,000 according to the twelve tribes of Israel, but when he looks he *sees* an innumerable international multitude. Once again, the vision clarifies the audition by portraying the same subject from a different perspective. In this case, the vision reveals that the figure of 144,000 is symbolic for the entirety of God's covenant people comprised of individuals from every nation. When we return to the vision of the new creation and observe that a cubic city with dimensions of 12,000 stadia results in city walls of 144,000,000 square stadia—which coordinates rather perfectly with the walls' thickness of 144 cubits—it becomes apparent that the dimensions of the new Jerusalem signify the entirety of God's covenant people.[26]

Second, not only does this vision present the new Jerusalem as God's people, it portrays God's people as a priesthood. That the new Jerusalem is depicted as a worldwide Most Holy Place implies the priestly character of God's people, as does the list of stones that adorn the foundations of the city wall (21:19–20). As many have observed, the twelve stones that decorate these foundations correspond to the twelve stones that adorned

---

26. For much of this discussion I am indebted to the insights of Gundry, "New Jerusalem," 256–60. See also Palmer, "Imagining Space in Revelation," 42–43.

the breastplate of the Israelite high priest (Exod 28:15–20).[27] Eight of these stones are identical to the list in the LXX and four are synonyms; the difference may be explained either by John providing his own translation of the Hebrew or his listing the stones from memory, which is reasonable given his exilic situation.[28] In Exodus these twelve stones represented God's covenant people, since each stone bore the name of one of the twelve tribes of Israel (Exod 28:21). In Revelation these twelve stones do not adorn the city gates on which the names of the twelve tribes of Israel are written, but rather the city foundations that bear the names of the twelve apostles. This implies that the high priestly function of Aaron and his descendants who entered the Most Holy Place and represented God's people has been democratized and applied to the church as a whole. The worldwide Most Holy Place of the new creation is thus portrayed as filled with a worldwide priesthood consisting of the entirety of God's people.

Third, this final apocalyptic vision portrays God's people as kings in the new creation. We have already explored how this vision portrays God as King at the beginning and the end through the image of his throne. In line with this, the vision ends by highlighting the royal function of God's people who will reign alongside God and the Lamb in the new creation. After noting the absence of any curse and the worship-centered function of God's eternal throne, John concludes this section by declaring that God's servants "will reign forever and ever" (Rev 22:5). In the letter to the church at Laodicea Jesus had promised, "The one who conquers, I will grant him to sit with me on my throne, as I also conquered and sat down with my Father on his throne" (3:21). In 5:5–6 a heavenly elder tells John not to weep because the Lion/Lamb has conquered, and here in the final vision we see the culmination the Lamb's conquest as his promise to the Laodiceans becomes a reality for all of God's faithful people.[29]

Finally, this vision of the new creation portrays God's people as an international multitude. This is implied by the architectural dimensions of 12,000 stadia and 144 cubits (21:16–17), which as we saw above recall the roll call of God's 144,000 sealed servants (7:4–8), a figure that is interpreted as an innumerable international multitude (7:9). Further reflecting the international character of God's people is the allusion to Lev 26:11–12 in Rev 21:3. This covenant formula ("I will be your God, and you will be

---

27. Mathewson, *New Heaven and a New Earth*, 138–40; Beale, *Revelation*, 1080; Osborne, *Revelation*, 756–58; Keener, *Revelation*, 496.

28. Osborne, *Revelation*, 756.

29. Resseguie, *Revelation*, 258.

my people") occurs in various permutations throughout the Bible,[30] though the use in Rev 21:3 is unique in pluralizing the reference to God's people. Literally the text says, "He will dwell with them, and they will be his *peoples* (*laoi*), and God himself will be with them as their God."[31] This pluralization of God's partner in the covenant formula is best understood as reflecting the multinational character of God's people in the new covenant era.[32]

Reinforcing this is the eschatological influx of the nations portrayed in Rev 21:23–27. John observes that the new Jerusalem will have "no need of sun or moon to shine on it, for the glory of God gives it light, and its lamp is the Lamb" (v. 23), and therefore the nations will walk by this light and "the kings of the earth will bring their glory into it" (v. 24). The city's "gates will never be shut by day—and there will be no night there" (v. 25), and "the glory and the honor of the nations" will be brought into it (v. 26). The anticipation of such an international pilgrimage appears in a variety of Old Testament texts,[33] though the passage most immediately in view behind this description of the new Jerusalem is Isaiah 60. In this latter text, the city to which the nations will bring their tribute has no need for sun or moon because God will provide its light (v. 19), and its gates will never be shut (v. 11a) so that the nations can bring their wealth into it (vv. 3, 5, 11b).[34]

Although this final vision of Revelation employs this image of the eschatological influx of the nations, we should not view this pilgrimage as occurring on an ongoing basis in the new creation. That is, it is not the case that the new creation will contain space that is external to the new Jerusalem from which these kings and nations will bring material tribute. As we have seen, Revelation 21 presents the new creation as the new Jerusalem; the renovated earth is portrayed as this worldwide temple-city and therefore to be outside the city is to be outside the new creation.[35] Instead, these kings and nations who bring their "glory" and "honor" into the city represent the same multitude comprised of every tribe, language, people, and nation whom the Lamb saved and for which he receives praise in 5:9–10 and 7:9–11.

---

30. E.g., Jer 7:23; 11:4; 24:7; 30:22; 31:33; 32:38; Ezek 11:20; 14:11; 36:28; 37:23, 27; Zech 8:8; 2 Cor 6:16; Heb 8:10; cf. Hos 1:9.

31. I have followed the ESV here except for pluralizing "peoples." Some English translations render *laoi* as a singular in conformity with the covenant formula elsewhere (e.g., NIV [1984, 2011], NASB, ESV, HCSB), while others translate it as a plural in this unique instance (e.g., ASV, NRSV, CSB).

32. So also Osborne, *Revelation*, 734.

33. E.g., Isa 2:2–4; Jer 3:17–18; Mic 4:1–5; Hag 2:6–9; Zech 8:20–23.

34. See the analysis of Beale, *Revelation*, 1093–94.

35. Gundry, "New Jerusalem," 263–64.

Supporting this is the observation that the only other contexts in Revelation where the terms "glory" (*doxa*) and "honor" (*timē*) appear together are the heavenly worship scenes in the opening throne room vision (4:9, 11; 5:12–13) and the first intercalation (7:12) of the visionary section. In these passages, the act of giving "glory" and "honor" to God describes praising him (4:8–9) for his work of creation (4:11) and as a response to the Lamb's redemption of individuals from every people group of the world (5:12–13; cf. v. 9; 7:12; cf. v. 9). Since God repeatedly receives "glory" and "honor" for redeeming this international multitude, it seems most probable that the kings and nations who bring him "glory" and "honor" in the new creation are none other than this same international multitude redeemed by the blood of the Lamb. The background text of Isaiah 60 reinforces this understanding, since that passage parallels bringing material tribute ("gold and frankincense") with bringing "the praises of the LORD" (v. 6).

Consequently, this portrayal of the eschatological influx of the nations does not describe end-time kings bringing material wealth into a city that is spatially distinct from its surroundings.[36] Rather, this is another image of the ethnolinguistically comprehensive nature of God's people whom the Lamb has redeemed, who have been brought into his eternal kingdom, and who will praise him in the new creation as their Creator and Redeemer. Solidifying this is the final verse of the chapter, which contrasts the unclean who will never enter the new Jerusalem with those who will: "only those who are written in the Lamb's book of life" (21:27).

SUMMARY

In this chapter we have seen that the book of Revelation presents a multifaceted yet consistent portrayal of the mission of God as fulfilled. The book portrays God as the great King seated on his throne, executing judgment against his enemies, providing redemption for his people, and exercising sovereign rule through the Davidic/Danielic reign of Jesus, the Lamb who was slain. God's people are depicted as an international priestly kingdom redeemed by the blood of the Lamb and comprised of individuals from every tribe, language, people, and nation. In the vision of the new creation these images coalesce and reach their climax as God's temple presence through his people is portrayed as coterminous with the entire earth. God's people are presented as an eschatological high priesthood who has filled the earth, thereby characterizing the new creation as a worldwide temple-city. God's throne is a central element in this temple-city, to which the nations

---

36. See also Beale, *Revelation*, 1098–99; Gundry, "New Jerusalem," 264.

are depicted as making their eschatological pilgrimage. In these ways the book of Revelation draws together various biblical images and provides the grand finale of the mission of God and the mission of God's people. At the eschatological renovation of creation, God's kingship will be represented to the ends of the earth.

11 MISSION TODAY
The Church's Call to Missions

The previous chapters have traced the theme of mission from Genesis to Revelation and sought to provide a coherent analysis of the mission of God and the mission of God's people. In this final chapter I will summarize this analysis and explore various ways in which this theology of mission ought to inform both the church's overall mission and the church's call to missions.

SUMMARY OF MISSION IN SCRIPTURE

In chapter 1 we saw that the creation account introduces both the mission of God and the mission of God's people. Based on God's depiction as King and humanity's portrayal as his representatives, I argued that God's mission in the world is for his kingship to be represented to the ends of the earth. The mission of God's people is therefore to fill the earth as God's royal representatives and thereby demonstrate that his kingship extends over the entire earth. This mission is introduced when God creates humanity as his image and commissions them to "be fruitful and multiply and fill the earth" (Gen 1:26–28). We then saw in chapter 2 that the creation account portrays God as a gracious King, and that humanity only represents God rightly by obeying his authoritative word (Gen 2:16–17). If humanity had been faithful to God they would have fulfilled the creation mandate, filled the earth, and accomplished their mission. This initial mission of Adam was therefore centrifugal in nature; he was to begin in the center (Eden) and expand God's representation to the ends of the earth.

Despite this privileged mission, as we examined in chapter 2, humanity rejects God's kingship and instead treats the serpent as king. This leads God to eject humanity from his temple presence in the garden and curse them with frustration in their mission. The subsequent narratives of the Primeval History illustrate this cursing by portraying humanity as inclined toward murder (Genesis 4; 6–9) and centralization (Genesis 11), which together represent the opposite of the creation mandate. At the end of the Primeval History, God judges the people of Babel by scattering them across the face of the earth, thereby actualizing his charge for humanity to fill the earth. However, since humanity has now filled the earth as rebellious images, they do not represent God's kingship rightly and therefore do not fulfill their mission. Nevertheless, hope is expressed throughout the Primeval History as God promises to redeem fallen humanity through the woman's offspring, who will crush the serpent's head in the midst of suffering. We traced this *protoevangelium* through the genealogies of Seth and Shem until we arrived at the call of Abram.

Chapter 3 explored how God resumes his mission by calling Abram and promising to bless the scattered nations of the earth through him. In Gen 12:1–3 God calls Abram to exercise faithful obedience to his word, and in response God promises to bless Abram in such a way that the nations recognize his blessed status. In recognizing Abram this way, the nations will respond either by blessing or dishonoring him, which will reflect their esteem or lack thereof for faithful relationship with God. Based on a person's response, God will either bless or curse them, and through this means all the families of the earth will be blessed. Throughout the preceding analysis I have referred to this process as "the Abrahamic formula." This formula is a centripetal development of the mission of God's people; rather than calling Abram to go out and bless the nations, God calls him to obey his word and receive blessing in such a way that the nations take notice and submit to God.

Since the nations have been scattered throughout the earth in actualization of the creation mandate, and since the Abrahamic formula is the means by which these scattered nations may be reconciled to God and begin to function properly as his images again, this call of Abram is presented as the avenue by which the creation mandate is fulfilled. Supporting this are the repeated allusions to the creation mandate throughout the patriarchal narratives. As we have seen, several repetitions of God's promise to bless the nations through Abram are linked to God's promise to make him fruitful and cause him to multiply.[1] Consequently, although the Abrahamic formula is centripetal in nature, it is best viewed as a redemptive development of the centrifugal mission given to Adam and therefore has the same goal in view: representing God's kingship to the ends of the earth.

---

1. Gen 22:17–18; 26:4; 28:3–4; see also 17:2, 6.

In chapter 4 we analyzed how the call of Abram is organized and given further clarity in the call of Israel. In Exod 19:3–6 God calls Israel to obey his voice and keep his covenant and thereby to teach the nations by example what it means to relate to God in a faithful way. The Torah specifies that such faithfulness on Israel's part will result in God fulfilling both the creation mandate and the Abrahamic formula through them. Israel's king is responsible for leading the people in this Torah faithfulness, and the temple is the location to which the nations may come and submit to God. In all these ways, as a continuation of the call of Abram, the call of Israel is centripetal in nature. However, as an extension of Abram's call, Israel's call is also an organized development of the creation mandate and therefore has the same goal in view: representing God's kingship to the ends of the earth.

As we saw in chapter 5, the Torah warns that Israel will fail in this mission if they refuse to respond to God's word with faith and repentance. Rather than making Israel numerous and blessing them in the sight of the nations, God will reduce their numbers and cause them to be a recognized recipient of cursing. As history unfolds, like Adam, Israel fails to obey God and therefore does not represent his kingship rightly. As a result, rather than fulfilling the creation mandate and the Abrahamic formula, Israel is decimated and receives the curses of the covenant, climaxing in their exile from God's temple presence in Jerusalem. Even in the midst of this judgment, however, God does not leave his people without hope but provides promises of future restoration for the sake of his name among the nations. According to the prophets, God will restore Israel in order that they might fulfill the Abrahamic formula, serve as a light for the nations, and realize the creation mandate. In the context of Israel's future restoration, Isaiah describes a representative servant who will achieve forgiveness for God's people through suffering, and according to Daniel, accompanying this restoration will be the heavenly ascension of "one like a son of man," a divine-human figure who will take his seat beside the Ancient of Days and rule over all peoples, nations, and languages. As the Old Testament narrative progresses, Israel experiences geographical restoration to the promised land, though the prophetic hopes for missional success are never realized in the postexilic period. This reveals that, despite being restored geographically, Israel remains in exile spiritually and in need of ultimate reconciliation with God.

Chapter 6 surveyed how Jonah, Psalms, and the Wisdom literature cohere with this Old Testament theology of mission. I concluded that neither the book of Jonah nor the Psalter contradicts the view that Israel's mission was centripetal; rather, Jonah focuses on God's gracious and compassionate character and the Psalter on God as Israel's ultimate King. Aligning with earlier observations about the missional function of the Torah, the Wisdom literature contributes to a theology of mission by highlighting the need for God's people to have a proper heart disposition before God: the action of Torah faithfulness must be combined with an attitude of "the fear of the LORD."

In chapter 7 we looked at how Jesus fulfills the various missional roles of the Old Testament. As the last Adam and true Israel, Jesus is faithful where these two Old Testament predecessors were unfaithful. As the suffering servant he atones for the sin of his people and reconciles them fully and finally to God. As the righteous Davidic King he leads his people in living faithfully before God and successfully executing their mission. As the Danielic Son of Man he ascends to his heavenly throne and rules over all peoples, nations, and languages. And finally, as the eschatological temple, Jesus is the climactic intersection of God's heavenly presence on earth to whom the nations are to come, find forgiveness, and express their allegiance. In these ways Jesus redeems the mission of God's people.

Chapter 8 then explored how Jesus reinstates the mission of God's people by calling and equipping the church. The Gospels and Acts record various post-resurrection commissions in which Jesus calls the church to fulfill their redeemed identity as God's representative people. We saw that the mission of the church is predicated upon Jesus' authority, involves incorporating people into the covenant community through the proclamation of repentance and forgiveness, and as an extension of Jesus' own ministry is executed by the power of the Holy Spirit. Jesus equips the church for this mission at Pentecost by pouring out the Holy Spirit and thereby transforming the church into the temple of God. This establishment of the ecclesial temple is the mechanism that changes the missional methodology of God's people from the centripetal pull of Israel's calling to the centrifugal spread of the church's witness. This outpoured presence of the Holy Spirit is also what ensures that the church will succeed in this mission where both Adam and Israel failed.

In chapter 9 we examined the centrifugal mission of the early church through the narrative of Acts as well as the inspired reflection on this mission in the epistles. We saw that both Acts and the epistolary literature display a repeated preoccupation with the geographical expansion of the church. In line with this, the New Testament depicts the church as fulfilling the creation mandate, the call of Abram, the call of Israel, the Isaianic servant, and the eschatological temple. Just as Jesus fulfills each of these Old Testament missional roles, as an extension of Jesus' earthly ministry the church also fulfills these roles and therefore fulfills the mission of God's people. Further supporting this is the overarching theme of the kingdom of God in the early church's gospel proclamation. By fulfilling these Old

Testament missional roles and proclaiming the good news of the kingdom to all nations, the church executes the mission formerly assigned to both Adam and Israel: representing God's kingship to the ends of the earth.

Finally, in chapter 10 we analyzed how the book of Revelation portrays the mission of God's people as fulfilled. When Jesus returns to judge the world at the eschaton, God will renovate the cosmos into a new heaven and a new earth. The book of Revelation presents this new creation as an earth-wide Most Holy Place that is filled with God's people, who are presented as a priestly kingdom comprised of individuals from every nation, with God ruling over them as King. This apocalyptic depiction of the new creation is designed to encourage God's people to persevere as they engage in their mission between Jesus' ascension and return. By seeing the final result of history—an earth filled with God's allegiant representatives—God's people may find strength to endure in carrying out their mission to the ends of the earth today.

This survey reveals that the mission of God's people throughout the Bible is consistently designed to be executed by means of the creation mandate. Before the fall, humanity was to fulfill the mandate by abundant procreation and centrifugal geographical spread. After the fall—and specifically after the scattering at Babel—God promises to fulfill the mandate through his covenant people in response to their faithful obedience, resulting in a centripetal witness among the nations. After Jesus atones for sin and pours out his Spirit on the church, the mandate is fulfilled once again in a centrifugal manner as the word of God is fruitful and multiplies and fills the earth through the church's proclamation of the gospel. In the remainder of this chapter I will offer some reflections on various ways in which this theology of mission ought to direct and inform the church's call to missions today.

MISSION IS GROUNDED IN CREATION

The first observation to make is that mission is grounded in creation. In their biblical theology of mission, Köstenberger and O'Brien write, "There was no 'mission' in the Garden of Eden and there will be no 'mission' in the new heavens and the new earth (though the results of 'mission' will be evident)."[2] Similarly, Christopher Wright states, "God's mission is what spans the gap between the curse on the earth of Genesis 3 and the end of the curse in the new creation of Revelation 22."[3] In contrast to these views, I have argued that God's mission began not in Genesis 3 but in Genesis 1.

2. Köstenberger and O'Brien, *Salvation to the Ends of the Earth*, 251.
3. Wright, *Mission of God's People*, 46.

God created the world with a mission and communicated that mission to humanity through the creation mandate. This original mandate receives a redemptive reassertion in the calls of Abram and Israel and finds eschatological fulfillment in the work of Jesus and the call of the church. This organic relationship between the creation mandate and subsequent redemptive history reveals that, in the biblical storyline, mission precedes redemption. Mission existed for the sake of God's kingly glory before there was any need for human salvation. By viewing mission this way, we see that the work of missions is first and foremost an extension of a creation ordinance rather than a redemptive ordinance. That is, missions is fundamentally a proactive endeavor aimed at representing God's kingship to the ends of the earth rather than a reactive response to the presence of sin in the world. Missionaries are therefore better conceived of as royal couriers sent to represent the authority of the great King rather than rescue workers seeking to save lost souls. Of course, in a fallen world, salvation is a central aspect of the message that missionaries proclaim and the means by which rebellious images are forgiven and restored to their proper function. However, by grounding mission in creation we see that salvation *in itself* is not the ultimate goal of missions. Rather, the ultimate goal of missions is the creational concern to fill the earth with allegiant representatives of God.

REDEMPTION REPOSITIONS GOD'S PEOPLE FOR MISSION

For this reason, in missiological reflection, the anthropocentric element of salvation should be viewed as a means to the theocentric goal of worldwide representation. In chapter 2 we observed that the fall of humanity resulted not only in a broken relationship with God but also in a frustration of our mission. The curses that God pronounced against humanity when they first sinned directly affected their ability to execute their task of being fruitful, multiplying, and filling the earth. This set the stage for redemption to be viewed not simply as relational reconciliation with God but also as a restoration for mission. This broadened understanding of redemption substantially affects our view of the scope and effect of the gospel. Contemporary evangelicalism has often reduced the gospel to two major components:

(1) We are sinful and deserve God's judgment.

(2) Jesus died for us and brought us forgiveness.

Although individual justification is certainly a central and precious aspect of the gospel, failure to see the missional implications of the fall has often resulted in failure to see the missional implications of our redemption. Instead of summarizing the gospel with two major components, we do better to describe it in four:

(1) We were created to fill the earth as God's representatives.

(2) We are sinful and deserve God's judgment, and part of that judgment results in our inability to fulfill our mission.

(3) Jesus died for us and brought us forgiveness.

(4) In our forgiven state we are now reconciled with God and restored in order to fill the earth as God's representatives.

Redemption therefore has significant implications beyond individual justification; it repositions God's people to engage in the mission for which we have been created. Contrary to popular usage, the gospel is best viewed not simply as the good news that we are forgiven of our sin but also the announcement that our forgiving King has conquered death, called us into his royal service, and commissioned us to serve as his representatives throughout the world.

MISSION IS FUNDAMENTALLY EXPANSIONISTIC

This mission for which Jesus has redeemed his people is presented throughout the canon as fundamentally expansionistic in nature. In chapter 1 we discussed the recent trend to broaden the term "missions" and apply it to a whole spectrum of ministries. In certain evangelical circles the term "missions" includes domestic church planting, campus ministry, prison chaplaincy, mercy ministry, and all sorts of other wonderful endeavors that are *evangelistic* in nature but not *expansionistic*. The problem with this trend is that it obscures our ability to assess whether or not the church as a whole is strategically fulfilling the mission that God has given us. Since our mission is to fill the earth with allegiant representatives of God, we as the church must always be seeking ways to expand geographically and ethnolinguistically in order to represent God's kingship to the ends of the earth. If we have no terminology to distinguish between evangelistic ministry and expansionistic ministry, we can easily draw the false conclusion that we are fulfilling the mission that God has given us when in fact we are not.

I was once part of a church that financially and prayerfully supported ten "missionaries," none of whom lived outside the continental United

States, and all of whom ministered to major American people groups who already have access to the greatest amount of Christian resources in the history of the world. This support went to church planting efforts in our region, which even amidst the highly churched United States was already above average in its church-to-population ratio. We supported several campus ministers who served university students in areas that were densely populated with Bible-believing churches. We supported a prison chaplain who counseled the incarcerated, a mercy minister who served families in a low-income area, and we even included our financial contributions to our regional Presbytery as part of our "missions" budget. All of these were good, gospel-centered ministries, but none of them were *expansionistic* in nature; none of them extended gospel witness to people groups where such is lacking. Rather, each of these ministries continued to saturate a region that already had an established gospel witness, even though we as a church were under the impression that we were participating well in the work of "missions." If every local church were to adopt this philosophy of "missions," we would never fill the earth with allegiant representatives of God and therefore we would never fulfill our mission. Although ministries such as these are certainly *part* of the church's mission—since gospel witness in its various facets is needed everywhere—the church cannot limit itself to such non-expansionistic endeavors and expect to *fulfill* our mission. For this reason, distinguishing expansionistic ministry from non-expansionistic ministry is critical for the church to assess accurately whether or not we are contributing to the fulfillment of our mission.

In light of this, it seems wisest to reserve the term "missions" for those efforts aimed at expanding the church's witness into new geographical and ethnolinguistic areas. In chapter 1 we discussed the issue of *access* to the gospel as a distinguishing characteristic of missions. Those people who do not believe the gospel but have access to it are in a different missiological category from those who neither believe the gospel nor have access to it. In order to fill the earth, the church must endeavor to expand and establish witnessing communities among those peoples without sufficient access to the gospel; to do so strategically requires distinguishing expansionistic from non-expansionistic ministry. If my former church had made such a distinction, we would have seen clearly that our ministry involvement was imbalanced; we were heavily involved in outreach and evangelism among people who already had access to the gospel, yet we were uninvolved in the expansionistic endeavor to fill the earth by extending gospel witness into new areas. By distinguishing our terminology, we are better positioned to assess our involvement and thus able to adjust our methodology to align more strategically with God's mission.

MISSIONS IS NOT SIMPLY MINISTERING CROSS-CULTURALLY

This need to distinguish expansionistic from non-expansionistic ministry also leads to the conclusion that missions should not be fundamentally conceived of in terms of crossing cultures. While the tendency is still growing to refer to any and every evangelistic ministry as "missions," in most circles it is a foregone conclusion that anyone who crosses cultures for the sake of the gospel is a "missionary." Yet it is not the case that ministering cross-culturally *in itself* results in a geographical or ethnolinguistic expansion of gospel witness. If a person leaves the United States and moves to South Korea in order to plant a church, they have crossed cultures and geographical boundaries, though they have simply gone from one nation with a sufficient indigenous gospel witness to another nation with a sufficient indigenous gospel witness. Such a cross-cultural move does not expand the church's witness into an area where no sufficient witness exists. This type of cross-cultural ministry is categorically different from a person who goes to plant a church among the Shaikh people of Bangladesh, which is the largest unreached people group in the world. In this latter case the crossing of cultures results in the expansion of the church's witness into an area where gospel access is highly limited. It follows therefore that crossing cultures in itself should not be viewed as the essential element that classifies a particular ministry as "missions." For this reason, Michael Goheen has suggested that we distinguish between "missions" and "cross-cultural partnership."[4] Goheen uses the latter phrase to describe those who cross cultures for gospel purposes but are not actively working toward expanding the geographical and ethnolinguistic reach of the church's witness. By making distinctions such as this we are able to assess more accurately whether or not our cross-cultural involvement is contributing to the expansion of the church's witness and thus the fulfillment of our mission.

In light of this, in order to develop a strategic missiology based on this biblical theology of mission, it is unhelpful to universalize the work of missions with geographically indiscriminate summaries such as "the gospel from everywhere to everyone,"[5] or "mission from everyone to everywhere."[6] These phrases capture the reality that the missionary enterprise is no longer a movement "from the West to the rest" as it used to be, since the Majority World of the global south has become the center of gravity for world

---

4. Goheen, *Introducing Christian Mission Today*, 403.
5. This is the subtitle to Escobar, *New Global Mission*.
6. This is the subtitle to Yeh, *Polycentric Missiology*.

Christianity and thus a vibrant source for sending missionaries. However, these sorts of phrases overstate the case and imply that crossing cultures into people groups that have sufficient access to the gospel is equally strategic missiologically as crossing cultures into people groups without sufficient access. Yet based on the nature of the church's mission, the most coordinated way for the church to fill the earth is to send missionaries not simply to *other* people groups but to people groups without a sufficient indigenous gospel witness. Once a people group has a sufficient indigenous gospel witness, it is no longer necessary to send cross-cultural workers there. Of course, this does not mean that it is inappropriate for a person to engage in "cross-cultural partnership" or that such ministry does not have a positive gospel impact; it simply means that we should not conflate this type of work with expansionistic ministry by referring to both of them as "missions." The most strategic way for the church to fill the earth is not simply by taking the gospel "from everywhere to everyone" but "from where the church is established to where it is not."

MISSION IS FULFILLED BY REACHING ALL PEOPLE GROUPS

Another way of stating the above conclusion is that God's people will fill the earth not simply by reaching *other* people groups but by reaching *all* people groups. In chapter 2 we saw that fallen humanity's rejection of the creation mandate culminated in the rebellion at Babel, which gave rise to the various people groups of the world and caused them to be scattered across the earth. As we explored in chapter 3, the call of Abram and subsequent biblical history is aimed at extending God's redemptive blessing—eschatologically revealed in the good news of Jesus—to these scattered people groups. Since the call of Abram is portrayed as a redemptive reassertion of the creation mandate, it follows that reaching the scattered people groups of the world is the means by which God's people will fill the earth. We saw this concept developed in the New Testament, where the word of God was fruitful and multiplied as God's people expanded gospel witness to locations farther and farther away from Jerusalem. Consequently, the reason we take the gospel to the nations is not because God simply likes diversity.[7] Rather, we go to

---

7. I am unclear how Wright concludes that the "nations are simply 'there' as a given part of the human race as God created it to be," that there is a "rich diversity of the original creation," and that there is a "creational given of ethnic diversity" (*Mission of God*, 456). On the contrary, no biblical datum indicates any sort of ethnic or linguistic diversity among humanity on the historical level prior to the dispersion at Babel. This is not to say that diversity in itself is bad or will be done away with in the new creation,

the nations because they have been dispersed throughout the earth, and by reaching all people groups we will fill the earth with allegiant representatives of God.

Therefore, in our age of immigration and globalization it is insufficient to say, "The nations are coming to us," implying that the church does not need to send missionaries to places without a sufficient indigenous gospel witness. This way of thinking mistakes ethnic and cultural diversity as the goal of missions rather than recognizing it as the means of reaching our goal. Instead, our ultimate missional goal is inherently geographical in character: to *fill the earth* with allegiant representatives of God. Reaching immigrants is an important element for a church's local witness and often has broader missional effects when redeemed immigrants from unreached peoples return to their homeland. However, ministering to immigrants is no replacement for actively seeking avenues for establishing indigenous witnessing communities among every people group *in their geographical locale*. It is only when individuals from every people group in every location throughout the world submit to Jesus that his kingship will truly be represented to the ends of the earth.

MISSIONS MUST MAINTAIN A PEOPLE-GROUP MENTALITY

For this reason, we must maintain a "people group mentality" when strategizing our work of missions. The missional significance of people groups first emerges when God calls Abram and promises to bless "all the *families* (*mišpᵉḥōṯ*) of the earth" through him (Gen 12:3); it reaches its climax when Jesus issues the Great Commission and sends his followers to "all nations (*ethnē*)" (Matt 28:19); and it receives its fullest expression in Revelation when John sees the heavenly throne room populated with worshipers "from every nation, from all tribes and peoples and languages" (Rev 7:9). We have already noted that neither *mišpᵉḥōṯ* in the call of Abram nor *ethnē* in the Great Commission refers to geopolitical entities but rather to smaller kinship units, something at either the tribe or clan level. In missiological studies these kinship units have come to be referred to as "people groups."

In 1982 a working group sponsored by the Lausanne Committee for World Evangelization composed a definition of "people group" that has become widely used in missiological discussions. According to this definition, a people group is

---

but it is to say that diversity is not the biblical fuel that drives the work of missions.

a significantly large grouping of individuals who perceive themselves to have a common affinity for one another because of their shared language, religion, ethnicity, residence, occupation, class or caste, situation, etc., or combinations of these.[8]

A people group thus refers to a collection of individuals who are connected more deeply than simply sharing a passport. Individuals from the same people group are sufficiently similar to one another in terms of language, customs, and worldview that they do not cross into a different social culture when engaging with one another. This is significant for purposes of evangelism and church planting, as the Lausanne definition goes on to specify: "For evangelistic purposes, [a people group] is 'the largest group within which the gospel can spread as a church-planting movement without encountering barriers of understanding or acceptance.'"[9] In other words, within a particular people group, the gospel can be explained clearly and churches can be planted that naturally fit the culture of that group. Once a person goes beyond their own people group and ministers in the same fashion, however, they begin to encounter "barriers of understanding or acceptance."

As we have seen, the means by which God's people are to fill the earth is by spreading the good news of Jesus and making disciples of all people groups by establishing self-sustaining, gospel-witnessing churches. Once a sufficient indigenous gospel witness is established within a people group, the gospel can spread internally through evangelism and church planting without requiring external, cross-cultural assistance. To fulfill our mission as God's people, therefore, we must view the world not geopolitically but in terms of people groups and endeavor to reach these smaller units by establishing indigenous gospel witnesses in those places.

In contrast to this approach, I once met with the chairperson of a church's missions committee who told me that their philosophy of missionary support was to get the "most bang for their buck." What this person meant is that they prefer to support missionaries who serve in areas where the gospel spreads the fastest and the easiest. Although at first glance this strategy may seem to maximize results, ultimately it does not attend well to the Scriptural teaching that the church is to fill the earth by making disciples of all people groups. A "most bang for your buck" approach to missions assumes that the goal of the church's mission is to convert as many individuals as quickly as possible, which suggests that we should pursue the path of least resistance when choosing where to send missionaries. A logical byproduct of such a strategy is to neglect the people groups of the world that are most

8. Winter and Koch, "Finishing the Task," 19.
9. Winter and Koch, "Finishing the Task," 19.

resistant to the gospel. However, if we pursue such a path and neglect certain ethnolinguistic segments of the world, we will never fulfill our mission of filling the earth. Instead of pursuing the path of least resistance, we need to acquaint ourselves with the global missiological landscape, identify which people groups lack a sufficient indigenous gospel witness, and prioritize taking the gospel to those places.

MISSIONS IS DIRECTED TOWARD UNREACHED PEOPLE GROUPS

In other words, in order to fulfill our mission as God's people, the church must prioritize the discipleship of unreached people groups. Missiologically, a people group is classified as unreached when "there is no viable indigenous community of believing Christians with adequate numbers and resources to evangelize their own people without outside (cross-cultural) resources."[10] Traditionally this has been understood as a people group in which the indigenous population is less than 5 percent Christian or 2 percent evangelical. Since mission is fundamentally expansionistic, I have argued that a strategic missiology must distinguish expansionistic ministry (missions) from nonexpansionistic ministry. Such a strategic missiology must also distinguish between people groups in which the indigenous church is able to evangelize the rest of the group (reached) and people groups where the indigenous church cannot do so without external assistance (unreached). Since we will only fulfill our mission by filling the earth with allegiant representatives of God, and since the means by which we fill the earth is making disciples of all people groups, it follows that if we fail to prioritize the establishment of an effective indigenous gospel witness among unreached people groups, we will fail to fulfill our mission.

Despite this assessment, it is a well-known missiological reality that the church overall is not prioritizing the evangelization of unreached peoples. Although statistical analyses vary, a conservative estimate finds that more than 90 percent of human and financial resources devoted to "missions" from the Western church go toward cross-cultural partnership.[11] Rather than filling the earth by expanding the reach of the gospel into unreached areas, we are primarily sending people from one reached people group to another. We currently send the vast majority of our cross-cultural workers to labor among people groups where cross-cultural workers are unnecessary

---

10. Johnstone, *Future of the Global Church*, xiii.

11. Goheen, *Introducing Christian Mission Today*, 420. See also Guthrie, *Missions in the Third Millennium*, 24; Winter and Koch, "Finishing the Task," 22.

for the gospel to spread, while neglecting to send such workers to places where external assistance is necessary. Contributing to this imbalance is a deficit of understanding regarding the church's global mission as well as the universalizing of the term "missions" as noted above. The only way to remedy this imbalance is to reevaluate how we understand the church's mission, how we define the work of missions, and how we allocate our resources to fulfill our calling as God's representative people.

In opposition to this way of thinking, David Sills has argued strenuously against prioritizing unreached people groups in missiological strategy. Sills criticizes both the validity and reliability of the statistical method used to classify unreached peoples,[12] argues that a focus on unreached peoples marginalizes cross-cultural workers who labor among reached peoples,[13] and suggests that a focus on reaching the unreached results in a shallow and unfinished discipleship. Concerning this last point Sills writes, "Unfortunately, many missionaries have reached people groups and then hurriedly gone in search of UPGs, leaving unfinished work in the hands of untaught, ill-prepared national believers."[14] Instead of focusing on prioritizing unreached people groups, Sills advocates a missiology based on "receptivity" in which we adjust our methods based on peoples' willingness to receive the good news. Sills states that "receptivity is not based on regions or countries but on the work of the Holy Spirit," and that we should "find where God is working and join Him there."[15]

In response, we must first note that, even if one wishes to take issue with the suitability of the 5 percent Christian/2 percent evangelical marker of an unreached people group or the reliability of surveys to yield accurate data for ascertaining Christian populations, this does not affect the *theoretical validity* of prioritizing unreached people groups. The 5 percent/2 percent figure is a statistical approximation of the threshold under which a Christian population lacks the internal resources to reach the remainder of their people group. If more compelling research were to suggest that an unreached people group is better classified as 8 percent Christian and 5 percent evangelical, or 10 percent and 7 percent, such would not affect the validity of the underlying missiological concept; it would simply refine how we apply that concept.[16] Furthermore, the need to establish a sufficient in-

12. Sills, *Reaching and Teaching*, 111–12.
13. Sills, *Reaching and Teaching*, 112–13.
14. Sills, *Reaching and Teaching*, 115.
15. Sills, *Reaching and Teaching*, 115. He takes the latter quote from Henry Blackaby, *Experiencing God* (no page number cited).
16. For a history of the term "unreached" and a helpful assessment of the benefits and limitations of the 5 percent/2 percent threshold, see Datema, "Defining

digenous gospel witness in places where none exists derives from a biblical theology of mission and is not contingent upon our confidence level in the results of population surveys. The fact that "the number of evangelical Christians in a population is difficult to ascertain,"[17] as Sills observes, should not lead us to abandon the effort to analyze the world and allocate our resources strategically. Keeping in mind that such research is never perfect and constantly in need of refinement, we must study the global landscape to the best of our ability and expand the church's witness according to the data we are able gather.

Second, Sills's concern that focusing on unreached people groups minimizes the calling of those who labor among reached peoples does not follow logically, though even if it did this would not be a meaningful argument against the concept. According to Sills,

> The assumption in efforts to classify levels of reachedness is that the less reached an area is, the more worthy it is of missionary investment. The pervasive thinking that the least reached should be our top priority leaves little room for the possibility that God might be leading someone to a harvest field.[18]

On the contrary, it does not follow that placing a *priority* on unreached people groups "leaves little room" for people to engage in cross-cultural partnership. Only if one were to suggest that the church should *solely* send cross-cultural workers to labor among unreached peoples would the work of cross-cultural partnership be called into question. Yet the call to prioritize the geographical and ethnolinguistic expansion of the church's witness must be retained in light of the nature of the church's mission. Moreover, as the statistics above demonstrate, at present the Western church is in no danger of overprioritizing its work among unreached peoples. The danger lies in continuing to saturate reached people groups through cross-cultural partnership and failing to fulfill our mission by neglecting to expand the representation of Jesus' kingship to the ends of the earth. Based on the current distribution of resources, future cross-cultural workers would do well to consider whether their prospective service is truly contributing to the advancement of the church's mission of reaching *all* people groups. Ecclesial communities who send cross-cultural workers are also wise to assess whether they are investing their human and financial resources in a balanced and strategic manner or whether they are simply transferring the bulk of their

---

'Unreached,'" 45–71.

17. Sills, *Reaching and Teaching*, 112.

18. Sills, *Reaching and Teaching*, 112–13.

gospel resources from one reached people group to another. Determining where in the world God is leading a person to invest their life or a church to invest their resources should not be based on subjective criteria or personal preference but rather on how God has revealed his mission for the world throughout the Scriptures.

Third, Sills's claim that a focus on unreached people groups leads to shallow discipleship is a straw man critique of this missiological concept. The definition provided above articulates well the foundational characteristic of an unreached people group as one in which the indigenous church lacks "adequate numbers and resources to evangelize their own people." If missionaries evangelize and convert people but do not teach and disciple them to the point that the indigenous church is equipped to reach the rest of their group, that people group should not be considered reached and the work of missions is not complete. Jesus has commissioned the church to make disciples of all peoples not only by baptizing them but also by teaching them to observe *all* that he has commanded. The rapid "convert and depart" missiological method, or what Sills calls "the need for speed,"[19] does not represent a legitimate application of an expansionistic missiology focusing on unreached peoples, and therefore Sills's criticism of the former does not undermine the legitimacy of the latter.

Finally, Sills's advocacy of "receptivity" as a guide for missiological strategy is essentially a refined version of the "most bang for your buck" approach. Sills distinguishes between a missiology "based on regions or countries" and one based on "the work of the Holy Spirit." However, as we have seen, the New Testament presents the work of the Holy Spirit as empowering Jesus' followers to expand and fill the earth by making disciples of *all* people groups. From creation to new creation we have seen a consistent biblical preoccupation with a missional geography, one in which God's kingship is represented to the ends of the earth. For this reason, it is a false dichotomy to pit a missiology "based on regions or countries" against "the work of the Holy Spirit." Rather, the outpoured Holy Spirit has come in order to equip the church to extend God's temple presence through the spread of the gospel into ever-expanding regions and countries in order that Jesus' kingship would be represented across creation. The only way this work of the Spirit will be finalized is for the gospel to break forth into resistant, unreached people groups who refuse to bow their knee to King Jesus.

---

19. Sills, *Reaching and Teaching*, 113.

MISSION IS CHARACTERIZED BY THE PROCLAMATION OF THE KINGDOM OF GOD

As the church fills the earth and expands gospel witness among all people groups, the message that God's people proclaim must be centered on the kingdom of God over which Jesus reigns now as the resurrected King. Since receiving the creation mandate, the mission of God's people has always been to represent God's kingship to the ends of the earth. In chapter 9 we saw this mission reflected in the early church's consistent proclamation of the kingdom of God and the resurrection of Jesus. Consequently, the manner in which we represent God's kingship now is by announcing the reality of Jesus' resurrection, ascension, and heavenly reign, and then calling all people everywhere to repent of their sin, seek his forgiveness, and submit to his supreme authority. What enables people to enter God's kingdom is Jesus' atoning work on the cross, which they must trust for the forgiveness of their sins. When people trust Jesus' sacrifice, submit to his kingship, and orient their lives around his word, their function as God's image is restored and they begin to represent his kingship rightly. As more and more people in increasingly numerous people groups enter the kingdom of God this way, God's original mission for humanity is fulfilled as the representation of his kingship expands to the ends of the earth.

This focus on the kingdom of God in the church's mission is critical for God's people to avoid the errors of individualism, antinomianism, and parochialism. Individualism makes the mistake of viewing the Christian life fundamentally as a relationship between God and the individual person. Although God certainly loves and interacts with his people individually, the preponderance of biblical revelation depicts God as a King who relates covenantally to his people *as a kingdom*. The Scriptures portray both Israel and the church as a kingdom of priests with a mission to mediate knowledge of God to the rest of the world, with God extending forgiveness to individuals not primarily for their sake but in order to incorporate them into this ever-expanding kingdom. A kingdom-focused proclamation teaches converts (and reminds the converted!) that by becoming a Christian they are not simply "changing religions" as a matter of intellectual persuasion but rather entering the kingdom of God and thereby shifting their priorities to align with those of the King.

A kingdom-focused proclamation also guards against antinomianism, which falsely views God's law as non-binding for the Christian. Although we are not justified by our obedience to the law but by faith in Jesus' sacrificial death, this justification by faith incorporates us into a kingdom over which Jesus reigns as King and within which we are to express our allegiance to him by endeavoring to keep his word through repentant obedience. As we have seen, such repentant obedience to God's law was the means by which Israel witnessed to his kingship among the nations, and it continues to be an avenue through which God's people publicize his authority throughout the world.

In addition, a focus on God's kingdom in the church's witness protects God's people against parochialism. By parochialism I mean the tendency to view the Christian life and gospel ministry in geographically and ethnolinguistically limited terms. Although individual Christians and churches must indeed seek ways to reach out both to their immediate and regional neighbors, every Christian serves a King who has decreed that his kingdom is to be globally comprehensive and therefore every Christian is responsible to have a global mindset when it comes to the spread of the gospel. As discussed in chapter 9, since the body of Christ comprises many different parts with various functions, the manner in which any given person participates in the work of missions varies depending on their specific gifts, resources, and calling. Yet it must be emphasized that missions is not the responsibility of a specialized subset of the church; all of God's people are called to participate in the work of missions in some way because all of God's people have entered a kingdom that is designed to fill the earth.

MISSION LEADS TO THE NEW CREATION

Finally, the destination to which this expansionistic mission of God's people leads is the new creation. In chapter 10 we saw that the book of Revelation portrays the new creation as a city, the new Jerusalem, which is in turn depicted as the people of God. Consequently, although the new creation will be the home of God's people as a renovated version of the present world—a *new* heaven and a *new* earth—through these interlocking apocalyptic images the book of Revelation presents the new creation *as* the people of God. This apocalyptic portrayal highlights the fact that the new creation is the culmination of the mission of God's people: an earth filled with allegiant representatives of God. For this reason, as the church engages in its mission and multiplies the number of disciples throughout the world, in a real sense we are building the new creation here and now. We do not build the new creation by planting trees, cleaning up neighborhoods, or establishing just societal structures, as good as such things are. Rather, we build the new creation by extending the representation of God's kingship as we fill the earth with God's redeemed images. This is why Paul says, "if anyone is in Christ— new creation!—the old has passed away; behold, the new has come" (2 Cor

5:17, author's translation).[20] To convert to Christ is to enter the inaugurated reality of the new creation, and therefore to preach Christ to the ends of the earth is to push this inaugurated reality toward its ultimate, eschatological fulfillment.

For this reason, we must disagree with DeYoung and Gilbert, who argue that "Christians do not build the holy city, New Jerusalem, from the ground up,"[21] and that it is "far beyond the biblical witness to talk as if we as Christians are somehow contributing to the building of the new heavens and the new earth."[22] In an effort to combat tendencies toward a social gospel this conclusion overstates the case and fails to account for the anthropological portrayal of the new Jerusalem and thus the eschatological effects of contemporary missionary activity. In Revelation's apocalyptic worldview, by increasing the number of God's people on the earth we are indeed contributing to the construction of the new Jerusalem and thus the new heaven and new earth. Although God himself inaugurated the new creation through Jesus' resurrection (1 Cor 15:20–23) and will consummate it at Jesus' return (Rev 21:5), in the intervening period the church has the extraordinary privilege to serve as "God's fellow workers" laboring to build "God's building" (1 Cor 3:9). This is what N. T. Wright refers to as "eschatology-shaped mission,"[23] a mission that is driven not by hope in a disembodied, non-earthly, eternal existence in "heaven" but by an understanding that our ultimate destination is a remade earth full of faithful representatives of God. This eschatological understanding deepens our view of the church's mission and ought to guide us as we endeavor to carry out the work of missions today.

CONCLUSION

Throughout this book I have argued that the church's call to missions is grounded on a biblical theology of mission stemming from the creation mandate. We have seen how God's original mission for humanity in the

---

20. I have adapted the ESV here to reflect the abrupt manner in which "new creation" follows the conditional clause, lacking an expressed subject or verb. Although these elements could be supplied from the context, resulting in the translation "he is a new creation" (ESV), "there is a new creation," or "such a one is a new creation" (Matera, *II Corinthians*, 128, note i), such a reading risks over-individualizing the concept of new creation rather than recognizing that those who repent and submit to Jesus become *part* of the new creation (see, e.g., Kruse, *2 Corinthians*, 175).

21. DeYoung and Gilbert, *What Is the Mission of the Church?*, 206.

22. DeYoung and Gilbert, *What Is the Mission of the Church?*, 208.

23. Wright, "Reading the New Testament Missionally," 177.

garden persists throughout the biblical narrative, taking various shapes within the different covenantal administrations, climaxing in Jesus' post-resurrection commissions, and finding eschatological fulfillment in the new creation. From Genesis 1 to Revelation 22 the mission of God's people has always been to fill the earth as God's representatives and thereby demonstrate that his kingship extends over the entire earth. This biblical-theological understanding of mission categorically disagrees with the view of DeYoung and Gilbert, who conclude that "as the biblical story unfolds, the role of picking up Adam's failed mandate and completing it is *not* ours. That role is assumed by the last Adam, the Lord Jesus Christ."[24] Yet as we have seen, that Jesus fulfills an Old Testament missional role does not preclude his followers from *continuing* to fulfill that same role through the indwelling presence of the Holy Spirit. Indeed, Jesus does pick up and complete Adam's failed mandate, though he does so not only through his own redemptive work but also by working in and through his people during the period between his ascension and return. In this way, an organic connection exists between the missions of Adam, Israel, Jesus, and the church: the failures of the first two are redeemed by third, who calls the empowers the fourth to succeed.

This biblical theology of mission provides a robust framework for understanding the church's call to missions today. It is only as the church expands geographically and multiplies numerically by reaching all people groups with the gospel of the kingdom that we will fulfill the mission that God has given us. The church's call to missions, therefore, is not contingent upon a handful of "missions verses" but is rooted in the entire breadth of the Scriptural metanarrative. By expanding the representation of God's kingship to the ends of the earth through the work of missions, we work toward the ultimate fulfillment of God's original commission to humanity at creation. Once this mission is complete, Isaiah's vision of the eschatological kingdom of the "shoot from the stump of Jesse" will finally become a reality:

> The wolf shall dwell with the lamb,
>   and the leopard shall lie down with the young goat,
> and the calf and the lion and the fattened calf together;
>   and a little child shall lead them.
> The cow and the bear shall graze;
>   their young shall lie down together;
> and the lion shall eat straw like the ox.
> The nursing child shall play over the hole of the cobra,
>   and the weaned child shall put his hand on the adder's den.
> They shall not hurt or destroy

---

24. DeYoung and Gilbert, *What Is the Mission of the Church?*, 212 (emphasis original).

in all my holy mountain;
for the earth shall be full of the knowledge of the LORD
as the waters cover the sea. (Isa 11:6–9)

BIBLIOGRAPHY

Abernethy, Andrew T. *The Book of Isaiah and God's Kingdom: A Thematic-Theological Approach*. NSBT. Downers Grove: InterVarsity, 2016.

Alexander, T. Desmond. *From Paradise to the Promised Land: An Introduction to the Pentateuch*. 3rd ed. Grand Rapids: Baker Academic, 2012.

———. "Further Observations on the Term 'Seed' in Genesis." *TynBul* 48 (1997) 363–67.

Alter, Robert. *The Art of Biblical Narrative*. Rev. ed. New York: Basic, 2011.

———. *The Art of Biblical Poetry*. Rev. ed. New York: Basic, 2011.

———. *The Book of Psalms: A Translation with Commentary*. New York: Norton, 2007.

Amit, Yairah. *The Book of Judges: The Art of Editing*. Leiden: Brill, 1999.

Aquinas, Thomas. *Summa Theologica: Volume I, Part I*. Translated by Fathers of the English Dominican Province. New York: Cosimo, 1912.

Arnold, Bill T. "The Love-Fear Antinomy in Deuteronomy 5–11." *VT* 61 (2011) 551–69.

Arnold, Bill T., and John H. Choi. *A Guide to Biblical Hebrew Syntax*. Cambridge: Cambridge University Press, 2003.

Ashbaucher, Reid A. *Made in the Image of God: Understanding the Nature of God and Mankind in a Changing World*. Collierville, TN: Innovo, 2011.

Ashford, Bruce Riley, and Heath A. Thomas. *The Gospel of Our King: Bible, Worldview, and the Mission of Every Christian*. Grand Rapids: Baker Academic, 2019.

Ashley, Timothy R. *The Book of Numbers*. NICOT. Grand Rapids: Eerdmans, 1993.

Baker, David W. *Joel, Obadiah, Malachi*. NIVAC. Grand Rapids: Zondervan, 2006.

———. "רעע." In *NIDOTTE* 3:1154–58.

Ballenger, Isam. "Missiological Thoughts Prompted by Genesis 10." *RevExp* 103 (2006) 391–401.

Bandstra, Barry L. *Reading the Old Testament: Introduction to the Hebrew Bible*. 4th ed. Belmont, CA: Wadsworth, 2008.

Bauckham, Richard. *Bible and Mission: Christian Witness in a Postmodern World*. Grand Rapids: Baker Academic, 2003.

———. *The Climax of Prophecy: Studies on the Book of Revelation*. Edinburgh: T. & T. Clark, 1993.

———. "The Eschatological Earthquake in the Apocalypse of John." *NovT* 19 (1977) 224–33.

Bavinck, J. H. *An Introduction to the Science of Missions*. Translated by David Hugh Freeman. Phillipsburg, NJ: P. & R., 1960.

Beale, G. K. *The Book Revelation: A Commentary on the Greek Text*. NIGTC. Grand Rapids: Eerdmans, 1999.

———. "The Descent of the Eschatological Temple in the Form of the Spirit at Pentecost: Part 1: The Clearest Evidence." *TynBul* 56.1 (2005) 73–102.

———. "The Descent of the Eschatological Temple in the Form of the Spirit at Pentecost: Part 2: Corroborating Evidence." *TynBul* 56.2 (2005) 63–90.

———. *A New Testament Biblical Theology: The Unfolding of the Old Testament in the New*. Grand Rapids: Baker Academic, 2011.

———. *The Temple and the Church's Mission: A Biblical Theology of the Dwelling Place of God*. NSBT 17. Downers Grove: InterVarsity, 2004.

———. "The Use of Hosea 11:1 in Matthew 2:15: One More Time." *JETS* 55 (2012) 697–715.

Beale, G. K., and Mitchell Kim. *God Dwells Among Us: Expanding Eden to the Ends of the Earth*. Downers Grove: InterVarsity, 2014.

Beale, G. K., with David H. Campbell. *Revelation: A Shorter Commentary*. Grand Rapids: Eerdmans, 2015.

Beckwith, Roger. *The Old Testament Canon of the New Testament Church*. Grand Rapids: Eerdmans, 1985.

Beers, Holly. *The Followers of Jesus as the 'Servant': Luke's Model from Isaiah for the Disciples in Luke-Acts*. LNTS 535. London: Bloomsbury T. & T. Clark, 2015.

Beetham, Christopher A. *Echoes of Scripture in the Letter of Paul to the Colossians*. BIS 96. Leiden: Brill, 2008.

Berkof, Louis. *Manual of Christian Doctrine*. 2nd ed. Arlington Heights, IL: Christian Liberty, 2003.

Berlin, Adele. *Lamentations*. OTL. Louisville: Westminster John Knox, 2002.

Bird, Michael F. "'A Light to the Nations' (Isaiah 42:6 and 49:6): Inter-textuality and Mission in the Early Church." *RTR* 65 (2006) 122–31.

Blackaby, Henry. *Experiencing God: Knowing and Doing the Will of God*. Nashville: Broadman & Holman, 2008.

Blauw, Johannes. *The Missionary Nature of the Church: A Survey of the Biblical Theology of Mission*. New York: McGraw-Hill, 1962.

Blenkinsopp, Joseph. *Ezra-Nehemiah*. OTL. Philadelphia: Westminster John Knox, 1988.

Blocher, Henri. "The Fear of the Lord as the 'Principle' of Wisdom." *TynBul* 28 (1977) 3–28.

Block, Daniel I. *The Book of Ezekiel Chapters 25–48*. NICOT. Grand Rapids: Eerdmans, 1998.

———. *Deuteronomy*. NIVAC. Grand Rapids: Zondervan, 2012.

———. "Eden: A Temple? A Reassessment of the Biblical Evidence." In *From Creation to New Creation: Biblical Theology and Exegesis. Essays in Honor of G. K. Beale*, edited by Daniel M. Gurtner and Benjamin L. Gladd, 3–32. Peabody: Hendrickson, 2013.

———. *For the Glory of God: Recovering a Biblical Theology of Worship*. Grand Rapids: Baker Academic, 2014.

———. *Judges, Ruth*. NAC 6. Nashville: Broadman & Holman, 1999.

———. "The Privilege of Calling: The Mosaic Paradigm for Missions (Deut 26:16–19)." In *How I Love Your Torah, O Lord! Studies in the Book of Deuteronomy*, 140–61. Eugene, OR: Cascade, 2011.

———. "The Prophet of the Spirit: The Use of RWḤ in the Book of Ezekiel." *JETS* 32 (1989) 27–49.
Bock, Darrell L. *Acts*. BECNT. Grand Rapids: Baker Academic, 2007.
Boda, Mark J. *Haggai, Zechariah*. NIVAC. Grand Rapids: Zondervan, 2004.
Bodner, Keith. *1 Samuel: A Narrative Commentary*. HBM 19. Sheffield: Sheffield Phoenix, 2009.
Boring, M. Eugene. *Mark: A Commentary*. NTL. Louisville: Westminster John Knox, 2006.
Bosch, David J. *Transforming Mission: Paradigm Shifts in Theology of Mission*. Maryknoll, NY: Orbis, 1991.
Bosma, Carl J. "Jonah 1:9—An Example of Elenctic Testimony." *CTJ* 48 (2013) 65–90.
———. "A Missional Reading of Psalms 67 and 96." In *Reading the Bible Missionally*, edited by Michael W. Goheen, 151–71. Grand Rapids: Eerdmans, 2016.
Boxall, Ian. *The Revelation of St. John*. Peabody: Hendrickson, 2006.
Branson, Mark Lau, and Nicholas Warnes, eds. *Starting Missional Churches: Life with God in the Neighborhood*. Downers Grove, IL: InterVarsity, 2014.
Briggs, Richard S. "Humans in the Image of God and Other Things Genesis Does Not Make Clear." *JTI* 4 (2010) 111–26.
Brown, Michael L. "ברך." In *NIDOTTE* 1:755–57.
Brueggemann, Walter. *Genesis*. IBC. Louisville: Westminster John Knox, 1982.
Bullock, C. Hassell. "Wisdom, the 'Amen' of Torah." *JETS* 52 (2009) 5–18.
Burge, Gary M. *John*. NIVAC. Grand Rapids: Zondervan, 2000.
Cardoza-Orlandi, Carlos F., and Justo L. Gonzalez. *To All Nations From All Nations: A History of the Christian Missionary Movement*. Nashville: Abington, 2013.
Carey, William. *An Enquiry into the Obligations of Christians to Use Means for the Conversion of the Heathens*. Leicester: Ireland, 1792.
Carroll, John T. *Luke: A Commentary*. NTL. Louisville: Westminster John Knox, 2012.
Carroll R., M. Daniel. "Blessing the Nations: Toward a Biblical Theology of Mission from Genesis." *BBR* 10 (2000) 17–34.
Carson, D. A. *The Gospel According to John*. PNTC. Grand Rapids: Eerdmans, 1991.
Cartledge, Tony W. *1 & 2 Samuel*. SHBC. Macon: Smyth & Helwys, 2001.
Cate, Robert L. "The Fear of the Lord in the Old Testament." *The Theological Educator* 35 (1987) 41–55.
Chalmers, Aaron. *Exploring the Religion of Ancient Israel: Prophet, Priest, Sage and People*. Downers Grove: InterVarsity, 2012.
Chapman, Stephen B., and Laceye C. Warner. "Jonah and the Imitation of God: Rethinking Evangelism and the Old Testament." *JTI* 2 (2008) 43–69.
Chapple, Allan. "Paul and Illyricum." *RTR* 72 (2013) 20–35.
Childs, Brevard S. *Isaiah*. OTL. Louisville: Westminster John Knox, 2001.
Chisholm, Robert B., Jr. *1 & 2 Samuel*. TTC. Grand Rapids: Baker, 2013.
———. "The Christological Fulfillment of Isaiah's Servant Songs." *BSac* 163 (2006) 387–404.
———. *A Commentary on Judges and Ruth*. Grand Rapids: Kregel, 2013.
———. "When Prophecy Appears to Fail, Check Your Hermeneutic." *JETS* 53 (2010) 561–77.
Clements, R. E. *God and Temple: The Idea of the Divine Presence in Ancient Israel*. Eugene, OR: Wipf & Stock, 2016.
Clifford, Richard J. *Psalms 1–72*. AOTC. Nashville: Abingdon, 2002.

Cohen, Jeremy. *Be Fertile and Increase, Fill the Earth and Master It: The Ancient and Medieval Career of a Biblical Text*. Ithaca: Cornell University Press, 1989.
Cole, R. Dennis. *Numbers*. NAC 3B. Nashville: Broadman & Holman, 2000.
Collett, Don. "The Christology of Israel's Psalter." *CurTM* 41 (2014) 390–95.
Collins, Adela Yarbro. *The Combat Myth in the Book of Revelation*. Harvard Dissertations in Religion 9. Missoula: Scholars, 1976.
Collins, C. John. *Genesis 1–4: A Linguistic, Literary, and Theological Commentary*. Phillipsburg: P. & R., 2006.
———. "The (Intelligible) Masoretic Text of Malachi 2:16 or, How Does God Feel About Divorce?" *Presbyterion* 20 (1994) 36–40.
———. "A Syntactical Note (Genesis 3:15): Is the Woman's Seed Singular or Plural?" *TynBul* 48 (1997) 139–48.
Coloe, Mary L. *God Dwells With Us: Temple Symbolism in the Fourth Gospel*. Collegeville: Liturgical, 2001.
Coxhead, Steven R. "The Cardionomographic Work of the Holy Spirit in the Old Testament." *WTJ* 79 (2017) 77–95.
Craigie, Peter C. *The Book of Deuteronomy*. NICOT. Grand Rapids: Eerdmans, 1976.
Creach, Jerome F. D. *Yahweh as Refuge and the Editing of the Hebrew Psalter*. JSOTSup 217. Sheffield: Sheffield Academic, 1996.
Crowe, Brandon D. *The Last Adam: A Theology of the Obedient Life of Jesus in the Gospels*. Grand Rapids: Baker Academic, 2017.
———. *The Obedient Son: Deuteronomy and Christology in the Gospel of Matthew*. BZNW 188. Göttingen: de Gruyter, 2012.
Das, A. Andrew. "Paul of Tarshish: Isaiah 66.19 and the Spanish Mission of Romans 15.24, 28." *NTS* 54 (2008) 60–73.
Datema, Dave. "Defining 'Unreached': A Short History." *IJFM* 33 (2016) 45–71.
Davids, Peter H. *The First Epistle of Peter*. NICNT. Grand Rapids: Eerdmans, 1990.
Davies, John A. *A Royal Priesthood: Literary and Intertextual Perspectives on an Image of Israel in Exodus 19.6*. JSOTSup 395. London: T. & T. Clark, 2004.
Davis, Jud. "Acts 2 and the Old Testament: The Pentecost Event in Light of Sinai, Babel and the Table of Nations." *CTR* 7 (2009) 29–48.
Dearman, J. Andrew. "Daughter Zion and Her Place in God's Household." *HBT* 31 (2009) 144–59.
deClaissé-Walford, Nancy, et al. *The Book of Psalms*. NICOT. Grand Rapids: Eerdmans, 2014.
Dempster, Stephen G. *Dominion and Dynasty: A Theology of the Hebrew Bible*. NSBT 15. Downers Grove: InterVarsity 2003.
DeRouchie, Jason S. "The Heart of YHWH and His Chosen One in 1 Samuel 13:14." *BBR* 24 (2014) 467–89.
De Vaux, Roland. *Ancient Israel: Its Life and Institutions*. Grand Rapids: Eerdmans, 1997.
DeYoung, Kevin, and Greg Gilbert. *What Is the Mission of the Church? Making Sense of Social Justice, Shalom, and the Great Commission*. Wheaton: Crossway, 2011.
Dietrich, Walter. *The Early Monarchy in Israel: The Tenth Century B.C.E.* Biblische Enzyklopädie. Translated by Joachim Vette. Atlanta: Society of Biblical Literature, 2007.
Dozeman, Thomas B. *Exodus*. ECC. Grand Rapids: Eerdmans, 2009.

———. "Inner-Biblical Interpretation of Yahweh's Gracious and Compassionate Character." *JBL* 108 (1989) 207–23.
Dumbrell, William J. *Covenant and Creation: An Old Testament Covenant Theology*. Rev. ed. Milton Keynes: Paternoster, 2013.
———. *The Faith of Israel: A Theological Survey of the Old Testament*. 2nd ed. Grand Rapids: Baker Academic, 2002.
du Preez, Jannie. "People and Nations in the Kingdom of God According to the Book of Revelation." *JTSA* 49 (1984) 49–51.
Eichrodt, Walther. *Theology of the Old Testament*. Translated by J. A. Baker. 2 vols. OTL. Philadelphia: Westminster, 1961, 1967.
Enns, Peter. *Exodus*. NIVAC. Grand Rapids: Zondervan, 2000.
———. *Inspiration and Incarnation: Evangelicals and the Problem of the Old Testament*. Grand Rapids: Baker Academic, 2005.
Escobar, Samuel. *The New Global Mission: The Gospel from Everywhere to Everyone*. Christian Doctrine in Global Perspective. Grand Rapids: IVP Academic, 2003.
Evans, Craig A. "A Light to the Nations: Isaiah and Mission in Luke." In *Christian Mission: Old Testament Foundations and New Testament Developments*, edited by Stanley E. Porter and Cynthia Long Westfall, 93–107. MNTSS. Eugene, OR: Pickwick, 2011.
Ferdinando, Keith. "Mission: A Problem of Definition." *Themelios* 33 (2008) 46–59.
Filbeck, David. *Yes, God of the Gentiles, Too: The Missionary Message of the Old Testament*. Wheaton: Billy Graham Center, 1994.
Filho, Jose Adriano. "The Apocalypse of John as an Account of a Visionary Experience: Notes on the Book's Structure." *JSNT* 25 (2002) 213–34.
Fokkelman, Jan P. *Reading Biblical Narrative: An Introductory Guide*. Translated by Ineke Smit. Louisville: Westminster John Knox, 1999.
Foster, Robert L. "A Plea for New Songs: A Missional/Theological Reflection on Psalm 96." *CurTM* 33 (2006) 285–90.
———. "Shepherds, Sticks, and Social Destabilization: A Fresh Look at Zechariah 11:4–17." *JBL* 126 (2007) 735–53.
Foster, Stuart J. "The Missiology of Old Testament Covenant." *IBMR* 34 (2010) 205–8.
Fowl, Stephen E. *Ephesians: A Commentary*. NTL. Louisville: Westminster John Knox, 2012.
Frame, John M. *Salvation Belongs to the Lord: An Introduction to Systematic Theology*. Phillipsburg: P. & R., 2006.
France, R. T. *The Gospel of Mark: A Commentary on the Greek Text*. NIGTC. Grand Rapids: Eerdmans, 2002.
———. *Matthew: An Introduction and Commentary*. TNTC 1. Downers Grove: InterVarsity, 1985.
Fretheim, Terence E. *Exodus*. IBC. Louisville: John Knox, 1991.
Futato, Mark D. *Interpreting the Psalms: An Exegetical Handbook*. Grand Rapids: Kregel, 2007.
Gentry, Peter J., and Stephen J. Wellum. *Kingdom through Covenant: A Biblical-Theological Understanding of the Covenants*. Wheaton: Crossway, 2012.
Gilbert, Pierre. "The Missional Relevance of Genesis 1–3." *Direction* 43 (2014) 49–64.
Gladd, Benjamin L. "The Last Adam as the 'Life-Giving Spirit' Revisited: A Possible Old Testament Background of One of Paul's Most Perplexing Phrases." *WTJ* 71 (2009) 297–309.

Glasser, Arthur F., et al. *Announcing the Kingdom: God's Mission in the Bible*. Grand Rapids: Baker Academic, 2003.
Goheen, Michael W. *Introducing Christian Mission Today: Scripture, History and Issues*. Downers Grove: InterVarsity, 2014.
———. *A Light to the Nations: The Missional Church and the Biblical Story*. Grand Rapids: Baker Academic, 2011.
Goheen, Michael W., ed. *Reading the Bible Missionally*. The Gospel and Our Culture. Grand Rapids: Eerdmans, 2016.
Goldingay, John. *Old Testament Theology, Volume 1: Israel's Gospel*. Downers Grove: IVP Academic, 2003.
———. *Psalms, Volume 3: Psalms 90–150*. BCOTWP. Grand Rapids: Baker Academic, 2008.
Goldsworthy, Graeme. "The Great Indicative: An Aspect of a Biblical Theology of Mission." *RTR* 55 (1996) 2–13.
Goswell, Greg. "The Fate and Future of Zerubbabel in the Prophecy of Haggai." *Bib* 91 (2010) 77–90.
Greear, J. D. *Gospel: Recovering the Power that Made Christianity Revolutionary*. Nashville: Broadman & Holman, 2011.
Green, Douglas J. "'The LORD Is Christ's Shepherd': Psalm 23 as Messianic Prophecy." In *Eyes to See, Ears to Hear: Essays in Memory of J. Alan Groves*, edited by Peter Enns et al., 33–46. Phillipsburg: P. & R., 2010.
Green, Joel B. *The Gospel of Luke*. NICNT. Grand Rapids: Eerdmans, 1997.
Greidanus, Sidney. *Preaching Christ from the Old Testament: A Contemporary Hermeneutical Method*. Grand Rapids: Eerdmans, 1999.
Grisanti, Michael A. "Israel's Mission to the Nations in Isaiah 40–55: An Update." *MSJ* 9 (1998) 39–61.
Gross, Jerry. "Missions and the Glory of God." *ResQ* 25 (1982) 150–57.
Grüneberg, Keith N. *Abraham, Blessing and the Nations: A Philological and Exegetical Study of Genesis 12:3 in its Narrative Context*. BZAW 332. Berlin: de Gruyter, 2003.
Guder, Darrell L., ed. *Missional Church: A Vision for the Sending Church in America*. Grand Rapids: Eerdmans, 1998.
Gundry, Robert H. "The New Jerusalem: People as Place, Not Place for People." *NovT* 29 (1987) 254–64.
Gupta, Nijay K. "Which 'Body' Is a Temple (1 Corinthians 6:19)? Paul Beyond the Individual/Communal Divide." *CBQ* 72 (2010) 518–36.
Guthrie, Stan. *Missions in the Third Millennium: 21 Key Trends for the 21st Century*. Eugene, OR: Wipf & Stock, 2014.
Hafemann, Scott J. "The Kingdom of God as the Mission of God." In *For the Fame of God's Name: Essays in Honor of John Piper*, edited by Sam Storms and Justin Taylor, 235–52. Wheaton: Crossway, 2010.
Halas, Stanislas. "Sens dynamique de l'expression λαὸς εἰς περιποίησιν en 1 P 2,9." *Bib* 65 (1984) 254–58.
Hall, Sarah Lebhar. *Conquering Character: The Characterization of Joshua in Joshua 1–11*. LBS. New York: T.& T. Clark, 2010.
Hamilton, James. "The Seed of the Woman and the Blessing of Abraham." *TynBul* 58 (2007) 253–73.
Hamilton, Victor P. *The Book of Genesis: Chapters 1–17*. NICOT. Grand Rapids: Eerdmans, 1990.

———. *The Book of Genesis: Chapters 18–50*. NICOT. Grand Rapids: Eerdmans, 1995.
———. *Exodus: An Exegetical Commentary*. Grand Rapids: Baker Academic, 2011.
Hansen, Steven E. "Forgiving and Retaining Sin: A Study of the Text and Context of John 20:23." *HBT* 19 (1997) 24–32.
Hare, Douglas R. A. *Matthew*. IBC. Louisville: Westminster John Knox, 2009.
Harland, P. J. "Vertical or Horizontal: The Sin of Babel." *VT* 48 (1998) 515–33.
Harris, Murray J. *The Second Epistle to the Corinthians: A Commentary on the Greek Text*. NIGTC. Grand Rapids: Eerdmans, 2005.
Harris, R. Geoffrey. *Mission in the Gospels*. Eugene, OR: Wipf & Stock, 2004.
Hedlund, Roger E. *The Mission of the Church in the World: A Biblical Theology*. Grand Rapids: Baker, 1991.
Hill, Andrew E. "Daniel." In *The Expositor's Bible Commentary*, Vol. 8. Rev. ed. Edited by Tremper Longman III and David E. Garland. Grand Rapids: Zondervan, 2008.
———. *Haggai, Zechariah and Malachi*. TOTC. Downers Grove: InterVarsity, 2012.
Hill, David. "The Spirit and the Church's Witness: Observations on Acts 1:6–8." *IBS* 6 (1984) 16–26.
Hoekema, Anthony A. *Created in God's Image*. Grand Rapids: Eerdmans, 1986.
Holwerda, David E. "The Church and the Little Scroll (Revelation 10, 11)." *CTJ* 34 (1999) 148–61.
Horner, David. *When Missions Shapes the Mission: You and Your Church Can Reach the World*. Nashville: Broadman & Holman, 2011.
Horton, Michael. *Ordinary: Sustainable Faith in a Radical, Restless World*. Grand Rapids: Zondervan, 2014.
Huey, F. B., Jr. *Jeremiah, Lamentations*. NAC 16. Nashville: Broadman & Holman, 1993.
Humphreys, W. Lee. *The Character of God in the Book of Genesis: A Narrative Appraisal*. Louisville: Westminster John Knox, 2001.
Hunter, Kent R. *Who Broke My Church? 7 Proven Strategies for Renewal and Revival*. New York: FaithWords, 2017.
Hurtado, Larry W. *Lord Jesus Christ: Devotion to Jesus in Earliest Christianity*. Grand Rapids: Eerdmans, 2005.
Hwang, Jerry. "The *Missio Dei* as an Integrative Motif in the Book of Jeremiah." *BBR* 23 (2013) 481–508.
Janzen, J. Gerald. *Abraham and All the Families of the Earth: A Commentary on the Book of Genesis 12–50*. ITC. Grand Rapids: Eerdmans, 1993.
Jobes, Karen H. *1 Peter*. BECNT. Grand Rapids: Baker, 2005.
Johnson, Dennis E. "Jesus Against the Idols: The Use of Isaianic Servant Songs in the Missiology of Acts." *WTJ* 52 (1990) 343–53.
Johnson, Raymond. "The Church's Mission: John 20:19–23 Reconsidered." *CurTM* 43 (2016) 22–28.
Johnstone, Patrick. *The Future of the Global Church: History, Trends and Possibilities*. Milton Keynes: Authentic Media Limited, 2011.
Joüon, Paul, and T. Muraoka. *A Grammar of Biblical Hebrew*. Subsidia Biblica 27. Rome: Editrice Pontificio Istituto Biblico, 2006.
Kaiser, Walter C., Jr. "Divorce in Malachi 2:10–16." *CTR* 2 (1987) 73–84.
———. *Mission in the Old Testament: Israel as a Light to the Nations*. 2nd ed. Grand Rapids: Baker Academic, 2012.
Kaminski, Carol M. *From Noah to Israel: Realization of the Primaeval Blessing after the Flood*. JSOTSup 413. London: T. & T. Clark, 2004.

———. *Was Noah Good? Finding Favour in the Flood Narrative*. LBS. London: Bloomsbury, 2014.

Keener, Craig S. *A Commentary on the Gospel of Matthew*. Grand Rapids: Eerdmans, 1999.

———. "Why Does Luke Use Tongues as a Sign of the Spirit's Empowerment?" *JPT* 15 (2007) 177–84.

Kerr, Alan R. *The Temple of Jesus' Body: The Temple Theme in the Gospel of John*. JSNTSup 220. Sheffield: Sheffield Academic, 2002.

Kessler, John. "Haggai, Zerubbabel, and the Political Status of Yehud: The Signet Ring in Haggai 2:23." In *Prophets, Prophecy, and Prophetic Texts in Second Temple Judaism*, edited by Michael H. Floyd and Robert D. Haak, 102–19. LHBOTS 427. New York: T. & T. Clark, 2006.

Kessler, Martin, and Karel Deurloo. *A Commentary on Genesis: The Book of Beginnings*. New York: Paulist, 2004.

Kidner, Derek. "The Distribution of Divine Names in Jonah." *TynBul* 21 (1970) 126–28.

Kilgallen, John J. "Paul's Speech to the Ephesian Elders: Its Structure." *ETL* 70 (1994) 112–21.

Kim, Chil-Sung. "A Study on Paul's Missiological Thoughts in Romans." *The Korean Society of Mission Studies* 43 (2016) 73–103.

Kirk, J. Andrew. *What Is Mission? Theological Explorations*. Minneapolis: Fortress, 2000.

Kissling, Paul J. *Genesis, Volume 1*. The College Press NIV Commentary. Joplin, MO: College Press, 2004.

Klein, George L. *Zechariah*. NAC 21B. Nashville: Broadman & Holman, 2008.

Klein, Ralph W. "Psalms in Chronicles." *CurTM* 32 (2005) 264–75.

Kodell, Jerome. "'The Word of God Grew': The Ecclesial Tendency of λόγος in Acts 6,7; 12,24; 19,20." *Bib* 55 (1974) 505–19.

Köstenberger, Andreas J. *John*. BECNT. Grand Rapids: Baker Academic, 2004.

Köstenberger, Andreas J., and Peter T. O'Brien. *Salvation to the Ends of the Earth: A Biblical Theology of Mission*. NSBT 11. Downers Grove: InterVarsity, 2001.

Kruse, Colin G. *2 Corinthians*. Rev. ed. TNTC. Downers Grove: InterVarsity, 2015.

Kutsko, John F. *Between Heaven and Earth: Divine Presence and Absence in the Book of Ezekiel*. BJS 7. Winona Lake, IN: Eisenbrauns, 2000.

Landon, Michael. "The Psalms as Mission." *ResQ* 44 (2002) 165–75.

Lapsley, Jacqueline E. *Can These Bones Live? The Problem of the Moral Self in the Book of Ezekiel*. BZAW 301. Berlin: de Gruyter, 2000.

Layton, Scott C. "Remarks on the Canaanite Origin of Eve." *CBQ* 59 (1997) 22–32.

Lee, Chee-Chiew. *The Blessing of Abraham, the Spirit, and Justification in Galatians: Their Relationship and Significance for Understanding Paul's Theology*. Eugene, OR: Pickwick, 2013.

———. "Once Again: The Niphal and Hithpael of ברך in the Abrahamic Blessing for the Nations." *JSOT* 36 (2012) 279–96.

Legrand, Lucien. *Unity and Plurality: Mission in the Bible*. Translated by Robert R. Barr. Maryknoll, NY: Orbis, 1990.

Leim, Joshua E. "In the Glory of His Father: Intertextuality and the Apocalyptic Son of Man in the Gospel of Mark." *JTI* 7 (2013) 213–32.

———. *Matthew's Theological Grammar: The Father and the Son*. WUNT 2/402. Tübingen: Mohr Siebeck, 2015.

Leithart, Peter J. "Adam, Moses, and Jesus: A Reading of Romans 5:12–14." *CTJ* 43 (2008) 257–73.
Léonas, Alexis. "A Note on Acts 3,25–26: The Meaning of Peter's Genesis Quotation." *ETL* 76 (2000) 149–61.
Lessing, R. Reed. "Isaiah's Servants in Chapters 40–55: Clearing up the Confusion." *Concordia Journal* 37 (2011) 130–34.
Lim, Johnson T. K. *Grace in the Midst of Judgment: Grappling with Genesis 1–11*. BZAW 314. Berlin: de Gruyter, 2002.
Limburg, James. *Jonah: A Commentary*. OTL. Louisville: Westminster John Knox, 1993.
Litwak, Kenneth D. "The Use of Quotations from Isaiah 52:13—53:12 in the New Testament." *JETS* 26 (1983) 385–94.
Long, V. Philips. "1 and 2 Samuel." In *Zondervan Illustrated Bible Backgrounds Commentary*, Vol. 2. Edited by John H. Walton. Grand Rapids: Zondervan, 2009.
Ludwig, Alan. "Mission in the Psalms." *Logia* 23 (2014) 11–19.
Luhrmann, Tanya M. *When God Talks Back: Understanding the American Evangelical Relationship with God*. New York: Knopf, 2012.
Lyons, Michael A. "Paul and the Servant(s): Isaiah 49,6 in Acts 13,47." *ETL* 89 (2013) 345–59.
Mainville, Odette. *The Spirit in Luke-Acts*. Translated by Suzanne Spolarich. Eugene, OR: Wipf & Stock, 2018.
Maller, Allen S. "Isaiah's Suffering Servant: A New View." *Dialogue & Alliance* 20 (2006) 9–16.
Marlowe, W. Creighton. "Music of Missions: Themes of Cross-Cultural Outreach in the Psalms." *Missiology* 26 (1998) 445–56.
Marshall, I. Howard. "Acts." In *Commentary on the New Testament Use of the Old Testament*, edited by G. K. Beale and D. A. Carson, 513–606. Grand Rapids: Baker Academic, 2007.
———. *The Book of Acts: An Introduction and Commentary*. TNTC. Grand Rapids: Eerdmans, 1980.
Martens, Elmer. "Ezekiel's Contribution to a Biblical Theology of Mission." *Direction* 28 (1999) 75–87.
———. "Impulses to Mission in Isaiah: An Intertextual Exploration." *BBR* 17 (2007) 215–39.
Mascarenhas, Theodore. *The Missionary Function of Israel in Psalms 67, 96, and 117*. Lanham: University Press of America, 2005.
Mason, Steven D. "Getting a 'Handle' on Holistic Christian Mission: The Contribution of Isaiah 61 as a Discrete Old Testament Voice." *Missiology* 40 (2012) 295–313.
Matera, Frank J. *II Corinthians: A Commentary*. NTL. Louisville: Westminster John Knox, 2003.
Mathews, Kenneth A. *Genesis 1–11:26*. NAC 1A. Nashville: Broadman & Holman, 1996.
———. *Genesis 11:27–50:26*. NAC 1B. Nashville: Broadman & Holman, 2005.
Mathewson, David. *A New Heaven and a New Earth: The Meaning and Function of the Old Testament in Revelation 22.1—22.5*. JSOTSup 238. Sheffield: Sheffield Academic, 2003.
Mays, James L. *The Lord Reigns: A Theological Handbook to the Psalms*. Louisville: Westminster John Knox, 1994.
McCann, J. Clinton. *Judges*. IBC. Louisville: Westminster John Knox, 2011.

———. *A Theological Introduction to the Book of Psalms: The Psalms as Torah.* Nashville: Abingdon, 1993.
McCann, J. Clinton, ed. *The Shape and Shaping of the Psalter.* JSOTSup 159. Sheffield: Sheffield Academic, 1993.
McCarter, P. Kyle, Jr. *1 Samuel: A New Translation with Introduction, Notes & Commentary.* AB 8. Garden City, NY: Doubleday, 1980.
McComiskey, Douglas S. "Exile and Restoration from Exile in the Scriptural Quotations and Allusions of Jesus." *JETS* 53 (2010) 673–96.
McConville, J. Gordon. *Deuteronomy.* AOTC 5. Leicester: InterVarsity 2002.
McDonnell, Kilian. *The Baptism of Jesus in the Jordan: The Trinitarian and Cosmic Order of Salvation.* Collegeville: Liturgical, 1996.
McKenzie, Tracy J. "The Hebrew Bible and the Nations." In *Theology and Practice of Mission: God, the Church, and the Nations*, edited by Bruce Riley Ashford, 146–59. Nashville: Broadman & Holman, 2011.
McKeown, James. *Genesis.* THOTC. Grand Rapids: Eerdmans, 2008.
McLean, John A. "Did Jesus Correct the Disciples' View of the Kingdom?" *BSac* 151 (1994) 215–27.
Middleton, J. Richard. *The Liberating Image: The Imago Dei in Genesis 1.* Grand Rapids: Brazos, 2005.
———. "A New Heaven and a New Earth: The Case for a Holistic Reading of the Biblical Story of Redemption." *JCTR* 11 (2006) 73–97.
Milgrom, Jacob. *Leviticus: A Book of Ritual and Ethics.* Minneapolis: Augsburg, 2004.
Miller, Patrick D., Jr. *Deuteronomy.* IBC. Louisville: John Knox, 1990.
———. "Syntax and Theology in Genesis XII 3a." *VT* 34 (1984) 472–75.
Moberly, R. W. L. *At the Mountain of God: Story and Theology in Exodus 32–34.* JSOTSup 22. Sheffield: JSOT, 1983.
———. "Preaching for a Response? Jonah's Message to the Ninevites Reconsidered." *VT* 53 (2003) 156–68.
Modrzejewski, Joseph Mélèze. "The Septuagint as *Nomos*: How the Torah Became a 'Civic Law' for the Jews of Egypt." In *Critical Studies in Ancient Law, Comparative Law and Legal History*, edited by John W. Cairns et al., 183–99. Portland, OR: Hart, 2001.
Moloney, Francis J. "Constructing Jesus and the Son of Man." *CBQ* 75 (2013) 719–38.
Moo, Douglas J. *The Epistle to the Romans.* NICNT. Grand Rapids: Eerdmans, 1996.
———. *The Letters to the Colossians and to Philemon.* PNTC. Grand Rapids: Eerdmans, 2008.
Moore, Thomas S. "'To the End of the Earth': The Geographical and Ethnic Universalism of Acts 1:8 in Light of Isaianic Influence on Luke." *JETS* 40 (1997) 389–99.
Moran, William L. "The Ancient Near Eastern Background of the Love of God in Deuteronomy." *CBQ* 25 (1963) 77–87.
Moreau, A. Scott, et al. *Introducing World Missions: A Biblical, Historical, and Practical Survey.* Grand Rapids: Baker Academic, 2004.
Mounce, Robert H. *The Book of Revelation.* NICOT. Rev. ed. Grand Rapids: Eerdmans, 1998.
Murphy, S. Jonathan. "Is the Psalter a Book with a Single Message?" *BSac* 165 (2008) 283–93.
Neill, Stephen. *Creative Tension.* London: Edinburgh House, 1959.
Nel, Philip J. "כבש." In *NIDOTTE* 2:596.

Nelson, Richard D. *Raising Up a Faithful Priest: Community and Priesthood in Biblical Theology*. Louisville: Westminster John Knox, 1993.

Niehaus, Jeffrey J. *Ancient Near Eastern Themes in Biblical Theology*. Grand Rapids: Kregel, 2008.

Noonan, Benjamin J. "Abraham, Blessing, and the Nations: A Reexamination of the Niphal and Hitpael of ברך in the Patriarchal Narratives." *HS* 51 (2010) 73–93.

O'Brien, Peter T. "Mission, Witness, and the Coming of the Spirit." *BBR* 9 (1999) 203–14.

O'Dowd, Ryan. *The Wisdom of Torah: Epistemology in Deuteronomy and the Wisdom Literature*. FRLANT 225. Göttingen: Vandenhoeck & Ruprecht, 2009.

Okoye, James Chukwuma. *Israel and the Nations: A Mission Theology of the Old Testament*. ASMS. Maryknoll, NY: Orbis, 2006.

Olson, C. Gordon. *What in the World Is God Doing? The Essentials of Global Missions: An Introductory Guide*. Rev. 5th ed. Cedar Knolls, NJ: Global Gospel, 2003.

Osborne, Grant R. *Revelation*. BECNT. Grand Rapids: Baker Academic, 2002.

Oschwald, Jeffrey. "The Word of the Lord Grew—and Multiplied—and Showed its Strength: The Word of God in the Book of Acts." *Concordia Journal* 44 (2018) 41–60.

Oswalt, John. *The Book of Isaiah, Chapters 40–66*. NICOT. Grand Rapids: Eerdmans, 1998.

O'Toole, Robert F. *Luke's Presentation of Jesus: A Christology*. Subsidia Biblica 25. Rome: Editrice Pontificio Istituto Biblico, 2004.

Ott, Craig, et al. *Encountering Theology of Mission: Biblical Foundations, Historical Developments, and Contemporary Issues*. Grand Rapids: Baker Academic, 2010.

Palmer, Erin. "Imagining Space in Revelation: The Heavenly Throne Room and New Jerusalem." *JTAK* 39 (2015) 35–47.

Parsons, Gregory W. "The Structure and Purpose of the Book of Job." *BSac* 138 (1981) 139–57.

Patrick, Dale. "The Covenant Code Source." *VT* 27 (1977) 144–57.

Patrick, James E. "The Fourfold Structure of Job: Variations on a Theme." *VT* 55 (2005) 185–206.

Paul, Shalom M. *Isaiah 40–66: Translation and Commentary*. ECC. Grand Rapids: Eerdmans, 2012.

Peskett, Howard, and Vinoth Ramachandra. *The Message of Mission: The Glory of Christ in All Time and Space*. BST. Downers Grove: InterVarsity, 2003.

Peters, George W. *A Biblical Theology of Missions*. Chicago: Moody Bible Institute, 1972.

Petersen, David L. *Haggai and Zechariah 1–8*. OTL. Philadelphia: Westminster John Knox, 1984.

Peterson, David G. *The Acts of the Apostles*. PNTC. Grand Rapids: Eerdmans, 2009.

Pikkert, Peter. *The Essence and Implications of Missio Dei: An Appraisal of Today's Foremost Theology of Missions*. Ancaster, ON: Alev, 2017.

Piper, John. *Let the Nations Be Glad! The Supremacy of God in Missions*. Rev. 2nd ed. Grand Rapids: Baker Academic, 2003.

Plantinga, Cornelius, Jr. *Engaging God's World: A Christian Vision of Faith, Learning, and Living*. Grand Rapids: Eerdmans, 2002.

Platt, David. *Radical: Taking Back Your Faith from the American Dream*. Colorado Springs: Multnomah, 2010.

Plummer, Robert L. *Paul's Understanding of the Church's Mission: Did the Apostle Paul Expect the Early Christian Communities to Evangelize?* PBM. Milton Keynes: Paternoster, 2006.

———. "A Theological Basis for the Church's Mission in Paul." *WTJ* 64 (2002) 253–71.

Polhill, John B. *Acts*. NAC 26. Nashville: Broadman & Holman, 1992.

Porter, Stanley E., and Cynthia Long Westfall. "A Cord of Three Strands: Mission in Acts." In *Christian Mission: Old Testament Foundations and New Testament Developments*, edited by Stanley E. Porter and Cynthia Long Westfall, 108–34. MNTSS. Eugene, OR: Pickwick, 2011.

Poythress, Vern Sheridan. *In the Beginning was the Word: Language—A God-Centered Approach*. Wheaton: Crossway, 2009.

Pratt, Richard L., Jr. *Designed for Dignity: What God Has Made it Possible for You to Be*. 2nd ed. Phillipsburg: P. & R., 2000.

———. "Historical Contingencies and Biblical Predictions." In *The Way of Wisdom: Essays in Honor of Bruce K. Waltke*, edited J. I. Packer and Sven Soderlund, 180–203. Grand Rapids: Zondervan, 2000.

Priest, Robert J., and Robert DeGeorge. "Doctoral Dissertations on Mission: Ten Year Update, 2002–2011 (Revised)." *IBMR* 37 (2013) 195–202.

Reichenbach, Bruce R. "Genesis 1 as a Theological-Political Narrative of Kingdom Establishment." *BBR* 13 (2003) 47–69.

Renz, Thomas. *The Rhetorical Function of the Book of Ezekiel*. Leiden: Brill, 1999.

Resseguie, James L. *The Revelation of John: A Narrative Commentary*. Grand Rapids: Baker Academic, 2009.

Rhoads, David. "Children of Abraham, Children of God: Metaphorical Kinship in Paul's Letter to the Galatians." *CurTM* (2004) 282–97.

Riecker, Siegbert. "Missions in the Hebrew Bible Revisited: Four Theological Trails Instead of One Confining Concept." *Missiology* 44 (2016) 324–39.

Robertson, O. Palmer. *The Flow of the Psalms: Discovering Their Structure and Theology*. Phillipsburg: P. & R., 2015.

Rose, Wolter H. *Zemah and Zerubbabel: Messianic Expectations in the Early Postexilic Period*. JSOTSup 304. Sheffield: Sheffield Academic, 2000.

Rosner, Brian S. "Temple Prostitution in 1 Corinthians 6:12–20." *NovT* 40 (1998) 336–51.

Ross, Allen P. *A Commentary on the Psalms: Volume 1: (1–41)*. KEL. Grand Rapids: Kregel, 2011.

Rotenberry, Paul. "Blessing in the Old Testament: A Study of Genesis 12:3." *ResQ* 2 (1958) 32–36.

Roxburgh, Alan J., and M. Scott Boren. *Introducing the Missional Church: What It Is, Why It Matters, How to Become One*. Grand Rapids: Baker, 2009.

Ryrie, Charles C. *Basic Theology: A Popular Systematic Guide to Biblical Truth*. Chicago: Moody, 1999.

Sailhamer, John H. "Hosea 11:1 and Matthew 2:15." *WTJ* 63 (2001) 87–96.

Sarna, Nahum M. *Exodus*. The JPS Torah Commentary. Philadelphia: JPS, 1991.

———. *Genesis*. The JPS Torah Commentary. Philadelphia: JPS, 1989.

Schmutzer, Andrew J. *Be Fruitful and Multiply: A Crux of Thematic Repetition in Genesis 1–11*. Eugene, OR: Wipf & Stock, 2009.

Schmutzer, Andrew J., and Randall X. Gauthier. "The Identity of the 'Horn' in Psalm 148:14a: An Exegetical Investigation in the MT and LXX Versions." *BBR* 19 (2009) 161–83.

Schnabel, Eckhard J. *Early Christian Mission, Volume One: Jesus and the Twelve*. Downers Grove: InterVarsity, 2004.

———. *Early Christian Mission, Volume Two: Paul and the Early Church*. Downers Grove: InterVarsity, 2004.

———. "Israel, the People of God, and the Nations." *JETS* 45 (2002) 35–57.

———. *Paul the Missionary: Realities, Strategies and Methods*. Grand Rapids: IVP Academic, 2008.

———. "Paul's Missionary Strategy: Goals, Methods, and Realities." In *Christian Mission: Old Testament Foundations and New Testament Developments*, edited by Stanley E. Porter and Cynthia Long Westfall, 155–86. MNTSS. Eugene, OR: Pickwick, 2011.

Schreiner, Thomas R. *1 Corinthians: An Introduction and Commentary*. TNTC. Downers Grove: InterVarsity, 2018.

———. *1, 2 Peter, Jude*. NAC 37. Nashville: Broadman & Holman, 2003.

Schriever, Henry R. "As the Father Has Sent Me." *Missio Apostolica* 20 (2012) 16–22.

Scobie, Charles H. H. "Israel and the Nations: An Essay in Biblical Theology." *TynBul* 43 (1992) 283–305.

Scott, James M. *Paul and the Nations: The Old Testament and Jewish Background of Paul's Mission to the Nations with Special Reference to the Destination of Galatians*. WUNT 84. Tübingen: Mohr Siebeck, 1995.

Senior, Donald, and Carroll Stuhlmueller. *The Biblical Foundations for Mission*. Maryknoll, NY: Orbis, 1983.

Shanor, Jay. "Paul as Master Builder: Construction Terms in First Corinthians." *NTS* 34 (1988) 461–71.

Sibley, Jim R. "You Talkin' to Me? 1 Peter 2:4–10 and a Theology of Israel." *SJT* 59 (2016) 59–75.

Sills, M. David. *The Missionary Call: Find Your Place in God's Plan for the World*. Chicago: Moody, 2008.

———. *Reaching and Teaching: A Call to Great Commission Obedience*. Chicago: Moody, 2010.

Silva, Moisés. "Abraham, Faith, and Works: Paul's Use of Scripture in Galatians 3:6–14." *WTJ* 63 (2001) 251–67.

Skreslet, Stanley H. "Doctoral Dissertations on Mission: Ten Year Update, 1992–2001." *IBMR* 27 (2003) 98–133.

Smith, Brandon D. "The Identification of Jesus with YHWH in the Book of Revelation: A Brief Sketch." *CTR* 14 (2016) 67–84.

Smith, Christopher R. "The Structure of the Book of Revelation in Light of Apocalyptic Literary Conventions." *NovT* 36 (1994) 373–93.

Smith, Gary V. *Isaiah 40–66*. NAC 15B. Nashville: Broadman & Holman, 2009.

Spitters, Denny, and Matthew Ellison. *When Everything Is Missions*. Orlando: Bottomline Media, 2017.

Stead, Michael R. *The Intertextuality of Zechariah 1–8*. LHBOTS 506. New York: T. & T. Clark, 2009.

Stein, Robert H. *Luke: An Exegetical and Theological Exposition of Holy Scripture*. NAC 24. Nashville: Broadman & Holman, 1992.

Steinmann, Andrew E. "The Structure and Message of the Book of Job." *VT* 46 (1996) 85–100.
Sternberg, Meir. *The Poetics of Biblical Narrative: Ideological Literature and the Drama of Reading.* Bloomington: Indiana University Press, 1985.
Stetzer, Ed. "The Missional Church." In *Missiology: An Introduction to the Foundations, History, and Strategies of World Missions,* edited by John Mark Terry, 99–110. 2nd ed. Nashville: Broadman & Holman, 2015.
Stetzer, Ed, and Philip Nation. *Compelled by Love: The Most Excellent Way to Missional Living.* Birmingham: New Hope, 2008.
Stevenson, Jeffery S. "Judah's Successes and Failures in Holy War: An Exegesis of Judges 1:1–20." *ResQ* 44 (2002) 43–54.
Steyn, Gert J. "Psalm 2 in Hebrews." *Neotestamentica* 37 (2003) 262–82.
Stoebe, Hans Joachim. "רעע." In *TLOT* 3:1249–54.
Stott, John R. W. *Christian Mission in the Modern World: What the Church Should Be Doing Now!* Downers Grove: InterVarsity, 1975.
Strandenæs, Thor. "The Missionary Speeches in the Acts of the Apostles and Their Missiological Implications." *SMT* 99 (2011) 341–54.
Strauss, Steve. "Missions Theology in Romans 15:14–33." *BSac* 160 (2003) 457–74.
Strawn, Brent A. "Jonah's Sailors and Their Lot Casting: A Rhetorical-Critical Observation." *Bib* 91 (2010) 66–76.
Strelan, Rick. "'We Hear Them Telling in Our Own Tongues the Mighty Works of God' (Acts 2:11)." *Neotestamentica* 40 (2006) 295–319.
Strong, John. "Ezekiel's Use of the Recognition Formula in His Oracles Against the Nations." *PRSt* 22 (1995) 115–33.
Stuart, Douglas K. *Exodus.* NAC 2. Nashville: Broadman & Holman, 2006.
Sylva, Dennis D. "The Temple Curtain and Jesus' Death in the Gospel of Luke." *JBL* 105 (1986) 239–50.
Tanner, J. Paul. "James' Quotation of Amos 9 to Settle the Jerusalem Council Debate in Acts 15." *JETS* 55 (2012) 65–85.
Tavo, Felise. "The Structure of the Apocalypse: Re-examining a Perennial Problem." *NovT* 47 (2005) 47–68.
Tennent, Timothy C. *Invitation to World Missions: A Trinitarian Missiology for the Twenty-first Century.* ITSS. Grand Rapids: Kregel, 2010.
———. "William Carey as a Missiologist: An Assessment." In *Expect Great Things, Attempt Great Things: William Carey and Adoniram Judson, Missionary Pioneers,* edited by Allen Yeh and Chris Chun, 15–26. Eugene, OR: Wipf & Stock, 2013.
Thiessen, Henry C. *Lectures in Systematic Theology.* Revised by Vernon D. Doerksen. Grand Rapids: Eerdmans, 1979.
Thiselton, Anthony C. *1 Corinthians: A Shorter Exegetical & Pastoral Commentary.* Grand Rapids: Eerdmans, 2006.
Thompson, J. A. *The Book of Jeremiah.* NICOT. Grand Rapids: Eerdmans, 1980.
Timmer, Daniel C. "Jonah and Mission: Missiological Dichotomy, Biblical Theology, and the *Via Tertia.*" *WTJ* 70 (2008) 159–75.
Tsumura, David Toshio. *The First Book of Samuel.* NICOT. Grand Rapids: Eerdmans, 2007.
Tucker, W. Dennis, Jr. "Hortatory Discourse and Psalm 96." *VT* 61 (2011) 119–32.
Turner, David L. *Matthew.* BECNT. Grand Rapids: Baker Academic, 2008.
Turner, Laurence A. *Announcements of Plot in Genesis.* Eugene, OR: Wipf & Stock, 1990.

———. *Genesis*. Readings: A New Biblical Commentary. Edited by John Jarick. Sheffield: Sheffield Phoenix, 2009.
Van Gelder, Craig, and Dwight J. Zscheile. *The Missional Church in Perspective: Mapping Trends and Shaping the Conversation*. Grand Rapids: Baker Academic, 2011.
Van Winkle, D. W. "The Relationship of the Nations to Yahweh and to Israel in Isaiah 40–55." *VT* 35 (1985) 446–58.
Van Zyl, Danie C. "Exodus 19:3–6 and the Kerygmatic Perspective of the Pentateuch." *OTE* 5 (1992) 264–71.
Verhoef, Pieter A. *The Books of Haggai and Malachi*. NICOT. Grand Rapids: Eerdmans, 1987.
Verkuyl, Johannes. *Contemporary Missiology: An Introduction*. Translated and edited by Dale Cooper. Grand Rapids: Eerdmans, 1978.
Viands, Jamie. *I Will Surely Multiply Your Offspring: An Old Testament Theology of the Blessing of Progeny with Special Attention to the Latter Prophets*. Eugene, OR: Pickwick, 2014.
von Rad, Gerhard. *Old Testament Theology, Volume 1: The Theology of Israel's Historical Traditions*. Translated by D. M. G. Stalker. New York: Harper & Row, 1962.
Wagner, J. Ross. *Heralds of the Good News: Isaiah and Paul in Concert in the Letter to the Romans*. Leiden: Brill, 2002.
Wallace, Daniel B. *Greek Grammar Beyond the Basics: An Exegetical Syntax of the New Testament*. Grand Rapids: Zondervan, 1996.
Waltke, Bruce K. *The Book of Proverbs, Chapters 1–15*. NICOT. Grand Rapids: Eerdmans, 2004.
———. "The Fear of the Lord." In *Alive to God: Studies in Spirituality Presented to James Houston*, edited by J. I. Packer and Loren Wilkinson, 17–33. Downers Grove: InterVarsity, 1992.
———. *An Old Testament Theology: An Exegetical, Canonical, and Thematic Approach*. Grand Rapids: Zondervan, 2007.
Waltke, Bruce K., and M. O'Connor. *An Introduction to Biblical Hebrew Syntax*. Winona Lake: Eisenbrauns, 1990.
Waltke, Bruce K., with Cathi J. Fredricks. *Genesis: A Commentary*. Grand Rapids: Zondervan, 2001.
Walton, John H. *Ancient Near Eastern Thought and the Old Testament: Introducing the Conceptual World of the Hebrew Bible*. Grand Rapids: Baker Academic, 2006.
———. *Genesis*. NIVAC. Grand Rapids: Zondervan, 2001.
———. "The Mesopotamian Background of the Tower of Babel Account and Its Implications." *BBR* 5 (1995) 155–75.
———. "The Object Lesson of Jonah 4:5–7 and the Purpose of the Book of Jonah." *BBR* 2 (1992) 47–57.
Webster, Edwin C. "A Rhetorical Study of Isaiah 66." *JSOT* 34 (1986) 93–108.
Weinfeld, Moshe. "Jeremiah and the Spiritual Metamorphosis of Israel." *ZAW* 88 (1976) 17–56.
Wells, Jo Bailey. *God's Holy People: A Theme in Biblical Theology*. JSOTSup 305. Sheffield: Sheffield Academic, 2000.
Wenham, Gordon J. *Genesis 1–15*. WBC 1. Waco: Word, 1987.
Westermann, Claus. *Genesis 1–11: A Commentary*. Translated by John J. Scullion. Minneapolis: Augsburg, 1984.

———. *Isaiah 40–66*. Translated by D. M. G. Stalker. OTL. Philadelphia: Westminster, 1969.

Wheeler, Aaron. "The Commissioning of All Believers: Toward a More Holistic Model of Global Discipleship." *Missiology* 43 (2015) 148–62.

Willis, Avery T., Jr., and Henry T. Blackaby. *On Mission with God: Living God's Purpose for His Glory*. Nashville: Broadman & Holman, 2002.

Willis, Timothy M. *Jeremiah-Lamentations*. The College Press NIV Commentary. Joplin, MO: College Press, 2002.

Wilson, Gerald H. *The Editing of the Hebrew Psalter*. Chico, CA: Scholars, 1985.

———. "The Structure of the Psalter." In *Interpreting the Psalms: Issues and Approaches*, edited by Philip S. Johnston and David G. Firth, 229–46. Grand Rapids: IVP Academic, 2005.

———. "The Use of Royal Psalms at the 'Seams' of the Hebrew Psalter." *JSOT* 35 (1986) 85–94.

Wilson, Lindsay. "The Book of Job and the Fear of God." *TynBul* 46 (1995) 59–79.

Winter, Ralph D. "Unreached Peoples: The Development of the Concept." In *Reaching the Unreached: The Old-New Challenge*, edited by Harvie M. Conn, 17–43. Phillipsburg: P. & R., 1984.

Winter, Ralph D., and Bruce A. Koch. "Finishing the Task: The Unreached Peoples Challenge." *IJFM* 19 (2002) 15–25.

Witherington, Ben, III. *The Acts of the Apostles: A Socio-Rhetorical Commentary*. Grand Rapids: Eerdmans, 1998.

———. *The Gospel of Mark: A Socio-Rhetorical Commentary*. Grand Rapids: Eerdmans, 2001.

———. *The Indelible Image: The Theological and Ethical Thought World of the New Testament, Vol. 1: The Individual Witnesses*. Downers Grove: InterVarsity, 2009.

———. *John's Wisdom: A Commentary on the Fourth Gospel*. Louisville: Westminster John Knox, 1995.

Wright, Christopher J. H. *The Mission of God: Unlocking the Bible's Grand Narrative*. Downers Grove: IVP Academic, 2006.

———. *The Mission of God's People: A Biblical Theology of the Church's Mission*. Biblical Theology for Life. Edited by Jonathan Lunde. Grand Rapids: Zondervan, 2010.

———. *Old Testament Ethics for the People of God*. Downers Grove: InterVarsity, 2004.

Wright, N. T. "Reading the New Testament Missionally." In *Reading the Bible Missionally*, edited by Michael W. Goheen, 174–93. Grand Rapids: Eerdmans, 2016.

Yeh, Allen. *Polycentric Missiology: Twenty-First Century Mission from Everyone to Everywhere*. Downers Grove: IVP Academic, 2016.

Yeh, Allen, and Chris Chun, eds. *Expect Great Things, Attempt Great Things: William Carey and Adoniram Judson, Missionary Pioneers*. Eugene, OR: Wipf & Stock, 2013.

Youngblood, Ronald F. "1, 2 Samuel." In *The Expositor's Bible Commentary*, edited by F. E. Gaebelein, 3:551–1104. Grand Rapids: Zondervan, 1992.

Zehnder, Markus. "A Fresh Look at Malachi II 13–16." *VT* 53 (2003) 224–59.

———. "Why the Danielic 'Son of Man' Is a Divine Being." *BBR* 24 (2014) 331–47.

SCRIPTURE INDEX

OLD TESTAMENT/ HEBREW BIBLE

Genesis

1–2	23
1:1—2:3	11
1	11n21, 13, 14, 35, 184, 269, 284
1:1	168n1, 169, 184n29
1:3	12
1:4	12, 69n7
1:5	12, 12n22, 13
1:7	12n23
1:8	12
1:9–10	13
1:9	12n22, 12n23
1:10	12, 69n7
1:11	12n22, 12n23
1:12	12, 69n7
1:14–19	13
1:14	12n22
1:15	12n23
1:18	12, 69n7
1:20–21	19
1:20	12n22
1:21	12, 69n7
1:24–25	19
1:24	12n22, 12n23
1:25	12, 69n7
1:26–28	265
1:26	12n22, 14, 20
1:28–30	17
1:28	11n21, 15, 17, 17n39, 18n41, 19n45, 21, 30, 32, 33n21, 61n28, 67, 225, 228, 229
1:29	23
1:30	12n23
1:31	12, 69n7
2	23
2:2–3	12, 12n25
2:2	12
2:4	37n26, 168
2:7–8	23
2:7	198, 199
2:9	23
2:15	23, 86
2:16–17	24, 265
2:16	25
2:17	24, 25, 26, 36, 41
2:18	24
2:21–23	24
2:23	28
2:25	24
3–11	35
3	109, 269
3:1	25, 26
3:2–3	25
3:3	41
3:4	26, 36, 41
3:6–7	26
3:6	36
3:8–19	26
3:8	85, 209
3:12	41
3:14–15	27
3:15	35, 35n25, 37, 40, 41, 45, 56, 109, 131n2

Genesis *(continued)*

3:16–19	27, 40
3:16	27, 28
3:17–19	43
3:17–18	27
3:20	40
3:22	23
3:24	209
4–11	22, 28, 31
4–9	28
4	43, 266
4:1–2	36
4:1	28
4:2	28
4:3	41
4:4	41
4:8	28, 36
4:9	29, 36
4:12	42
4:14	28
4:15	28
4:16	42, 42n41, 43
4:17–22	37
4:17–18	28
4:17	28, 42
4:18	28
4:20	28
4:22	28
4:23–24	28, 43
4:24	29
4:25	37
4:26	41
5	42, 43, 168
5:1–32	37, 44, 45
5:1	37n26, 168
5:5	41
5:8	41
5:11	41
5:14	41
5:17	41
5:20	41
5:21–24	42
5:22	43
5:24	43
5:27	41
5:28–31	42–43
5:29	43
5:31	41
5:32	37, 38, 38n28
6–9	266
6:1	29
6:2–4	29
6:3	29
6:5–7	43
6:5	29, 107
6:8	43, 44
6:9	37n26, 44
6:10	38n28
6:11	30
6:13	30
7:1	44
7:13	38n28
8:19	55
8:20–22	30
8:21	44
9:1	19n45, 30, 32, 32n16, 33n21, 61n28
9:6–7	30, 74
9:6	31n14
9:7	31n14, 32, 61n28, 67
9:18	38n28
9:24	38
9:25–27	38
10:1	37, 37n26, 38, 38n28
10:2–5	38
10:2	38
10:3	38
10:4	38
10:5	55, 56, 57
10:6–20	38
10:6	38
10:7–12	38
10:13–14	38
10:15–19	38
10:18	55
10:20	55, 56, 57
10:21–31	38, 40
10:22	38
10:23	38
10:24–25	38
10:24	38
10:26–29	38
10:31	55, 56, 57
10:32	37n26, 55, 57
11	32, 266

11:1–9	40	18:17–19	58
11:1–2	31	18:18–19	61, 114
11:1	56, 57n23, 58	18:18	52, 56, 70, 112
11:2	42n41	19	91
11:3	68n3	22	47, 59
11:4	32, 33, 33n21, 57n23, 58, 68, 68n3	22:16–18	59
11:7–9	57	22:17–18	61–62, 63, 70, 266n1
11:7–8	33, 33n21	22:17	62, 227n12
11:7	68n3	22:18	52, 56, 62, 112, 124n37, 230, 230n19
11:8	32n16, 33, 57n23	24:1–2	54
11:9	33, 56, 57n23	24:35	54
11:10–26	39, 40, 45	24:49	149n43
11:10	37n26	25:12–18	37
11:18	38	25:12	37n26
11:26	40, 45	25:19—35:29	37
11:27	37n26, 46	25:19	37n26
11:29	46–47	26:4–5	59
11:30	47, 47n1	26:4	52, 56, 62, 63, 112, 227n12, 230n19, 266n1
12–50	34	26:12–13	54
12	35, 35n24, 40, 50, 52n19, 53, 230	26:24	54, 227n12
12:1–3	47, 51, 53, 54, 57, 58, 61, 113, 230, 266	26:25	41n36
		27:6–10	16
12:1	58, 70	27:29	16, 17
12:2	50, 51, 58, 61, 70, 81	27:37	16
12:3	8, 11n20, 50, 50n15, 51, 54, 55, 55n21, 56, 58, 61, 63, 64, 70, 96, 112, 112n15, 132, 133, 195, 230, 232, 233, 275	28:3–4	62, 63, 266n1
		28:3	62, 227n12
		28:4	62
		28:10–22	62
12:4	58	28:13–14	63
12:8	41n36	28:13	63
13:4	41n36	28:14	52, 56, 63n31, 64, 112, 230n19
14:18	116	28:19	64n32
14:19	49	29:15	149n43
15	60–61	32:12	31n14
15:15	31n14	35:11	64, 89
15:18	70	35:15	64n32
17	60n27, 61	36:1–43	37
17:1–7	60, 62, 64	36:1	37n26
17:1	48	36:9	37n26
17:2	61, 61n28, 70, 227n12, 266n1	37:2—50:26	37
17:4–5	61	37:2	37n26
17:6	61, 61n28, 89, 227n12, 266n1	37:16	149n43
17:7	61	38:29	63n31
17:16	89	41:39	80n34, 152n48
17:20	61	42:18	48
17:21	61	45:17–18	52

Genesis (continued)

47:27	62, 66
48:3–4	64
48:4	227n12
49:10	89

Exodus

1:7–10	225n9
1:7	62, 66, 67, 225, 228
1:8–10	67
1:10	68, 68n3
1:11	68
1:12	63n31, 68
1:13–14	68n5
1:14	68n3
1:15–16	69
1:15	69n6
1:19	69
1:20	69
1:21	69
1:22	69, 70
2	69
2:2	69
2:3	69
2:6	70
2:7–9	70
2:10	70
2:11–22	70
2:23–24	70
2:24	72
4:22–23	173
6:3	20
6:4–5	72
9:30	31n14
14	105n4
14:26–29	105n4
17:1–2	175
17:9	175
19	73, 75, 76, 234
19:3–6	71, 75, 80, 233, 234, 267
19:4	71, 76
19:5–6	8, 73, 74
19:5	73, 76, 81, 234
19:6	76, 234
19:7–8	72
19:22	63n31, 76
19:24	63n31
20:1	72
20:2–17	72
20:22—23:33	72
21:12	85n38
21:16	85n38
23:14–17	212
23:33	106
25:10–21	209
26:34	209
28:12	76n31
28:15–20	261
28:21	261
28:29	76n31
28:30	76n31
28:35	77n31
28:38	77n31
29:4	110n13
32:9–10	134
32:12–13	134
32:12	135
32:13	136
32:14	134, 135–36
33:13	151n47
33:20	214
34	137
34:6–7	134, 134–35, 136
34:12–16	106
34:18–23	212
40:29	176
40:34–38	176
40:34–35	209
40:34	211

Leviticus

1:3	44
4	82, 83
4:1–2	82
4:3	82, 83
4:4–12	83
4:13	82, 83
4:14–21	83
4:20	83
4:22	83
4:23–26	83

4:26	83	26:45	155n58
4:27	83		
4:28–31	83		
4:31	83	## Numbers	
5–6	84		
5	83	3:7–8	23
5:1	83	6:22–27	76n28
5:2–4	83	6:24–26	146
5:5–6	83	8:7	110n13
6:1–7	83–84	8:26	23
6:4–5	84	10:35	76n25
6:4	84	13:2	101
6:6–7	84	13:30–33	102
10:10–11	76n29	13:32	117
10:10	24, 86	14:1–4	102
13–14	76n26	14:1	117
13:40–46	24, 86	14:11–12	102
16	214	14:15–16	102
16:4	110n13	15:28–31	84
20:10	85n38	15:30	84
24:17	85n38	18:5–7	23
26	78, 103, 104	21:4–5	174
26:1–13	103, 104	24:17–19	89n46
26:3	78	25:1–3	175
26:4–5	79	27:21	76n27
26:4	104n2	32:22	86
26:5	104n2	32:29	86
26:6	79, 104n2	35:16–21	85n38
26:7–8	79, 104n2		
26:9	78, 103, 104n2, 240, 257		
26:10	79, 104n2	## Deuteronomy	
26:11–12	79, 239, 239n36, 240, 256, 259, 261	1–3	80
26:14–16	103	1:10	78
26:16–17	104n2	1:40	31n14
26:16	104	4	81
26:17	91, 104	4:1–43	80
26:18–20	104n2	4:4	31n14
26:20	104, 126n38	4:5–8	80
26:21–22	104n2	4:5–7	150
26:22	103	4:6–8	80
26:23–26	104n2	4:6	80
26:25	104	4:7	80
26:26	104, 126n38	4:10	161n74
26:29	104	4:22	31n14
26:30–32	104	4:27	34n22, 102
26:33	102, 104	4:34	98n60
26:37–39	104	4:44	80

Deuteronomy (continued)

Reference	Page
5:15	98n60
5:29	161n74
5:30–31	31n14
6:1–2	161n74
6:3	78
6:13–15	175
6:16	175
6:24	161n74
7:1–4	107
7:6	72, 86
7:7–8	73
7:12–13	78
7:16	106
7:17–19	106
7:19	98n60
7:25–26	88
8:1	79
8:2–3	174
8:3	151n47
8:6	161n74
10:8	76n24, 76n28
10:12–13	98, 161n74
11:2–4	98n60
11:22–24	87
12:4–7	98
12:5	85n39, 97
12:11	85n39
12:21	85n39
13:4	161n74
13:17–18	79
14:2	72
14:23–24	85n39
16:2	85n39
16:6	85n39
16:16	212
17	92
17:14–20	90, 93, 120
17:15	90
17:16	90
17:17	90
17:18–20	90
17:18–19	93
17:19	90, 161n74
17:20	90
18:13	44
18:15	230
18:19	230
20:1–3	106
20:4	106
20:16–17	86
20:18	86
21:5	76n28
22:22	85n38
23:3	107
24:7	85n38
26:1–2	85n39
26:8	98n60
26:16–19	81, 150
26:18	72, 81
26:19	81
28	104
28:1–2	81, 202
28:3	79
28:4	79
28:5	79
28:6	79
28:7	80
28:8	80
28:10	81–82, 150
28:11	79
28:12	80
28:13	80
28:16	104
28:17–18	126n38
28:17	104
28:18	104
28:19	104
28:21	104
28:22	104
28:25	91, 104
28:27	104
28:28–29	104
28:30–31	104
28:30	126n38
28:32–34	104
28:35	104
28:36	104
28:37	104
28:38–40	104, 126n38
28:41	104
28:43–44	104
28:49	204n38
28:58	161n74
28:62–63	103

28:62	34n22	2:11–23	106
28:64	34n22, 102	2:11–13	91, 106n7
30:5	104	2:14–15	91
30:6	105, 128, 218	2:16	91
30:16	79	2:17	91
31	161	2:19	106n7
31:9	76n24	3–16	106, 106n7
31:12–13	161, 161n74	3:4	91
33:8–11	75	3:7—16:31	91
33:23	17	16:6	149n43
		16:10	149n43
		16:13	149n43
		17:1—21:25	91

Joshua

		17:6	91
1:6–9	87	18:1	91
1:7	87	19–21	91
1:14	31n14	19:1	91
2:8–11	155n58	21:25	91
2:10	155n58		
3:3	76n24		
3:6	76n24	## Ruth	
3:8	76n24		
3:13–15	76n24	4:4	149n43
3:17	76n24		
4:9–10	76n24		
4:16	76n24	## 1 Samuel	
4:18	76n24		
6:1	88	3:15	149n43
7:3	88	4:4	209n47
7:4–5	88	4:13	149n44
7:16–17	55	5:6	20
7:20–21	88	5:9	20
9:3	156n58	5:12	20
9:24–25	156n58	6:2	151n47
11:1–9	105n4	6:4	20
17:17–18	106	6:5	20
18:1	86	6:8	20
24:14–26	161n74	6:19–20	76n25
		7:3–14	92
		8	89
## Judges		8:5	89, 92
		8:7	88, 92
1:1—3:6	91	8:10–18	92
1	106	8:19–20	89, 92
1:19	105	9:2	92
1:21–36	106	9:18	149n43
2:1–3	106	10:15	149n43
2:10	91	12:14	161n74

1 Samuel (continued)

13	93
13:8–9	92
13:14	92, 93, 120
14:43	149n43
15:11	92
15:24	93
15:28	93
23:6–12	76n27
28:15	151n47

2 Samuel

1:20	149n44
5:20	63n31
6:2	209n47
6:8	63n31
7	94, 180, 240
7:2	94
7:5	94
7:11	94
7:12–13	94
7:13	239n36, 240
7:14	94, 180, 180n20, 181, 239, 239n36, 240
7:15	94
7:16	94, 180
7:21	152n48
12:13–23	94n57
12:15	28
17:16	149n43

1 Kings

2:28	184n31
3:2	85n40
3:28	80n34
4:29	80n34
5:3	85n40
5:5	85n40
5:12	80n34
6:20	258
8:10–11	97, 209
8:10	212
8:16–20	85n40
8:20	97
8:27	32n20
8:29	85n40
8:41–43	97
8:41	32n20
8:42	97
8:43	32n20, 98, 98n61
8:59–61	99
8:60	99
9:4	94
10:1–13	156n60
10:24	80n34
11:1–3	107
11:3	90n47
11:4	94, 107
11:6	107
11:34	94
12:8	29n10
12:10	29n10
12:14	29n10
14:8	94
15:3	94
15:26	107n8
15:34	107n8
16:7	107n8
16:19	107n8
16:25	107n8
16:30	107n8
17:21	198
18:24	41n36
21:20	107n8
21:25	107n8
22:52	107n8

2 Kings

3:2	107n8
8:18	107n8
8:27	107n8
9:15	149n44
13:2	107n8
13:11	107n8
14:13	63n31
14:23–27	138n15
14:24	107n8, 138n15
14:25	138n15
14:26	138n15

15:9	107n8
15:18	107n8
15:24	107n8
15:28	107n8
17	107
17:2	107n8
17:8	107
17:9–18	107
17:17	107n8
17:27	76n29
19:15	209n47
21:2	107n8
21:6	107n8
21:9	107n8
21:16	107n8
21:20	107n8
23:32	107n8
23:37	107n8
24:9	107n8
24:10–17	107
24:19	107n8

1 Chronicles

13:6	209n47
16	153, 154
16:1	76n25
16:8	41n38, 152
16:23	154n55
16:24	154n55
16:27	154n55
16:29–32	154
16:29	154n55
16:30	154n55
16:32	154n55
16:33	154n55
28:2	209
29:3	73

2 Chronicles

7:1	209n47
9:1–12	156n60
15:3	76n29
36:22–23	113

Ezra

1:1–4	113
2:63	76n27
3:2	125
3:4–5	125
3:8	125
4:1–5	125
4:24	125
6:14–15	126, 126n39
7	126
7:11–12	76n29
7:21	76n29
7:25	80n34
9	126

Nehemiah

5:1–19	126
5:9	127
7:65	76n27
8	126
8:7–8	76n29
8:12	152n49
9	126
9:36	166
10	126
13:10	127
13:13–31	126
13:15–22	127
13:18	127
13:26–27	127

Job

1–2	162
1:1	163
1:8	163
1:9–11	163
2:3	163
2:4–6	163
3–27	162
4:21	199
10:12	151n47
28	162
28:1–12	162

Job (continued)

28:13–20	162
28:21–27	162
28:28	162
29–41	162
29–31	162n80
32–37	162n80
37:19	151n47
38–41	162n79, 162n80
38:3	151n47
40:3–5	162n79, 163
40:7	151n47
42:1–6	162n79, 163
42:4	151n47
42:7–17	162

Psalms

1–2	158, 159n68
1	158
1:1	159n68
1:2	159n68
2	158, 159
2:1–3	158
2:1	159n68
2:4	159
2:5–9	159
2:7	179–80, 180, 180n20, 181
2:8–9	180
2:8	157n61
2:9	253, 254, 254n16
2:10–12	159
2:12	159n68
3–41	158
7:7–8	157n62
7:7	157
9	149n42, 150, 152
9:5	157n62
9:8	157n62
9:11	149, 150, 150n44, 151, 152, 155, 164
9:13–14	150–51
9:19–20	157n62
10:16	157n62
16:8–11	179
16:10	180
18	156
18:43	157n61
18:47	157n61
18:49	155, 156, 164
19:1	153
19:7–9	161n74
22:27	148n40
22:28	157n62
24:3–6	152
25:4	151n47
25:10	144n31
25:14	151n47
26:3	144n31
27:4–8	151n47
33:6–9	147
33:6	184
33:8	49, 145, 145n34, 153
33:10	157n62
37:26	48n10
39:4	151n47
40:10–11	144n31
41:13	158
42–72	158
44:14	156
45:5	157n62
45:17	148n40
46:10	148n40
47:1	142n26
47:2	157n63
47:7–9	157n63
47:9	143, 158n65
48:10	148
51	94n57
51:11	217n64
51:16–17	85n38
56:7	157n62
57	156
57:3	144n31
57:5	153
57:7	153
57:9	149n41, 155, 155n57, 156, 164
57:10	144n31
59:5	157n62
59:13	157n62
61:7	144n31
65:1–2	157
65:5–8	157n64
66:1	142n26

SCRIPTURE INDEX 313

66:3	143, 158n65	79:6	157n62
66:4	50, 148	79:10	157n62
66:5	143	80:1	209n47
66:6	143n28	82:8	157n62
66:7	157n63	83	157n62
66:8	142n26	84:1	184n31
66:16	143	85:10	144n31
67	146, 147	86:9	148, 148n40
67:1	145n36, 146n37	86:11	161n74
67:2	145n36, 146, 146n37	86:15	144n31
67:3	145n34, 147	89	13, 159
67:4	145n34, 147, 157n63	89:3–4	94
67:5	145n34, 147	89:5–8	13
67:6–7	145n36	89:9–14	13
67:7	145n36, 147	89:9	13
68:29	143	89:10	13
68:31	143	89:11–12	14
68:32	142n26	89:13	14
69:13	144n31	89:14	14, 144n31
72	95, 96, 97, 157, 159	89:30–32	94
72:1–4	95	89:33–34	94
72:5	95	89:38–45	159
72:7	95	89:49	159
72:8–11	95	89:52	158
72:8	157n61	90–106	158
72:10–11	157	90	159
72:10	96, 157	90:1	159
72:12–14	96	93	159
72:15	96, 157	95–99	159
72:16	96	96	149n41, 152, 153, 154
72:17	50, 50n15, 96, 157	96:1	152, 153, 154n55
72:18–19	97	96:2	154n55
72:19	158	96:3	153
72:20	95n58	96:6	154n55
73–89	158	96:7–8	142n26
74	13	96:7	153
74:1–11	13	96:8	143, 154n55
74:12–17	13	96:9–11	154
74:12	13	96:9	153
74:13–14	13	96:10	153, 154, 154n55
74:13	13	96:11	153
74:16	13	96:13	154n55, 157n62
76:12	148	97:6	148
77	155	98	144
77:14–15	155	98:1–3	143–44, 144n29
77:14	157n64	98:2–3	157n64
77:16–20	155	98:4	142n26, 144n29
78:5	152n49	98:9	157n62

Psalms (continued)

99:1–3	147
99:1	145n34, 209n47
99:2	157n63
99:5	157, 209
99:6–8	41n37
99:9	158
100:1	142n26
100:2	143
100:4	143
102:15	148n40
102:18–22	148
102:22	148n40
104:3	124
105	151, 152, 153
105:1–3	152
105:1	41n38, 149, 151, 152, 155, 164
105:4	152
105:6	151
106	153
106:48	158
107–150	158
108	156
108:3	155, 155n57, 156, 164
108:4	144n31
108:5	153
110	160
110:2–3	157n61
110:5–6	157n62
112:1	161n74
113:4	157n63
115:1	144n31
116:4	41n37
116:17	41n36
117	144
117:1–2	144
117:1	142, 142n26
117:2	144
119:46	149n41, 156n60
119:63	161n74
126:1–2	157n64
126:2	149n41
128:1	161n74
132	160
132:5	184n31
132:7	209
135:4	72n15
135:7	204n38
138:2	144n31
138:4	148n40
143:8	151n47
144:2	157n61
145:11–12	149n41
145:12	152n49
145:21	149n41
146–150	158
148	147
148:7	145n34
148:11	145n34, 147
148:13–14	147
148:13	145n34, 147
148:14	147
149:6–7	157
149:7	156
150:6	145n34

Proverbs

1:7	161
1:8—9:18	162
1:29	162n77
2:5	162n77
2:6	80n34
3:7	162n77
8:13	162n77
9:9	152n49
9:10	162
10–31	162
10:7	48–49n10
10:27	162n77
14:2	162n77
14:26–27	162n77
15:16	162n77
15:33	162n77
16:6	162n77
19:23	162n77
22:4	162n77
22:21	151n47
23:17	162n77
24:21	162n77
31:30	162

Ecclesiastes

1:1	163
1:2—12:8	163
1:2-11	163
1:12—12:7	163
2:8	73
2:26	80n34
12:8	163
12:9-14	163
12:13-14	163

Song of Songs

1:7	149n43

Isaiah

2:1-5	210
2:2-4	262n33
2:2-3	212-13
2:2	212
8:9	204n39
10:2	117n27
11:6-9	284-85
12:2-4	41n37
12:2	117n27
12:4	151n47
13:9-10	182n26
17:10	117n27
19	49
19:1	124
19:19-20	49
19:21	49
19:22	49
19:23	49
19:24-25	49
19:24	49, 49n10, 50
19:25	49, 50
20:1-4	132
24:1	34n22
24:6	34n22
25:9	117n27
26:1	117n27
33:2	117n27
33:6	117n27
33:22	117n27
34:4-5	182n26
35:4	117n27
37:16	209n47
37:20	117n27
37:35	117n27
38:20	117n27
40-55	113
40:3-4	235
41:8-9	114
41:21-29	114
42	115
42:1-4	113n18, 116, 235
42:1	114, 114n20, 116
42:3	114
42:4	114
42:6	113, 114, 115, 177, 178
42:7	114, 235
42:8	114
42:19	114
42:21-22	114-15
43:1-7	115
43:10	115
43:12	117n27
43:20-21	234
43:20	234
43:21	234
44:1-5	115
44:21-22	115
45:1-7	115
45:8	117n27
45:17	117n27
45:22	117n27, 204n39
48:20	115, 204n38
49	115
49:1-6	113n18, 115
49:3	115
49:5	115, 177
49:6-7	235
49:6	9, 113, 115, 117, 117n27, 118, 177, 178, 204, 204n39, 235, 236
49:8	117n27
49:25	117n27
50:4-9	113n18
50:6	116
51:4-5	115
51:5	117n27
51:6	117n27

Isaiah (continued)

51:8	117n27
52:7	236
52:10	117n27, 240
52:11	239, 239n36, 240
52:13—53:12	113n18, 240
52:15	116, 118, 235, 236, 240
53	176n14
53:3	116, 180n21
53:4-6	116
53:4	176
53:7-8	176
53:7	116
53:11	116
53:12	116, 176
55:3	180
56:1	117n27
56:6-7	98-99, 186
56:6	117n27
56:7	185
59:1	117n27
59:16	117n27
59:17	117n27
60	262, 263
60:1-3	116, 118, 119
60:2	119
60:3	119, 262
60:5	262
60:6	263
60:11	262
60:19	262
61:1-3	166n85
61:1-2	166
61:1	235
61:9	111
61:10	117n27
62:11	117n27, 204n38
63:1	117n27
63:5	117n27
63:9	117n27
64:2	152n49
65:17-18	257-58
66:1	12, 12n25, 209
66:10-14	165
66:12	165
66:15-18	165
66:15	165
66:18-19	164, 165
66:18	164n82, 165
66:19	149n44, 150n44, 164, 165
66:20-21	165
66:20	165
66:22-24	165
66:24	165

Jeremiah

3	121
3:13-14	119
3:15-17	119-20, 121, 178, 210
3:15	120
3:16-17	120
3:16	120, 120n30
3:17-18	262n33
3:17	120
4:1-2	112
4:2	112
4:5	149n44
5:20	149n44
6:22	204n39
7:11	185
7:23	262n30
10:13	204n38
10:25	55
11:4	262n30
11:18	151n47
16:19	204n39
18:7-8	132
18:15-17	107n9
18:18	76n29
19:8	107n9
21-22	120
22:24	121
22:25-26	121
23	120, 121
23:1-6	121, 178
23:1-2	121
23:2	121
23:3	121
23:4	121
23:5	121, 128
23:6	121
24:7	262n30
25:9	107n9

25:18	107n9	5:15	107n9
25:32	204n39	6:2	123n34
29:18	107n9	7:26	76n29
30:22	262n30	10–11	209
31:8	204n39	11:20	262n30
31:10	149n44	14:11	262n30
31:27–30	216n61	16:2	152n48
31:31–34	216	20:4	151n47
31:32–33	216	20:9	108
31:32	216	20:14	108
31:33	217, 217n66, 262n30	20:22	108
31:34	216n61	20:34	239
32:38	262n30	21:31	199
33:7–9	111	22:4	107n9
33:14–16	122n32	22:26	76n29
36:20	149n44	23:32–34	107n9
38:25	149n43	29:12	34n22
44:8	104	32:7–8	182n26
46:14	149n44	34:26	49n10
48:19	150	36:8–15	122
48:20	149n44, 150	36:10–11	122
50:2	150n44	36:15	122
50:28	149n44	36:19–20	108, 109
50:49	204n39	36:21	109
51:16	204n38	36:22–29	110, 112
		36:22–23	110
		36:22	110

Lamentations

		36:23	110
		36:24	110
2:6	184n31	36:25	110, 110n13, 113
		36:26–27	128
		36:26	110, 113

Ezekiel

		36:27–28	217
		36:27	111, 176, 217n66
2:1	123n34	36:28	111, 262n30
2:3	123n34	36:29–36	112–13
2:6	123n34	36:29–30	113
2:8	123n34	36:29	111
3:1	123n34	36:31	113
3:3	123n34	36:33–34	113
3:4	123n34	37	199n27
3:10	123n34	37:9	198, 199
3:17	123n34	37:23	262n30
3:25	123n34	37:26–27	257n20
4:1	123n34	37:27	239, 262n30
4:12–15	132	43:1–5	209
4:16	123n34	43:11	152n48
5:1	123n34		

Daniel

1–6	123
2:15	152n49
2:17	152n49
2:23	80n34
2:28	152n49
2:29	152n49
2:45	152n49
3:12	124n35
3:14	124n35
3:17–18	124n35
3:28	124n35
5:8	152n49
6:16	124n35
6:21	124n35
7–12	123
7:1–8	123
7:9–10	123, 252
7:11	123
7:12	123, 124
7:13–14	123–24, 124n37, 181, 182
7:13	124, 182, 183, 252
7:14	124, 183, 190
7:17	123
7:23	123
8:17	123

Hosea

1:2	132
1:9	262n30
4:7	107
11:1	171, 172, 172n9, 173

Joel

2:10–11	182n26
2:28–32	212
2:28	212
2:30–31	182n26
2:32	41n37
3:14–16	182n26

Amos

8:9	182n26
9:11–12	9

Jonah

1	136, 140n22
1:1–3	136
1:2	132
1:4	137
1:5	136, 137
1:8	149n43
1:9	137
1:10	136, 137
1:16	136, 137
1:17	137
2	140n22
2:9	137
3:2	132
3:4	132, 133, 140n22
3:5–9	133
3:5	136
3:9	135
3:10	133, 135–36, 136n12, 139, 139n18
4	133, 134, 138, 140n22
4:1–4	134
4:1	134, 139
4:2	134
4:3	140
4:5–11	134
4:6	138, 139, 139n18
4:7	138
4:8	140
4:9–11	138
4:9	140
4:10–11	138, 140
4:11	7

Micah

3:11	76n29
4:1–5	210, 262n33

Nahum

2:1	199

Habakkuk

3:1	95n58
3:17	229

Haggai

1:3–4	125
1:6	125
1:9	125
1:10–11	125
1:12–15	126
1:15	126n39
2:6–9	262n33
2:23	127

Zechariah

3:8	128
4:1–10	127
6:9–15	210
6:13	128
8:8	262n30
8:12	113
8:13	49, 49n10, 50, 113
8:20–23	262n33
12:7–9	128
12:10	128
13:7–9	128
13:9	41n39
14:9	128
14:16	128–29

Malachi

1:5	129
1:6–14	126
1:11	129
1:14	129
2:1–9	126

2:10–12	126
2:13–16	126
3:6–9	127
3:10–12	126

NEW TESTAMENT

Matthew

1:1	56, 168, 171, 178
1:21	176
1:22	172n10
2:13	171, 191, 192
2:14–15	171
2:15	171, 172n10, 173
2:17	172n10
2:19–23	172
2:23	172n10
3:2	242
3:15	172
3:17	173
4:1–11	173
4:3–4	174
4:3	174
4:4	174
4:5–7	174
4:5–6	174
4:7	174
4:8–10	174
4:8–9	174
4:8	26n7
4:10	174
4:14	172n10
4:17	242n39, 243
4:23	242n39, 243
5:3	243
5:10	243n42
5:17	172n10
5:19	243n42
6:10	243
6:33	242
7:11	6
7:21	243n42
7:28–29	192n11
8:11	242
8:17	172n10, 176
8:20	181n24

Matthew (continued)

9:6	181n24
9:27	178n18
9:35	242n39, 243
10:7	242n40
10:23	181n24
11:19	181n24
12:1–2	184
12:3–5	185
12:6	185, 185n33
12:8	181n24
12:17	172n10
12:23	178n18
12:28	242
12:32	181n24
12:40	181n24, 185
12:41	185
12:42	185n33
13:11	242
13:35	172n10
13:37	181n24
13:41	181n24
13:48	172n10
15:22	178n18
16:13	181n24
16:18	241
16:19	242
16:27	181n24
16:28	243n41
17:9	181n24
17:12	181n24
17:22	181n24
18:3–4	243n43
19:14	243n43
19:23–24	243n45
19:28	178–79, 181n24
20:18	181n24
20:20–28	243n43
20:28	181n24
20:30	178n18
21:4	172n10
21:9	178n18
21:12–13	185n34
21:12	185
21:15	178n18
21:31–32	243n42
21:43	243
23:32	172n10
24:1–3	182
24:1–2	186
24:27	181n24
24:29–30	182
24:29	182
24:30	181n24, 182
24:31	183
24:37	181n24
24:39	181n24
24:44	181n24
25:31	179, 181n24
25:34	242
26:2	181n24
26:24	181n24
26:45	181n24
26:54	172n10
26:56	172n10
26:64	179, 181n24, 183
26:65–66	183
27:9	172n10
27:50–51	186
27:51–53	186
27:51	215
28:18–20	1, 8, 8n12, 189, 190, 241n37
28:18–19	10
28:18	206
28:19–20	206
28:19	10, 191, 195, 201, 207, 215, 275
28:20	207n45

Mark

1:1	168n1
1:15	242n39
2:10	181n24
2:28	181n24
4:11	242
8:31	181n24
8:38	181n24
9:1	243n41
9:9	181n24
9:12	181n24
9:31	181n24
9:35	39
9:47	243n42
10:14–15	243n43

10:23–25	243n45	4:43	242n39, 244
10:33	181n24	6:20	243
10:45	181n24	8:1	242n39, 244
10:47	178n18	8:10	242
11:15–17	185n34	9:2	242n40
11:17	185	9:11	242n39
12:28–34	243n42	9:27	243n41
13:10	8n12	9:60	242n40
13:24–25	182	9:61–62	243
13:26	181n24, 182	10:9	242n40
13:27	183	10:10–12	243
14:9	8n12	11:2	243
14:21	181n24	11:13	6
14:41	181n24	11:20	242
14:62	179, 181n24, 183	12:31	242
14:63–64	183	12:32	243n42
15:37–38	186	13:28–29	242
15:38	215	16:16	242n39, 244
16:9–20	188n1	17:20–21	242
		18:16–17	243n43
		18:24–25	243n45
		18:29–30	243
		18:36	178n18

Luke

		19:45–46	185n34
1:1—2:52	168	19:45	185
1:27	178	21:20	182n27
1:32–33	178	21:25–27	182
2:4	178	21:27	182, 203
2:22–24	177	21:31–32	243n41
2:29–32	177	22:20	202, 217
2:30	177	22:37	176
2:32	177	22:69	179, 183, 203
3:1–22	168	23:45	215
3:4–5	235	24	204
3:22	169, 169n4	24:25	203
3:23–38	169	24:38	203
3:23	169	24:44–49	8n12, 193, 241n37
3:38	169, 169n4	24:44–47	9
4	166n85	23:44–45	186
4:3–4	169n4	23:45–46	186
4:3	169	24:45	10
4:9–12	169n4	24:46–47	10
4:9	169	24:46	194
4:16–21	8	24:47	10, 195, 204, 207
4:18–19	166	24:48	203, 207
4:18	235	24:49	201, 206, 207n45, 211, 215
4:21	166		

John

1:1	169, 184, 184n29
1:2–3	184
1:3	169
1:14	169, 184
2:14–21	185n34
2:18	185
2:19	185
2:21	185
3:3–5	242
3:16	200, 200n30
3:18	200n30, 200n31
3:36	200n30
4:34	198n22
5:23–24	198n22
5:24	200n30, 200n31
5:30	198n22
5:36–38	198n22
6:29	198n22
6:38–39	198n22
6:39–40	200
6:40	200n30
6:44	198n22
6:47	200n30
6:57	198n22
7:16	198n22
7:28–29	198n22
7:33	198n22
7:39	199
8:16	198n22
8:18	198n22
8:24	200n31
8:26	198n22
8:29	198n22
8:34	33n21
8:42	198n22
8:44	36
12:31	26n7
14:26	199
14:30	26n7
15:26	199
16:7	199, 211
16:8	199
16:11	26n7
16:13–14	199
18:36	242
20:11–18	197
20:21–23	197, 241n37
20:21	8n12, 207
20:22	198, 199, 201, 207n45
20:23	200n29, 207
20:31	200

Acts

1–7	204, 225
1	196
1:1	201, 207
1:3	202, 244
1:4–5	211
1:4	201, 206
1:6–8	201, 202
1:6	202
1:8	8n12, 203, 204, 204n40, 205, 205n43, 206, 207, 207n45, 219–20, 231, 235, 241n37, 247
1:9	201, 220
1:10–11	220
1:12–26	203
1:12	220
1:13–26	220
1:16	217n64
1:22	196n19, 247
2	212
2:1–13	220
2:2	211, 212
2:5	211, 212
2:6	212
2:11	211
2:14–41	220
2:14–39	246n49
2:22–28	179
2:22	203
2:23	246, 246n50
2:24	246n51
2:30–31	179
2:31	246n51
2:32	196n19, 247
2:33	203
2:36	179
2:39	231–32
2:41	212, 220
2:42–47	220
2:47	220

SCRIPTURE INDEX

3–7	220	8:13	203
3	195, 220	8:14–19	203
3:1–10	230	8:14	226n11
3:11–16	230	8:25	226n11
3:12–26	246n49	8:26–35	237
3:12	203	8:26	220
3:15	196n19, 246, 246n50, 246n51, 247	8:32–35	176
		8:40	220
3:17–24	230	9:1–9	235
3:25–26	55, 56, 230	9:3	220
3:25	230, 230n19, 231, 233	9:10–12	235
3:26	231, 232, 246n51	9:11	235
4:7	195, 203	9:12	235
4:8–12	203, 246n49	9:15–16	235
4:10	195, 246, 246n50, 246n51	9:20–25	220
4:12	195	9:26–31	220
4:16	220	9:31	220, 221
4:19–20	246n49	9:32	220
4:25	217n64	9:35	221
4:31	203, 226n11	9:36	220
4:33	203	9:42	221
5:12	220	10	231
5:14	220	10:1–48	220
5:16	220	10:15	232
5:21	220	10:34–43	246n49
5:28	220	10:34–35	232
5:29–32	246n49	10:38	203
5:30–32	196n19, 246, 247	10:39–41	196n19, 247
5:30	246n50, 246n51	10:39	246, 246n50
5:42	220	10:40	246n51
6:2	225	10:44–45	232
6:4	225	11:1–18	221
6:7	220, 225, 226, 228, 241	11:1	226n11
6:8—8:1	226	11:18	232
6:8	203	11:19	221
6:13	220, 247	11:21	221
7:2–53	220	11:24	221
7:17–19	225n9	12:1–5	226
7:17	225	12:6–11	226
7:49	12	12:7	226
7:55	248	12:12–17	226
7:56	220, 248	12:19–23	221
7:58	247	12:20–23	226
7:59–60	220	12:23	227
8–12	204, 220, 225	12:24	225, 226, 227, 228, 241
8:1	220, 226	12:25	221, 227
8:5	220	13–28	221, 225
8:12	244	13–14	221

Acts (continued)

13	204
13:1–3	227
13:5	226n11
13:7	226n11
13:9–12	203
13:16–41	246n49
13:22	93
13:27–28	246
13:29	246, 246n50
13:30–31	196n19
13:30	246n51
13:31	247
13:32–35	179
13:33	246n51
13:34	180, 180n21, 246n51
13:37	246n51
13:44	226n11
13:46–47	236
13:46	226n11
13:47	9, 116, 117, 204, 236
13:48	226n11
13:49	221
14:1	221
14:15–17	246, 246n49
14:21	221
14:22	243n44, 244
14:26	223
15:1–35	221
15:13–18	9
15:36—18:22	221
16:5	221
16:32	226n11
17:13	226n11
17:18	247
17:21	246
17:22–31	246, 246n49
17:31	247
18:10	221
18:11	226n11
18:23—20:38	221
19:8	244
19:11–12	227
19:11	203
19:13–16	227
19:16	228
19:17	227
19:18	227
19:19	227
19:20	221, 225, 225n8, 227, 228, 241
19:21	228
20:24–27	244
20:24	245
20:25	245
20:27	245
21–28	221
22:14–15	247
22:20	248
26:16	247
26:18	235
26:22–23	10
28:17–22	245
28:23	228, 245
28:24–27	245
28:25	245n47
28:28	245
28:30–31	228, 245

Romans

1:3	178
2:28–29	217
3:25	195
5	171
5:1–11	169
5:12	170
5:14	170, 172n8
5:15–19	170
5:15	172
5:16	170, 170n6
5:17	170n6
5:18	170, 170n6
5:19	170, 170n6
5:21	170n6
7:14	33n21
8:7	33n21
8:23	238
10:14–15	236
11:13	9
12:4–8	223
14:17	243
15:14–29	222
15:14–16	222

15:17–19	222	15:50	243
15:19	222		
15:20	3, 223, 236		
15:21	118, 236, 240	**2 Corinthians**	
15:23	223		
15:24	223	4:4	26n7
15:28	223	5:17	282–83
		6	239
		6:14–15	239
1 Corinthians		6:16–18	239, 241
		6:16	239, 240, 262n30
1:23	246n48	6:17	239, 240
2:2	246n48	6:18	239, 240
3	238	11:2	259
3:3–4	237		
3:5–9	237		
3:6	223	**Galatians**	
3:9	283		
3:10–15	237	1:15–16	223
3:10	223	2:11–12	223n22
3:16–17	210, 237	2:15–21	223
3:16	196	3:2	232, 232n23
4:20	243	3:3–4	232
6	238, 239	3:5	232, 232n23
6:9–10	243n46	3:6	232, 232n23
6:12–20	237	3:7	232
6:12–13	238	3:8–9	55, 232
6:13	238	3:8	51n16, 53, 56, 230, 232, 233
6:14–15	238	3:9	233
6:15–17	238	3:10–14	233
6:15	238	3:14	55
6:18	238	5:19–21	243n46
6:19–20	238	6:14	246n48
6:19	238		
10:1–2	173		
10:5	173	**Ephesians**	
12:1–11	223		
12:12–26	223	2	241
12:27–31	223	2:1–10	241
15	171	2:1–2	26n7
15:1–11	171	2:8–10	44
15:12–19	171	2:11–12	241
15:20–23	283	2:13	241
15:20	171	2:14–18	241
15:21–22	171	2:19–22	241
15:24	243	2:20	259
15:45	171	2:21	241

Ephesians (continued)

4:4–16	223
4:24	14n28
5:5	243n46
5:22–30	259
6:4	17

Colossians

1	228
1:1–5	228
1:4	229
1:5–6	228–29
1:5	229
1:6	229
1:7–8	229
1:9–10	229
1:10	229
1:13–14	243
1:15–16	229
3:10	14n28
4:11	243

1 Thessalonians

2:12	243

2 Thessalonians

1:5	243n44

1 Timothy

2:3–4	7

2 Timothy

2:8	178
3:16–17	9
4:17	223
4:18	243

Hebrews

1:1–3	180
1:3–5	181
1:5	180n20
7:23–28	215
8:7–8	216
8:9	216
8:10	262n30
9:1—10:18	216n61
9:7	214
10:11–14	215
10:19–20	215
10:21–22	215
11:4	41
11:5	42
11:7	44
11:8	54, 59
11:17	59
12:28	243

James

2:5	243
2:20–22	59
2:23	6

1 Peter

2	233
2:1	233
2:2–7	233
2:8	233, 234
2:9	233
2:12	234
2:21–25	176

2 Peter

1:10–11	243n42
1:21	217n64
3:10	186
3:11–13	186n38

1 John

3:12	36
5:19	26n7

Revelation

1:1–8	249
1:4	252
1:5–6	254
1:5	252, 254
1:7	252, 254
1:9—3:22	249
1:9	251, 254
1:10	249
1:13–15	252
1:13	252
2:7	251n10
2:9	254n16
2:11	251n10
2:17	251n10
2:26–27	254
2:26	251n10
3:5	251n10
3:12	251n10, 259
3:21	251n10, 261
4:1—22:5	249
4:1—16:21	249, 250, 252
4–5	251
4	253
4:2	249, 252n13
4:3	252n13
4:4	252n13
4:5	250, 250n4, 252n13
4:6	253n13
4:8–9	263
4:9–10	252n13
4:9	263
4:10	253n13
4:11	263
5:1	252n13
5:5–6	261
5:5	178, 253n15, 260
5:6	253n13, 260
5:7	252n13
5:9–10	255, 262
5:9	56, 263
5:11–12	253n13
5:12–13	263
5:13	252n13
6–16	251
6:16	253n14
7	260
7:1–17	250
7:1–8	260
7:4–8	261
7:4	250n6
7:9–17	253
7:9–11	262
7:9–10	253n13, 255
7:9	255, 260, 261, 263, 275
7:12	263
8:1–5	253
8:3	253
8:5	186n38, 250, 250n4, 253
8:12	186n38
10:1—11:13	250
10:6–7	250
10:11	255n17
11:2–3	250n6
11:7	250n6
11:9	255
11:15–19	250, 253
11:15	26n7, 253
11:19	186n38, 250, 250n4
12–14	250, 250n6, 251
12:5	253, 253n15, 254
12:6	250n6
12:10	253
12:11	251
12:14	250n6
13:5	250n6
13:7	250n6, 255
13:10	252
14:1	250n6
14:3	253
14:4	255
14:6	255, 255n18
14:12	252
14:14	253
15:1	250
15:3	253
16:2	250n6
16:10	186n38, 250n6
16:13	251n6

Revelation (continued)

16:17–21	253	21:2	256, 257, 258, 259
16:17	253, 253n14	21:3	253, 256, 259, 261, 262
16:18	186n38, 250, 250n4	21:5	253, 256, 257, 283
16:19	251n6	21:7	251
17:1—22:5	251	21:9—22:5	250, 251
17:1—21:8	250, 251	21:9–27	257
17:1-2	251	21:9	251, 251n8, 256, 259
17:1	251n8	21:10	249, 251, 259
17:3	249, 251	21:12–14	259
17:15	255n17	21:16–17	261
19:4	253n14	21:16	258, 260
19:11	253	21:17	258
19:15	253, 253n15, 254	21:18	258
19:16	254	21:19–20	260
20:4	254	21:23–27	262
20:6	254	21:23	262
20:11–15	254, 256	21:24	262
20:11–12	253n14	21:25	262
20:11	253	21:26	262
21:1—22:5	214n59, 256	21:27	263
21	257, 262	22	269, 284
21:1-2	257	22:1	253, 257
21:1	256, 257	22:3	253, 257
		22:5	261
		22:6–21	249
		22:16	178, 253n15